Islam
in
Southeast
Asia

The **Institute of Southeast Asian Studies (ISEAS)** was established as an autonomous organization in 1968. It is a regional centre dedicated to the study of socio-political, security and economic trends and developments in Southeast Asia and its wider geostrategic and economic environment.

The Institute's research programmes are the Regional Economic Studies (RES, including ASEAN and APEC), Regional Strategic and Political Studies (RSPS), and Regional Social and Cultural Studies (RSCS).

ISEAS Publications, an established academic press, has issued more than 1,000 books and journals. It is the largest scholarly publisher of research about Southeast Asia from within the region. ISEAS Publications works with many other academic and trade publishers and distributors to disseminate important research and analyses from and about Southeast Asia to the rest of the world.

ISEAS Series on Islam

Islam in Southeast Asia

Political, Social and Strategic Challenges for the 21st Century

EDITED BY
K. S. Nathan
Mohammad Hashim Kamali

ISEAS INSTITUTE OF SOUTHEAST ASIAN STUDIES
Singapore

First published in Singapore in 2005 by
Institute of Southeast Asian Studies
30 Heng Mui Keng Terrace
Pasir Panjang
Singapore 119614

E-mail: publish@iseas.edu.sg
Website: <http://bookshop.iseas.edu.sg>

© 2005 Institute of Southeast Asian Studies, Singapore

ISEAS Library Cataloguing-in-Publication Data

Islam in Southeast Asia : political, social and strategic challenges for the 21st century / edited by K.S. Nathan and Mohammad Hashim Kamali.
1. Islam—Asia, Southeastern—History.
2. Islam—21st century.
3. Islam and state—Asia, Southeastern.
4. Islam and politics—Asia, Southeastern.
5. Terrorism—Religious aspects—Islam.
6. September 11 Terrorist Attacks, 2001—Influence.
I.   Nathan, K.S.
II. Kamali, Mohammad Hashim, 1944–
III. Series.
BP63 A9I823   2005

ISBN 981-230-282-4 (soft cover)
ISBN 981-230-283-2 (hard cover)

Typeset by Superskill Graphics Pte Ltd
Printed in Singapore by Utopia Press Pte Ltd

CONTENTS

PART TWO: POLITICS, GOVERNANCE, CIVIL SOCIETY AND GENDER ISSUES IN SOUTHEAST ASIAN ISLAM

PART THREE: MODERNIZATION, GLOBALIZATION AND THE 'ISLAMIC STATE' DEBATE IN SOUTHEAST ASIA

PART FOUR: IMPACT OF SEPTEMBER 11 ON ISLAMIC
THOUGHT AND PRACTICE

PREFACE

This book is a revised version of the proceedings of the Conference on "Islam in Southeast Asia: Political, Social, and Strategic Challenges for the 21st Century" held at the Institute of Southeast Asian Studies, Singapore on 2–3 September 2002. To the extent possible, all chapters have been revised and updated to include recent developments that highlight the role, relevance and challenges, as well as the political and strategic dimensions of Islam in contemporary Southeast Asia.

In producing this special volume, we wish to express our deep appreciation and gratitude to several individuals whose support, assistance and co-operation have in no small measure contributed to the materialization of this publication. Firstly, the former ISEAS Director, Professor Chia Siow Yue who played a key role in initiating the idea of this seminar, and Mr. K. Kesavapany, the present Director whose enthusiastic commitment has enabled the final stages of editing and publication to proceed without a hitch. Our thanks are also due to the valiant efforts of three Research Associates whose editorial assistance has been crucial to the completion of this project: Ravi A. Menon, Graham Gerard Ong, and S. Thyaga Rajan. In the final stages, Thyaga worked very diligently with both of us in tying up loose ends and in improving the technical quality of the final drafts.

We wish to thank all the contributors for their fine papers and their full co-operation in responding promptly to requests for chapter revisions. We are also grateful to Mrs. Triena Ong, Head of the Publications Unit in ISEAS for providing valuable suggestions and handling production and marketing of this book, Ms Ch'ng Kim See and staff of the ISEAS Library for extending research support, and Mrs. Y.L. Lee and her staff in the Administration for their kind assistance.

K.S. NATHAN
MOHAMMAD HASHIM KAMALI
Singapore
September 2004

INTRODUCTION
Understanding Political Islam
Post-September 11

K.S. Nathan and Mohammad Hashim Kamali

The process of globalization has taken us out of isolation and brought us into a truly new phase of human co-existence which, for the present, is unsettled and dangerous. Globalization initially promised to be a vehicle for promotion of human development and democracy addressing issues like freedom and opportunities for progress. However, it seems to have brought greater concentration of wealth and power in the hands of the industrialized West. September 11 further accentuated the negative dimensions of globalization. The U.S. military intervention in Afghanistan and Iraq heightened the sense of insecurity over the prospects of world peace and people were alerted to the stark reality of the militarist overtones of globalization. Terrorism is heinous and frightening wherever it occurs and when it extends to suicide bombing and becomes an engaging theme of world civilizations, its negative repercussions are bound to overshadow every other aspect of East-West relations, especially relations between the Muslim world and the United States.

The West's relentless drive to fight terrorism with military means has brought espionage activities and intelligence agencies to a new prominence that is reminiscent of similar tendencies following WWI when fifth columnist activities overshadowed the climate of understanding among countries and nations. Mutual suspicion has became dominant and the world has seen, as per Subroto Roy, "a collapse of the global conversation". The crimes of September 11 were ones of political protest, but they were not something inexplicable or *sui generis*. They symbolized a total breakdown of the centuries-old cosmopolitan conversation with Islam. There exists today a fundamental disconnect in communication between the United States and Muslims around the world. At its root lies the inescapable truth that each side sees the world through a very different prism. That basic misunderstanding brought into sharp relief by September 11 has widened ever since by an increasingly polarized media on both sides. The unilateralist tendencies in U.S. foreign policy, exhibited not just in its relations with Muslims, but also with its allies in Europe and elsewhere often stand in the way of genuine dialogue. This may not be easy to penetrate in the face of the entrenched American self-image of the supremacy of its values and vision, and the expectation therefore that others must accept them and comply.

A great deal of American values may admittedly be said to be shared by others, including the Muslims. This is shown by the fact, even to this day, that the United States has many friends and allies among Muslims countries, some of which may still entertain a positive image and a historical memory of friendship with the United States. That invaluable sentiment has been shaken and in most cases overshadowed by hostile and polarized media, and of course, the United States' unwavering support for Israeli militarist policies in Palestine.

Efforts are being made in the meantime at international forums and conferences, interfaith dialogues and persons of goodwill to open up avenues of communication and draw attention to the more enduring themes of shared values on both sides. The present volume of essays also aims at widening the horizons of understanding between the West and the world of Islam. Notwithstanding the latent dominance of negative trends in East-West relations and the historical obsession on both sides to focus on the differences between them, often at the expense of the much wider scope of their common values, it remains to be said that Islamic and Western civilizations maintain similar perspectives on basic human values such as the sanctity of life, justice, human dignity and freedom.

If one were to characterize aspects of the two cultures, the Arab culture, one might say Islam generally, accentuates human dignity whereas Western culture tends to emphasize liberty. Bedouin culture in the history of the Arabs had a highly developed methodology and nexus of dignity and honour. These dignitarian concepts penetrated the wider culture of the Arabs and had enormous consequences on the gender question and issues of war and peace. Arab culture in turn had considerable influence on the religion of Islam worldwide. In those cases where Muslims are in rebellion against the *status quo*, a substantial cultural reason for the rebellion is perceived collective indignity. This is true, as Ali Mazrui noted in a 2002 article, of rebellions of Muslims in Chechnya, Palestine, Macedonia, Kashmir, Kosovo and even Nigeria.

A clash of cultures did occur when President Bush used, when addressing the Taliban, the language of ultimatum and no negotiation over surrendering Osama bin Laden: "Just hand over Osama bin Laden and his thugs. There is nothing to talk about." He did not give the Taliban any line of dignified retreat. Admittedly the Western culture also puts a high premium on dignity. The United States even stood up for the dignity of the colonized people of the Muslim world and elsewhere. Even as late as in the 1960s, President John F. Kennedy was emphasizing that "Africa was for the African" — and not for the white settlers or minority governments. Yet the Americans arguably saw their anti-colonialism as a defence basically of liberty, whereas for the Muslims the fight against European colonialism was above all a struggle for collective dignity.

Meanwhile a Jewish state had been created in a region which for a thousand years had been overwhelmingly Muslim. What is more, it was created in ways which violated dignity. There was an ethnic cleansing which displaced thousands of Palestinians to make room for Jews. Someone from the Ukraine who claimed to have had a Jewish ancestor two thousand years ago had a greater right under Israel's Law of Return than a Palestinian who ran away from within the Israeli borders in 1948. In the face of the new waves of Israeli military actions in 2000–01 against street processions of the Palestinian youth, new Jewish settlements and destruction of Palestinian homes, it was baffling to the Muslims, and one would assume to most people, to hear President Bush's description of Ariel Sharon as "a man of peace". The Palestinian issue is basically not a religious issue but the consequence of an unjust situation over occupation of territory.

Ever since its inception in 1969 the Organization of Islamic Conference (OIC), which is a representative forum of fifty-seven Muslim and Muslim majority countries, indeed the largest Muslim forum in existence, had consistently exhibited a pro-U.S. posture and generally aligned itself with its policies during the Cold War years. But the OIC grew critical and took an anti-American stance over the Palestinian issue on basically the following four grounds:

1. The U.S. opposition to giving Palestinians their rights;
2. Its continuous military, economic and political support for Israel;
3. Its use of veto power in the UN Security Council on issues pertaining to Jerusalem and Palestine;

4. Its diplomatic and propaganda campaign against the Palestine Liberation Organization (PLO).

Moreover, the United States moved to deal with OIC countries outside the framework of the OIC. It acted as a catalyst in getting Egypt, an OIC member country, to recognize Israel and sign a treaty with it. The OIC consequently condemned the United States. The signatory of that treaty, Pesident Anwar Sadat of Egypt, was soon assassinated.

Terrorism is not condoned by the vast majority of moderate Muslims who subscribe to the belief that Islam abhors terrorism and it can never be justified in its name. Malaysia's Prime Minister, Abdullah Badawi, who is the current OIC Chairman, was only recently quoted in the media to reiterate what he had said on several occasions:

> There were those who claimed that terrorist acts perpetrated by some Muslims were representative of Islam, and others who see the religion as intolerant and promoted violence. This is patently untrue as Islam is a religion of peace. It abhors violence and the unnecessary taking of life. (*The Star*, Kuala Lumpur, 6 August 2004).

The perception also holds among Muslim leaders and intellectuals that radical Islamism advocated by violent methods is misrepresentative of Islam itself. In a post September 11 article, Edward Said pointed out that "the carefully planned and horrendous, pathologically motivated suicide attacks and mass slaughter by a small group of deranged militants has been turned into proof of Huntington's thesis" ("The Clash of Ignorance", *The Nation* (USA), 22 October 2002). Suicide bombing has been condemned by numerous Muslim commentators and political leaders across the Muslim world as criminal acts by a small group of hateful individuals. Terrorism violates the fundamental Islamic norm of the sanctity of life. Suicide bombing intentionally violates innocent life and also violates the religion.

Political Islam in the sense of radical Islamism was in a state of decline in the 1990s in the belief that it failed to offer a viable alternative for a system of government within the Muslim lands and failed also to facilitate resolution of disputed issues. Just as moderate Islam was beginning to emerge at the centre state, September 11 and its aftermath was a shot in the arm for radical Islamism, and gave a new lease of life to Muslim extremism. It is now obvious that Muslims themselves are the principal victims of terrorism and the world is witness to a vicious circle where extremism on the part of a few is given the unwarranted respectability of dictating the course of the U.S. presidential election, of world affairs generally, and of robbing the moderate thinkers of their initiative.

In Southeast Asia as elsewhere, since September 11, the concept and phenomenon of "political Islam" has somehow impacted upon our imagination even more than in the pre-9/11 era, as we attempt to come to grips with the political and strategic dimensions of a religious ideology that has global political, social, cultural and security implications. Given Southeast Asia's generally open societies and economies, the region's survival, progress and prosperity in the twenty-first century is a matter of concern to all — policymakers, scholars, diplomats, businessmen, media professionals, military strategists, students and researchers of political economy — and even the ordinary man in the street. In the wake of Islamic globalization since the Khomeini Revolution in Iran in the late seventies, the spread of contemporary Islamic influence in Southeast Asia is marked both by a process of active cultural expansion, as well as a reactive process to modernization and secular globalization originating from the West, especially since the end of the Cold War.

For Muslims, Islam apparently furnishes a complete if not comprehensive system in which politics, economy, religion and society are all interwoven into a complex whole. Non-Muslims, however, who have become accustomed to secular political, economic and social processes since independence in the 1940s and 1950s in Southeast Asia, do not quite understand the rationale or significance of this fusion of religion and politics in Islam. It also needs to be mentioned that Muslims equally fail to appreciate the concerns of Non-Muslims when attempts are made by certain sections of Muslims in the current nation-state system in Southeast Asia, to vigorously pursue the path of Islamization without due regard to the political, social, economic, and strategic consequences of such an approach in culturally diverse and pluralistic societies such as ours.

The events following the September 11 terrorist attacks in the United States attest to the fact that perceptions of Islam and rising Islamic militancy in Southeast Asia require a much deeper analysis of the origins and growth of this religion, its socio-political and ideological character, organizational impulse, and cultural impact on government and society in the region. More importantly, further intellectual inquiry and debate on the strategic impact of global Islam have become more relevant in the light of September 11, as all state actors — big, medium and small — begin to grapple with the pressing need to maintain domestic order and regional stability — and to contain all forms of terror, whether religiously motivated or not — that threaten to undermine the very fabric of social order and prosperity the region has thus far achieved.

The chapters that follow reflect a sound knowledge and expertise on the part of scholars and activists in the field of doctrinal and political Islam — and its strategic implications for Southeast Asia. Part I outlines Islamic doctrine and traces the history and growth of Islam in Southeast Asia as well as the role and development of Islamic economic institutions in the region. In Part II, politics, governance, civil society and gender issues are examined in the context of Southeast Asian Islam. Part III devotes itself to the impact of modernization and globalization on Muslim society and the ongoing debate about the merits, problems and challenges of establishing an "Islamic State" in the context of the modern international system based on the nation-state structure. Part IV examines and evaluates the impact of the 11 September 2001 terrorist attacks on the icons of the American superpower, and attempts to explore the significance of this event and impact if any on Islamic thought and practice. The Conclusion attempts to offer some perspectives on the challenges and prospects for Islamic doctrine and practice in the context of Southeast Asia.

In Chapter 1, Azyumardi Azra expounds on the complexity of Islamic thought in the philosophical, dogmatic, theoretical, and conceptual aspects especially in the context of recent international developments such as the September 11 tragedy. He adds that the complexity is also great in the discussion of Southeast Asian Islam which, in addition to having a lot of affinities with Middle Eastern Islam, possesses a number of distinctive characteristics. He concludes that despite little traces of Shi'ism and the attempts to spread Shi'ism after the Iranian revolution in the 1980s, Southeast Asian Islam remains Sunni. But, again, within the Sunni themselves, there exist groups that have differing if not conflicting religious, intellectual, and political tendencies. This creates not only disunity among Sunni Muslims, but also social and political struggles that characterize the dynamics of the Muslim world, including Southeast Asia.

The history of Islam in Southeast Asia is traced by Johan H. Mueleman in Chapter 2. He argues that any approach that fails to consider a diversity of factors and a variety of successive stages in its history will also misunderstand contemporary Southeast Asian Islam. Mueleman examines the position of the Southeast Asian Muslim community in past and present globalization, Islamic "counter-globalization" and localization processes, and offers an explanation for some contemporary dissimilarities of the situation and characteristics of Islam in the various countries of the region by referring to differing styles of colonization and decolonization.

In Chapter 3, Carmen A. Abu Bakar discusses the spread and growth of Islam in the Philippines. She suggests that trade has been a crucial factor in the advent of Islam to the Philippines, adding that the role of the Sufi movement in consolidating the Muslims into organized communities that served as the bulwark against the onslaught of colonialism in the sixteenth century was equally important. More recently, in the post-9/11 era, she argues that the the Philippine Government's high profile in the anti-terrorist campaign has caused Muslims to suffer, thereby prompting a growing number of people to revert to Islam — a phenomenon known as "*balik* Islam" which is invariably linked to the worldwide Islamic resurgence.

The evolution of Islamic economic institutions in Indonesia is the subject of discussion by Bahtiar Effendy in Chapter 4, while Mohamed Aslam Haneef focuses on similar developments in Malaysia in Chapter 5. Effendy considers the founding of an Islamic bank (Bank Mualalamt Indonesia) in 1991 as a historical landmark in the creation of Islamic financial institutions in the country, as the existence of this institution enables Muslims to perform their religious obligation in the field of economy. However, he notes that what constitutes *riba* (usury) is still a debatable subject with no finality or consensus emerging from the *fiqh* (Islamic jurisprudence) scholars themselves — and there is no prospect of such a consensus emerging in the near future. Haneef in his expose categorically argues that the need for development programmes after political independence, and the perceived failures of both the capitalist and socialist models, provided a fresh opportunity for Muslims to seek "indigenous solutions" to their socio-economic problems. Taking a broader view of the region, he maintains that the "Islamization" of modern economics has been the basis of the efforts in Southeast Asia rather than any attempt to impose traditional models and views that may not necessarily be contextually relevant.

Chapters 6–10 engage the reader in several issues of major significance to the practice of contemporary Islam in the context of modernization and globalization. In Chapter 6, Shamsul A.B. suggests that globalization has contributed to "political Islam" being highly profiled internationally leading to the suggestion by Samuel Huntington that it is one of the Eastern civilizations that would challenge Western civilization. In his essay, Shamsul discusses the kind of political Islam that has become embedded in a highly pluralistic Southeast Asian environment, and how it has affected directly and indirectly state formation and governance in the region. However, Zainah Anwar in Chapter 7 prefers to focus specifically on the efforts and attempts of Islamist party, PAS, to impose the *hudud* law in the Malaysian states of Terengganu and Kelantan. Through this case study, she draws out issues and raises questions on the relationship between religion and politics, and the fundamental challenges posed to democratic governance when Islam is used as a political ideology to mobilize support for political power. She concludes by examining the implications of the politicization of Islam for women's rights, human rights and fundamental liberties when religion is used as a source of laws and public policies.

The course of events in Malaysia tends to confirm the scenario painted by Zainah. In 1993 the Islamic Party of Malaysia (PAS) introduced the *Shari'a* Criminal Enactment, known as the *Hudud* Bill, following their victory in the 1990 elections. The bill was passed by the State Legislature of Kelantan and even signed by the Sultan, but it remains in abeyance ever since due to its disapproval by the federal government. This is because the bill proposes a range of severe penalties for offences which fall outside the jurisdictional limitations of the *shari'a* courts as stipulated in the Federal Constitution. The *Hudud* Bill has been politicized so much so as to engage the state government of Kelantan and the federal government of Malaysia in a decade-long political controversy. The *hudud* became a topical issue for the media and the years of publicity on it left the juridical aspects of that issue altogether in the background.

The *Hudud* Bill remained a hot issue also in the 1999 elections which in which PAS won further ground and acquired control of a second state, namely Terengganu. The *Hudud* Bill debate acquired fresh prominence as a result and it was no surprise that Terengganu followed the same route as that of Kelantan over this issue. In the March 2004 elections the PAS governments in the two states declared that if they won the elections they would proceed to implemnent the *hudud* penalties. On this occasion, however, PAS lost ground and lost not only Terengganu but barely managed to retain Kelantan with a narrow majority. This phenomenal election defeat overwhelmed and disillusioned the PAS leaders far beyond expectations. One wonders once again whether it was due to the politicization of *shari'a*. Why should an essentially juridical issue be so politicized as to be included in party election manifestos? Is it possible at all to recall any other criminal legislation, or any proposed enactment for that matter, that has topped the party political agenda the way the *Hudud* Bill did?

One clear message of the 2004 elections in Malaysia is that the vast majority of Muslims in that country do not support radical Islamism, nor even politicization of Islamic issues, the way PAS was able to do during the 1990s. Prime Minister Abdullah Badawi won a landslide electoral mandate due mainly to his moderate approaches to issues of concern to religion and ethnic relations. Badawi's administration has committed itself to the politics of accommodation and compromise in relations among the religious and ethnic groups of Malaysia. Badawi has advocated not only greater tolerance but adjustment and integration of ethnic and religious groups. He has also spoken of Islam *Hadhari*, or action-oriented progressive Islam that maintains a perspective over the civilizational dimensions of interfaith relations, and the desire to accentuate aspects of Islam that strike common ground with the best values of other civilizations.

Civil society issues in Islam are the subject matter of discussion by both Patricia A. Martinez (Chapter 8) and Peter G. Riddell (Chapter 9). Martinez begins her discussion by raising a very fundamental question: Is it civil society versus Islam, in Malaysia? She notes that many writers have excluded Islamists from definitions of civil society largely on the grounds that Islam and Islamism are part of traditional and primordial formations, and partly on the perceived incompatibility of a religious-based society, sought by Islamism, with pluralist democracy. This latter idea is reinforced by the totalitarian and authoritarian manifestations of many Islamic movements, especially in the Middle East. In the context of contemporary Islam in Malaysia, she attempts to describe the various actors and layers of complexity that are fluid and eemerging quickly in the evolution of Islam, the "Islamic state" claimed by the ruling polity and its political opposition, and the Islamization agendas of both the ruling party and the Islamist opposition. She concludes by exploring whether the conundrum in Malaysia is the Islamists versus civil society dilemma, or whether there are other possibilities and problems that define their engagement. In furtherance of this debate, Peter Riddell outlines in Chapter 9 key elements in the Islamization process in recent years in Malaysia at the state and non-state levels. However, the major focus of his presentation is on the impact of Islamization on religious minorities in Malaysia, especially the Christian community — their perspectives, concerns and responses in the midst of a struggle taking place among Malaysian Muslims to define the future direction of the nation.

The last essay in this section takes an analytical view of gender issues in Islam. In Chapter 10, Lily Zakiyah Munir seeks to understand the age-old debates over the subject of Islam and gender with particular focus on the issues in Islamic family law most affecting women: marriage, sexuality, polygamy, divorce, and inheritance. Her central argument is that the arduous and relentless struggle for the realization of Islam as a women-liberating religion has been exacerbated by the entrenched patriarchy pervasive among most Muslim societies. She elaborates that despite explicit provisions in the

Qur'an that do not prohibit women's rights to participate in politics, business and employment, these issues remain controversial in most Muslim societies. Women's veiling, regardless of its theological debate, has apparently become a social pressure for women in Southeast Asia for the last two decades in the aftermath of the Iranian Revolution. Shaped by gender-biased socio-cultural backgrounds, Lily Munir concludes that most Muslim societies appear to have fallen into the patriarchal reading and interpretations of religious scriptures thus subduing Islam's basic mission of justice, equality and freedom for all, both men and women. There is no mandate in the Qur'an on the practice of veiling or of any particular dress form. The text instead speaks of the virtue of modesty in the encounter among members of the opposite sex. Radical Islamists have on the other hand chosen to read the relatively open terms of the Qur'anic text in favour of their much stricter puritanical positions.

Chapters 11–14 in Part Three enter into some theoretical discussion and debate on the meaning, context and significance of modernization and globalization for discourses on the need and relevance/irrelevance of establishing an "Islamic state" to best serve the spiritual and material needs of Muslims today. According to Syed Farid Alatas (Chapter 11), modernity refers to the end result of the process of modernization. The traits of modernization include the rationalization of economic and political life, rapid urbanization, industrialization, differentiation in the social structure, greater popular involvement in public affairs, and globalization. Using this broad context, Alatas observes that in Islamic economics, there is still no empirical work on existing economic systems, and the nature, function and effects of interest in these systems in a manner that could be regarded in theoretical and methodological terms as specifically Islamic. On democracy and civil society or *masyarakat madani,* he concludes that thus far, calls for a *masyarakat madani* have been made without a deeper understanding by Muslim scholars of the contextual realities of modern political economy so that there appears to be a disjuncture between proponents of democracy on the one hand and those seeking an Islamic order on the other.

In Chapter 12, Abdul Rashid Moten provides a critical perspective of Muslim experiences and responses to modernization and the process of globalization. He maintains that contrary to widespread belief, most of the principles (such as toleration, plurality, justice, unity) espoused by Islam are in harmony with those inherent in modernization and the processes of globalization. As a general rule civilizations should unite under common values, belief systems and histories. They did not. While America and Europe are obsessed with globalization, Muslims are apprehensive about Francis

Fukuyama's annihilation of history and the triumphalism about the hegemony of Western values, ideas and civilization. From a Muslim point of view, the conduct of foreign relations and the imposition of the so-called "modernization and globalization" agenda by the West have been both Machiavellian and coercive. There exists, throughout the Muslim world, a great sense of grievance and resentment toward the West. Moten then goes on to identify the three Muslim responses: first, the mass response, which is frequently expressed in the form of spontaneous and, at times, violent acts of protest against all forms of radical Westernization and colonial invasion. Second, the theoretical and intellectual response, which recognizes and emphasizes the inextricable ties between Western modernity and Western imperialism. The third response comes from the governing elites in the Muslim world who believe that globalization is inevitable and that there is no conflict between Islam and the values upheld by modernization and globalization, but demand an opportunity to reinterpret and modify the rules of the game "to prevent discrimination and favouritism", and to ensure an equitable distribution of the benefits of globalization. Moten concludes rather emphatically that the three Muslim responses are in essence a rejection of the disruptive nature of Western dominance and the suppression of their own (Muslim) politics and cultures, not actually against modernization and globalization.

In Chapters 13 and 14, Shad Saleem Faruqi and Mohammad Hashim Kamali discuss the problems of conceptualization, definition and interpretation of what constitutes an "Islamic state" in the context of contemporary politics and international relations. Faruqi suggests in Chapter 13 that to a large extent the debate whether Malaysia is an Islamic or secular state is attributable to semantics. The problem is compounded by the fact that there is no ideal or prototype secular or Islamic state that one could hold up as a shining model of one or the other. In the midst of this debate a number of deeply divisive and sensitive issues are coming to the foreground — the right of the state to punish "deviationists"; the branding by some Muslims of other Muslims as *kafirs* (infidels); the constitutional claim of some Muslims to convert to other faiths versus the right of the Islamic state to punish apostates; and the conflict between *shari'a* and civil courts. In this emerging context Faruqi asks: Will the Islamic tide sweep away the existing "mixed" Constitution and replace Malaysia's cherished multi-cultural mosaic with something more "ideal" and "pure" is a question on many lips? He argues that it is unlikely that Islam will have a "walkover" in Malaysia and sweep away everything in its path. Malaysia will remain a plural society. Islam in Malaysia will continue to co-exist with modernity, with Malay nationalism, with Malay *adat* (custom) and with the dominant American and European culture that shapes the world view and the thinking processes of most Malaysians including Malaysian Muslims.

Mohammad Hashim Kamali sets out in Chapter 14 some of the uncertainties concerning the concept and definition of an Islamic state, a brief history of developments, and a literature review. He then discusses the salient attributes of an Islamic state: whether the Islamic state proposes a limited as opposed to a totalitarian government, whether it can be characterized a civilian state as opposed to theocracy, and whether it would be justified to characterize the Islamic state as a qualified democracy. Finally, Kamali briefly addresses the Islamist demand for the establishment of an Islamic state, and provides some comments on recent developments in Malaysia, including his observation that the Islamic state is more an idea and concept than an institutional form. He concludes objectively that any state that is committed to the principles of equality, justice, basic rights and liberties of the people including religious freedom for non-Muslims to practice their own faith free of interference, supports a civilian, constitutional and representative system that upholds people's welfare and the morality and dogma of Islam — can be regarded as an Islamic state. The disjuncture that Farid Alatas has noted concerning Islamic economics also obtains, according to Kamali, in the existing literature on Islamic state and government. A certain gap thus remains in the writings of Muslim jurists on constitutional law between the theoretical orientations of an Islamic polity and the more developed aspects of the modern nation state.

The impact of September 11 on Islamic thought and practice constitutes the substance of the discussion in the final part, Part IV. Noorhaidi Hasan examines in Chapter 15 the rise of Islamic militancy in Indonesia in the post-9/11 context. He argues that in the aftermath of September 11, the radical Islamist discourse has become increasingly dominant in the public sphere of Indonesia and interlocked with the radical Islamist discourse all over the world — in which Osama bin Laden has become the key point of reference. He concludes that instead of reducing the space for Islamic militancy which has engulfed Indonesia since the collapse of the New Order regime, the September 11 incident and its aftermath has empowered various radical Islamist groups to be more vocal and effective in producing their discourse. In the final chapter (Chapter 16), Bernard Adeney-Risakotta argues that whereas it is always dangerous to generalize about Islam anywhere, let alone in a region as large and diverse as Southeast Asia, it is useful to reflect on commonalities in Muslim responses to September 11, before going on to observe the differences. While Islam is not a monolith, it is striking that almost all Muslim leaders in Southeast Asia condemned the attack on September 11, including those from Islamic groups considered "radical" and those considered "moderate". Even more striking is the fact that almost all Muslims, from all parties, also condemned the attack on Afghanistan. Indeed, Muslim responses to September 11 cannot be considered in isolation from the broader contexts of Afghanistan and the Middle East. Thus, he maintains, Muslim definitions of terrorism and differing perceptions about who are the terrorists cannot be ignored. He suggests that the modern nation-state is losing credibility in the eyes of many Muslims, as the sole legitimate wielder of force. September 11 strengthened solidarity among Muslims and weakened nationalism in Southeast Asia. Muslim resistance to Western capitalistic hegemony is not primarily waged on the basis of local, particularistic values, but rather is based on a competing universal ideology. The tragedy of September 11 brought forth conflicting and ambivalent emotions among Southeast Asian Muslims. In fact, Risakotta notes that many viewed Osama Bin Laden as simultaneously a scapegoat, sacrificial victim and heroic martyr. The political impact of September 11 is quite distinct from, although connected to, the emotional response of Muslims. He concludes with some reflections on the political impact of September 11 in Indonesia, Malaysia, Thailand, Philippines and Singapore.

PART ONE

Islamic Doctrine, History, Growth and Institutions in Southeast Asia

1

ISLAMIC THOUGHT: THEORY, CONCEPTS AND DOCTRINES IN THE CONTEXT OF SOUTHEAST ASIAN ISLAM

Azyumardi Azra

INTRODUCTION

There is little doubt that Islamic thought is very complex. The complexity of Islamic thought is even greater in philosophical, dogmatic, theoretical, and conceptual aspects especially if one puts it in the context of recent international developments such as the 11 September 2001 terrorist attack in the United States. The complexity is also great in the context of Southeast Asian Islam which, in addition to having a great deal of affinities with Middle Eastern Islam, possesses a number of distinctive characteristics due to its different historical, social, cultural and political realities.

There has been a lot of discussion whether Islam is one or many and, by extension, also if Islamic thought is monolithic or pluralistic. There are many among Muslims who maintain that Islam is only one; they refuse the perception that Islam is many. Responding to this matter, I would argue that at the level of the Qur'an — the original and primary source of Islam — Islam is one. There is no disagreement among Muslims that the Qur'an is God's revelation sent down to the Prophet Muhammad. But, Muslims from the time of post-Prophet Muhammad have been in disagreement about the Prophetic tradition (*hadith*, the second source of Islam), a portion of which is considered false and fabricated by Muslim religious scholars (*ulama*).

However, it is important to make it clear that the Qur'an and valid *hadith* need interpretation (*ijtihad*) from the *ulama* in order to formulate workable and implementable doctrines. The formulation of the *ulama* especially in the field of *aqidah* (beliefs) and *fiqh* (detailed interpretation of general principles of *shari'a* contained in the Qur'an) are generally very detailed. Influenced by certain sociological, cultural, historical and political factors, differing if not conflicting interpretation of certain verses of the Qur'an and *hadith* among Muslim *ulama* have been existing not long after the death of the Prophet Muhammad. As a result, at the sociological level, there are many "Islams" or, to put it in a more precise way, there are many expressions of Islam throughout Islamic history.

SUNNISM AND SHI'ISM

It is important to point out that much of the differences among Muslims had its origins not in the religious discourse, but in the political disputes and conflicts between the followers of Uthman ibn Affan, the third caliph, and of Ali ibn Abi Talib, the fourth caliph of the four rightly-guided caliphs (*al-khulafa' al-rashidun*). The conflicts, involving civil wars (*al-fitan al-kubra*), among Muslims, resulted not only in the continued political struggles in the subsequent periods of Islamic history, but also in the rise of a great number of theological schools (*kalam*).

The first small splinter group was the Kharijites (seceders) who seceded from the *ummah* (Muslim nation) because they believed that other Muslims who had been involved in the conflicts were sinners and, therefore, had become infidels (*kafir*). Taking a literal interpretation of Islam, the Kharijites maintained that all differences and conflicts among Muslims should be resolved (*tahkim*) according to the Qur'an. Citing a verse in the Qur'an, they insisted that Muslims who did not resolve their conflicts using the law of God, had become infidels (*kafir*s). Based on this belief, the Kharijites launched subversive and violent activities against rulers in the region (which includes the present-day Middle East). Violent and radical Muslim groups in the Middle East today are reminiscent of the Kharijites and they are in fact referred to as "neo-Kharijite" groups.

The second group, which is much larger, are the followers of Ali ibn Abi Talib, who had been persecuted by Mu'awiyah ibn Abi Sufyan, the most prominent and a shrewd leader of the Uthman ibn Affan group. Claiming the caliphate for himself at the expense of Ali, Mu'awiyah's son, Yazid, killed

Husayn, Ali's son, in the battle of Karbela, Iraq. Since then the followers of Ali have been known as the Shi'ite, which simply means the "party of Ali", and later developed distinct religio-political doctrines. The growth of doctrine had a lot to do with the Shi'ite's bitter political experience during much of their history since the time of Ali ibn Abi Talib, the first *imam* of the Shi'ites.

In terms of theology, however, the Shi'ites have not developed their own. Rather, they generally adopted the rational and philosophical theology that had been formulated by the Sunnis, more precisely by the Mu'tazilah, as will be discussed briefly below. The case is also the same in Sufism, where the Shi'ites mainly adopted philosophical or theoretical Sufism as proposed by great Sunni thinkers such as Ibn Arabi. In terms of *fiqh* (Islamic jurisprudence) there are more affinities and similarities rather than differences between the Shi'ites and Sunnis. The differences between them relate mainly to the issue of *nikah mut'ah* (marriage for convenience), which is generally accepted by the Shi'ite *ulama* but is despised by the Sunni *ulama*.

The most distinctive trait of Shi'itism lies in the religio-political field. Again, this has much to do with the Shi'ites' bitter political experiences in much of their history. Religiously and politically, the Shi'ites were led by the *imam* by way of a hierarchical rigid structure of the *ulama*. Generally there were twelve *imam* who were responsible for leading the Shi'ite masses in political struggles against any ruler who was regarded as having had usurped the *imam*'s sole right to political power. During the medieval period of Islam, there were a number of Shi'ite dynasties in the Middle East such as the Buwaihid and the Fatimids, but they did not last very long after the early sixteenth century during which the Muslim world saw the rise of the Safavid dynasty in Persia. In contemporary times, Shi'itism has had its strongest following in Iran, Iraq and the Yemen.

The third largest group — in fact the majority of Muslims — is the *Ahl al-Sunnah wa al-Jama'ah*, or better known simply as the Sunni. Despite their dislike of the way Mu'awiyah and Yazid treated 'Ali ibn Talib, Hasan ibn 'Ali, and Husayn ibn 'Ali, the Sunnis preferred to keep the unity of Muslims (*jama'ah*) under the banner of the "caliphate" of the Umayyad, Abbasids, Ottoman, and other Sunni Muslim political entities. In political thought and tradition, as we will elaborate below, the Sunnis have been very submissive to the rulers who were able not only to co-opt the *ulama* but also to gain religious justification from the *ulama* for their absolute power.

In terms of theology, as a response to the Kharijites, a limited number of the Sunni *ulama* developed Mu'tazilite theology, which basically proposed that Muslims who had been involved in conflicts between the followers of Mu'awiyah ibn Abi Sufyan and Ali ibn Abi Talib were neither Muslim nor *kafir* (infidels), but rather were in between two places (*al-manzilah bayn manzilatayn*). The Mu'tazilites developed very intricate theological doctrines relating to the "nature" of God. Basically, the Mu'tazilites formulated an anthropocentric theology, which emphasized human free-actism and free will.

Therefore, Mu'tazilite theology was known as the "rational" and "free will" kind of Islamic theology and was regarded by mainstream Sunni as having gone astray. It was only since the early twentieth century that certain aspects of Mu'tazili rationalism have been accepted by particular groups of Sunni Muslims. The person who has been held responsible for the re-introduction of Mu'tazilite theology was Muhammad Abduh, one of the greatest *mujaddid* (reformer) of Islam in the late nineteenth and early twentieth century. In fact, the Egyptian Abduh has been regarded by some Muslim scholars as a "neo-Mu'tazili". In contemporary Southeast Asia, the most prominent proponent of the "neo-Mu'tazilite" doctrines was the late Harun Nasution, professor of Islamic theology and former rector of State Institute for Islamic Studies in Jakarta. Neo-Mu'tazilite doctrines gained popularity among certain circles of Indonesian Muslims since 1980s for their relevance to the concepts and ideas on modernity and national development (Nasution 1987, 1998; Martin, Woodward and Atmaja 1997).

Refusing both the Kharijite and Mu'tazite theologies, the Sunni mainstream developed its own distinctive theology (*kalam*). Sunni mainstream *ulama* formulated the Ash'arite (Ash'ariyah) and Maturidite (Maturidiyyah) theologies. Different from the Mu'tazilite theology which put too much emphasis on '*aql* (reason), the Ash'arite emphasized the importance of the *naql* (verses of the Qur'an and valid *hadith*), though not always in very literal ways as the Kharijites did. Another distinctiveness of the *Ash'arite* theology was that human acts had been predestined by God himself; there was no free will and free-action. The most important figure in the formulation of Sunni religious ideology was Imam al-Ghazali. Thus in the post-Ghazalian period, the Sunni religious ideology was to consist of Ash'arite theology, Shafi'i *fiqh*, and Ghazalian Sufism.

It is clear from the above accounts that there were already a great deal of differences among Muslims in the fields of theology (*kalam*) and law (*shari'a/ fiqh*), though most of them were related to non-fundamental issues (*furu'iyyah*). As a result, there were groups within the Sunnis who have had different interpretation of the verses of the Qur'an and, different religious practices as well. In the contemporary times, there are categories like "traditionalist" and "modernist" groups; there are Sunni "literalists" and "radicals" — like the Wahhabis — and, on the other hand, there are Sunni "liberals".

The problem becomes more complicated because Sunni Islam is lacking in a central and monolithic leadership like that of Shi'ite Islam. There is no single institution, let alone individual, among the Sunnis that can dominate the interpretation and meaning of Islam. Therefore, neither institution nor individual can claim the leadership of the *ummah* (Muslim nation). The *imam* is of course also present among the Sunnis, but an *imam* is simply the leader of prayers or the chief functionary of a mosque. Or, an honorific title granted for great *ulama* like Imam al-Shafi'i or Imam al-Ghazali. The imam, in the Sunni tradition, is not a political leader like the one in the Shi'ite tradition.

The history of Sunni Muslim politics from medieval times up to more recent times by and large was marked by what I would term "submissive politics". When the period of the four Rightly Guided Caliphs (*al-khulafa' al-rashidun*) was over, there arose absolute Muslim political entity under the Umayyads and more especially during the period of the Abbasids. The succession of the caliph was not based on merit as in the period of *al-khulafa al-rashidun*, but rather, on bloodline. Therefore, as Ibn Khaldun argues, the rulers of the Umayyads and the Abbasids were not caliphs (*khulafa'*), but rather, kings; and their political entities were not caliphates but kingdoms (*al-mamlakah*).

The absolutism of the Sunni Muslim rulers was strengthened when the Abbasids adopted the absolute political culture and tradition of Persia. Not unlike the Sasanid kings they declared themselves as the shadow of God on earth (*zill Allah fi al-ard*). They built magnificent palaces that created an aura of absolutism as well as enigma in the eyes of the people. The life in the palaces seemed to be very hedonistic as described vividly in the story "One Thousand and One Nights".

The absolutism of Sunni Muslim rulers and the decaying state of their dynasties continued until the expansion of European imperialism to the Muslim world. Particularly from the eighteenth century, the European colonial powers not only ruled much of the Muslim world, but also introduced their political ideas, concepts and institutions. The introduction of concept and practices such as "nation", "nationalism" and "nation-state" by the Europeans presented difficult challenges for Muslim rulers, intellectuals and the *ulama*.

As one might expect, there were a number of different responses to these challenges by Muslims. In general, I would suggest there were three kinds of responses. First, confronting the Europeans through *jihad*, which eventually failed. Second, accommodating and adopting European ideas, concepts and practices. This second type of response was the most common one that resulted in the adoption of European ideas, concepts and institutions such as "nationalism", "nation-state", "modernism", "secularism", and the like. The third response was proposing alternative concepts and institutions by returning to the romanticized and ideal Islamic concepts. With respect to this, some Muslim scholars and activists such as al-Afghani and 'Abd al-Rahman al-Kawakibi, for instance, appealed for the re-invigoration of the caliphate (*al-khilafah*) as the single, universal Islamic political entity, which, it was believed, would unify the fragmented *ummah*. Other Muslim theologians, who found that it was very difficult to establish such a caliphate, proposed another alternative concept, namely the *dawlah Islamiyyah* (Islamic state), which would be founded in a certain Muslim country.

In the end, after War War II, most of the newly independent Muslim countries adopted the Western model of the nation-state together with secular ideologies that, in most cases, were regarded as being incompatible and even hostile to Islam. This failure of secular states in their modernization programmes has only provided another impetus for the "Islamists" to consolidate their efforts in replacing their respective regimes. This marked the rise of political Islam, aimed at the establishment of God's sovereignty (*hakimiyyah Allah*). It is not unusual that the Islamists' struggle to achieve this end involves the use of violence. The practice of "state terrorism" that seems to be common in many Muslim countries today has given rise to an unbroken use of violence or even worse, a "circle of terrorism" (Azra 1996).

MAINSTREAM SUNNI: SOUTHEAST ASIAN REALITIES

Southeast Asian Islam is overwhelmingly Sunni. Since the twelfth century, wandering Sufi teachers and traders — coming mostly from Arabia — had introduced Sunni Islam to Southeast Asia. As a result, the majority of Muslims throughout Southeast Asia now adhere to Sunni Islam. There have been assertions from some historians in the Malay-Indonesian world that Shi'ism was also introduced to the archipelago in the seventh and eighth centuries; if fact they, like Hasymi, argue that the Shi'ites founded the Perlak Kingdom in the Aceh area after expelling the Sunnis. But, there is no convincing evidence that supports this assertion (Azra 2000).

In contemporary times, the success of Ayatullah Khomeini's Islamic revolution in Iran has inspired a limited number of Muslims in Indonesia to adopt Shi'ism. Since the early 1980s a number of Shi'ite foundations have been established in various cities in the country; a growing number of Indonesian students have travelled to Iran in search of Shi'ite Islamic knowledge; and many publications on Shi'ism have also appeared. Despite all of these efforts, it seems that there is no strong evidence that many Indonesian

Sunni Muslims converted to Shi'ism. Whereas the Shi'ites are relatively free in Indonesia, they face a great deal of difficulties in other countries in Southeast Asia. In both Malaysia and Brunei Darussalam, Shi'ism is regarded as a deviant teaching and, therefore, the governments in the two countries keep a watchful eye on Shi'ism and its possible spread. (Azra 2002).

The fact that the majority of Southeast Asian Muslims are Sunnis have contributed a great deal to the formation of distinct Islamic traditions that can still be observed today. Doctrinally speaking, Southeast Asian Muslims generally follow the Ash'arite theology (*kalam*), Shafi'ite school of law (*madhhab*), and Ghazalian Sufism. The Muslims who adhere to these schools of Islamic thought and practices, as mentioned above, are called the followers of *Ahl al-Sunnah wa al-Jama'ah*, indicating those who follow the way (*sunnah*) of the Prophet Muhammad and hold fast to the unity of Muslims (*jama'ah*).

Even though *Ahl al-Sunnah wa al-Jama'ah* is the dominant Islamic group in Southeast Asia, it is important to point out that in Indonesia, since its independence on 17 August 1945, the state has not declared this officially. In fact Islam itself is not the official religion of the Indonesian state, despite the fact that the majority of the Indonesian people are Muslims. The state, instead, officially recognizes the existence of religion in the 1945 Constitution, which contains the Pancasila (five pillars), the first pillar of which is the belief in One Supreme God. All the other four pillars of Pancasila are regarded by most Muslim leaders — if not all — as being compatible with Islamic principles and teachings. As far as Islam and the other religions in Indonesia are concerned, the role of the state is confined to administrative matters rather than interfering in theological and doctrinal issues of any religion.

In contrast, in Malaysia, where Islam has been declared the official religion, the state recognizes the *Ahl al-Sunnah wa al-Jama'ah* as the only valid doctrine. In fact religious matters have been in the hands of the traditional rulers, the Sultans (*kerajaan*) since the colonial administration. The *kerajaan* performs a deciding role not only in administrative matters, but also in doctrinal ones (Gullick 1992; 1987; Milner 1995). It is the *kerajaan* which controls and decides on the most valid interpretation — according to the doctrines of the *Ahl al-Sunnah wa al-Jama'ah* — and bans any other interpretation and practice regarded as invalid (*sesat*) such as the *Dar al-Arqam*. In contrast, the *Dar al-Arqam* has never been banned in Indonesia and, in fact, it is gaining new momentum in this country after the fall of President Suharto in 1998.

It is important to point out that Sunni doctrines in Southeast Asia, or at least in Indonesia, have undergone some changes despite a great deal of continuity. In Indonesia, at least since the 1980s, there has been some convergence in the teachings and practices of various groups of Muslims. This is mainly due to the fact that there is no institution or Muslim group and organization that can claim to have the most valid interpretation of Islam. Not least importantly, various streams of Islamic thought coming from elsewhere in the Muslim world have contributed to the hybdridity of contemporary Islamic thought and practices in Indonesia.

By comparison, in Malaysia and Brunei, the *kerajaan* have tended to resist religious changes, and maintain Sunni traditionalism. In Brunei Darussalam, the doctrines of Sunnism are integrated into the national ideology called "MIB" (*Melayu,* Islam, *Beraja,* or Malay, Islam, and Kingship). In Malaysia, the Malay rulers are continuously very sensitive to what they regard as "deviant teaching" (*ajaran menyimpang*), and take very harsh measures against any group considered to deviate from the official Sunni doctrines (Abdullah 1997; 1990).

The formation of Sunni tradition in Southeast Asia had taken place more strongly from the seventeenth to the second half of the nineteenth centuries. In this period, there lived a number of Malay-Indonesian students, who later became *ulama* and obtained their education for many years in the Mecca and Medina in Saudi Arabia. They were involved in the cosmopolitan networks of the *ulama* centered in Mecca and Medina, and formed connections to Africa, South Asia, Central Asia and, of course, Southeast Asia. Most of them returned to the archipelago thus becoming the most important channel of transmission of Islamic doctrines from the Middle East to the Malay-Indonesian world (Azra 2004; Ishak and Othman 2000; Laffan 2003).

The most important among these Malay-Indonesian *ulama* were: Nur al-Din al-Raniri (better known in the Malay-Indonesian world as Nuruddin ar-Raniri), Abd al-Ra'uf al-Sinkili (Abdurrauf Singkel), Muhammad Yusuf al-Makassari (Syekh Yusuf Makasar) all in the seventeenth century; Abd al-Samad al-Palimbani (Syekh Abdussamad Palembang), Daud al-Patani (Southern Thailand), Abd al-Malik ibn Abd Allah (better known in the Malay Peninsula as Tok Pulau Manis Trengganu), Muhammad Arshad al-Banjari (Syekh Arsyad Banjar), Muhammad Nafis al-Banjari (Syekh Nafis Banjar) all in the eighteenth century; and Ahmad Rifa'i Kalisalak (Ahmad Ripangi of Pekalongan Central Java), Muhammad Nawawi al-Bantani (Nawawi Banten), Muhammad Mahfuzh al-Termasi, Muhammad Saleh Darat al-Samarani, Ahmad Khatib Sambas, Ahmad Khatib al-Minangkabawi, Hasan Mustafa Bandung and some others in the nineteenth century.

Most of them — if not all — were prolific writers who produced the earliest works written in the Malay language. To take some examples, al-Raniri was the first writer who produced a work entitled *al-Sirat al-Mustaqim* on *fiqh ibadah* (rituals); al-Sinkili was the first scholar who wrote a book on *fiqh mu'amalah* (social intercourse) entitled *Mir'at al-Tullab*, as well as a book on *tafsir* (Qur'anic exegesis) entitled *Tarjuman al-Mustafid*. Taken together, all these scholars produced a great number of works relating to various disciplines of Islamic knowledge, such as *fiqh* (*shari'a*), *tafsir*, *hadith* (the tradition of the Prophet Muhammad), *tasawwuf* (Sufism), and *tarikh* (history). All of their works introduced the orthodox teachings of the most authoritative Sunni *ulama* in Arabia or in the area now is known as the Middle East.

Furthermore, all of these great *ulama* and their networks of students played an instrumental role in strengthening the position of Sunnism in the Malay-Indonesian world. When they returned to the archipelago together with their students, they founded essential Islamic institutions such as *pesantren* or *pondok*, which were traditional Islamic boarding schools. It is true that some of *pesantren*s or *pondok*s had been founded since the early period of Islam in the archipelago, but it is from the nineteenth century onwards that these educational institutions gained a new momentum. The continued increased in the number of the returning students and *haj* pilgrims from Mecca, had been mainly responsible for the rapid foundation of *pesantren*s and *pondok*s in various places in the Malay-Indonesian world.

The *pesantren* and *pondok* play a very crucial role in at least three things. First, the transmission of Islamic knowledge from the *ulama* (or *kiyai* in Java) to the *santri*s (students of *pesantren* or *pondok*). This transmission and transfer of knowledge is generally smooth since most of the *santri*s live in the *pesantren*'s compound. Second, As far as Islamic tradition is concerned, the *pesantren* hold fast to the Sunni doctrines and practices as described above, thus maintaining Islamic tradition while the *santri*s were taught in the orthodox Sunni tradition. Thirdly, one of the most important tasks of the *kiyai*s is to prepare their *santri*s to become *ulama*, thus ensuring the reproduction of the *ulama* themselves. Of course not all of the *santri*s would eventually become *ulama*, but some of them do, and they in turn founded their own *pesantren* or *pondok*. Most of the *pesantren*s or *pondok*s in Indonesia and Malaysia have been associated with Islamic traditionalism, that in the Indonesian case is generally represented by the Nahdlatul Ulama (NU) as discussed below.

I would argue that the Malay-Indonesian *ulama*, particularly of the seventeenth century were mostly responsible for the earliest reforms of Islamic teachings and Muslim life in the archipelago. It has been widely known that the Islam that spread in the Malay-Indonesian world from the end of the twelfth century had mixed with local beliefs and practices. This is due to the fact that — as has been said above — Islam was introduced mainly by wandering Sufi teachers who tended to be very accommodating and inclusive, by accepting pre-Islamic beliefs and practices that continued to hold sway among newly converted Muslims. The *ulama* from the seventeenth century onwards, through their works and preaching, reformed this kind of religious life by introducing a more scripturally oriented brand of Islam. They, for instance, appealed for a more *shari'a*-oriented Sufism as taught, for instance, by al-Ghazali. They put a great emphasis on the importance of the *shari'a* in Muslims' life.

The peaceful and moderate reforms among Southeast Asian Muslims were disrupted by the rise of the Padri movement in the Minangkabau area (West Sumatra) in the nineteenth century. Strongly influenced by the Wahhabi ideology in Arabia, a group of *ulama* led by Tuanku Nan Renceh, Tuanku Imam Bonjol and others introduced radical reforms aimed at purifying Islam in the area, from pre-Islamic belief and practices as well as from un-Islamic *adat* (customs). The Padri radicalism was confronted by a majority of Muslims led by Tuanku Nan Tuo, who preferred peaceful reforms, thus resulting in the famous Padri Wars that ended only after the interference of the Dutch (Azra 1988).

Even though the Padris were able to strengthen the position of Islam in the Minangkabau, the radical movement was short-lived and failed to spread elsewhere in the Malay-Indonesian archipelago. The Padri was the only precedence of the Wahhabi-like radicalism throughout the Asian region. In fact the very word "Wahhabi" remains an anathema for many Muslims in the region. There are radical groups in Southeast Asia that have come to assert themselves after the Padri movement, but their religious ideology and praxis — as we will see below — are different from the Padris of West Sumatra.

Another wave of Islamic reformism came to the shores of the Malay-Indonesian world in the early twentieth century. Transmitted mostly by returning Malay-Indonesian students from Cairo and the spread of reformist literature, Islamic modernism, as we will be discussed further below, soon gained momentum in the Malay-Indonesian world. The most important proponents of this new brand of reformism were Jamal al-Din al-Afghani, Muhammad Abduh, Muhammad Rashid Rida and others who were centred mostly in Cairo, Egypt (Laffan 2003; Azra 1999; Noer 1973; Roff 1967; Abu Bakar 1994; Hamzah 1981; Eliraz 2002).

This new reformism is also usually categorized as "Islamic modernism". The term "Islamic modernism", which refers to this new wave should be qualified, since it actually contains a mixture of various streams. One distinct colour of thought in this wave is Salafism, meaning the return to the pure and original Islam as practised by the Prophet Muhammad and his companions. Therefore, unwarranted innovations (*bid'ah*), and superstitions (*khurafat*) were opposed, and with appeals for independent reasoning (*ijtihad*) instead. In line with this appeal, Muslims were also urged to adopt modern institutions in the field of education, economy, social and other aspects of life. With all of these emphases, it is no surprise that this wave of Islamic reformism is called "Islamic modernism".

MAINSTREAM SUNNI ORGANIZATIONS

The most loyal and "perfect" representation of a Muslim group who claim to adhere strictly to the Sunni doctrine in Southeast Asia, or more precisely Indonesia, is the Nahdlatul 'Ulama (literally "the awakening of Muslim religious scholars). Founded in 1926, the NU now is the largest Muslim organization in Indonesia with a claimed membership of some forty million Muslims. Holding fast to the Sunni tradition, the NU religious ideology is based on the doctrines of "*Aswaja*" (*Ahl al-Sunnah wa al-Jama'ah*). Again, the majority of Indonesian Muslims are of course Sunnis, but it is the NU, which is claimed time and again by its members to be the most authentic representation of the Sunni religious ideology. Therefore, the NU is called the "traditionalist" organization for its strict following of the Sunni doctrine (van Bruinessen 1994; Barton and Fealy, eds. 1996; Feillard 1999; Qomar 2002).

There are some other traditionalist Muslim organizations throughout Indonesia, but most of them are provincially based. They include al-Washliyyah in North Sumatra, Perti in West Sumatra, Mathlaul Anwar in West Java, Nahdlatul Watan in Nusa Tenggara Barat, al-Khairat and Dar ud-Dakwah wa al-Irsyad Indonesia (DDII) in Sulawesi. Even though each organization is independent and has no official affiliation with each other, they have a strong network with the NU.

The NU has long been associated with rural Islam. In fact its strong base is the rural area, mostly in East and Central Java. The NU *ulama*, better known as *kiyai*, in turn have their strong base in the *pesantrens*, or Muslim traditional educational institutions, which, as stated above, were mostly founded in the nineteenth century. Resisting Dutch or Western educational systems, the *pesantrens* only began modernizing in the 1970s through the inclusion of modern subjects in their curricula. Modernization of the *pesantrens* and the affiliated *madrasahs* continued with the adoption of the curricula of 1994 issued by Ministry of National Education and complemented by the

Ministry of Religious Affairs. The modernization of the *pesantrens* has brought this Muslim educational institution into the mainstream of national education.

Considering the religious ideology (*aswaja*) of the NU — that is "Islamic traditionalism — as well as the adoption of national curricula by the *pesantrens* and *madrasahs*, it is wrong to assume that these two Islamic educational institutions are the breeding ground of radicalism. In fact, the religious ideology of Islamic traditionalism with its strong colour of Sufism is inclusive and accommodating, not only in religious belief and practices, but also in the political life. Therefore, it is absurd to expect that the *pesantrens* and *madrasahs* would produce radical *santris*.

It is necessary to keep in mind, however, that even though the NU and its *kiyais* and *pesantrens* have long been regarded as traditionalist — as far as their religious beliefs and practices are concerned — there are a lot of changes that can be observed within this traditional wing of Indonesian Islam. After having experienced bitter political disappointments in the period between the late 1960s and 1970s under President Suharto, the NU under the leadership of Abdurrahman Wahid pulled itself out from politics and returned to the "*Khittah 1926*", that is, it focused itself on being a socio-religious organization. Since then NU religious doctrines have undergone rethinking and reassessment. Conscious efforts were carried out by Wahid and some of his younger colleagues to liberate NU religious worldview without discarding its "traditionalism" in order to be more relevant to the contemporary Indonesian context and challenges. Wahid's efforts now have resulted in the birth of new offshoot of young NU thinkers, who have introduced the idea of "contextual", "indigenous" and "liberal" Islam that has sometimes caused controversies among Indonesian Muslims (Qomar 2002).

The second largest Muslim organization in Indonesia, the Muhammadiyah (founded in 1912) is a Sunni organization as well. But the Muhammadiyah's understanding of Sunnism is, to a certain extent, different from that of NU. Even though Muhammadiyah basically accepts the basic principles of the Sunni doctrine, it is very critical of certain Sunni traditional beliefs and practices that it considers religiously "impure" for having no strong religious grounding (*bid'ah*). In line with my argument above concerning the "reformism" of al-Afghani, Abduh and others in the Middle East, Muhammadiyah can be categorized as a Salafi organization, which appeals to the Muslims to return to "pure" and "pristine" Islam as practised by the Prophet Muhammad and his companions. At the same time Muhammadiyah is opposed to unwarranted innovations (*bid'ah*) and superstitions (*khurafat*).

Muhammadiyah, claiming the following of some thirty-five million Indonesian Muslims, contrary to the NU, had in fact introduced the reforms of Islamic beliefs and practices through the following: first, purification of Islam from unwarranted innovations; second, opening the gate of personal religious decision (*ijtihad*); and third, adoption of modern approaches to modernize Muslims, particularly through education, health and other social services (Noer 1973; Nakamura 1983; Alfian 1989).

To a large extent, Muhammadiyah's religious ideology was influenced by Salafi thinkers in Arabia and Egypt, prominent among them were Ibn Taymiyyah, Muhammad ibn 'Abd al-Wahhab, Jamal al-Din al-Afghani, Muhammad Abduh and Rashid Rida. All of these thinkers espoused Islamic reforms through purification of Islamic beliefs and practices. But it is important to point out that Muhammadiyah had not adopted the radical approach introduced by al-Wahhab, the founder of the Wahhabi movement; Muhammadiyah, rather, adopted peaceful methods of reform through modern education and preaching (*dakwah*).

Given this brand of Islamic religious ideology and outlook, Muhammadiyah has previously been involved in conflicts with the NU. But, again, most of the conflicts resulted from differences in trivial religious matters (*furu'*) regarding certain aspects of Islamic ritual, and from competition and struggles to gain political influence and power. But since the 1980s, there has in fact been convergence in much of religious matters and rituals where they differed in the past. But rivalry between the members of two organizations can still be observed in the political field.

Muhammadiyah has often been categorized as a "modernist" Muslim organization that has its strongest base in urban areas. This is true as far as Muhammadiyah's adoption of modern schooling and social services are concerned. On the other hand, Muhammadiyah, at the level of ideology at least, is a rather "conservative" organization. Compared with the NU, which now tends to be more liberal, the Muhammadiyah seems to be more reserved and very cautious in its approach to renew and reform of Islamic beliefs and practices; Muhammadiyah now tends to stick only to the idea of purification of Islam without providing any substantive intellectual discourse regarding many issues that are under discussion among the Muslim public.

Despite their differences, the NU and Muhammadiyah remain Sunni organizations. Thanks to their nationwide networks, both continue to exert a great influence among Indonesian Muslims apart from much rapid political and social changes that have taken place in Indonesia in the two decades at least, and more importantly after the fall of President Suharto from his long-held power in 1998. Both remain at the forefront of a moderate and nationalistic brand of Indonesian Islam despite the rise of smaller Muslim groups, some of which preach a very literal understanding of Islam as well as having a Middle Eastern orientation.

It is clear that one cannot find organizations such as NU or Muhammadiyah in Malaysia, or anywhere else in Southeast Asia. As argued above, Islamic life is tightly controlled by the state, giving only very limited room for Muslims to express themselves. Therefore, Muslim organizations in Malaysia are very limited not only in terms of their number, but also in terms of their influence, activities, and institutions affiliated with them. All mainstream Muslim organizations are also known as *dakwah* organizations, because of their strong emphasis on Islamic preaching (*dakwah*) rather than anything else.

It seems that the most important mainstream Muslim organization in Malaysia is the *Angkatan Belia Islam Malaysia* (ABIM, or Malaysian Youth Movement), founded in 1969 not long after the 13 May 1969 racial riots between Chinese and Malays. The ABIM is very active in *dakwah,* especially among university students and youth in general; it encourages lobbying efforts and active participation in politics (Peletz 1997, p. 235; Shamsul 1997, pp. 212–19).

Another important organization is the Jamaah Islah Malaysia (JIM), which was originally named the Islamic Representative Council (IRC), establihed in 1974 in the United Kingdom by Malaysian students studying there. With the conversion into JIM, and registered officially as an NGO, this organization also includes in its membership ex-students who studied in other countries (Salleh 199, pp. 44–45).

There is little doubt that in terms of religious belief and practices, the ABIM and IRC are within the realm of mainstream Sunni. It is suggested that with respect to religious ideology, both organizations are largely traditional, even though they are "modern" in terms of programmes and activities. But in the 1980s the two organizations were considered "radical" by the government because they were unequivocally vocal, and critical of the regime. This attitude is related to their main aim, which that was to alter public life styles and change the prevailing secular establishment into an Islamic system. Despite this "radical" aim, both organizations by no means resorted to violence. In the 1990s, however, the ABIM and IRC have adopted a relatively non-confrontational stance, and have become much more aligned with the government, which dominates the interpretation of Islam. This change can be attributed to a more accommodating attitude of the government, which was followed by the entrance of Anwar Ibrahim, former leader of ABIM, into the establishment.

Other than the above two organizations, one probably should mention only another two organizations; they are the United Malay National Organization (UMNO) and PAS (Partai Islam Se-Malaysia, All Malaysian Islamic Party). It is clear that UMNO and PAS are political parties, not *dakwah* organizations. But, there is little doubt that the two organizations play an important role in state-sponsored Islamization in Malaysia. In fact, UMNO and PAS have been involved in bitter struggles in their efforts to dominate the meaning and interpretation of Islam among the Malays.

It seems that UMNO tends to be more liberal in its interpretation of Islam, while the PAS tends to be more literal, even though in religious practices both tend to be "traditional". The PAS, however, is considered radical not only because it aims at establishing an Islamic state in Malaysia, but also because of its vocal and critical attitude towards the Mahathir government. Furthermore, as a political party, PAS adopts campaigning methods such as the use of religious and ethnic issues that are sometimes considered offensive by the government. The PAS is considered to have toned down its radicalism in the 1990s when it came under *ulama* leadership. This change, combined with the growing resentment against then Prime Minister Mahathir who sacked and accused Anwar Ibrahim of misconducts, allowed PAS to score some success in the 1999 elections.

SUNNI MUSLIMS: SPLINTER GROUPS

There is yet another splinter and "radical" Muslim group in Malaysia that is the Darul Arqam, which had been regarded by the Malaysian Government as being outside of the mainstream and, therefore, was outlawed in 1994. As has been shown by Salleh (1992) and Hamid (1999), the Darul Arqam, an apolitical Sufi-messianic revivalist organization, which in addition to concentrating its activities on Islamic spirituality, conducted a number of successful economic enterprises. The Malaysian Government, however, considered it a deviant (*sesat*) group and, therefore, made it illegal. But many observers maintained that the banning was actually politically motivated.

There were attempts to also ban the Darul Arqam in Indonesia. This created a great deal of controversy. The government, supported by the Muhammadiyah on the one hand, wanted it to be banned. But the NU on the other hand, opposed the move, since it regarded that there was nothing wrong with the beliefs and practices of the Darul Arqam. In fact, the NU found a great deal of similarities and affinities with the Darul Arqam. In the end, the Indonesian Government took no serious action against the Darul Arqam, even though it went "underground" for sometime, before it openly reinvigorated itself in the post-Suharto period.

From a theological point of view, the present-day hardliner Muslim groups in Indonesia like Lasykar Jihad (LJ), Front Pembela Islam (FPI), Majelis Mujahidin Indonesia (MMI), and Hizb al-Tahrir, and the Jama'ah Islamiyyah (JI) in Malaysia and Singapore — if it exists at all — are Sunni. None of these groups is *Shi'ite*. It is important to make it clear that they are far from monolithic; there are a lot of differences among these small groups, not only in terms of their religious attitudes, but also in their political views and action.

But as in the past history of the interpretation and understanding of Islamic doctrines, there are individuals or Muslim groups which tend to be more literal in their religious outlook, and more radical in their approach to religious and political matters. In this regard, most of the groups are radical Salafi, if not "neo-Kharijite". They are Salafi for one obvious reason, that is, their appeal for and espousal of the "pure" and "pristine" Islam practised in the time of the Prophet Muhammad and his companions (*sahabah*).

To achieve that end, however, they tend to use radical approaches, not peaceful means like education and preaching (*dakwah*). In this last respect they are not unlike the Wahhabis, and even — to a certain degree — the Kharijites. But their radicalism is much less compared to the classic Kharijites who formulated three radical steps; first, *takfir*, proclaiming other Muslims as non-believing; second, *hijrah*, migrating from "corrupted areas" that are occupied by other Muslims and non-Muslims to an Islamic area; third, *jihad*, waging wars against mainstream Muslims who refuse to accept their doctrines. As one might observe, the three steps have not been publicly adopted by these groups.

However, one should not jump to the conclusion that the theological reason is the only motive for the rise of radical Muslim groups in Southeast Asia. In fact there are many other factors and root causes that have nothing to do with Islam that are working to provide momentum for them to express themselves in a more visible, vocal, militant, and radical manner. In the case of Indonesia, some other very important root causes that gave rise to radicalism are, among others, liberalization of the political system, fragmentation and conflicts among the political elite and parties, failure of law enforcement, economic deprivation, and socio-cultural dislocation and alienation (Azra 2003).

To conclude, it is terribly wrong to assume that these radical groups are influential in Southeast Asia. The history and sociology of Southeast Asian Muslim societies have shown us that this kind of fringe groups have never been able to exercise significant influence among Muslim society as a whole. One can expect, most of such groups will disappear through time simply because their literal interpretation and radicalism cannot be accepted by other Muslims. In the meantime, however, moderate Muslim leaders and organizations should pay more attention to this tendency of radicalism, and find ways to address it.

References

Abdullah, Abdul Rahman Haji. *Pemikiran Islam di Malaysia: Sejarah dan Aliran.* Jakarta: Gema Insani Press, 1997.

Abdullah, Abdul Rahman Haji. *Pemikiran Umat Islam di Nusasntara: Sejarah dan Perkembangannya hingga Abad 19.* Kuala Lumpur: Dewan Bahasa dan Pustaka, 1990.

Abdullah, Firdaus Haji. *Radical Malay Politics: Its Origins and Early Development.* Petaling Jaya: Pelanduk Publication, 1985.

Abu Bakar, Ibrahim bin. *Islamic Modernism in Malaysia: The Life and Thought of Sayid Syekh al-Hadi 1867–1934.* Kuala Lumpur: University of Malaya Press, 1994.

Alfian. *Muhammadiyah: The Political Behavior of a Muslim Modernist Organization under Dutch Colonialism.* Yogyakarta: Gadjah Mada University Press, 1989.

Azra, Azyumardi. *The Origins of Islamic Reformism in Southeast Asia: Networks of Malay-Indonesian and Middle Eastern 'Ulama' in the 17th and 18th Centuries.* Canberra: AAAS & Allen-Unwin, 2004.

Azra, Azyumardi. "Southeast Asian Islam in the Post-Bali Bombing: Debunking the Myth", paper presented at Workshop "After Bali: The Threat of Terrorism in Southeast Asia", Institute of Defence and Strategic Studies (IDSS), Nanyang Technological University, Singapore, 27–28 January, 2003.

Azra, Azyumardi. "Globalization of Indonesian Muslim Discourse: Contemporary Religio-Intellectual Connections between Indonesia and the Middle East", in J. Meuleman (ed.), *Islam in the Era of Globalization: Muslim Attitudes towards Modernity and Identity*, London & New York: RoutledgeCurzon, 2002.

Azra, Azyumardi. "Syi'ah di Indonesia: Antara Mitos dan Realitas", introduction in *Syi'ah dan Politik di Indonesia: Sebuah Penelitian*, edited by A. Rahman Zainuddin and Hamdan Basyar. Bandung: Mizan, 2000.

Azra, Azyumardi. "The Transmission of al-Manar's Reformism to the Malay-Indonesian World: The Cases of al-Imam and al-Munir". *Studia Islamika: Indonesian Journal for Islamic Studies* 6, III, 1999.

Azra, Azyumardi. *Pergolakan Politik Islam: Dari Fundamentalisme, Modernisme hingga Post-Modernisme*. Jakarta: Paramadina, 1996.

Azra, Azyumardi. "The Rise and Decline of Minangkabau Surau: A Traditional Islamic Educational Institution in West Sumatra during the Dutch Colonialism", M.A. thesis, Columbia University, New York, 1988.

Barton, Greg and Greg Fealy, eds. *Nahdlatul Ulama: Traditional Islam and Modernity in Indonesia*. Clayton: Monash Asia Institute, 1996.

Elizar, Giora. "The Islamic Reformist Movement in the Malay-Indonesian World in the First Four Decades of the 20th Century: Insights Gained from a Comparative Look at Egypt". *Studia Islamika: Indonesian Journal for Islamic Studies* 9, I, 2002.

Feillard, Andree. *NU Vis-à-vis Negara: Pencarian Isi, Bentuk dan Makna*, Yogyakarta: LkiS, 1999.

Gullick, J.M. *Rulers and Residents: Influence and Power in the Malay States 1870–1920*. Oxford: Oxford University Press, 1992.

Gullick J.M. *Malay Society in the Late Nineteenth Century*. Singapore: Oxford University Press, 1987.

Hamid, Ahmad Fauzi Abdul. "New Trends of Islamic Resurgence in Contemporary Malaysia: Sufi-Revivalism, Messianis, and Economic Activism". *Studia Islamika: Indonesian Journal of Islamic Studies* 6, III, 1999.

Hamzah, Abu Bakar. *Al-Imam: Its Role in Malay Society 1906–1908*. Kuala Lumpur: Media Cendekiawan, 1981.

Ishak, Md. Sidin Ahmad and Mohamad Redzuan Othman. *The Malays in the Middle East*. Kuala Lumpur: University of Malaya Press, 2000.

Laffan, M.F. *Islamic Nationhood and Colonial Indonesia: The Umma below the Winds*. London: RoutledgeCurzon, 2003.

Martin, R.C., M.R. Woodward and D.S. Atmaja. *Defenders of Reason in Islam: Mu'tazilism from Medieval School to Modern Symbol*. Oxford: Oneworld, 1997.

Milner, A. *The Invention of Politics in Colonial Malaysia: Contesting Nationalism and the Expansion of the Public Sphere*. Cambridge: Cambridge University Press, 1995.

Mutalib, Hussin. *Islam in Malaysia: From Revivalism to Islamic State*. Singapore: Singapore University Press, 1993.

Nagata, J. *The Reflowering of Malaysian Islam: Modern Religious Radicals and Their Roots*. Vancouver: University of British Columbia Press, 1984.

Nakamura, Mitsuo. *The Crescent Arises over the Banyan Tree: A Study of the Muhammadiyah Movement in a Central Javanese Town*. Yogyakarta: Gadjah Mada University Press, 1983.

Nasution, Harun. *Islam Rasional*, edited by Saiful Mujani. Bandung: Mizan, 1998.

Nasution, Harun. *Muhammad Abduh dan Teologi Rasional*. Jakarta: Universitas Indonesia Press, 1987.

Noer, Deliar. *The Modernist Muslim Movement in Indonesia 1900–1942*. Kuala Lumpur: Oxford University Press, 1973.

Peletz, M.G. "Ordinary Muslim" and Muslim Resurgents in Contemporary Malaysia: Notes on an Ambivalent Relationship". In *Islam in an Era of Nation-States*, edited by R.W. Hefner and P. Horvatich. Honolulu: University of Hawaii Press, 1997.

Qomar, Mujamil. *NU "Liberal": Dari Tradisionalisme Ahlussunnah ke Universalisme Islam*. Introduction. Azyumardi Azra, Bandung: Mizan, 2002.

Roff, W.R. *The Origins of Malay Nationalism*. Kuala Lumpur: University of Malaya Press, 1967.

Salleh, Muhammad Syukri. "Recent Trends of Islamic Revivalism in Malaysia". *Studia Islamika: Indonesian Journal for Islamic Studies* 6, II, 1999.

Salleh, Muhammad Syukri. *An Islamic Approach to Rural Development: The Arqam Way*. London: Asoib International, 1992.

Shamsul A.B. "Identity Construction, Nation Formation, and Islamic Revivalism in Malaysia". In *Islam in an Era of Nation-States*, edited by R.W. Hefner and P. Horvatich. Honolulu: University of Hawaii Press, 1997.

Van Bruinessen, M. *NU: Tradisi, Relasi-relasi Kuasa, Pencarian Wacana Baru*. Yogyakarta: LKiS, 1994.

2

THE HISTORY OF ISLAM IN SOUTHEAST ASIA: SOME QUESTIONS AND DEBATES

Johan H. Meuleman

INTRODUCTION

Islam probably reached Southeast Asia in the very first century of the Islamic era. Although this early period may be considered as the starting point of the Islamization process, the most recent events have shown that its end has yet to come. Many theories have been offered on the origin and development of Islam in this region. Any approach that fails to consider a diversity of factors and a variety of successive stages in its history will also misunderstand contemporary Southeast Asian Islam. This chapter will present a few details to substantiate this thesis. It will also analyze some debates on the history of Islam in the region and highlight the inter-related scholarly and political dimensions of these discussions.

The chapter will pay particular attention to the role of international networks in the development of Southeast Asian Islam and the existence of various international, regional, and local intellectual references. As cases in point, it will offer some details on the development of Islamic educational institutions and the circulation and translation of books produced in various parts of the world. It will also examine the position of the Southeast Asian Muslim community in past and present globalization, Islamic "counter-globalization", and localization processes.

To complete this historical survey, this chapter will explain some contemporary dissimilarities of the situation and characteristics of Islam in the various countries of the region by referring to differing styles of colonization and decolonization. Although much research has been done on the history of Islam in Southeast Asia, many questions remain unanswered and various debates undecided. This condition is not only of an academic or scholarly nature, but has ideological and political dimensions too.

THE PROBLEM OF ORIGIN

The very starting point of Islamic history in the region is matter of controversy. Estimations vary from the first century of the Islamic era, that is, approximately the latter half of the seventh and the first half of the eighth century of the Christian or "common" era, to somewhere around the twelfth century of this common era. The question of the time in which Islam was introduced into Southeast Asia is closely related to questions of the region it came from, and of the people who brought it. This relationship is both of a technical and of an ideological nature.

By a technical connection I mean the obvious link between the region from which Islam was introduced into Southeast Asia, the people or ethnic group who did so, and the period in which this group was involved in contacts with the latter. The nature of these contacts, commercial, intellectual, military, or otherwise, is another object of discussion, to which we shall return later.

The ideological relationship is based on the widespread conviction that the purest form of Islam is the form that existed at the very birth of the religion, among the Arabs, on the Arabian peninsula. This standpoint has been shared by many Muslims and non-Muslims. These Muslims consider that one of these criteria being met is positive, two better, and three the ideal. In addition, most Muslim scholars of the region tend to emphasize the pureness and vigour of Islam in their home countries. On the other hand, the European historians of Islam living in the colonial period were inclined to highlight the syncretic, superficial, or derived nature of Southeast Asian Islam.[1] These attitudes, although not always conscious or the result of deliberate policies, are in conformity with the different political and social positions and interests of both groups. Their shared idea on what was "real" Islam combined with their diametrically opposed judgements on Islam in this region led both groups to curiously contrasting theories on the Islamization of Southeast Asia.

Let us follow the debate in some detail. Until well beyond the middle of the nineteenth century, most European specialists ascribed the spread of Islam in Southeast Asia to Arabs. Examples from the middle of the nineteenth century are the Dutchmen S. Keyzer, G.K. Niemann, J.J. de Hollander, and P.J. Veth. A few decades earlier, the Scotsman, John Crawfurd had indicated a mixed origin: Arabs and "Mahomedans of the Eastern coast of India". He was followed by T.W. Arnold. None of them specified where these Arabs came from.[2] Only Keyzer claimed that Southeast Asian Islam originated from Egypt. His opinion was based on the argument that the same Shafi'ite school of jurisprudence was dominant both in Egypt and Southeast Asia. This was quite a weak argument since many other regions in the Middle East and South Asia adhere to this school too.[3] Most later European authors, however, defended the theory that Southeast Asian Islam originated from India. Those who upheld this standpoint included the Dutchmen, J. Pijnappel, C. Snouck Hurgronje, J.P. Moquette, R.A. Kern, B.H.M. Vlekke, J. Gonda, B.J.O. Schrieke, and more recently G.W.J. Drewes; the Britons, R.O. Winstedt and more recently D.G.E. Hall; and the Frenchman, G.H. Bousquet. They assumed that Islam had arrived in the region from the twelfth century of the Christian era or later.[4] Their main arguments related to the existence of international maritime trade routes, the identity of schools of Islamic jurisprudence, and the similarity of gravestones or literary styles and themes between particular Indian regions and places in the Malay-Indonesian archipelago. They did not agree on the question of which part of the Indian sub-continent had been the first source of Southeast Asian Islam. In 1872, Jan Pijnappel claimed that Arabs from Gujarat and Malabar had spread Islam in the Indonesian archipelago.[5] In a 1912 article, Moquette mentioned Gujarat and he was followed by most later European authors. During the last two decades of the nineteenth century however, Christiaan Snouck Hurgronje argued that South India was much more probable as the origin of Indonesian Islam. He ascribed the first stage of this Islamization process to Indian middlemen of the international maritime trade and the refining, finishing touch to Arabs.[6] More than half a century later, a British author, G.E. Marrison, restated that South India was the origin. His main arguments were that Islam became only established in Gujarat after it was brought to the Malay-Indonesian archipelago, whereas South India became Muslim several centuries earlier; that the Shafi'ite tradition was dominant in South and not in West India, and that early Malay Muslim literature contained references to South India, not to Gujarat.[7] Drewes, in his own 1968 survey of the continuing debate, concluded that the South India theory was the most reliable one indeed.[8]

After the Indonesian people recovered its independence, it revised the established theories about is history, including the arrival of Islam. A number of regional and national seminars on Islamic history were organized. The most pertinent was the seminar on the Coming of Islam to Indonesia (*Seminar Masuknya Islam ke Indonesia*), held in Medan from 17 to 20 March 1963. In a rather formal way, it adopted a series of conclusions, the first of which was as follows: "[the participants conclude] that according to sources which we know, Islam entered for the first time in Indonesia during the first century of the *hijrah* (seventh/eighth century of the Christian era) and directly from Arabia".[9] In Malaysia, the Indian origin theory found a prominent opponent in S.M. Naguib al-Attas. He based his thesis of the Arab origin of Islam in the region on his observation that the Arabic rather than the Indian worldview was expressed through the religious literature that was produced in the Indonesian/Malay archipelago from the tenth century onwards.[10]

In view of the existence of maritime commercial relations between the Middle East and China since before the birth of the new religion, it is very probable that the coastal zones of Southeast Asia have had some contact with Muslims from the very first period of Islam. Among the many traders sailing from the Arab peninsula and the rest of the Middle East to the ports of South, then Southeast, and finally East Asia, some must have been Muslims. Not much more than this can be said, however. Drewes even warns against the use of certain Chinese texts from the first centuries of the Islamic era as proof of early cases of Islamization by Arabs in Sumatran ports. A number of authors, including Arnold, have considered references in these works to Arabs who resided in these ports as evidence. Drewes deemed it inconclusive, however, because some Chinese authors confounded the west coast of Sumatra and Arabia.[11] Nevertheless, very early contacts with Muslim traders in Southeast Asia are probable and they may be considered as the starting point of the Islamization process. As for the end point, the most recent developments in the area have shown that it has yet to come.

Not only do various viewpoints exist regarding the chronological, geographical, and ethnic origin of Southeast Asian Islam but opinions also differ on the mechanisms through which the new religion spread in the region. Many adherents both of the early Arab origin theory and of the later Indian origin standpoint indicated international maritime trade as the main mechanism. J.C. van Leur, an eminent Dutch specialist of early Asian trade, considered this analysis too simplistic and rather emphasized a combination of commercial and political motives that brought inhabitants of Javanese ports to embrace Islam.[12] A.C. Milner has suggested a similar explanation and stressed the pragmatic or utilitarian side of Islamization: Southeast Asian princes were attracted by the suprahuman position of the Muslim kings, whose power was enhanced by the Persian royal tradition and certain aspects of Islamic mysticism; traders were attracted by the advantage they would acquire by adopting the same religion as their foreign partners.[13] A.H. Johns preferred a totally different approach. He highlighted the role of Sufism and international scholarly networks. In his opinion, Sufism became a particularly strong vehicle for the international expansion of Islam after the fall of the Abbasid caliphate to the Mongols (Baghdad fell in 656/1258).[14] Azyumardi Azra has been inspired by Johns's work in his study of later, seventeenth and eighteenth centuries, international networks linking Southeast Asia, South Asia, and the Middle East. However, referring to R. Bulliet, he argues that the large-scale international expansion of Islamic mysticism started about three centuries earlier than Johns had claimed.[15]

THE ORIGIN OF THE PROBLEM

How should one cope with such a bewildering diversity of more or less contradictory opinions and theories on the development of Islam in Southeast Asia? Firstly, one should be aware that, in this question as in other scientific and scholarly issues, various theories often complete and refine rather than totally exclude each other. Secondly, scholarly opinions and attitudes are often related to ideological and political positions, although often this relationship is unconscious. It tends to be particularly strong in matters of great sensitivity and strategic interest such as religion and national history. Thirdly, adherents of opposing theories may very well take the same stereotypes or simplifications as their point of departure.

To start with the first question, one should abandon the widespread tendency to attempt to attribute the origin of Southeast Asian Islam to one ethnic group or region, or to explain its spread and development to a single mechanism. Furthermore, one should distinguish successive stages in the process of Islamization, some of which may have existed at a very early period, while other ones are still continuing today or may not even have begun yet. The first instance of a foreign Muslim trader setting foot on a Southeast Asian shore, the first moment such a trader settles in a local port, when he marries a local woman, Islam becomes the common religion of their family; the time a Southeast Asian ruler, through military submission, commercial interest, mystical fascination, and/or yet other factors, embraces Islam; the period public institutions and local culture begin to be influenced by Islamic principles and Muslim traditions; the period Southeast Asians, instead of consuming ideas and writings produced by foreign Muslims, start to create their own Islamic jurisprudence, educational institutions, and writings; all these moments should be distinguished. They have been mentioned in a more or less natural, successive order, but not all stages need to have produced themselves everywhere or in this order. Part of the confusion in debates on the development of Islam in Southeast Asia is due to a lack of distinction between these different stages. This lack of precision is also one of the causes by which various participants in these debates use the same terms of "Islamization" or "Islam" with different meanings.[16]

Another fact serious scholars should pay attention to is that notions like "Southeast Asian Islam" or "Indonesian Islam" are basically simplified concepts of some utility as analytical tools and should not lead to ignoring the differences between Muslim societies and ideas in Malacca, the northern coast of Java, the Javanese interior, and the island of Buton, to mention a few places, nor the contrast between the various colonial territories and post-colonial states of the region.

Finally, the numerous detailed studies of particular periods should be completed by analyses from a long-term perspective. The works of Denys Lombard and Anthony Reid are cases in point. Both scholars have in particular addressed the question of why Islam (Lombard) or Islam, Christianity, and Theravada Buddhism (Reid) have become dominant characteristics of large parts of Southeast Asia since the fifteenth, sixteenth, or early seventeenth centuries only, although these religions were present before. These observers of the *longue durée* in Southeast Asia, have each in his own way explained that one of the main mechanisms inducing this religious revolution was the opening up of its populations to new, international horizons. Both external and internal factors played a role. On the one hand, this period was characterized by the expansion and intensification of rivalling international trade networks: a Muslim one that had its basis in the Middle East and South Asia, a Catholic one that had its basis in Portugal, and later a predominantly Protestant one directed from the Dutch provinces. On the other hand, the period witnessed the transformation of various parts of Southeast Asia, especially its innumerable islands and the coastal zones, from relatively closed societies based on agriculture to extraverted societies in which maritime trade was a fundamental activity.[17] As is the case in other historical processes, in this one too external and internal factors were not totally independent nor can they always be clearly distinguished. Moreover, although the long-term perspective lends a particular attractiveness to this type of historical explanation, they too arouse questions. S.O. Robson, for example, has argued that, at least in the case of Majapahit, the theory which relates Islamization to the transformation of an agricultural into a maritime society, is not convincing.[18]

The second and third observations on the causes of so many different opinions on the history of Islam in Southeast Asia, and the way to deal with them, are related. They may be illustrated by having a look at the idea that Arab Islam, especially in its earliest form, is the purest form of Islam. It was explained above that this idea was and continues to be shared by many Western, non-Muslim and Southeast Asian Muslim scholars — as well as by politicians and administrators. This shared convention is supported by a static vision of Islam, which is also shared by many Muslim and non-Muslim specialists of Islamic studies. These shared ideas, however, become the foundation of totally opposing conclusions on the history of Islam in the region.[19] Those who, by national pride as Indonesians or Malaysians, for example, and by religious pride as Muslims, are eager to find evidence of the purity and seriousness of Islam in their countries will tend to exploit the smallest indication as proof of an early and preferably Arab origin of Islam in the region. They will quickly jump to the conclusion that the religion was present there from the very first century of the Islamic era. Their Western and non-Muslim opponents will tend to underscore the non-existence or inconclusiveness of any evidence of large-scale Islamization that had a profound impact on the Southeast Asian societies before the thirteenth century of the Christian era. Very probably, both parties are right, but the deeper truth lies in the combination of their conclusions and a dynamic understanding of Islam and Islamization.

MISUNDERSTANDINGS BETWEEN PAST AND PRESENT

Any approach that does not take into consideration a diversity of factors and a variety of successive stages in the development of Islam in Southeast Asia will not only fail to analyse its history properly, but also misunderstand contemporary Southeast Asian Islam. Short analyses of a number of additional debates relating to the history of Islam in Southeast Asia will substantiate this thesis. They will also show, once again, that these discussions have inter-related scholarly and political dimensions. They will bring one additional clarification: the opposition between Western, generally non-Muslim and Southeast Asian, especially Muslim specialists, which, without being absolute, often manifested itself during previous periods of scholarly debate, has become less sharp in more recent times.

The first case in point is the debate on the alleged syncretic character of Southeast Asian Islam. As mentioned above, one of the ways in which many Western scholars have tended to depreciate the importance and strength of Islam in this area has been to characterize it as syncretic. The nature of the mystical tradition and its prominent place in the region has often been considered as evidence in support of this judgement. Javanese Islam especially, has been treated this way. Clifford Geertz, in the title of one of his best-known books, even avoided the term "Islam" and used "The Religion of Java" instead.[20] Recently however, several authors have criticized this judgement. In his dissertation, another American, Mark Woodward, has concluded that the allegedly numerous Hindu or Buddhist elements are insignificant in Javanese Islam and that, moreover, mysticism cannot rightly be contrasted with "orthodox" Islam.[21] Furthermore, in a number of case studies, contemporary Indonesian Muslim scholars have tried to correct the traditional view that Indonesian, and especially Javanese, mysticism is unorthodox.[22]

A discussion that is connected to the preceding one concerns the relationship of mysticism and *fiqh* and their respective roles in the development of Southeast Asian Islam. The established opinion among Western scholars is that, after a possible earlier wave of Islamization which left no noteworthy traces, from about the thirteenth century of the Christian era, Islam spread in the Malay-Indonesian archipelago in a form dominated by mysticism, while the influence of Islamic law and jurisprudence remained reduced. A contemporary Dutch scholar, Karel Steenbrink, has corrected this opinion and argued that mysticism was not the only aspect of Islam that took root in the archipelago from this century onwards.[23] It has also been suggested that during a later period the legal and doctrinal rather than the mystical side of Islam was strengthened by intensive scholarly contacts with Mecca and Medina. Woodward, however, has shown that, at least before the Wahhabite ideology became established in the Arabian peninsula, these contacts became the vehicle of mystical doctrines as well.[24] This thesis was confirmed by Azyumardi, whose work offers many details.[25]

Another question relating to the Islamization of the region, although less subject to intense debate, concerns the peaceful nature of this process. Many authors have supported this characterization. It is certainly true that, in comparison to many parts of the Middle East, North Africa, and India, violence has played a relatively small role in the spread of the new religion. It would be inexact, however, to deny its existence completely. An example among the limited cases of Islamization through war in this region are the *Musu' Selleng*, the series of wars waged by the Kingdom of Gowa against the *Tellunpoccoe* alliance, consisting of the kingdoms of Bone, Soppeng, and Wajo, from 1607 to 1611 of the common era. This violent episode in the generally peaceful Islamization of South Sulawesi has been analyzed by Ahmed M. Sewang, who, in addition to the religious motive, has indicated the political and economic reasons for this series of expansionist campaigns.[26]

The non-violent character of the Islamization process, together with the prevalence of its mystical dimension and, according to some, even its unorthodox character, have been considered an important cause of the peacefulness and moderateness that have often been highlighted as particularities of Islam in this region. Once again, these viewpoints are justified from a perspective of comparison with many other Muslim societies. One should avoid oversimplification, however. The early nineteenth century Padri wars, on Western Sumatra, were quite an exceptional case of a violent Islamic reform movement in the region and the most recent dramatic developments in the Moluccas and other parts of the Indonesian Republic show that Indonesian Islam is not always pacific. The relationship of Islam and violence — or the absence of violence — is an extremely complicated question. Only in-depth analysis of a series of cases of conflict and — at least on the surface — absence of conflict will produce a balanced and comprehensive understanding of this relationship. As mere hints of the type of results a similar study might lead to, two short remarks may be made: serious analysis shows that the famed harmony within the Muslim community and between the various religious communities in New Order Indonesia was partly the result of repressive government policies; the recent inter-religious violence in the country, on the other hand, cannot be attributed to religion alone.[27]

Yet another recurring issue in the study of the history of Islam in Southeast Asia is the role of Arabs. It was explained above that the question of whether it was Arabs who introduced Islam to the region, has been hotly debated and that this debate has not been free of ideological and political elements. Even those scholars who admitted that Arabs had played a significant role disagreed on some points. Keyzer, as mentioned earlier, assumed it was Egyptian Arabs who had first brought Islam to the region. Later authors rejected the argument he based his theory on, that is, that both Egyptian and Southeast Asian Muslims adhered to the Shafi'ite school of jurisprudence. Rather, they emphasized the role of Arabs from the Hadhramaut, also adherents of the Shafi'ite tradition. This did not solve the problem either: Drewes and L.W.C. van den Berg have pointed out that the Hadramis only began to play some role of importance in the region at a much later stage.[28]

The role of Arabs in Southeast Asian Islam, whether large or limited, positive or negative, has always remained a sensitive issue. In 1925, the re-edition of the last part of the *Sĕrat Dĕrmangandul* in the *Javanese Almanac* led to protests in Central Java. Earlier editions of this work, which contrasted Java with Islam and the Javanese with the Muslims and more in particular the Arabs, but also with the Chinese, had not provoked significant reactions.

According to Drewes, this difference in reactions was mainly the result of the development of stronger social and political tensions between the various ethnic groups in 1925, compared to earlier moments at which this and similar texts had been published.[29] Similar incidents have happened since, from time to time, even in reaction to less rude forms of critical remarks on the role of Arabs in Indonesian history. The attitude of the Arabs to the colonizers is a particularly delicate topic. A recent case is the reaction to a scholarly article that appeared in the spring 1995 issue of *Studia Islamika. Indonesian Journal for Islamic Studies,* published under the authority of IAIN Syarif Hidayatullah, Jakarta. The article was a balanced, but critical assessment of the role of Sayyid Uthman, a Hadrami assistant to the Dutch colonial administration, written by Azyumardi Azra, editor-in-chief of the journal. Partly because of the weak Indonesian abstract of the article, a number of Southeast Asian Arabs protested. They sent letters to the author or the rector of IAIN, Syarif Hidayatullah. One of them even published a counter-publication in the form of a booklet entitled *Menangkal Fitnah Berbisa* [Warding Off Poisonous Slander]. The rector of IAIN, Syarif Hidayatullah, himself of Hadrami descent, convoked the editorial board of the journal for some cordial exchange of words. Among the statements of Azyumardi that aroused particular indignation were those relating to the economic, non-religious motives of the immigration of most Hadramis to Indonesia and their activities in the country, which were not in conformity with the idealized image that all or most Arabs in the country were primarily motivated by the holy cause of spreading and defending Islam.[30]

The question of whether — or to what extent — Indonesian Islam is part of a universal religion and civilization or a particular, isolated phenomenon has been the object of another continuing debate, related to some of the discussions mentioned in the preceding paragraphs. In all these debates, academic, ideological, and political factors play a role and interact. For example, some of the scholars who emphasized the superficial character of Indonesian Islam, its particularity in comparison with the classical, Middle Eastern model, or the limited field of application of its legal prescripts in comparison with *adat* (customary) law, were among the prominent supporters of policies such as the assimilation of the Muslim population of the colonies into Dutch culture and civilization, the restriction of their religion to the domain of rituals, and their legal administration in the framework of a large number of different *adat* systems rather than Islamic law. In post-colonial Southeast Asia, almost the same scholarly debates continue to be related to ideological and political issues, such as the attitude of Indonesian or Malaysian Muslims towards Arabs and the Middle East, to the West, to their fellow-countrymen who adhere to other religions, to the place of Islamic law in their states and societies, and to their understanding of Islam and Islamic law.[31]

LOCAL ISLAM IN GLOBAL INTERACTION

The preceding discussions have shown that Southeast Asian Islam has been shaped in the course of a long, continuing process of various stages, by multiple mechanisms, and through manifold contacts. At the same time, Islam has been conditioned by the particular local traditions and situations. We therefore understand what Southeast Asian Islam — or Islam as it has developed in any of the numerous states and regions of this large zone — is not: it is not an exact copy of any model existing elsewhere in the Muslim world, nor a phenomenon totally isolated from and unrelated to Islam as a universal and global religion and civilization, nor a static entity beyond all transformation in the course of time. A series of short notes on diverse aspects of Southeast Asian Islam, concerning various moments of its historical development, will clarify this point.

Several authors have paid attention to the international contacts Southeast Asian Muslims have had, from the very introduction of their religion in the region up to the present, through various commercial, mystical, and scholarly networks. Lombard and Reid have explained that the very conversion to Islam of large parts of the inhabitants of Southeast Asia brought them a new and wider understanding of time, space, and human civilization and their position within these frames of reference.[32] Other authors have concentrated on scholarly and mystical contacts, through the circulation of students, teachers, and texts. Among them are Johns and al-Attas, who have tried to reconstruct which texts and which literary and religious styles were transmitted, and also from which points of origin to which places in the Malay-Indonesian archipelago. They conclude that these networks were very extensive. They included contacts in India, but went beyond to the Arab core of the Muslim world. Johns discusses a series of works that were produced in the archipelago from the end of the sixteenth century of the Christian era, but had adapted ideas from other nodes in these spiritual networks.[33] Azyumardi has chosen a later period to make a detailed study of the transmission of a specific category of ideas to Indonesia, namely Islamic reformism. He has discovered that this transmission had started in the second half of the seventeenth century, well before the nineteenth century usually considered as the era in which Southeast Asia became exposed to Middle Eastern reformist ideas. He has also shown that during the period he studies, that is, the second half of the seventeenth century and the eighteenth century, many scholars taught, studied, and transmitted several mystical traditions and various other branches of religious and related sciences, such as *fiqh* and history, together. The combination of mysticism, based on various mystical orders, and *shari'a*-oriented studies was characteristic of this period of what Azyumardi calls "neo-Sufism", in contrast to earlier periods, in which most intellectual exchange was limited to mysticism and the legal aspects of Islam were less strongly developed in the archipelago. During the period Azyumardi studies, at least in the fields of mysticism and jurisprudential studies, Southeast Asia appears mainly as a consumer and receptor in these international networks, although most Malay-Indonesian students became teachers in their turn, some of them in one of the two holy cities, Mecca and Medina.[34]

The participation of Southeast Asian Muslims in international intellectual networks has continued up to the present day. The intensity of these contacts has even increased as a consequence of technological and economic developments. So have the diversity of contacts and intellectual references. Two recent studies may be mentioned in this connection.

Howard Federspiel points out the diversity and multipolarity of the references of contemporary Southeast Asian intellectuals. They may refer to Middle Eastern sources, but also, more cautiously, to Western and to Iranian works. References to intellectual products from Southeast Asia itself are the most frequent in the work of part of these intellectuals, however. One of Federspiel's most interesting observations is the existence of a competition between these different zones.[35]

A special form of intellectual transmission is the translation of texts. The phenomenon of Islamic translation has existed for centuries. In recent times, it has become even more important. This fact is related to the expansion of mass education, globalization, and the "upsurge" of Islam. In addition to an increase in the quantity of translations, there have also been shifts in their nature. Although translations from Arabic and Middle Eastern originals remain very important, translations of publications written in English and other Western languages and produced in regions like South Asia, Europe, and Northern America occupy a growing portion of the market for Islamic literature in Indonesia. This trend, for its part, is connected with various social and cultural transformations, such as shifts of the demographic and intellectual centres within the Muslim world at large and the rise of new categories of Muslims in the archipelago, with types of education, language skills, interests, and tastes that differ from the traditional groups of educated Muslims. Moreover, in the context of the complicated relationship between the tendencies to stress their being part of universal Islam on the one hand, and the particularity of local Islam on the other hand, many contemporary Southeast Asian Muslims take a particular interest in those Islamic creations that are part of global Islam, but not typical of the Middle Eastern tradition. Examples would be books by a Muslim residing in the United States on Islam and science, by an Iranian philosopher on Islam and social revolution, or by a Pakistani and a Moroccan Muslim feminist on Islam and gender.[36] In this way, adherence to universal Islam does not necessarily mean adherence to the Middle Eastern tradition. The world of Islamic translations in Southeast Asia also reveals a competition between various styles, ideologies, and regions. A related phenomenon is the existence of various parallel markets for Islamic translations, each for a public with different social backgrounds and intellectual tastes.[37]

Whereas documents such as biographical dictionaries contain useful information on the intellectual networks of the past, contemporary technology offers a new tool for tracking the spiritual and scholarly connections of Southeast Asian Muslims: the web links and other references included in the websites of various persons and organizations. It would be interesting to compare the references to books and the notes on various contemporary authors mentioned on the website of the *Islam Liberal* group, and the educational institutions visited and books studied by the leaders and adherents of organizations such as Laskar Jihad.[38] A quite different, but not totally unrelated question is whether the latter type of organizations is somehow involved in an international terrorist network, as Singapore intelligence reports and authors like Rohan Gunaratna seem to suggest.[39]

In addition to places visited by students and texts copied, imported, or translated, the orientation of Southeast Asian institutes for Islamic education adds to our understanding of the development and nature of Islam in this area. Cases in point are the Indonesian *Institut Agama Islam Negeri* or State Institutes for Islamic Sciences. In a recent publication, I have shown that they basically refer to three different models in the structure and contents of their study programmes: the Middle Eastern model, especially al-Azhar; the Western, especially Dutch model; and the local tradition and specific needs.[40] Similar studies have been made about other Islamic educational institutions of Southeast Asia. Mona Abaza has just published a book on a related subject: the development of the "Islamization of knowledge" idea in the different local contexts of Egypt and Malaysia — rather than Indonesia, in which different political and intellectual conditions were much less in favour of this type of developments.[41] Still more analyses of other aspects and other periods might be added to substantiate the thesis that Southeast Asian Islam has been shaped in the course of a long historical process through the interaction of the local traditions and situations with those of various other regions of the world.

FORMS AND ASPECTS OF GLOBALIZATION

In view of the unprecedented expansion of Islam during the first centuries of its history and the involvement of Muslims in international mystical, scholarly, and commercial networks ever since then, globalization is not wholly a new process in relation to Islam. Although the present situation is not identical to the past, there is no need to go into detail on the contemporary globalization process[42] except for some brief remarks.

In the context of Islam, two different forms of globalization may be distinguished: on the one hand, globalization may be understood as the intensification of the involvement in universal Islam, away from Malay or Moroccan idiosyncrasy, for example; on the other hand, it may be understood as a movement towards a more or less uniform, global civilization, away from particular reference to Islam or the Muslim community. In contemporary Southeast Asia, both forms exist and they are not always clearly distinct from each other. How to typify, for example, the case of "Islamic feminism", or, more concretely, the case of an American Muslim feminist who visited Malaysia, and of whom a book was published in Malaysia, which then became a reference work in certain Indonesian Muslim circles?[43] Another distinction that should be made is between the different positions communities occupy in various types of contemporary or historical globalization processes; these may be a position as (co-)actor, as re-actor, or as victim. In the contemporary world, certain types of re-active mechanisms exist in the Muslim world that might be called Islamic counter-globalization.

Not only texts and ideas — or, from a more general and sophisticated perspective, discourse — may be analyzed as objects of globalizing and localizing mechanisms. Other cultural products are subject to the same type of processes. Kees van Dijk recently presented a historical analysis of the interaction and competition between European or Western, local, and Islamic celebrations and dress codes among Indonesian Muslims. He concludes that the most recent globalizing trend has tended to be related to international Islam.[44] One might consider this as a form of counter-globalization. However, although Southeast Asia has often been a consumer of foreign models, the flourishing "Muslim dress" industry of Malaysia and Indonesia, complete with luxurious fashion shows, has by now shown much creativity and originality.

COLONIAL AND POST-COLONIAL DIVERSITY

European colonization — or, for present-day Thailand, the absence of colonization — has had a great impact on the Muslim societies of Southeast Asia. So have the decolonization and state formation processes of the various contemporary states. In addition to dissimilarities already existing before the era of European expansion, later variations should be taken into consideration in the analysis of contemporary developments. Differences of colonial styles as well as of administrative systems and government policies in the independent states all have their impact on the contemporary Muslim communities of the region.

An important difference between the policies of the two main colonial powers in the Muslim part of the area, Great Britain and the Netherlands, concerns their attitude towards Islamic law and its administration. Generally speaking, Great Britain did not interfere much in the administration of justice among its Malay subjects and left this task to the sultans and other pre-colonial, indigenous leaders. It also treated Islamic jurisprudence as the principal source for legal procedures and decisions among its Muslim subjects. On the other hand, the Dutch colonial administration interfered much more in the administration of justice among its Muslim subjects. Moreover, at least since the period of the great scholars-cum-colonial administrators, Christiaan Snouck Hurgronje and Cornelis van Vollenhoven, it made numerous regional and local systems of so-called *adat* law the main reference in this administration, limiting the domain of *fiqh* to a few aspects of family law. This divergence in colonial style has led to significant differences between contemporary Malaysia and Indonesia. Firstly, the autonomy of the various states forming the Malaysian federation and the power of their respective administrations is much larger than those of the various parts of the Indonesian Republic, especially in Islamic religious matters. Very probably, the ongoing Indonesian decentralization process will somewhat reduce the difference between the two countries from this point of view. Secondly, the administration of Islamic justice, its organization, and its rules are much more developed in Malaysia than in Indonesia. This difference remains manifest even more than ten years after the latter country adopted its Law on Religious Justice. Another important difference between both countries, due to historical processes that do not need to be analyzed here, relates to the status of Islam. Malaysia has adopted Islam as its official religion, Indonesia has not.

One example will suffice to illustrate the impact of this type of historical dissimilarities on contemporary politics: the official reactions in various Southeast Asian countries against the Darul Arqam organization, also known as al-Arqam. This relatively recent mystical order distinguished itself by numerous small enterprises and other social and economic activities — according to its own spokesmen in seventeen countries. In 1994, it was banned by the Malaysian Government. This ban was an almost automatic follow-up of negative *fatwas* by the religious authorities of all Malaysian states. Its official motivation was mainly religious: the Darul Arqam was considered deviating from the Islamic doctrine. Political motives very probably played a role as well. In Indonesia, the Darul Arqam faced an entirely different fate. Although a number of provincial councils of *ulama* declared it a deviating religious sect and called for its ban, the national government never took such a decision. The influence of councils of religious scholars on the local and national government was much weaker, and what the regime was primarily interested in was not purely from the viewpoint of religious doctrine but the harmonious relationship between the various communities composing the nation. Although the New Order banned hundreds of religious sects for this reason, the Darul Arqam was not considered a threat to communal harmony. In Thailand, the attitude to this originally Malaysian organization was characterized by indifference: it formed only a marginal problem in this country in which Islam is the religion of a relatively small minority. In Singapore, the Muslim community as a small minority is forced to remain united in its pluralism. Therefore, as is the case in Indonesia and much less so in Malaysia, pluralism is accepted within Singapore Islam. However, the Majelis Ugama Islam Singapura (MUIS — Islamic Centre of Singapore) banned the Darul Arqam from the institutions under its authority because it considered the organization a threat to family life and to the Muslim effort to catch up with the Singapore "mainstream".[45]

CONCLUSION

The study of history is not a mere pastime without relevance to contemporary developments and problems. Present-day social, cultural, and political dynamics cannot be fully understood without considering their historical dimensions. Islam in Southeast Asia is a perfect illustration of this fact. The existence of a large number of opinions on many fundamental questions is a complicating factor. In this chapter, ways to cope with this situation have been suggested. One of our most important conclusions would be that contemporary ideological and political positions influence our understanding of history, often in a negative way; on the other hand, our understanding of the present and the solution of its problems can only be attained by improving our understanding of the past. The circle is almost vicious, but the patient, critical examination and combination of different opinions on the history of Islam in the region will help us to stand up to the challenges of the twenty-first century.

Notes

1 Cf. William R. Roff, "Islam Obscured? Some Reflections on Studies of Islam and Society in Southeast Asia", *Archipel* (Paris) 29 (1985), pp. 7 f.

2 Gerardus Willibrordus Joannes Drewes, "New Light on the Coming of Islam to Indonesia?", *BKI* (The Hague) 124 (1968), pp. 438 f.; Azyumardi Azra, *The Transmission of Islamic Reformism to Indonesia: Networks of Middle Eastern and Malay-Indonesian 'Ulamâ' in the Seventeenth and Eighteenth Centuries* (Ph.D. dissertation, Columbia University, New York, 1992) [Indonesian translation: *Jaringan Ulama: Timur Tengah dan Kepulauan Nusantara Abad XVII dan XVIII. Melacak Akar-Akar Pembaruan Pemikiran Islam di Indonesia* (Bandung: Mizan, 1994)], pp. 31 ff.

3 Drewes, op. cit., p. 439.

4 Ibid., pp. 439 ff.; Azyumardi, op. cit., pp. 27 ff.

5 Drewes, op. cit., pp. 439 f.

6 Ibid., pp. 440 f.

7 Marrison wrote in 1951; see Drewes, op. cit., pp. 444 f.

8 Ibid., pp. 459.

9 A. Hasymy, *Sejarah Masuk dan Berkembangnya Islam di Indonesia (Kumpulan Prasaran pada Seminar di Aceh* [The History of the Arrival and Development of Islam in Indonesia (Collection of Preliminary Reports to the Aceh Seminar)] (s.l. [Bandung]: Almaarif 1989), p. 7 (quote translated from the Indonesian).

10 Azyumardi, op. cit., pp. 33 ff.

11 Drewes, pp. 453 f.; contrary to Drewes, Azyumardi, op. cit. pp. 31 f. accepts Arnold's use of this source material to prove this theory of Islamization.

12 Jacobus Cornelis van Leur, *Indonesian Trade and Society: Essays in Asian Social and Economic History* (The Hague: Van Hoeve, 1955) (reprint Dordrecht/ Providence, Foris, 1983 [K.I.T.L.V.-reprint]), especially p. 115.

13 Anthony Crothers Millner, "Islam and Malay Kingship", *JRASGBI* 1 (1981), pp. 46–70; idem, "Islam and the Muslim State", in *Islam in Southeast Asia*, edited by Michael Barry Hooker, Leiden: Brill, 1983, pp. 23–49.

14 Anthony Hearle Johns, "Sufism as a Category in Indonesian Literature and History", *JSEAH* 2, no. 2 (1961): 10–23; idem, "Islam in Southeast Asia: Reflections and New Directions", *Indonesia* 19 (April 1975), pp. 33–55; idem, "Islam in Southeast Asia: Problems of Perspective", in *Southeast Asian History and Historiography: Essays Presented to D.G.E. Hall*, edited by Charles Donald Cowan and Oliver William Wolters, Ithaca: Cornell University Press, 1976): 304–20.

15 Azyumardi, op. cit., 42 ff.
16 Cf. Johns, "Islam in Southeast Asia", pp. 35 f; Christian Pelras, "Religion, Tradition and the Dynamics of Islamization in South Sulawesi", *Archipel* 29 (1985): 107–35; Azyumardi, op. cit., pp. 22, 38, 118 f.
17 Denys Lombard, "L'horizon Insulindien et son Importance pour une Compréhension Globale de l'Islam", *Archipel* 29 (1985): 47 ff.; idem, *Le Carrefour Javanais: Essai d'Histoire Globale*, Paris: EHESS, 1990, especially vol. 2, "Les Réseaux Asiatiques", section 3c, "Vers la Conception d'un Espace Géographique et d'un Temps Linéaire" (176 ff.); Anthony Reid, *Southeast Asia in the Age of Commerce: 1450–1680*, New Haven and London: Yale University Press, vol. 2 (1993), "Expansion and Crisis", chapter 3, "A Religious Revolution" (132 ff.).
18 Stuart Owen Robson, "Java at the Crossroads. Aspects of Javanese Cultural History in the 14th and 15th Centuries", *BKI* 137 (1981): 260 ff., especially p. 262.
19 This question has been developed in Johan Hendrik Meuleman, "Indonesian Islam between Particularity and Universality", *Studia Islamika. Indonesian Journal for Islamic Studies* 4, no. 3 (July–Sept. 1997), especially pp. 110, 116.
20 Clifford Geertz, *The Religion of Java*, Glencoe: Free Press, 1960. Cf. Azyumardi, op. cit., p. 17.
21 Mark Rhey Woodward, *Islam in Java. Normative Piety and Mysticism in the Sultanate of Yogyakarta* (Tucson: University of Arizona Press, 1989).
22 For example Simuh, *Mistik Islam Kejawen Raden Ngabehi Ranggawarsita. Suatu Studi Terhadap Serat Wirid Hidayat Jati* [The Javanese Islamic Mysticism of Raden Ngabehi Ranggawarsita. A Study on the *Serat Wirid Hidayat Jati*] (Jakarta: Penerbit Universitas Indonesia, 1988); Moh. Ardhani, *Al Qur'an dan Sufisme Mangkunagara IV (Studi Serat-Serat Piwulang)* [The Quran and the Sufism of Mangkunagara IV (A Study of the *Serat-Serat Piwulang*)], Yogyakarta: Dana Bhakti Wakaf, 1995.
23 Karel A. Steenbrink, *Beberapa Aspek tentang Islam di Indonesia Abad ke-19* [Some Aspects of Islam in Nineteenth Century Indonesia], Jakarta: Bulan Bintang, 1984, pp. 173 f.
24 Woodward, op. cit., especially 244 ff.
25 Azyumardi, op. cit., passim.
26 Ahmad M. Sewang, *Islamisai Kerajaan Gowa (Pertengahan Abad XVI sampai Pertengahan Abad XVII)* [The Islamization of the Kingdom of Gowa (From the Middle of the Sixteenth Century until the Middle of the Seventeenth Century)], unpublished dissertation, IAIN Syarif Hidayatullah, Jakarta, 1997, 142 ff.
27 On the latter point, see Johan Hendrik Meuleman, "From New Order to National Disintegration. The Religious Factor between Reality, Manipulation, and Rationalization", to be published in *Archipel* 64 (autumn 2002).
28 Drewes, op. cit., p. 439; Lodewijk Willem Christiaan van den Berg, *Le Hadhramout et les Colonies Arabes dans l'Archipel Indien*, Batavia: Landsdrukkerij, 1886, 105 f.

29   Gerardus Willibrordus Joannes Drewes, "The Struggle between Javanism and Islam as Illustrated by the Serat Dermangandul", *BKI* 122 (1966): 310 f.

30   The incident was provoked by Azyumardi Azra, "Hadhrâmî Scholars in the Malay-Indonesian Diaspora: A Preliminary Study of Sayyid 'Uthmân", *Studia Islamika* 2, no. 2 (April–June 1995): 1–33; the counter-publication was HMH Alhamid Alhusaini, *Menangkal Fitnah Berbisa*, Jakarta: published by the author, s.a. [1995]; the author of the present text attended the meeting with the rector, Prof. Dr M. Quraish Shihab, as a member of the editorial board of *Studia Islamika*.

31   For a more detailed study of this question, see Meuleman, "Indonesian Islam between Particularity and Universality" (pp. 99–122). For Malaysia, similar questions have been addressed in Mona Abaza, "Islam in Southeast Asia: Varying Impact and Images of the Middle East", in *Islam, Muslims and the Modern State: Case-studies of Muslims in Thirteen Countries*, edited by Hussin Mutalib and Taj ul-Islam Hashimi, London: MacMillan/New York: St. Martin Press, 1994, 148 f.

32   Lombard, "L'horizon insulindien", loc. cit; idem, *Le Carrefour Javanais*, loc. cit.; Reid, loc.cit.

33   For example in Johns, "Islam in Southeast Asia".

34   Azyumardi, op. cit.

35   Howard M. Federspiel, "Contemporary Southeast Asian Muslim Intellectuals. An Examination of the Sources for Their Concepts and Intellectual Constructs", in *Islam in the Era of Globalization. Muslim Attitudes towards Modernity and Identity*, edited by Johan Hendrik Meuleman, London and New York: RoutledgeCurzon, 2002, pp. 327–50.

36   The references are to Isma'il Raji Al-Faruqi [Ismā'īl Rājī al-Fārūqī], *Islamisasi Pengetahuan* (Bandung: Pustaka, 1984), a translation by Anas Mahyuddin of *Islamization of Knowledge: General Principles and Workplan*, Washington, D.C.: International Institute of Islamic Thought, 1982; Ali Shariati ['Alī Shari'ātī,], *Tugas Cendekiawan Muslim* [The Task of the Muslim Intellectual], Jakarta: Rajawali, 1987, a translation by Amien Rais of *Man and Islam*, Mashhad: University of Mashhad Press, 1982 [a translation of the Persian original]; Fatima Mernissi and Riffat Hassan, *Setara dihadapan* [corrected in the second edition, 1996: *di Hadapan*] *Allah. Relasi Laki-laki dan Perempuan dalam Tradisi Islam Pasca Patriarkhi* [Facing God on Equal Footing. Men-Women Relations in Post-Patriarchal Muslim Tradition] (Yogyakarta: LSPPA — Yayasan Prakarsa, 1995), a collection of translations by a team of various short writings by both authors; and many other translations of works by these same and other Muslim authors.

37   Johan Hendrik Meuleman, *Modern Trends in Islamic Translations* (paper presented at the Sèvres workshop, 2–5 April 2002, in the framework of the History of Translation in Indonesia and Malaya project, Association Archipel, Paris and to be published with the other contributions to this project, edited by Henri Chambert-Loir and Monique Zaini-Lajoubert).

[38]   The address of the Islam Liberal group website is <http://www.islamlib.com>.
[39]   Rohan Gunaratna, *Inside Al Qaeda. Global Network of Terror*, London: Hurst, 2002, 174 ff.
[40]   Johan Hendrik Meuleman, "The Institut Agama Negeri Islam at the Crossroads: Some Notes on the Indonesian State Institutes for Islamic Studies", in idem, ed., *Islam in the Era of Globalization*, 283 ff.
[41]   Mona Abaza, *Debates on Islam and Knowledge in Malaysia and Egypt: Shifting Worlds*, Richmond: Curzon Press, 2001.
[42]   See Johan Hendrik Meuleman, "Southeast Asian Islam and the Globalization Process", in idem, ed., *Islam in the Era of Globalization*, pp. 13–29, for more details on this question.
[43]   The reference is to Amina Wadud-Muhsin and her *Qur'an and Woman: Rereading the Sacred Text from a Woman's Perspective*, Kuala Lumpur: Fajar Bakti, 1992; later republished in New York, etc.: Oxford University Press, 1999. This is only one illustration of a widespread phenomenon.
[44]   Kees van Dijk, "The Indonesian Archipelago from 1913 to 2013: Celebrations and Dress Codes Between International, Local, and Islamic Culture", in Meuleman, ed., *Islam in the Era of Globalization*, pp. 51–69.
[45]   See Johan Hendrik Meuleman, "Reactions and Attitudes towards the Darul Arqam Movement in Southeast Asia", *Studia Islamika* 3, no. 1 (Jan.–March 1996): 43–78 for more details.

References

Abaza, Mona. "Islam in Southeast Asia: Varying Impact and Images of the Middle East". In *Islam, Muslims and the Modern State; Case-studies of Muslims in Thirteen Countries*, edited by Hussin Matulib and Taj ul-Islam Hashimi. London: MacMillan/New York: St. Martin Press, 1994, pp. 139–51.

Abaza, Mona. *Debates on Islam and Knowledge in Malaysia and Egypt: Shifting Worlds*. Richmond: Curzon Press, 2001.

Ahmad M. Sewang, *Islamisai Kerajaan Gowa (Pertengahan Abad XVI sampai Pertengahan Abad XVII)* [The Islamization of the Kingdom of Gowa (From the Middle of the Sixteenth Century until the Middle of the Seventeenth Century)]. Unpublished dissertation, IAIN Syarif Hidayatullah, Jakarta, 1997.

Al-Faruqi, Isma'il Raji [Ismā'īl Rājī al-Fārūqī]. *Islamisasi Pengetahuan*. Bandung: Pustaka, 1984.

Alhamid Alhusaini, HMH. *Menangkal Fitnah Berbisa*. Jakarta: published by the author, s.a. [1995].

Ardhani, Moh. *Al Qur'an dan Sufisme Mangkunagara IV (Studi Serat-Serat Piwulang)* [The Quran and the Sufism of Mangkunagara IV (A Study of the *Serat-Serat Piwulang*)]. Yogyakarta: Dana Bhakti Wakaf, 1995.

Azyumardi Azra. "Hadhrâmî Scholars in the Malay-Indonesian Diaspora: A Preliminary Study of Sayyid 'Uthmân". *Studia Islamika* 2, no. 2 (April–June 1995): 1–33.

Azyumardi Azra. *The Transmission of Islamic Reformism to Indonesia: Networks of Middle Eastern and Malay-Indonesian 'Ulamâ' in the Seventeenth and Eighteenth Centuries.* Ph.D. dissertation, Columbia University, New York, 1992 [Indonesian translation: *Jaringan Ulama. Timur Tengah dan Kepulauan Nusantara Abad XVII dan XVIII: Melacak Akar-Akar Pembaruan Pemikiran Islam di Indonesia* (Bandung: Mizan, 1994)].

Berg, Lodewijk Willem Christiaan van den. *Le Hadhramout et les colonies arabes dans l'archipel indien.* Batavia: Landsdrukkerij, 1886.

Dijk, Kees van. "The Indonesian Archipelago from 1913 to 2013: Celebrations and Dress Codes Between International, Local, and Islamic Culture". In *Islam in the Era of Globalization. Muslim Attitudes towards Modernity and Identity*, edited by Johan Hendrik Meuleman. London and New York: RoutledgeCurzon, 2002, pp. 51–69.

Drewes, Gerardus Willibrordus Joannes. "New Light on the Coming of Islam to Indonesia?". *BKI* 124 (1968), pp. 433–59.

Drewes, Gerardus Willibrordus Joannes. "The Struggle between Javanism and Islam as Illustrated by the Serat Dermangandul". *BKI* 122 (1966), pp. 309–65.

Federspiel, Howard M. "Contemporary Southeast Asian Muslim Intellectuals. An Examination of the Sources for Their Concepts and Intellectual Constructs". In *Islam in the Era of Globalization. Muslim Attitudes towards Modernity and Identity*, edited by Johan Hendrik Meuleman. London and New York: RoutledgeCurzon, 2002, pp. 327–50.

Geertz, Clifford. *The Religion of Java.* Glencoe: Free Press, 1960.

Gunaratna, Rohan. *Inside Al Qaeda. Global Network of Terror.* London: Hurst, 2002.

Hasymy, A. *Sejarah Masuk dan Berkembangnya Islam di Indonesia (Kumpulan Prasaran pada Seminar di Aceh* [The History of the Arrival and Development of Islam in Indonesia (Collection of Preliminary Reports to the Aceh Seminar)]. s.l. [Bandung]: Almaarif, 1989.

Johns, Anthony Hearle. "Islam in Southeast Asia: Problems of Perspective". In *Southeast Asian History and Historiography: Essays Presented to D.G.E. Hall*, edited by Charles Donald Cowan and Oliver William Wolters. Ithaca: Cornell University Press, 1976, 304–20.

Johns, Anthony Hearle. "Islam in Southeast Asia: Reflections and New Directions". *Indonesia* 19 (April 1975): 33–55.

Johns, Anthony Hearle. "Sufism as a Category in Indonesian Literature and History". *JSEAH* 2, no. 2 (1961): 10–23.

Leur, Jacobus Cornelis van. *Indonesian Trade and Society: Essays in Asian Social and Economic History.* The Hague: Van Hoeve, 1955 (reprint Dordrecht/Providence, Foris, 1983 [K.I.T.L.V.-reprint]).

Lombard, Denys. "L'horizon Insulindien et son Importance pour une Compréhension Globale de l'Islam". *Archipel* 29 (1985): 35–52.

Lombard, Denys. *Le Carrefour Javanais: Essai d'Histoire Globale.* Paris: EHESS, 1990, 3 vols.

Mernissi, Fatima and Riffat Hassan. *Setara dihadapan* [corrected in the second edition, 1996: *di Hadapan*] *Allah. Relasi Laki-laki dan Perempuan dalam Tradisi Islam Pasca Patriarkhi* [Facing God on Equal Footing. Men-Women Relations in Post-patriarchal Muslim Tradition]. Yogyakarta: LSPPA — Yayasan Prakarsa, 1995.

Meuleman, Johan Hendrik. "Indonesian Islam between Particularity and Universality". *Studia Islamika. Indonesian Journal for Islamic Studies* 4, no. 3 (July–Sept. 1997): 99–122.

Meuleman, Johan Hendrik. "Reactions and Attitudes towards the Darul Arqam Movement in Southeast Asia". *Studia Islamika* 3, no. 1 (Jan.–March 1996): 43–78.

Meuleman, Johan Hendrik. "The Institut Agama Negeri Islam at the Crossroads: Some Notes on the Indonesian State Institutes for Islamic Studies". In *Islam in the Era of Globalization. Muslim Attitudes towards Modernity and Identity*, edited by Johan Hendrik Meuleman. London and New York: RoutledgeCurzon, 2002, pp. 281–97.

Meuleman, Johan Hendrik. "From New Order to National Disintegration. The Religious Factor between Reality, Manipulation, and Rationalization" to be published in *Archipel*, 64 (autumn 2002).

Meuleman, Johan Hendrik. "Southeast Asian Islam and the Globalization Process". In *Islam in the Era of Globalization. Muslim Attitudes towards Modernity and Identity*, edited by Johan Hendrik Meuleman. London and New York: RoutledgeCurzon, 2002, pp. 13–29.

Meuleman, Johan Hendrik. *Modern Trends in Islamic Translations*. paper presented at the Sèvres workshop, 2–5 April 2002, in the framework of the History of Translation in Indonesia and Malaya project, Association Archipel, Paris and to be published with the other contributions to this project, edited by Henri Chambert-Loir and Monique Zaini-Lajoubert.

Millner, Anthony Crothers. "Islam and Malay Kingship". *JRASGBI* 1 (1981): 46–70.

Millner, Anthony Crothers. "Islam and the Muslim State" In *Islam in Southeast Asia*, edited by Michael Barry Hooker. Leiden: Brill, 1983, pp. 23–49.

Pelras, Christian. "Religion, Tradition and the Dynamics of Islamization in South Sulawesi". *Archipel* 29 (1985): 107–35.

Reid, Anthony. *Southeast Asia in the Age of Commerce: 1450–1680*. New Haven and London: Yale University Press, 2 vols. (1988 and 1993).

Robson, Stuart Owen. "Java at the Crossroads. Aspects of Javanese Cultural History in the 14th and 15th Centuries". *BKI* 137 (1981): 259–92.

Roff, William R. "Islam Obscured? Some Reflections on Studies of Islam and Society in Southeast Asia". *Archipel* 29 (1985): 7–34.

Shariati, Ali ['Alī Sharī'ātī,]. *Tugas Cendekiawan Muslim* [The Task of the Muslim Intellectual]. Jakarta: Rajawali, 1987.

Simuh. *Mistik Islam Kejawen Raden Ngabehi Ranggawarsita. Suatu Studi Terhadap Serat Wirid Hidayat Jati* [The Javanese Islamic Mysticism of Raden Ngabehi

Ranggawarsita. A Study on the *Serat Wirid Hidayat Jati*]. Jakarta: Penerbit Universitas Indonesia, 1988.

Steenbrink, Karel A. *Beberapa Aspek tentang Islam di Indonesia Abad ke-19* [Some Aspects of Islam in Nineteenth Century Indonesia]. Jakarta: Bulan Bintang, 1984.

Wadud-Muhsin, Amina. *Qur'an and Woman: Rereading the Sacred Text from a Woman's Perspective*. Kuala Lumpur: Fajar Bakti, 1992; later republished in New York, etc.: Oxford University Press, 1999.

Woodward, Mark Rhey. *Islam in Java. Normative Piety and Mysticism in the Sultanate of Yogyakarta*. Tucson: University of Arizona Press, 1989.

3

THE ADVENT AND GROWTH OF ISLAM IN THE PHILIPPINES

Carmen A. Abubakar

INTRODUCTION: THE PROCESS OF ISLAMIZATION

The National Geographic Magazine in its September 1980 issue[1] published a map which showed the different countries with significant Muslim populations. A glance at this map reveals that Muslim communities pioneered by the Islamic expansion that began in the seventh century have largely remained and in many cases have grown in spite of political changes inimical to Islam.

The process of Islamization that took place in these countries may vary in detail but certain general patterns can be detected, especially in areas where similar historical circumstances prevailed. In this sense, the Islamization of Southern Philippines cannot be treated as an isolated incident but belongs in its proper context to the Islamic expansion that occurred after the death of the Prophet Muhammad in 632.

This general expansion can be classified into two types of movements. The first was characterized by the military conquests that expanded the Islamic empire out of Arabia to the Middle East, North Africa, Spain, Central Asia and later to Eastern Europe. The second was the expansion of Islam towards Southeast Asia and to Sub-Saharan Africa. This was characterized by the movement of dedicated Muslim individuals either as merchants or as missionaries.

The Islamization of the Malayo-Indonesia archipelago and Southern Philippines belongs to this second movement. Islamization in this phase involved the interplay of many different factors. The first and foremost was the acceleration of trade and the existence of trade routes. One of the oldest trade routes was the Silk Route,[2] an overland connection that linked China to Sumatra and the Middle East over mountains and deserts. Another was an overland caravan route that linked West and North Africa to the Middle East, while still another led to the Volga lands.

The sea routes,[3] which developed later on account of the spice trade started from Malacca on the Malay archipelago across the Indian Ocean and into the Persian Gulf, to Basrah in Iraq and up the Tigris River to Baghdad; or up the mountains of Asia Minor and Armenia to Trebizond on the Black Sea thence to Europe via Constantinople. The Arab market thus extended overland through Central Asia and overseas to Africa, India, China, and Southeast Asia. These routes made possible the tremendous exchange not only of goods but also of people and ideas. Along these great routes countless merchants, travellers, monks, friars, missionaries, moved freely between East and West especially during the hundred years from about 1245.[4] Arab trade, however, started to flourish from the beginning of the ninth century.

Climatic conditions also facilitated the movement of trade and determined to some extent the places at which merchants were most likely to stop for longer periods of time. For instance, the Southwest monsoon blowing from May to October carried merchant ships from the Red Sea and India out to the Straits of Malacca and blew them on with the homeward-bound Chinese vessels to the Far East. The Southeast monsoon between November and April brought the Chinese junks down to the Straits and carried Indian and Arab traders back to their home ports.[5] These conditions made the trade traffic between Southeast Asia, China, India and the Middle East a fairly regular one.

The trade winds, however, blew on a six-month interval and the merchants had to wait for the favourable wind to take them back home. They began therefore to establish temporary way stations in the ports where they conducted business. In time, these temporary dwellings grew into permanent residences as their commercial interests in the area expanded.[6] Since many of these merchants can be presumed to be males, intermarriage with the local population was inevitable. In this manner, foreign traders of different nationalities established communities. Among such communities would be one made up entirely of Muslims. Let us stop here a moment and consider another development which helped to accelerate the Islamization process.

From the seventh to the eighth centuries, a movement known as Sufism was taking place within Islam. This was essentially a reaction against the wealth, luxury and worldly enjoyment that came to prevail in the Muslim community with the establishment and consolidation of the vast new empires.[7] By the twelfth century, Sufism had turned into a mass movement in the form of organized brotherhoods or *Tariqas*.[8] These brotherhoods invaded the entire Muslim world from East to West. Of the fourteen or more orders to be organized, at least three were known to have spread to Southeast Asia, notably to Sumatra, Java and to the Malay archipelago.[9] These Sufi missionaries found their way to the Muslim communities where their work in advancing Islam remains incalculable.

Thus far, we can identify three complementary developments in the Islamization process: 1) Trade which created a favourable condition for the deployment not only of goods but also of people and ideas, 2) the Sufi movement which fielded indefatigable missionaries, 3) the establishment of Muslim communities outside Islam's principal boundaries. These communities provided a supportive environment for the growth and propagation of Islam.

Muslim Communities

Let us now consider these Muslim communities. The intermarriages with the local people created families and their natural growth contributed to the increasing membership in the community. Because trade brought considerable wealth to the traders, the communities became influential and powerful. They began to acquire status and to attract the attention of local rulers, who began to appoint Muslims to high government positions. Thus, in China during the Sung dynasty (960–1278), a Muslim rose to the rank of Minister and during the Yuan dynasty (1297–1369), a Muslim became adviser to the emperor.[10] Similarly, in West Africa, in the Kingdom of Ghana, founded in the eighth century, Muslims served as the king's interpreter, controller of the treasury and as ministers.[11] It is, however, in Malacca[12] where the influence of the local Muslim group can best be demonstrated. By successfully backing a palace coup in 1445, they were able to install a rajah whose first official act was to declare Malacca a Muslim state and Islam as the state religion.[13]

While these developments cannot be regarded as the "necessary conditions" for the growth of Islam, nevertheless, they helped hasten the process. This is because Islam, not having a clearly defined clerical body to carry out its missionary activities, must depend on individuals imbued with religious zeal and dedication to fulfil the function that an organized clergy does for other religions. The Sufi, the trader, and the preacher, therefore became the primary instruments in the dissemination of Islam during this period.

To stop at this juncture, however, is to negate the contributions of other factors. In Malacca, for instance, it was the conversion of the ruler, Parameswara, that facilitated the Islamization process. Later Rajah Kasim, together with his minister, Tun Perak, extended Islam to nearby areas such as Pahang, Trengganu and Kedah; southwards to the Sumatran river ports of Siak, Kampas, Indragani and Jamai. Their greatest accomplishment was the Islamization of Java formerly a Hinduized kingdom. This expansion was achieved through the judicious use of royal marriages, war, and diplomacy. Thus by 1450, Malacca had become the centre of Islam in the Malay archipelago.[14]

The question of whether the conversions of rulers and their subjects were directed either by political expediency or by personal convictions is difficult to assess or to answer categorically. Both reasons may well be present. For let us not underestimate the pull and attraction of Islam as a religion and as a way of life. It meant among other things: literacy, a tradition of learning, a code of laws, an individual sense of worth, and a system of action.[15] Hence, it is not by accident that Muslim states or kingdoms were centres of learning during this period. Baghdad, Cordova, Timbuktu, Delhi, and Malacca, were all flourishing centres of learning and culture at the height of Islamic rule.

Islam in Sulu

The Islamization of Southern Philippines followed the same general patterns. These activities, however, were recorded only in local documents such as the Sulu Genealogy and in the various *tarsilas* (genealogies) of both Sulu and Mindanao.[16] These will be our primary sources for the purpose of this discussion.

According to the Sulu Genealogy, the first person to introduce Islam to Sulu was a certain Tuan Mashaika who is estimated to have arrived in Sulu in the thirteenth century,[17] and whose descendants constituted the core of the Muslim community in Sulu.[18] When a later missionary by the name of Karim ul-Makhdum arrived during the second half of the fourteenth century, he found ready acceptance among a presumably Muslim community in Buansa. His religious activities thus served to reinforce the growing Islamic community established by the descendants of Tuan Mashaika.

An interesting postscript to the Makhdum episode is the number of places in Sulu, which claims the honor of having his grave. Scholars have come to the conclusion that there could have been many Makhdums who visited and preached in Sulu for the term Makhdum was used in India and Malaysia to refer to learned men or teachers. On the other hand, Majul notes the possibility of accretion whereby the activities of many persons became combined into one through the passage of time.

At the beginning of the fifteenth century, another Muslim came to Sulu bearing the title of "Baginda" a Menangkabaw honorific for prince.[19] His name was Rajah Baginda and his coming carried a different significance from that of his predecessors. At first the local natives tried to sink his boats but their behaviour dramatically changed when it became known that the Rajah was a Muslim. At this point, it is worthwhile noting that the Islamization process had reached a stage where being a Muslim had become an acceptable passport into the community.

Another point also becomes obvious. The fact that Baginda was a foreign prince travelling with his own men introduces the political element into the Islamization process. That Baginda exercised political authority was evident. He even designated his son-in-law Abu Bakr[20] as his successor, an unnecessary step had he been a common man. Sharif Abubakar was reportedly an Arabian preacher who came to Sulu via Johor.

Abu Bakr consolidated political power by introducing the sultanate as a political system and himself becoming the first sultan. His thirty years' reign saw the construction of *masajid* (mosques) and the establishment of *madaris* (religious schools). More important, he was able to Islamize the Buranun or the hill tribes of Sulu. By achieving this, Abu Bakr not only unified the sultanate but also intensified the Islamization of the community and turned Sulu into a flourishing part of the expanding *dar ul-Islam* in Malaysia by the sixteenth century.

Islam in Mainland Mindanao

The spread of Islam to Magindanao and Lanao is generally attributed to Sharif Kabungsuwan, also a foreign prince. However, much of the earlier works rested on the accomplishment of missionaries such as Sharif Awliya and Sharif Maraja.[21] Kabungsuwan is estimated to have arrived in the Mindanao area in the early sixteenth century. There are many *tarsilas* about his exploits but most agree on certain common features: 1) Kabungsuwan came with many followers, 2) his men were sea-faring people, 3) an element of force with the local people was initially involved upon his arrival, 4) his men built the town of Cotabato or Maguindanao (Silangan), 5) there were already Muslims in the area when Kabungsuan landed at the mouth of the Pulangi river.

The expansion of Islam to Lanao has been seen as the result of the various alliances undertaken by Kabungsuan with the different ruling families in the area, as well as with the ruling families of Sulu, Borneo and Ternate.[22] These alliances greatly accelerated Islamization so that by the nineteenth century, the whole of Lake Lanao had been Islamized, a situation which did not obtain in the late seventeenth century. This period, roughly the beginning of the fifteenth century to the sixteenth century, symbolized by the presence of Baginda, Abu Bakr and Kabungsuwan directs attention to the missionary activities ensuing from the Malay archipelago as well as to the way political, religious and educational institutions were utilized to advance Islam. Furthermore, the relatively easy acceptance of the authority of these personalities by the natives supplement the idea that Islam had imbued its adherents with a sense of identity that was at once able to transcend territorial and ethnic boundaries.

Islam in Luzon

The introduction of Islam to Luzon came via Brunei. It is reported that members of the Brunei Royal family married into the local ruling family. At the time of the coming of the Spaniards, a small community was already established. The ruler of what came to be known as Manila, was Rajah Soliman (also Sulayman). Some other Muslim communities also existed in Batangas and Cavite.

How Rajah Soliman and his people became Muslims is not well documented. Suffice it to say that Spanish chroniclers, like Antonio Pigafetta noted that the ruling families of Manila were Muslims related to the Bornean aristocracy. In his writings, Pigafetta relates about the capture of the "son of the king of Luzon" by the Spanish fleet while anchored off the coast of Brunei in 1521; further noting that their prisoner was "the Captain-General of the King of Brunei".[23] Some writers believed that the captured prince was Rajah Matanda (also known as Rajah Laya) and grandson of the Sultan of Brunei who was in Brunei at that time to marry a cousin. Rajah Matanda was also said to be the uncle and adviser of Rajah Soliman.

At any rate, the coming of Islam to Luzon could be seen as part of the pattern in the spread of Islam in Southeast Asia. Majul, speculates that "it is possible that what took place in Manila was that some Borneans formed a settlement among the older inhabitants at the mouth of the river Pasig".[24] These Borneans eventually established an understanding with the native people so that marriage amongst the royal families took place.

The Islamic penetration in Luzon was fairly underway when the Spaniards arrived in 1565. Spanish accounts however claimed that the Muslims of Luzon did not really understand the law of Mohamad since few could read the Alcoran (Qur'an) although they had already adopted the practice of circumcision and avoidance of pork.[25]

Features of Islamization

It can be observed from these events that the most striking features of Islamization as it developed in Southern Philippines are:

(1) Muslim missionaries and traders introduced Islam to the people in Southern Philippines. They intermarried with the local population and produced Muslim descendants who made up the core of the Muslim communities.
(2) Muslim political figures arrived later and introduced Islamic political, educational and religious institutions.
(3) Muslim ruling families of Sulu, Maguindanao, Lanao, Borneo and the Moluccas formed alliances that reinforced and deepened Islamic consciousness.

The process described should not be taken to mean that Islamization took on the same sequential manner presented in this chapter. Rather, it must be viewed as the convergence and interplay of all or some of the factors mentioned in a particular place during this particular period, the end result of which was the propagation and growth of Islam. Many theories have been presented regarding the Islamization process and this overview is an attempt at synthesizing these theories into a recognizable pattern so that what may appear as single strands in an otherwise scattered phenomena fuses into a significant whole.

THE GROWTH OF ISLAM IN THE PHILIPPINES: ISLAM AT THE CORE OF MOROS' POLITICAL STRUGGLE

It is often noted that Islam was already present in the Philippines before the coming of the Spanish, then the American colonizers. The Sulu Sultanate, established around 1450 was already seventy-one years old when Magellan came to Mactan in 1521. By the time Legazpi arrived in 1565, the Sulu Sultanate had existed for 115 years. By this time, it had developed into a centralized state with a distinct identity and worldview.

During the colonial period, Islam became the rallying point for resistance against the colonizers. It also became the core identity of the people whom the Spaniards called Moros, on account of their similarity to the Moors who ruled Spain for 800 years. Spanish colonial policy centred on subjugating and Christianizing the Moros, a policy that brought on the Moro wars. All throughout the colonial regime lasting around 350 years, the Moro label was the preferred reference when speaking of the Muslims. It was mostly used in a pejorative manner.

Having failed to conquer the Moros, the Spaniards signed them over to the Americans in the 1898 Treaty of Paris and the Americans in turn signed them over to the Filipinos through the grant of Philippine independence in 1946. The process of incorporation started first, when the American regime created the Moro Province in 1903 and later the Department of Mindanao and Sulu and second, by abolishing the sultanate as a political institution. This was accomplished through the conduct of a brutal war, then the imposition of socio-cultural, economic and political institutions on Moro societies, and capped by the formal signing of the Carpenter's Agreement abolishing the sultanate in 1915. Samuel Tan, a Filipino historian, has commented that the abolition of the sultanate as a political system may have meant Moros' loss of their capability to organize and mount collective resistance against the colonialists, but not their will to resist. The breakdown in collective resistance brought about the phenomenon called "Parang Sabil". This became one of the most effective methods of resistance the Moros used against colonial forces. The Spaniards introduced the word "*juramentado*" and the American used the word "*amok*" to describe this phenomenon.

The Moros protested the incorporation of their areas in what would be the Philippine Republic through petitions to the American Government, rallies, and other means but to no avail. The Bacon Bill introduced in the U.S. Congress intended to separate Mindanao and Sulu from the rest of the Philippines. Although not successful, it was a recognition of the fact that the Moros constituted a different community geographically, culturally and religiously, including having a political tradition of its own. Moreover, the bill took cognizance of the hostility and animosity that existed between the Moros and the Christian groups and the problem that may arise should the two groups be forced to live together where the former would become a minority community under the government of the latter.

The Moros' marginalization and minoritization was a direct result of the independence process as their territories were parcelled into provinces and their sovereign and political power completely reduced, if not totally obliterated in places which became majority Christian in population. The intense alienation of the Moros brought about peace and order problems that in the late sixties burst into open rebellion and the struggle for self-determination.

The Moro struggle in the 1970s relied on Islam as a consolidating and uniting factor of the various Moro ethnic groups in the same way it did during the colonial wars. Islamic identity and consciousness brought together different ethnic groups under the banner of the MNLF (Moro National Liberation Front). This core identity later became more pronounced in the MILF (Moro Islamic Liberation Front) that declared the formation of an Islamic state and the implementation of *shari'a* as its main goal. The Islamic identity became the overriding character of both the MNLF and the MILF as they appealed to the international Islamic community through the OIC (Organization of Islamic Conference) for moral, financial, and political support. The language and symbols used by the MNLF and the MILF were redolent with Islamic meanings. For example, MNLF/MILF forces were called *Mujahid* (one who conducts *jihad*), their struggle was identified as *jihad*, and their goal, an Islamic Republic. Islam became the language and symbol of the resistance.

It is not surprising that Islamic concepts and symbols resonate both among the civilians as well as the combatants. Neither was it so surprising that the Muslim identity become a much more preferred identity to that of the national identity of Filipino. However, in the 1970s, the name Bangsamoro was introduced by the MNLF and was entered into the 1987 Constitution in the context of defining regional autonomy and the Bangsamoro Homeland. There is no doubt however that the term generally refers to Muslims.

This development is understandable in the light of colonial experiences. The colonial wars divided the population along religious lines. Those who converted to Christianity became the friends of the colonizers and those who rejected Christianity became their bitter enemies. The biases and prejudices that accompanied the wars grew and became fixed in the minds of many Muslims and Christians so much so that relations between them became problematic. For example, during the Spanish period, the most popular entertainment was the Moro-Moro, a play that usually pitted the Muslim villain against the Christian hero. During the American period, derogatory slogans like "a good Moro is a dead Moro" and songs like "Moros have tails in Zamboanga" abound. Even after independence, Philippine history books carried the colonial imprint of characterizing Moros as pirates, traitors, *juramentados*. These stereotypes only intensified the ill feelings between Muslims and Christians. Over the years, these feelings may have been reduced to some extent through the efforts of progressive and church groups through interfaith dialogues and conscientization activities explaining Moro culture and the many dimensions of the Bangsamoro struggle for self-determination.

Although peace negotiations have been signed between the MNLF and the Philippine government, the implementation of the agreement had not been successful. Other groups, impatient for the attainment of declared goals (independent Islamic state) adopted more militant and radical lines. The case of the Abu Sayyaf easily comes to mind. This group has capitalized on the frustration of Muslim youths vis–a-vis the absence of development in their communities. Articulated as *jihad*, militant radicalism became an attractive alternative for those who were eager to advance the struggle they believed the MNLF had abandoned when it signed a peace agreement with the government. However, the ASG (Abu Sayyaf Group) *jihad* appears to be a misnomer. In a recent report, an ASG leader talked about the rift among them as caused by the unequal distribution of the ransom money they had collected and even boasted of his popularity (notoriety perhaps is the better word) as he is always seen in CNN and other world press. Asked if he was willing to surrender, his answer was: "A *mujahideen* cannot surrender. That is not allowed by Islam."[26] Yet for all intents and purposes, their actions no longer subscribed to the expectation of being *mujahideen*.

Many Muslims consider kidnapping and other atrocious activities of the ASG as unIslamic. In spite of this, the ASG was able to recruit members and rely on local support not so much due to religious convictions but more due to shared desire to strike against a perceived enemy, the government. Considered as a terrorist group with links to the Al Qaeda, the ASG became the object of intense military operations in Basilan. Speculations on its relation to the military continue to be made and denied. Recently however, the Senate subcommittee on National Defence and Security came up with a draft report implicating three military officers of possible culpability in the escape of the ASG from the Dr Jose Ma. Torres Memorial Hospital in Lamitan during the 2 June 2002 incident.[27] The Senate draft Report, signed by twenty senators, not only identified but also recommended Court Martial for the three suspects. AFP(Armed Forces of The Philippines) spokesperson, Brig. Gen. Eduardo Purificacion has stated that a board inquiry was formed after then Army Inspector General, Brig. Gen. Reynaldo Rivera came out with a report last year. However, he could not remember when the inquiry was conducted.[28]

Civil society as a third force to promote peaceful solutions to the Moro problem has surfaced. The Bangsamoro People's Consultative Assembly organized in Cotabato City is advancing the idea of a referendum to allow the Bangsamoro people the choice on what kind of political arrangement is appropriate for them: autonomy, federation, or independence. Its chairman, Abhoud Syed M. Lingga has read a statement at the Plenary Session of the twentieth Session of the United Nations Working Group on Indigenous Population at the Palais des Nations, Geneva, Switzerland on 23 July 2002 generally articulating this concern. Lingga concedes that unless a vigorous movement for referendum is conducted and sustained, such statements will just amount to no more than archival records. A Bangsamoro Civil Society Conference was held in Davao City on 17–18 October 2001.

Islam at the Core of Institution Building

A society is often defined by the vigour and strength of its institutions. One of the Islamic institutions that has flourished in the Muslim communities in the Philippines is the *madaris* (Islamic schools). It was introduced during the time of Shariful Hashim or Sultan Abubakar. Today, a Muslim community usually has one or two *madaris* teaching religion and Arabic language. In some communities, *madaris* reached the level of colleges.

For higher Islamic education, Muslims usually go to the Middle East, initially to Al Azhar in Egypt. Later, scholarships to some other countries for B.S. or M.A. in Islamic Law, and in Theology, became available. The International Islamic University in Malaysia has graduated a number of Muslim scholars for M.A. and Ph.D. In the Philippines, the Institute of Islamic Studies at U.P. Diliman offers an M.A. programme in Islamic Studies, while the MSU system offers B.S. in Islamic Studies in several of its Mindanao campuses. Sultan Kudarat Islamic Academy offers an integrated curriculum from elementary to college levels. Another integrated *madrasah* operates an elementary level education at Maharlika Village in Taguig, Rizal; while a pre-school in Cavite is operated by ISCAG (Islamic Call and Guidance), a Balik Islam (Muslim converts) NGO.

The government has now reactivated an old plan to integrate the *madrasah* to the public school system that started in the 1980s. Some Muslims see this move as an attempt to control the *madaris* and interfere in its curriculum and operations. For this reason, the initiative started in the 1980s died a natural death. But now the word being used for this process is mainstreaming and with World Bank funding, the new push for *madaris* development and integration may materialize. As of 1999, there was a total of 1,581 *madaris* in the country.[29] At one time, there was a proposal to seek funding for the *madaris* from Congress but the bill never reached the plenary.

The *masjid* as a religious institution has also grown in terms of numbers. No Muslim community is really complete unless a place of worship is designated. The distinctive designs of domes and minarets are often landmarks that identify Muslim communities. A *masjid* is constructed through the efforts of the community, a wealthy family or from donations from Muslim countries.

Another significant development was the establishment of the *shari'a* courts by virtue of Presidential Decree (PD) 1083. The courts handle cases having to do with family law for example, marriages, divorce, inheritance and succession. There are five district courts and eleven municipal courts today. Practitioners are qualified first by undergoing a forty-five-day training, then by taking a *shari'a* Bar examination administered by the Supreme Court. So far, the bar has qualified a total of 284 examinees since 1983.[30]

However, these *shari'a* courts are mostly located in the Autonomous Region in Muslim Mindanao (ARMM) provinces and cannot serve those who reside outside this area. For example, Muslims from Metro-Manila must file their cases in the provinces. Accessibility, inadequate number of judges and lack of funding and information dissemination are problems that beset these courts.

Less successful in terms of operation was the establishment of the Islamic Bank by PD 624, later Republic Act (RA) 6848 which created Al-Amanah Bank. Capitalized with only fifty million pesos, the bank has not been as active as other banks with bigger capital. It has not opened its Islamic component and functions as a regular commercial bank. Although privatization has been discussed, nothing definite has actually taken place. In the meantime, it has not provided the mechanism for the economic development of Muslim communities.

Of all these institutions, it is the *madrasah* that continues to develop in ways that respond to the needs of the Muslims for Islamic education. *Madaris* are often set up through Muslim self-initiatives without any government help. Although many of them are poorly equipped, nevertheless, they were able to give basic religious education to Muslim children.

The *shari'a* courts and the Islamic Bank were established as concessions to the Muslims during the 1970s when the war with the MNLF was at its height. Earlier, in the late 1960s, the government also created the Commission on National Integration (CNI) transformed later into the Office of Muslim Affairs (OMA) to help integrate the Muslim into mainstream polity. While given low budget priority by government, these institutions however demonstrate the latter's attempts to give some attention to Muslims' grievances without giving in to the political demands of the former.

War on Terrorism

After September 11, the Muslims in the Philippines, like other Muslim minorities elsewhere, began to feel the harsh and sometimes hostile perceptions of their society and religion. The September 11 attack brought back the biases and even bigotry to the fore as the association between Islam and the bombings became overly emphasized in the media. Local Muslims found that personal security was getting tied to this war. They felt that they were unjustly being associated with criminal elements like the ASG.

The "war on terrorism" has become a licence to raid Muslim communities and to apprehend members pointed out as ASG members or sympathizers. In Basilan, the military netted over 200 people of various ages suspected of being ASG members or sympathizers. About 90 of them are incarcerated in the Bicutan Detention Centre waiting for their court hearings. Recently, an additional 25 was added which included young teenagers with ages ranging from 13–14 who were caught fishing in Sulu waters. These people were pointed out by masked informers and were detained under the "warrantless arrest" policy of the government. The detainees have only one lawyer provided by an NGO to plead their cases. In Sulu, what Human Rights groups called a "silent war" has been going on without being reported in the media. Civilian casualties are often passed off as ASG.

The ASG became the focus of much attention as it became tied to the decision of the national government to ride on the U.S. "war on terror" to fight its own internal battle against rebel groups. The ASG became the first group to earn the terrorist label and also the focus of the Joint U.S.-Philippines military exercises known as Balikatan 02-1. At the height of the Balikatan controversy, the President called civil society groups protesting against the joint military exercises as "supporter of terrorism" and "Abu Sayyaf lovers". The war on terrorism dragnet has now drawn the Communist Party of the Philippines-New People's Army (CPP-NPA) into the list of the U.S. State Department's list of foreign terrorist organizations at the behest of the national government. Both the Philippine and the U.S. Governments have asked the Dutch Government to freeze the CPP-NPA assets and deport its leaders.[31]

The war on terrorism has extended even to the *madaris* since they have become the target of suspicion as the source of extremism. A *madrasah* was raided in Pangasinan and a group of Muslims were arrested and charged as terrorists. Some guns were reportedly found in the premises. The six suspects were Balik Islam (converts) and were being interrogated for alleged link to Al-Qaeda.[32] Now out on bail, they claimed that they were victims of false accusations by a neighbour who wanted to buy out their land and that the guns were planted. In a public hearing held at Congress, Gerry Salapuddin, Congressman of Basilan and Deputy Speaker for Mindanao said that the suspects suffered emotional distress and the raid had "maliciously imputed a sinister repute to *madrasah*, throughout the country", and therefore the incident needed to be clarified. Senior Supt. Rodolfo Mendoza, the Pangasinan police director during the raid conducted on 2 May, said that the area was not a *madrasah* "but a theoretical and practical training camp for small weapons". Muhammad Wali Santos, brother of the accused leader of the group, reputed this claim by stating that the area was being built into a model Islamic community.[33]

Other areas of life have also been at risk. For some, it has become more and more difficult to find employment whenever their biodata reveal them to be Muslims. Although not yet widespread, there have been reports of a few Muslims changing their names or religious affiliation in order to avail of employment opportunities. Women wearing headscarves are finding it hard to flag down taxis and their bags are often rigorously searched when entering business or public buildings.

An Anti-Terrorism Bill has been discussed in Congress. Introduced by Representative Imee Marcos of the Second District of Ilocos Sur, House Bill 3802 is "An Act Defining Terrorism, Providing Penalties Thereafter and for Other Purposes". Its shorter title is "Anti-Terrorism Act of 2001". This bill includes a definition of terrorism and identifies acts of terrorism and terrorist organization but excludes state terrorism among its concerns. The act calls for the creation of an Anti-Terrorist Action Council (ATAC), authority to intercept communications, authority to inquire into bank deposits, authority to freeze accounts, forfeiture of property, mutual assistance among states, refusal of entry of foreign nationals. The death penalty is prescribed for acts of terrorism. In addition, the Statute of Limitations does not cover crimes under this act.

Many of the acts listed are already included in the penal laws of the country and their inclusion in this bill elevates them to the status not only of national but also of global security concerns. Critics say that the bill, as crafted, intends to restrict the political space of opposition groups. Already marginalized minority groups like the Muslims will become more vulnerable to state coercive policies, since state terrorism is not recognized under this bill.

The recent spate of bombings in Bali, Indonesia (14 October 2002) and the explosion at the Philippine Consulate in Menadao and the bombings in Zamboanga (17 October) and in Metro Manila (19 October) has led the Philippines to initiate a meeting with officials from Indonesia, Malaysia and Cambodia in order to implement the regional trilateral anti-terrorism agreement. The Regional Joint Committee will monitor and implement the projects contained in the trilateral agreement which Brunei and Thailand are expected to sign at this meeting.[34] In addition to these moves, the government and congress have begun considering proposals including giving the President emergency powers to fight terrorism, adopting a national ID system and pushing the Anti-Terrorism Law through the legislative body both in the Lower and Upper Houses.[35]

Most, if not all, of the bombings in Indonesia as well as in the Philippines, have been attributed to Muslim extremist groups like the *Jama'ah Islamiyyah* and its local counterpart in the Philippines, the ASG. While there are those who think that these attacks are caused partly by the Philippines' support for the U.S.-led fight against global terrorism, there are those who do not think beyond the perceived stereotypes of Muslims as violent people in spite of the fact that Muslims were also casualties in the bombings.

The root of terrorism in the Philippines goes back to the lack of a comprehensive national policy regarding the development of Muslim areas. From the early "benign neglect" policy of the national government to the affirmative engagement being undertaken by the Macapagal administration today, national policies nevertheless tend to change with each new president. For example, in the short span of time from the Ramos to the Estrada presidency (1996–98), the policy changed from negotiation to total war. The effects of this later policy on Moro civilian population have been devastating. They suffered bombings, dislocations, and deaths of family members. Even now, there are still people in refugee centres and more are being displaced as the operations against the ASG goes on in Sulu and Basilan.

Continuing militarization has accentuated the Islamic content of the Moro political struggle since many Muslims have come to attribute these continued military presence as persecution because of their Islamic faith, in the same manner that other Muslim groups have been or are being persecuted elsewhere. This becomes more evident since the September attack has made their lives more insecure. Not only are they being targeted as terrorists, but their institutions are now suspected of being linked to terrorist organizations. The current deportation of Muslims from Sabah, Malaysia where hundreds of thousands had sought refuge from the continuing peace and order problems has increased the pressure of insecurity.

CONCLUSION: CONTINUING ISLAMIZATION

When Islam came to the Philippines, it absorbed many cultural elements that in time came to be recognized and accepted as Islamic. The Islamic resurgence in the early eighties to the present has largely been directed towards greater orthodoxy in terms of eliminating these elements deemed to be unIslamic. At the same time, it has also been directed towards propagating a higher Islamic awareness through both formal and informal means.

The attempts to Islamize culture has run into resistance from people who adhere to the idea that traditional practices are Islamic and not innovations as others would like to believe. The field of native performing arts, for example, music, singing, dancing, has been the object of much debate and criticisms, especially from foreign educated scholars who view these performances as *bida'a* (pernicious innovations) if not *haram* (forbidden). Some healing rituals have also fallen on hard times especially in urbanized areas, but their hold is still strong in rural communities where medical practitioners are not available. Esoteric spiritual knowledge is being slowly replaced by *shari'a*-based spirituality.

The main problem of Islamization in this situation however is the matter of interpretation. The tendency to interpret Islam more conservatively within a cultural milieu that is characterized by the flexibility exercised by customary law or *adat* has given rise to tension between the foreign trained scholars who are for purifying Islam of all accretions and the local *imam* who stand for protecting the customary practices of their ancestors. This has resulted in misunderstanding and some confusion among Muslims.

This internal debate has also influenced the work of *tabligh* (propagation) and *da'wah* (call to the faith) groups that have been at the forefront in the propagation of Islamic awareness amongst Muslims and non-Muslims. It means that the message they bring out is largely conservative especially in the context of gender relationships that among native Muslims tend to be more relaxed rather than role oriented. *Tabligh* and *da'wah* groups have been instrumental in accelerating the return-to-Islam outlook among native-born Muslims and converts known as Balik Islam. This latter community is growing in Mindanao, in the Visayas and in Luzon.

Secular culture at times acts as a countervailing weight against Islamization. For example, the increasing participation of Muslim women in the public arena is influenced by the general environment that promotes gender development, and at the same time by a growing number of Muslim women asserting a more progressive interpretation of women's role in society.

Islamization is further pushed by the globalized communication system so that Muslims worldwide are getting more information about Islam and on fellow Muslims — a trend that was not so marked during the Cold War era. Although access to the internet is still confined to the large urban centres in the Philippines, it has already accelerated the amount and volume of contact amongst the Muslims.

Notes

1   The National Geographic Magazine Special Map Supplement 158, no. 3, Washington, D.C.: The National Geographic Society (September 1980).
2   Starr, G. et al. *A History of the World*, Chicago: Rand McNally & Co., 1960, p. 11.
3   Ibid., p. 12.
4   Hilton, P.B. and D.J. Tate. *Southeast-Asia in World History*, Kuala Lumpur: Oxford University Press, 1963, pp. 89–90.
5   Harrison, B., *Southeast-Asia: A Short History*. London: MacMillan & Co. Ltd., 1954, pp. 61–62.
6   De Planhol, X.. "The Geographic Setting", in the *Cambridge History of Islam*, edited by Holt, Lambton and Lewis, Cambridge: Cambridge University Press, 1970, pp. 604–31.
7   Barberry, A.J., "Mysticism" in the *Cambridge History of Islam*, pp. 443–58.
8   Rahman, F., *Islam*. N.Y.: Anchor Books, Doubleday Co. Inc., 1968.
9   Lammens, H., *Islam Beliefs and Institutions*, London: Frank Cass & Co. Ltd., 1968.
10 According to Pe Cheou-i writing on The History of Islam in China, the main process by which Islam became propagated in China were: 1) personal contact in the case of people of the better class, 2) marriages, 3) the adoption of pagan children, the orphans; the conversion of adults in the employment or service of Muslims, 4) the fact that the clients of a man would follow the religion of their master. Pe Cheou-i, "History of Islam in China" in *Notes in Islam*, Calcutta: The Oriental Institute, St. Xavier's College, 1954, pp. 92–112.
11 Ghana later became a Muslim kingdom when it was conquered by the Berber Almoravids from Morocco in 1076. Lewis, B., "The Invading Crescent" in *The Dawn of African History*, edited by Oliver, R., London: Oxford University Press, 1968, p. 39.
12 Malacca was founded by Parameswara around 1400 when he was searching for sanctuary from political oppression. He adopted the name Muhammad Iskandar Shah after his conversion to Islam upon his marriage to a Pasai Muslim princess. H.J. de Graaf, de Steeg, "Southeast Asian Islam to the 18th Century", in the *Cambridge History of Islam*, edited by Holt, et al., Cambridge: Cambridge University Press, 1970.
13 Rajah Kasim took the title Sultan Muzaffar Shah. His mother was reportedly an Indian Muslim woman. He appointed his maternal uncle, Tun Ali, to the office of bendahara or chief minister but was later obliged to give the office to a rival,

Tun Perak became the architect of Moluccas' expansion into an empire. See
Gullick, J.M., *Malaysia*, N.Y.: Frederick A. Praeger, 1969.

[14] Hilton, P.B. and D.J. Tate, op. cit., pp. 46–51.

[15] Majul, *C.A. Muslims in the Philippines*, Quezon City: University of the Philippines
Press, 1973. See also Lewis, B. op. cit.

[16] See Majul, ibid. Also Sarangani, D.A. "Islamic Penetration in Mindanao Sulu".
Mindanao Journal 1, no. 1 (1974). Marawi: University Research Centre, MSU.

[17] Most dates are estimates due to the absence of exact periodization recorded in
the local documents.

[18] The Sulu Historical Notes confirms that Tuan Mashaika "begot Maumin". But
"*maumin*" according to Majul, may not be a proper name but rather a collective
term for believers (Arabic *mu*). The term could be taken to mean that Tuan
Mashaika begot Muslims. Majul further notes that "Tuan" is generally associated
with Muslims especially in Sulu. Majul, op. cit., p. 52.

[19] "Baginda" was used in Sulu in the sense of ruler. That Rajah Baginda came from
Sumatra is, however, no guarantee that he was a native Sumatran. Majul, op. cit.,
p. 56.

[20] Abu Bakr was reputedly the second Arab to come to Sulu in 1450 travelling
from Palembang Sumatra via Borneo. His arrival in Sulu is considered one of the
highlights of the Islamization process. He became Qadi (judge) and Imam of
Rajah Baginda. According to the *tarsilas*, he came to Malaysia to preach the
doctrines of Abu-Ishaq embodied in a book titled *Dar ul-Mazlum* [The House
of the Oppressed], Sarangani, op. cit., p. 65.

[21] Sharif Awliya probably arrived in Magindanao around 1460. He married, begot
a daughter, then left the place. Sharif Maraja was the brother of Sharif Hassan.
Both were reported to have come from Johor. Sharif Hasan proceeded to Sulu
while Sharif Maraja stayed in the Slangan area and married the daughter of
Sharif Awliya. Majul, op. cit., p. 65.

[22] In the latter part of the sixteenth century, the influence of the Sulu sultan was
already felt in Zamboanga and its neighbourhood. Bornean (and later Ternatan)
preachers were observed by the Spaniards to be operating in the Mindanao area
in the late sixteenth century. Governor-General Francisco Sande in his Letter of
Instruction enjoined the Captain to see that the Bornean preachers were not
admitted into Mindanao. Majul, p. 68. For more information about the linkages
between or among Mindanao ruling families, see Appendix A and D of the same
book.

[23] See Blair, Emma Helen D. and Robertson, James Alexander, eds., *The Philippine
Islands, 1493–1803*, Cleveland, Ohio: A.H. Clark, 1903–09, vol. 33, p. 2223.

[24] Majul, *Muslims in the Philippines*, 1973, p. 74.

[25] See Blair, Emma Helen D. and James Alexander Robertson, eds., *The Philippine
Islands, 1493–1803*, vol. 4. Cleveland, Ohio: A.H. Clark, 1903–09, p. 149.

[26] "Abu Leader Tells of Talking Peace With Army Officers", *Philippine Daily
Inquirer*, 24 August 2002, pp. 1–A16.

27 "AFP Officers in Lamitan Seige Face Axe", *Philippine Daily Inquirer*, 16 August 2002, pp. 1–21.

28 "AFP Clears 3 Officers of Collusion with Abu Sayyaf", *Philippine Daily Inquirer*, 20 August 2002, pp. 1–A18.

29 Office of Muslim Affairs (OMA), 2002.

30 Office of Muslim Affairs (OMA), 2002.

31 "US, RP Ask Netherlands to Freeze CPP Asset", *Philippine Daily Inquirer*, 13 August 2002, p. 1–14.

32 "6 Suspected Terrorists Nabbed in Pangasinan", *Philippine Daily Inquirer*, 4 May 2002, p. 4.

33 "House Probes Raid on Islam School", *Philippine Daily Inquirer*, 19 August 2002, p. 15.

34 "Anti-Terror Pact Pushed", *Philippine Daily Inquirer*, 21 October 2002, pp. A1–A20.

35 "Protesters Assail State-sponsored Poverty, Terrorism", *Philippine Daily Inquirer*, 22 October 2002, p. A2.

4

ISLAMIC ECONOMIC INSTITUTIONS IN INDONESIA: A RELIGIO-POLITICAL PERSPECTIVE

Bahtiar Effendy

INTRODUCTION

In 1991, an Islamic bank, Bank Muamalat Indonesia (BMI), was founded in Indonesia. In a way, this was a historical landmark considering the fact that the long-overdue project had finally materialized. Muslims in Indonesia had been aspiring to the creation of such an important financial institution since the 1970s. For many of them, the existence of an Islamic bank is a necessity to enable them to perform their religious obligation in the economic field. As widely understood Islam prohibits *riba* (usury).[1] What constitutes *riba*, however, is still a debatable subject. Among the *fiqh* (Islamic jurisprudence) scholars themselves, there has not been a final word regarding the issue. Different opinions and interpretations of *riba* are still very much in existence. In fact, discussions over the issue tend to develop into a more detailed, complex, and sophisticated manner, covering both the economic as well as religious dimensions. Yet, the likelihood is that Muslims will not come to a single understanding of it in the near future.[2]

Many Indonesian Muslims, like their counterparts throughout the Islamic world, believe that interest is one kind of *riba*. Thus, in their view, the existence of interest-based financial institutions does not seem to conform to Islamic teachings. A larger part of the Muslims, however, perceive otherwise. As such, they do not consider interest as a form of *riba*. Therefore, they do not seem to have any theological inconveniences in conducting economic and/or financial transactions with any existing conventional or non-Islamic banks. To make the question of interest more difficult to settle is the presence of the sizeable bulk of Muslims who take a middle stance. They argue that, given the strengths and weaknesses of each differing positions, interest can be identified as *mutasyabihat*, a legal issue that is not yet clear and therefore must be avoided. At best, they are of the opinion that until the foundation of an Islamically operated financial infrastructure is secured, the existence of a conventional banking system can be accepted as an emergency institution.

The fact that perceptions as to what constitutes *riba* are by no means unified does not appear to prevent Muslims from establishing Islamic financial institutions. Other than BMI, Indonesian Muslims now enjoy the presence of Bank Syariah Mandiri, a number of Unit Usaha Syariah (Islamic Banking Units under the management of Bank IFI, Bank Negara Indonesia, Bank Jabar, Bank Bukopin, Bank Danamon, and Bank Rakyat Indonesia), more than eighty Bank Perkreditan Rakyat Syariah (BPRS, Syariah or Islamic Rural Bank), and over 3,000 Bait al-Mal wa al-Tamwil (BMT, which literally means treasury and financing house).[3]

There are many views with regard to this new development. One dominant position is that the country's capitalism, and perhaps other important aspects as well, is undergoing the process of Islamization.[4] Others are of the opinion that in the end the state has to accommodate the specific interests of Muslims in order to enhance its own socio-cultural legitimacy.[5] Still, there are those who see this phenomenon in terms of economic opportunity for Muslim small and medium entrepreneurs to develop their business activities.[6] In any account, the existence of the already mentioned Indonesian Islamic economic institutions is a serious effort to provide necessary instruments or infrastructures for those who for religious or other reasons do not feel comfortable conducting financial and/or commercial transactions through the existing conventional banks. In this context, the establishment of BMI and other similar institutions are useful alternatives.[7]

Indonesia, being the largest Muslim country in the world, was once considered a lagger with regard to the development of Islamic economic infrastructure. Compared to its neighbouring state of Malaysia or even the Philippines for that matter, where Muslims constitute a minority — the Indonesian state seemed to be unwilling to take the interests of the country's

Muslims seriously. Included in this matter was their aspiration to form an Islamically-administered bank. For that reason, many believed that it was when the state emerged as a strong and hegemonic institution under the New Order regime, where no one could escape from its webs of influence and intimidation, which actually hindered the formation of such an important financial institution. At least, forces at work within the state were able to delay the materialization of an Islamic bank as well as other related financial instruments for nearly two decades. It was only when the relationship between Islam and the state became more amicable that the endeavour to establish an Islamic bank turned out to be a success. This is not only in the sense that the state no longer stood in the way, but it even formulated a possible loophole from the existing legal basis and assisted in the mobilization of the required capital.[8]

The significance of the state factor can hardly be denied. Not least important were theological perceptions which served as the basis of Muslims' endeavours in this venture. Theologically speaking, the need to establish an Islamic bank did not seem to have been shared by all Muslims. As suggested, even among the devout Muslim community (*santri*), there are many different views with regard to the issue of bank interest and the existence of an Islamic bank. The absence of a relatively unified stance in respect to the founding of an Islamic bank or other economic institutions will undoubtedly affect its further development and prospects. How can an Islamic economic institution survive, let alone develop and flourish, without the full-fledged support of Muslims? And how can such full-fledged support be devised in the midst of differing stances on the question of Islamic economy?

This chapter is an attempt to trace the history and development of Islamic economic institutions in Indonesia. Knowing that at least there were two major factors at work in the process of the founding of BMI and other related economic infrastructure, this essay will discuss the issue from two different but related perspectives — theological and political. Through this approach, it is expected that the development and prospects of the country's Islamic financial institutions can be ascertained.

THEOLOGICAL BASIS OF ISLAMIC BANK AND THE PROBLEM OF INTERPRETATION

Unquestionably, one of the most important factors in the creation of BMI and subsequently the other similar institutions, was theological in nature. It has every thing to do with how Muslims view their religion. Many have suggested that religion may be seen as a divine instrument to understand the world.[9] Islam in comparison to other religions is conceivably the one with the least difficulty in accepting such a premise. An obvious reason lies in one of Islam's most conspicuous characteristics: its omnipresence. This is a notion which recognizes that everywhere the presence of Islam should provide "the right moral attitude for human action".[10]

This notion has led many adherents to believe that Islam is a total way of life. The embodiment of this is expressed in the *shari'a* (Islamic law). A sizeable group of Muslims even push it further, asserting that Islam is an integrated totality that offers a solution to all problems of life. Undoubtedly, they "believe in the complete and holistic nature of revealed Islam. [Thus] Islam is an integrated totality that offers a solution to all problems of life. It has to be accepted in its entirety, and to be applied to the family, to the economy and to politics."[11]

In its present context, it is not surprising, though it is sometimes alarming, that the contemporary world of Islam witnesses many Muslims who want to base their socio-economic, cultural, and political life exclusively on Islamic teachings, without realizing their limitations and constraints. Their expressions are found in today's popularly symbolic terms such as Islamic revivalism, Islamic resurgence, Islamic revolution, Islamic reassertion, or Islamic fundamentalism. While such expressions are well motivated, they are not well thought out and in fact are rather apologetic in nature. Their central ideas, as Mohammed Arkoun has put it, "remain prisoners of the image of a provincial, ethnographic Islam, locked in its classical formulations inadequately and poorly formulated in contemporary ideological slogans". Furthermore, "[their] presentation [is] still dominated by the ideological need to legitimate the present regimes in Muslim societies".[12]

The holistic view of Islam as described above has its own implications. One of these is that it has excessively encouraged a tendency to understand Islam in its literal sense, emphasizing merely its exterior dimension. And this has been carried out so far at the expense of the contextual and interior dimensions of Islamic principles. Thus, what might lie beyond its textual appearances is almost completely neglected, if not avoided. In the extreme case, this tendency has hindered many Muslims from understanding the message of the Qur'an as a divine instrument which provides the right moral and ethical values for human action. On the question of the holistic nature of Islam, Qamaruddin Khan noticed that:

> There is a prevailing misconception in the minds of many Muslims that the Qur'an contains exposition of all things. This misunderstanding has been created by the following verse of the Qur'an: "And We have sent down on thee the Book making clear everything and as a guidance and

a mercy, and as good tiding to those who surrender"(16:89). The verse is intended to explain that the Qur'an contains information about every aspect of moral guidance, and not that it provides knowledge about every object in creation. The Qur'an is not an inventory of general knowledge.[13]

Recognizing the Islamic *shari'a* as a total way of life is one thing. Understanding it properly is quite another. In fact, it is in the context of "how is the *shari'a* to be known", as noted by Fazlur Rahman, that the crux of the problem is to be found.[14] There are a number of factors which can influence and shape the outcome of Muslims' understanding of the *shari'a*. Sociological, cultural, and intellectual circumstances, or what Arkoun describes as the "aesthetics of reception", are significant in determining the forms and substances of interpretation.[15] Different intellectual inclinations "whether the motive is to recover the true meaning of the doctrine as literally expressed in the text, or to find the general principles of the doctrine beyond its literal or textual expression" in the effort to understand the *shari'a* may lead to different interpretations of a particular doctrine. Thus while accepting the general principles of the *shari'a*, Muslims do not adhere to a single interpretation of it.

The emergence of several different schools of thought in Islamic jurisprudence or various theological and philosophical streams, for instance, shows that Islamic teachings are poly-interpretable. The interpretive nature of Islam has functioned as the basis of Islamic flexibility in history. In addition, it also confirms the necessity of pluralism in Islamic tradition. Therefore, as many have argued, Islam cannot and should not be perceived as monolithic.

This means that empirical or actually existing Islam, because of the divergence in the social, economic and political context, has meant different things to different people. Equally, it is both understood differently and utilized differently. To put this in the context of the contemporary discourse and practices of Islamic economy, the endeavour to establish and develop Islamic economic institutions even though its theological/religious necessity remains a debatable issue, may denote different meanings among Muslims.

Islamic economy cannot escape this "iron law" of poly-interpretability. The existence and development of various schools of thought with regard to the question of interest, for instance, is only a logical consequence of the poly-interpretative nature of Islam, as well as the fact that Islam values the practice of *ijtihad* (an act of independent judgement) and does not recognize the existence of an institution to render any kind of religious judgements. Different from many other religions, Islam gives ample opportunities and freedom to its adherents to form and develop their own religious thought as long as they do not contradict the Qur'an and Sunnah. They may differ from any authoritative *ulama* (religious scholar) or Muslim leaders, but they cannot deviate from what has been dictated by the two sources of Islam, the Qur'an and Sunnah or traditions of the Prophet Muhammad.

Indonesia's modern history does not seem to have enough information on when the idea of Islamic economic institutions and infrastructure was initially articulated. If theology is taken into consideration, then it should have been the case in time when the process of Islamization in Indonesia took place, beginning in the twelfth century. This becomes even more logical considering the fact that Islam arrived in the archipelago via trade routes. Furthermore, it was the trading activities which made the process of conversion relatively peaceful. And for several centuries, until the institutionalization of Dutch colonialism in the eighteenth century, Muslim traders became dominant economic practitioners.[16]

Perhaps because of the simple or traditional character of the business practices of the time, Muslim traders did not seem to have been in need of pertinent economic institutions, including trading organizations or associations. It was the Sarekat Dagang Indonesia (SDI) which appeared to be the first Islamic trading organization founded by Samanhudi in Solo in 1911. This organization was established not for religious reasons, but more for socio-economic reasons, to challenge the dominant position of Chinese traders in Java. In spite of its short life (SDI was transformed into a political organization in 1912, and was named Sarekat Islam), SDI had made Muslims aware of the importance of Islamic economic institutions which could provide loans without high rates of interest. In Solo, for instance, some Muslims had tried to form types of Islamic cooperatives or Islamic banks.[17]

The earliest discourse on the question of Islamic economy probably started in the 1940s or 1950s. According to M. Dawam Rahardjo, Indonesian Muslims had discussed this issue quite seriously around that period, sparked by the writings of Mohammad Hatta, a Dutch-trained economist who published before the Second World War on the question whether or not interest is usury. Like all Muslims, Hatta accepted the premise that *riba* is *haram* (forbidden). Given the fact that the Qur'an does not specify what *riba* really is, Hatta defined it as "a high percentage of additional charge on money lent for consumption purposes". Conversely, low or appropriate additional charge on money lent for productive purposes does not belong to the category of *riba*. Quoting the view of Syeikh Haji Abdullah Ahmad, a Minangkabau leading *ulama* at that time, Hatta came to the conclusion that "*rente* [interest] was not *riba*, if it was announced publicly beforehand, so that any body who wished to borrow already knew and agreed with it".[18]

Hatta's opinion represents one religio-intellectual current on the question of bank interest. Syafruddin Prawiranegara, a leading Muslim economist, an important figure in Masyumi's leadership, and former governor of Indonesia's first central bank, was also of the opinion that interest is not *riba*. A. Hasan, former leader of Persatuan Islam (Persis, or Union of Islam), a strict and puritan socio-religious organization, belonged to the same wagon.[19]

KH Mas Mansyur, former leader of Muhammadiyah, offered a somewhat different opinion. He contended that any bank interest is *riba*. And yet, because of public needs and demands on banking, he viewed interest as a permissible thing. This, however, should only be treated in a temporary manner.[20]

Finally, there are those who strongly believe that any form interest is *riba*. Therefore, it is forbidden for Muslims to deposit or save their money in a bank which charges and pays interest. In the absence of Islamically run economic or financial institutions, traditionally those who see interest as usury keep their wealth "under the bed". Should they feel it necessary to deposit it in the bank, they do not accept or take interest. For many Muslim entrepreneurs of this line of thought, however, they do not seem to provide further information as to how to avoid interest-charging should they decide to borrow money from the existing legal financial institutions.

At the level of organization, the country's two leading Islamic socio-religious organizations do not seem to adhere to a notion that bank interest is usury. In its national congress, held in 1936, Muhammadiyah, the oldest modernist Muslim organization founded in 1911, could not decide with full certainty regarding the question of bank interest. Thus, the legal position of bank interest was identified as *mutasyabihat*. For more than three decades after, the same position was preserved, including the decision adopted during its national gathering held in 1968. Many of its members believe that bank interest is usury, but as an organization Muhammadiyah is still unable to resolve the matter with full certainty. In fact, since the 1990s, Muhammadiyah has been lenient toward a stance that interest is not usury. This appeared to be the case when Muhammadiyah established its own credit banks in 1990[21] and acquired a conventional bank (Bank Persyarikatan) in 2001.[22]

Nahdlatul Ulama, the largest traditional socio-religious organization, formed in 1926, has been more clear on the issue since the beginning. In 1938, NU had affirmed that bank interest was allowed (*halal*). Between 1950 and 1960, this organization established three conventional banks. All three banks eventually collapsed, but the experience was revived in 1990 when under the leadership of Abdurrahman Wahid, this organization founded the Bank Perkreditan Rakyat (People's Credit Bank).[23] Nevertheless, it should not be construed that all members of NU view interest as not usury, or that they are religiously comfortable enough to do business transactions in a regular bank that offers and charges interest.[24]

Many have argued that the strength of Islam in part lies in its degree of flexibility. These characteristics contribute to the ability of Islam to adapt and adjust itself to different times and spaces. The fact that Islam is often believed to be timeless and universal (*shalih li kulli makan wa al-zaman*) is because of the nature of its flexibility and richness of ideas and practices, particularly on issues concerning the non-ritual matters, that is, socio-cultural, economical, and political.

Nonetheless, it is equally true (especially if managed poorly) that the diversity of religious opinions and views often become a hindrance to many Islamic endeavours. The long overdue project of Islamic banking is a case in point. This is in the sense that the absence of a unified-single opinion (not only on the question of whether or not bank interest is *riba*, but also on the necessity of the existence of Islamic banking) had minimized the aggregate-sum of the Muslims' interest on this matter. In fact, at some point, this fuelled the animosity of certain forces, and strengthened their objections toward the idea of establishing a legitimate Islamically oriented economic institution. As revealed by Robert Hefner,

> Though ... Muslim scholars from the Majelis Ulama Indonesia had been working behind the scenes for several years to win backing for the program, most military officials expected Soeharto to preserve the New Order's long established, if unwritten, policy that Islamic banks are unnecessary and only reinforce 'sectarian' or 'primordial' social interests.[25]

From what has been described with regard to the nature of Islamic teachings, expecting Muslims to arrive at a unified standpoint on the question of bank interest (or many other issues for that matter) is perhaps like a pie in the sky. This is precisely what the initiators of the founding of BMI (including Amin Aziz, Karnaen A. Perwataatmaja, M. Dawam Rahardjo, Adi Sasono, under the institutional tutelage of Majelis Ulama Indonesia (MUI, Indonesian Council of Ulama)) concluded. Inspired by the earlier attempt in the 1970s, they based their endeavour not on rejecting the practice of conventional banks, but on the fact that there are many Muslims who, because of their religious convictions, do not want to conduct business and commercial transactions with banks that offer and charge interest. Since the banking industry is licensed by the state, it is the duty of government to be responsive to its citizens' interests.[26]

Religion has been a prime mover for the establishment of BMI. Yet, the fact that opinions concerning the legal status of what constitutes usury are diverse, weakened the argument that the founding of an Islamic bank is a religious obligation. Surely, all Muslims believe that usury is forbidden. But the difficulty to achieve a single, unified decision concerning the legal position of bank interest has made the religious basis of a non-interest bank less rigorous. As the Indonesian experience indicated, only when the establishment of an Islamic bank was perceived as an alternative financial institution did the state give its consent. Being neither an Islamic nor secular state, Indonesia did not seem to have granted permission for the establishment of non-interest financial institutions based on religious considerations, but more on the basis of the state function to be responsive to the demands of the society.

THE POLITICAL ENVIRONMENT OF THE ESTABLISHMENT OF BMI

It is difficult to assess the history of the founding of BMI without putting it in the context of the development of the relationship between Islam and the state in the late 1980s or early 1990s. One simple reason is that Islam had been severely contained (especially in the fields of ideology, politics, and matters related to the inclusion of Islamic *shari'a* in the state law) for nearly four decades, beginning with the later years of Sukarno's leadership and for the most part of Suharto's administration. As such, this hampered Muslim efforts to articulate, *inter alia*, their economic interests. The source of this structural impediment was the hostile relationship between Islam and the state. In itself this was a startling phenomenon, given the preponderant position of Islam in the country, and being the religion of the majority of its inhabitants, the national and local leadership included. It was this bitter enmity and suspicion that had blocked any efforts by Muslims to relate their economic, political, or ideological aspirations to Islam. In a situation like this, to develop discourse on Islamic economy was never viewed by the state in the light of politics, especially when the efforts were undertaken in an academic or intellectual environment. Transforming the ideas into actions, however, would surely create political and ideological suspicions, as in the case of Muslims' endeavour to develop Islamic banking or other related financial institutions in the 1970s.

In Indonesia, Islam was once at an impasse in terms of its political relationship with the state. The regimes of former presidents Sukarno and Suharto had regarded political Islam as a potential power contender capable of undermining the nationalist basis of the state. Primarily because of this, for more than four decades, both governments worked to contain and domesticate political Islam. As a result, not only did leaders and activists of political Islam fail to make Islam the state ideology and religion in 1945 (prior to Indonesia's independence) and again in the late 1950s (during the Constituent Assembly debates over the country's constitutional future), but they also found themselves repeatedly labelled as "minorities" or "outsiders".[27] In those years, political Islam was constitutionally, physically, electorally, bureaucratically, and symbolically defeated.[28] Most distressing, political Islam was frequently a target of distrust, suspected as opposed to the state ideology of Pancasila.[29]

For their part, politically active Muslims looked with suspicion on the state. In spite of the willingness of the state to recognize and assist Muslims in the practice of their religious rituals, they considered the state as manoeuvering to dethrone the political significance of Islam and embrace the idea of a secular polity. In fact, this situation had often been treated as an indication that the state was applying a dual policy on Islam. That is, while allowing the ritual dimension of Islam to flourish, it provided no opportunities for political, ideological or symbolical Islam to develop.[30] In this respect, suffice it to say that a mutual suspicion between Islam and the state existed in a country in which the majority of its population is Muslim.[31]

A historical or chronological detailing of how such a hostile relationship evolved is not very important. And yet, by way of deconstructing the venture of the country's political Islam during the revolutionary (mid-1940s), liberal (mid-1950s), and early New Order (late-1960s) periods, observers of modern or contemporary Indonesian Islam realize that the formalistic or legalistic articulations of Islam, especially in terms of its political idealism and activism, played a crucial role in the evolution of a highly strained relationship between Islam and the state with regard to the role of Islam. In those years, the ideological aura of political Islam was at the height of its intensity, demanding, among other things, that Islam be adopted as the state ideology or religion along with its social, legal, and political ramifications.[32]

However, Indonesian Islamic legalism and formalism did not evolve out of a vacuum. To a large extent, these thoughts and actions were driven by negative encounters with the West, most notably Dutch colonialism. There was no doubt that this long and penetrating process of colonial control had a devastating impact. For a large part of the Muslim community, this was particularly evident in the obstruction of their economic, educational, and political opportunities. This, in turn, contributed to the limited availability of choices for political Muslims to express their self-realization in modern Indonesia. Thus, like Jamal al-Din al-Afghani in Egypt, who waged an ideological-political campaign of Pan-Islamism in the wake of European encroachment, they inwardly sought refuge in the holistic nature of Islam for the purpose of countering Westernism.[33]

Not all Indonesian Muslims supported this kind of politics. A large and powerful group of Indonesian political thinkers and activists, Sukarno, Hatta and Supomo being their primary representatives, were concerned mainly with the nature of Indonesia's nation state, rejecting these ideas and working hard to contain them in the mid-1940s and 1950s. The relative success of this politics of containment left political Islam as an outsider in the country's political process. Later, especially during the first twenty years of the New Order regime, political Islam in fact became a principal target of ideological-political distrust and the state's exclusionary policies, because it was suspected of being inherently against the state ideology, Pancasila.[34] Bad as it had been, in the eyes of Mohammad Natsir, "they [the government] have treated us like a cat with ring worm".[35]

It is this kind of dismal situation which the new generation of Muslim thinkers and activists, emerging in the early 1970s, intended to remedy. Operating with three different, but related and compatible, modes of intellectualism, "theological/religious renewal, political/bureaucratic reform, and social transformation", their primary purpose had been to transform the earlier outlook of political Islam, from formal-legalism to substantialism. Nurcholish Madjid, Abdurrahman Wahid, Munawir Syadzali, Mintaredja, Sulastomo, Sa'dillah Mursid, Mar'ie Muhammad, M. Dawam Rahardjo, and Adi Sasono were among the major figures who worked hard to reduce the hostility between Islam and the state.[36]

With their pioneering moves, political Islam was able to develop an alternative format. Its primary features, which include (1) the theological underpinning, (2) the goal, and (3) the approach of political Islam, are perceived to be congruent with the construct of Indonesia's unitary nation-state. In terms of its theological underpinnings, this new format of political Islam does not require a legalistic or formalistic connection between Islam and the state (or politics in general). As long as the state, ideologically as well as politically, operates on a value system which does not contradict Islamic teachings, it is sufficient for political Muslims to render it their loyalty and support. This makes them at ease with Pancasila which, as they themselves suggest, is in accord with Islamic precepts.[37]

Since the late 1980s, this more integrative approach has shown some encouraging signs of success. Political Islam seemed to have found ways to integrate itself into Indonesia's national politics. In addition, there were also a number of indications which suggested that the state began to see political

Islam not as a threat, but as a complementary force in the country's national development.

Evidence of this new development was the political relaxation of the state toward Islam, signified by the former's implementation of several policies perceived as being in accord with the latter's socio-cultural, economic, and political interests. Included in these accommodating actions were the passing of a religious court law which strengthens the position of Islamic courts in adjudicating marriage, divorce, reconciliation, inheritance, and endowment issues (1989), the foundation of ICMI, which adds a structural entry into policy decision-making (1990), the compilation of Islamic law (1991), and the establishment of an Islamic bank (1991).[38]

The changing political environment has certainly been a factor in the attempts of Muslims to assert their economic interests. As the narrative account of the ten years of BMI's development indicates, had it not been for the changing relationship between Islam and the state, from hostility to amicability, the founding of such an Islamic bank would have occurred at a much later time.[39]

It was actually against all odds when initiators of the founding of an Islamic bank began to embark on this venture in the mid-1980s. Other than religious impetus and a strong commitment to empower Muslim small and medium entrepreneurs, who comprise the larger segment of Indonesia's business practitioners, practically no substantial resources were behind them in the effort to create an Islamic bank. In the first place, the existing banking law No. 14/1967 stipulated that all banks have to offer and charge interest. The establishment of a free or non-interest bank did not seem to comply with such a regulation. At least, a profit and loss sharing principle, the major characteristic of an Islamic bank, was nowhere mentioned in the government policy on banking. And certainly, given the limited exposure to the practice of Islamically-oriented financial institutions, to convince them that a bank can be regulated by principles of *mudharabah* (profit sharing), *musyarakah* (partnership, or profit and loss sharing), *murabahah* (mark-up sale, cost-plus financing), *al-bai' bi al-thaman ajil* (sale with deferred payment or settlement), *al-ijarah* (leasing), *al-takjir* (acquisition of the leased asset by the lessee), *qard hasan* (benevolent loan), *al-wakalah* (bank serves as agent of transaction for customer), *al-kafalah* (bank serves as guarantor for customer's obligation to third party), and *wadiah* (deposit) was not an easy task to undertake.[40] In the meantime, there were no signs whatsoever that the state, especially President Suharto and the military, would not consider the effort as part of an ideological or political movement, and regard it as a simple economic aspiration. In addition, it was also still unclear where the base capital of 10 billion rupiah (just under US$5 million by exchange rate of that time) would be accumulated. Without extraordinary forces, collecting that sum of money from Muslims perceived to be sympathetic to such a cause was hardly possible "even the Jeddah based Islamic Development Bank (IDB) was reluctant to help financially".[41]

Under these circumstances, the idea of forming an Islamic bank seemed to be an impossible mission from the beginning. If the narrative account is true, then it was the state, which also played a pivotal role in the establishment of BMI. With Amin Azis' tireless effort, and MUI's institutional support at his disposal, important state apparatus were approached and persuaded to endorse the idea and lend a hand in the founding of such a bank. Not only was a legal loophole finally invented, by which it was suggested that the banking law could accommodate the principle of zero-percent-interests, but also on November 3, 1991, at the Bogor Palace, President Suharto announced the establishment of BMI and mobilized the sale of shares which amounted to the value of 110 billion rupiah.[42]

THE PROSPECT OF ISLAMIC FINANCIAL INSTITUTIONS

With the establishment of BMI in 1991, the theological controversy concerning the legal status of interest ended. While differences still remain, the existence of such an institution will no longer be debated in religious light. BMI and any other similar economic institutions will be regarded as necessary alternatives for those who, for religious or other reasons, choose to conduct business and commercial activities with interest-based banks.

Similarly, with the changing attitude of the state toward Islam, it is unlikely that the development of Islamic economic institutions will be seen in the light of ideological or political Islam. In 1992, through the revised version of the banking law No. 7, the state allowed any bank to operate on the basis of a profit and loss sharing principle. The new banking law No. 10/1998 gives even stronger legal basis for the operation of Islamic banking. Under this law, the state recognizes the existence of a dual banking system whereby conventional banks are allowed to set up Islamic banking units (*Unit Usaha Shari'a*). Under the law No. 23/1999, the Bank of Indonesia becomes the responsible agency to regulate and oversee the practice and performance of the existing Islamic banks. In line with such a role, the Bank of Indonesia also formed a research and development of *shari'a* banking team in 1999. And currently, the central bank has also established the Islamic Banking Bureau under the direct supervision of the Board of Governor. This means that

Islamically administered banking has become an integral part of the central bank's concern. Therefore, it is also the responsibility of the central bank to formulate policies to enhance their further development.[43]

More importantly, the current process of democratization, following President Suharto's forced withdrawal from the presidency in May 1998, is indeed an important step in abandoning the practice of exclusionary politics. With this new development, perhaps other than an attempt to make Indonesia an Islamic state, if such an aspiration is still around, there will always be room for Muslim interests to be negotiated and accommodated.

This leaves us to speculate that the prospect of Islamic banking (or other related institutions for that matter) depends more on its "internal environment", the ability to substantiate with brute figures that non-interest banking is a viable alternative to conventional (sometimes perceived as usurious) economic institutions. On the whole, prior to the crises, the performance of BMI had been generally good and promising. With nearly 90 billion rupiah to start, BMI experienced a growth rate of average 25–30 per cent. With no negative spread, in 1997 it gained 7,514 billion rupiah in profit, a 133.81 per cent increase compared to 1996.

The monetary crises that hit Indonesia hard, starting with the devaluation of the rupiah in August 1997, is the main reason for the collapse of the country's economy.[44] Under this circumstance, no single economic or financial institution was able to evade its contiguous and spiralling effects. The continuous ballooning of public distrust over the plummeting value of the rupiah in late 1997 to mid-1998 led to a rush where depositors withdrew their deposits in large sums to be exchanged into foreign currency, especially U.S. dollars, or spent on buying basic commodities. To prevent further rush, the government (among other things) issued a blanket warranty coverage on deposits and increased interest rates. This had a significant impact on BMI's performance. Individuals as well as collective depositors withdrew their deposits to be deposited in conventional banks which gave 40–50 per cent interest. Even the central bank offered up to 60 per cent interest. BMI suffered a huge loss amounting to 106 billion rupiah, leaving the available equity to only 39 billion rupiah and 65.61 per cent non-performance loan.

But, BMI has started to make improvements since 1999. Necessary measures were taken, including structural as well as operational adjustments. Though BMI still suffered a loss of between 1.5–2 billion rupiah, its non-performance loan decreased substantially (to only 46 per cent). It bounced back by the year 2000, beginning to (re)make a profit of over 1 billion rupiah (operational) and 20 billion rupiah (non-operational). A year later, BMI earned a substantial increase in profit, 21 billion rupiah (operational) and

40 billion rupiah (non-operational). By estimation, in 2002 profit is expected to increase to 40 billion rupiah (operational).[45]

If loan-to-deposit ratio has any significance to our judgement regarding the viability of a bank operating under certain Islamic principles, than perhaps we should also consider this aspect. According to some observers, as an intermediary banking institution, BMI has a 80–90 per cent loan-to-deposit ratio. Put together, Indonesia's conventional banks have only 38–40 per cent loan-to-deposit ratio, whereas all Islamic banks enjoy 110–115 per cent ratio.[46]

Institutionally, Indonesia's Islamic banks have experienced significant growth in the last ten years. If in 1991 it was only BMI which functioned as an Islamic economic institution, currently Indonesia has 2 Islamic commercial banks (BMI and Bank Syariah Mandiri), 6 Islamic banking units (under the management of Bank IFI, Bank Negara Indonesia, Bank Jabar, Bank Bukopin, Bank Danamon, and Bank Rakyat Indonesia), 81 Bank Perkreditan Rakyat Syariah (BPRS, Syariah or Islamic Rural Bank), and over 3037 Bait al-Mal wa al-Tamwil (BMT).[47] Other than these, there are also two insurance companies operated under Islamic principles, Asuransi Takaful (Takaful Insurance) and Al-Mubarakah; and two mutual fund units Danareksa and Permodalan Nasional Mandiri (PNM, Independence National Capital). While the former two are private institutions, the later two belong to the Department of Finance.[48]

CONCLUSION

From the above account, it is obvious that these Islamic economic institutions are not likely to replace the existence and function of conventional banking systems. So far, there has been no significant move in terms of clientele change from conventional banking to Islamic banking. Many Muslims remain customers of interest-banks, though some of them may also have accounts in one or two existing Islamic banks. Nevertheless, the already mentioned facts and figures concerning the development of Islamic economic infrastructures indicate the future prospects of these institutions.

Notes

[1]   According to *al-Mu'jam al-Mufahras li al-Alfadh al-Qur'an al-Karim*, the Quran mentioned the prohibition of *riba* eight times. Q.S. 2: 275–76; 2: 278; 3: 130; 4: 161; 30: 39.

2   An interesting view is given, among others, by M. Dawam Rahardjo. See, his "Eksperimen Konsep Bank Syariah", in M. Dawam Rahardjo, *Islam dan Transformasi Sosial-Ekonomi*, Jakarta: Lembaga Studi Agama dan Filsafat, 1999, pp. 404–24.

3   See, "Islamic Banking Statistics", Jakarta: Islamic Banking Bureau, Bank of Indonesia, March 2002. Also, personal interview with Mulya Siregar, Head of Research and Development of Syariah Banking Team, Bank of Indonesia.

4   See, Robert W. Hefner, "Islamizing Capitalism: On the Founding of Indonesia's First Islamic Bank", in *Toward A New Paradigm: Recent Developments in Indonesian Islamic Thought*, edited by Mark R. Woodward, Tempe: Programme for Southeast Asian Studies, Arizona State University, 1996, pp. 291–322.

5   See, for instance, Bahtiar Effendy, "Islam and The State: The Transformation of Islamic Political Ideas and Practices in Indonesia", Ph.D. dissertation, The Ohio State University, 1994.

6   See a range of essays collected by Baihaqi Abd. Madjid and Saifuddin A. Rasyid in *Paradigma Baru Ekonomi Kerakyatan Sistem Syari'ah*, Jakarta: Pinbuk, 1987. See also, M. Dawam Rahardjo, *Islam dan Transformasi Sosial-Ekonomi*, especially chapter 4, pp. 341–434.

7   Bahtiar Effendy, op. cit., pp. 341–42.

8   For a full account on the history of the establishment of BMI, see S. Sinansari ecip, Syu'bah Asa and Avesina, *Ketika Bagi Hasil Tiba: Perjalanan 10 Tahun Bank Muamalat*, Jakarta: Bank Muamalat, 2002.

9   This argument is advocated rather strongly by Robert N. Bellah. See, "Islamic Tradition and the Problems of Modernization", in Robert N. Bellah, *Beyond Belief: Essays on Religion in a Post-Traditionalist World*, Berkeley and Los Angeles: University of California Press, 1991, p. 146. See also Leonard Binder, *Islamic Liberalism: A Critique of Development Ideologies*, Chicago and London: University of Chicago Press, 1988, p. 4.

10 Fazlur Rahman, *Islam*, New York, Chicago, San Francisco: Holt, Rinehart, and Winston, 1966, p. 241.

11 Nazih Ayubi, *Political Islam: Religion and Politics in the Arab World*. London and New York: Routledge, 1991, pp. 63–64.

12 Mohammed Arkoun, "The Concept of Authority in Islamic Thought", in *Islam: State and Society*, edited by Klauss Ferdinand and Mehdi Mozaffari, London: Curzon Press, 1988, pp. 72–73 and 53.

13 Qamaruddin Khan, *Political Concepts in the Qur'an*, Lahore: Islamic Book Foundation, 1982, pp. 75–76.

14 Fazlur Rahman, *Islam*, p. 101.

15 Aesthetics of reception is defined as "how a discourse (oral or written) is received by listeners or readers". This issue "refers to the conditions of perception of each culture, or, more precisely, each level of culture corresponding to each social group in every phase of historical development". See his "The Concept of Authority in Islamic Thought", p. 58.

[16]   See, for instance, J.C. van Leur, *Indonesian Trade and Society*, Bandung: Sumur Bandung, 1960.

[17]   See, M. Dawam Rahardjo, "Pasang Surut Pengusaha Muslim: Tinjauan Sosiologis", in his *Islam dan Transformasi Sosial-Ekonomi*, p. 187; See also his "The Question of Islamic Banking in Indonesia", in *Islamic Banking in Southeast Asia*, edited by Mohamed Ariff, Singapore: Institute of Southeast Asian Studies, 1992, p. 140.

[18]   The quotations are of M. Dawam Rahardjo. See his "The Question of Islamic Banking in Indonesia", p. 138.

[19]   Ibid., p. 142.

[20]   Ibid., p. 143.

[21]   Robert W. Hefner, "Islamizing Capitalism: On the Founding of Indonesia's First Islamic Bank", p. 297.

[22]   Personal conversation with M. Din Syamsuddin, vice-chairman of Muhammadiyah.

[23]   Robert W. Hefner, op. cit., p. 296.

[24]   Personal interview with Ichwan Syam, former secretary-general of the Nahdlatul Ulama, in Jakarta.

[25]   Robert W. Hefner, op. cit., p. 305.

[26]   S. Sinansari ecip, Syu'bah Asa and Avesina, *Ketika Bagi Hasil Tiba: Perjalanan 10 Tahun Bank Muamalat.*

[27]   See, Ruth McVey, "Faith as the Outsider: Islam in Indonesian Politics", in *Islam in the Political Process*, edited by James P. Piscatory, Cambridge: Cambridge University Press, 1983, pp. 199–225; W.F. Wertheim, "Indonesian Moslems Under Sukarno and Suharto: Majority with Minority Mentality", *Studies on Indonesian Islam*, Townsville: Occasional Paper No. 19, Centre for Southeast Asian Studies, James Cook University of North Queensland, 1986.

[28]   Donald K. Emmerson, "Islam and Regime in Indonesia: Who's Coopting Whom?" A paper presented to the annual meeting of the American Political Science Association, Atlanta, Georgia, USA, 31 August 1989.

[29]   Introduced by Sukarno on 1 June 1945, it comprises five basic principles: (1) Belief in One God; (2) Just and civilized humanity; (3) Unity of Indonesia; (4) Democracy which is guided by the inner wisdom in unanimity arising out of deliberation amongst representatives; (5) Social justice for the whole people of Indonesia.

[30]   This approach is widely perceived as the legacy of the Dutch colonial policy on Islam, formulated by its chief architect Snouck Hurgronye. For a fuller account, see Harry J. Benda, *The Crescent and the Rising Sun: Indonesian Islam Under the Japanese Occupation 1942–1945*, The Hague and Bandung: W. Van Hoeve Ltd., 1958.

[31]   See, Deliar Noer, *The Modernist Muslim Movement in Indonesia 1900–1942*, Oxford: Oxford University Press, 1978; B.J. Boland, *The Struggle of Islam in Modern Indonesia*, The Hague: Martinus Nijhoff, 1971; Allan Samson, "Islam

and Politics in Indonesia", Ph.D. dissertation, University of California Berkeley, 1972.

32 See, Bahtiar Effendy, op. cit., pp. 63–140.

33 See, Bernard Lewis, *What Went Wrong?: The Clash Between Islam and Modernity in the Middle East*, London: Weindenfeld & Nicolson, 2002.

34 See, Bahtiar Effendy, op. cit., pp. 123–38.

35 See, Ruth McVey, "Faith as the Outsider: Islam in Indonesian Politics", op. cit.

36 See, Bahtiar Effendy, op. cit., pp. 141–95. See also, Fachry Ali dan Bahtiar Effendy, *Merambah Jalan Baru Islam: Rekonstruksi Pemikiran Islam Masa Orde Baru*, Bandung: Mizan, 1986.

37 See, Bahtiar Effendy, op. cit., pp. 196–65.

38 Ibid., pp. 303–45.

39 See, S. Sinansari ecip, Syu'bah Asa and Avesina, *Ketika Bagi Hasil Tiba: Perjalanan 10 Tahun Bank Muamalat.* See also, M. Dawam Rahardjo, "Eksperimen Konsep Bank Syariah" and "Bank Muamalat Islam", in his *Islam dan Transformasi Sosial-Ekonomi*, pp. 404–24 and pp. 425–33; Robert W. Hefner, "Islamizing Capitalism: On the Founding of Indonesia's First Islamic Bank", pp. 291–322.

40 The terms are taken from Sudin Haron, Norafifah Ahmad, and Sandra L. Planisek, "Bank Patronage Factors of Muslim and Non-Muslim Customers", *International Journal of Bank Marketing* 12, no. 1 (1994): 32–33.

41 See, S. Sinansari ecip, et al., op. cit., p. 53.

42 Ibid., pp. 103–09.

43 See, "Perbankan Syariah Nasional: Arah Kebijakan dan Perkembangan", Biro Perbankan Syariah, Bank Indonesia, August 2002.

44 For a useful account of the crises, see Richard Mann, *Economic Crisis in Indonesia: The Full Story*, Singapore: Times Books, 1998. See also his, *Plots & Schemes that Brought Down Soeharto*, Singapore: Gateway Books, 1998.

45 Description and figures are taken from S. Sinansari ecip, et al., op. cit., pp. 155–266.

46 Personal conversation with Mulya Siregar.

47 See, "Islamic Banking Statistics". Jakarta: Islamic Banking Bureau, Bank of Indonesia, March 2002.

48 Personal interview with Mulya Siregar.

5

THE DEVELOPMENT AND IMPACT OF ISLAMIC ECONOMIC INSTITUTIONS: THE MALAYSIAN EXPERIENCE

Mohamed Aslam Haneef

> If some have questioned whether Islam and modernity are compatible and warned of a clash of civilizations between Islam and the west, Malaysia is a Muslim nation that deflates such facile stereotypes. It has simultaneously emphasized its Muslim identity and promoted pluralism.
> (John Esposito, *Asiaweek*, 4 April 1997)

INTRODUCTION

The need for development programmes after political independence and the perceived failures of both the capitalist and socialist models provided a fresh opportunity for Muslim nations to seek "indigenous solutions" to their socio-economic problems. The main focus is on events in the last twenty-five years where actual policy documents are available and institutions established. This chapter* argues that the development of Islamic economic institutions has been due to both external and internal factors and that both Islamic legacy and modern economics have contributed to these institutions. The chapter will also argue that the developments of these institutions and related reforms in Malaysia have by and large been accommodating, flexible and relatively pluralist in nature. In this context, "Islamization" of modern economics has been the basis of the efforts in Malaysia rather than mere rejection of modern economics or attempts to impose traditional models and views that may not necessarily be relevant in the Southeast Asian context. The chapter also attempts to evaluate the impact of Islamic economic institutions on economic development in Malaysia. Financial statistics and figures may show that the impact has thus far been marginal. However, the chapter will also argue that Islam was actually mobilized by the Mahathir administration to try and provide a counter-balance to the increasing pace of economic/material development in the last two decades, especially among the Malays. Unfortunately, not much attention has been given to this important dimension in development studies in Malaysia.

THE MODERNIZATION THESIS AND ECONOMIC DEVELOPMENT IN SOUTHEAST ASIA: A ROLE FOR RELIGION?

In his 1968 article in the International Encyclopedia of Social Sciences, Lerner (1968) characterized modernization as a process in which less developed countries acquired the characteristics of developed countries.[1] Among these characteristics was the *diffusion of secular norms*[2] including *personality transformation*. The secular mind was seen as an important "attitudinal" ingredient in modernization, being rational and progressive as opposed to the irrationality of religious (and mythical/magical) predispositions. Von der Mehden (1986, p. 12) succinctly summarizes the view prevalent in Western scholarship as follows:

> In sum, then, modernization literature, particularly in the 1950s and 1960s, pictured a decline in religious values, attitudes and practices, and legitimacy as modernization proceeded in its inevitable forward progress. With this would come the weakening of the traditional, irrational, unscientific, or prescientific attitudes and behaviour that had permeated premodern society and the acceptance of 'modern' foundations of reasoning.

While in the mid-1970s, the development process was admitted to be more complex than previously thought of, accepting variations and modifications to the components of development and modernization, religion was still seen as a backward force. Even Weber's thesis on the role of the Protestant Ethic excluded "Asian religions" (Hinduism, Buddhism and Islam) as being a positive contributor to development. Notwithstanding the modernization/neoclassical models of the 1950s and the Marxist/dependencia alternatives of the 1960s, even variations of Weberian models were not inclined to support, in our case, a positive Islamic development model.

Nevertheless, the world and scholarship has changed in the last three decades. Rather than decline, the world has seen a resurgence of religion, especially led by Islam. Haynes (1999)[3] discusses the impact of religious resurgence in various parts of the world, in an era of globalization, and relates it to politics. Giving examples of the "Christian liberation theology" movements in Latin America, the Islamic movements in the Middle East and Indonesia, the Hindu resurgence in India and the Buddhist revival in Thailand/Myanmar, he posits the view shared by some that we are witnessing "an unsecularization of the world" (Weigel quoted in Huntington, 1993).[4]

In certain parts of the world like in Southeast Asia, religious resurgence has also occurred in an era of tremendous economic growth and transformation. This period of sustained economic growth, reduction of poverty, diversification of the economy and improved social and infrastructural facilities has been termed the Asian Miracle by the World Bank (1994). Although the 1997-98 financial/economic/political crisis that hit much of East and Southeast Asia (and continues to plague some countries) called into question many aspects of the "Asian Values-Development Model", the "official" incorporation of religious/moral values as a basis of economic development in the region in the last twenty years seems to question the modernization thesis. While personality transformation and science/scientific methods have and are being promoted, religion, in our case Islam, is being directly used as a reference point.

Von der Mehden's study on religion and modernization in Southeast Asia adds support to this view since he found no conclusive proof to support the pro-secular views on development. If anything, it provides valuable insights into the inaccuracies, outdated and inappropriate models used by many social scientists of the 1950s and 1960s. This supports the view of Mircea Elliade in his article in the *Encyclopedia of Religion* (1987, vol. 12) that the dichotomy between the religious and other aspects of life, that is, of secularization, was a product and experience of Christian/Western civilization since the seventeenth century. It need not be a universal truth to be followed by other peoples. Gellner (1994)[5] also seems to view the secularization thesis as not applying to Islam.

While some studies are available in the area of Islamic resurgence in Southeast Asia, these have more often than not been in the realm of politics. Not many studies have tried to look at the development of Islamic economics in the region and more importantly to evaluate the role, if any, of Islam in development efforts in Southeast Asia. Wilson's 1998 article in the Journal of Islamic Studies entitled "Islam and Economic Development in Malaysia", discusses the impact of Islam in Malaysia's economic development. Wilson's conclusion, based mainly on the data of the growth and performance of Islamic banking and finance, is that while Malaysia's economic success is a model for others, the "specifically Islamic" influence on it is marginal. Islam, he concludes, has not had a very great impact and effect on Malaysian economic development. However, he also states that there is no evidence to show that Islam has hindered economic development. This conclusion is also found in Von der Mehden (1986). In response to Wilson's article, Mohamed Aslam Haneef (2001) while agreeing with the conclusions of Wilson, tries to elaborate on some of the often "overlooked" developments in Malaysia and also argues that there was a need for greater intellectual effort to put forward logical, coherent and consistent conceptual frameworks of Islamic economics that can be used to evaluate economic thought and policy from "Islamic perspectives".

DEVELOPMENT OF ISLAMIC ECONOMIC INSTITUTIONS IN MALAYSIA

Official contemporary writings place the genesis of Islamic economic institutions in Malaysia in the 1960s, with the establishment of *Tabung Haji* or Pilgrim's Fund in 1969. However, the present writer is more inclined to view actual planned Islamic economic reforms as having started in 1981 when the Mahathir administration came to power.[6] Unlike its predecessors, and relating to the demands of the time, the Mahathir administration decided to utilize Islam as a positive ingredient in the development of the nation and its peoples, especially that of the Malays. The role of Islam, at the state level, went beyond ceremonial purposes.

This renewed interest in Islam was unquestionably partly motivated by political expediency, especially to counter the "Islamic challenge" of the opposition Partai Islam Se-Malaysia or PAS. However, it would not be incorrect to say that Dr. Mahathir was being consistent with views in his *The Malay Dilemma* (1970) where he argued that Islam had to be mobilized to help create a "new Malay", who was willing and able to compete with the Chinese for their legitimate share of the economic pie. In this, Muzaffar (1987) is partly correct when he places the Islamic resurgence in Malaysia as a consequence of ethnic-based policy making. However, the global Islamic resurgence in the 1970s that influenced individuals and organizations in

Malaysia must also be seen as a contributing factor that shaped the government's decision to initiate its "Islamization" agenda.

In March 1981, Dr. Mahathir (then Acting Prime Minister) announced that the government would be setting up an "Islamic Consultative Body" (ICB) to ensure that *national development programmes conformed to Islamic values*. This committee was to discuss and deliberate on various issues concerning Islam and development and to put forward these proposals to the government for consideration. For the first time since 1970, the NEP was being officially open to "Islamic input". Later in 1981, the government announced its Inculcation of Islamic Values (IIV) Policy, which was meant to cover government administration. No contemporary writer on Malaysian economics has seen these federal government's initiatives as being very significant to Malaysian economic development, preferring instead to focus on the developments in Islamic banking and finance. However, these "value-policies" are central in understanding the Malaysian attempt at modernization.

In order to convince the masses that the federal government was serious in its Islamic agenda and to challenge the opposition Islamic Party of Malaysia (PAS) Mahathir needed credible people in the party. Possibly one of the most important successes of Mahathir at the time was that he managed to convince Anwar Ibrahim, the then President of *Angkatan Belia Islam Malaysia* (ABIM, or the Malaysian Islamic Youth Movement), to join the government in 1982.[7] Not only was Anwar instrumental in the Islamic initiatives of the federal government, he was also their main spokesperson, given the role of criticizing the opposition's inability in actually doing anything constructive. Within a few years, Anwar and the initiatives undertaken by the government had managed to seriously challenge PAS' claim to being the only party working for Islam. Internationally, Malaysia had become a "model" Muslim nation.[8]

The Inculcation of Islamic Values Policy

The Inculcation of Islamic Values into the country's administration will create a Government which is more just and effective. All citizens irrespective of race or religion will benefit from an administration based on Islamic values.

(Dr. Mahathir Mohamad's speech before
the MNO General Assembly 1984)

The IIV policy, although announced in 1981, was left without any clear scope and elaboration. Over the years, the government crystallized this policy and it became clear that the policy was meant to instil universal Islamic values which would enable the country to have an effective, strong, just and progressive administration. This was to create a dynamic work ethic which would increase productivity. The important values stressed were: trust (*amanah*), responsibility, sincerity, dedication, moderation, diligence, cleanliness (incorruptibility), discipline, co-operation, integrity and thankfulness.[9]

In implementing this policy, various bodies were established, the most important one being the ICB which was made up of "Islamic experts" in administration, law, economics, medicine, engineering, agriculture, sociology, Islamic philosophy and politics whose task was to analyze and evaluate policies and technology with the intention of modifying them to ensure that they were in line with Islamic values.

Looking at the aims and general scope of the ICB, it would give the impression that the government was attempting some kind of "sifting" or "quality testing" for all development policies at the national level and seemed to indicate that the NEP was being "Islamized" or at least being injected with Islamic values. This would also imply that meeting the "Islamic standard" was going to be the requirement of all policies, thus elevating Islam to a central role in policy formulation and decision-making. However, further examination of the actual programmes planned under the IIV policy and the function of the ICB as it developed over the years, seem to indicate a relatively narrow scope and target group, that is, focusing on improving the work performance of government employees, who were predominantly Malay Muslims. What seemed to be argued was that Islam could be used to help in the economic development of the Malays/Muslims. In this sense, Islamic alternatives were being sought within the ethnically biased New Economic Policy framework.

The Mahathir administration was trying to balance the demands of both the Malays/Muslims and non-Muslims without causing too much tension. Modernization was being sought and religion was being mobilized in efforts at personality transformation and changing mind-sets. Rather than imposing Islamic law or other external aspects of Islam, the IIV policy was an attempt at improving individuals in their thinking, behaviour and value orientation. In this sense, Mahathir's views certainly are not neo-classical economic views that look at economics as an independent, objective discipline. Instead, culture (including values and attitudes) and religion play an important role in determining the success or failure of economic policies, something that Fukuyama (1995) refers to as "social capital".[10]

Talking about the IIV policy and evaluating it are two very different things. Unfortunately, no study evaluating the IIV policy has been undertaken to the knowledge of the present writer. Has the public administration become more trustworthy, honest, disciplined, loyal, clean (corrupt-free), responsible and efficient? Has the productivity level in the country increased over the years? Any study that tries to evaluate the efforts undertaken would have to take into consideration the effectiveness of the IIV policy and other stated "Islamic reforms" to reduce the number of corporate scandals and unethical practices in the country. It would also have to make a comparative study between the performance of Islamic institutions and organizations to that of its non-Islamic counterparts on a whole array of performance indicators before any meaningful conclusions could be put forward.

THE ESTABLISHMENT OF ISLAMIC INSTITUTIONS

While the IIV policy had in practice, a narrow target group and objective, the establishment of Islamic institutions in the country had a much greater audience and more ambitious aim.

A. Islamic Economic/Financial Institutions

> Malaysia has emerged as the first free-market economy to have a full-fledged Islamic banking system with the launch of the Islamic interbank money market.... first country to have a dual banking system.
>
> (*Malaysian Digest*, Jan./Feb. 1994)

As at the year end of 2001,[11] the Islamic financial system in Malaysia was represented by 2 Islamic banks, 14 commercial banks, 10 finance companies, 5 merchant banks and 7 discount houses participating in the Islamic Banking Scheme (IBS), an Islamic interbank money market and two *takaful* (Islamic insurance) companies offering a wide range of financial products. Islamic banking has been growing at a rate of 49 per cent in terms of assets for the period 1995–99. However, the share of Islamic banking as a percentage to overall banking is still only at about 8.5 per cent. To complement the Islamic banking system, the capital market has also seen a rapid growth of Islamic debt securities and equity markets, with the Labuan Islamic Offshore Financial Centre being set up in 1990 and which started offering Islamic facilities in 2001. The *takaful* growth has seen an annual growth of about 68 per cent over the period 1986–2000 but is still a very small percentage of the total market. Nevertheless, the efforts of the Malaysian Government have been acknowledged as very central in providing a viable alternative for investors looking for Islamic facilities and investment opportunities. In the Financial Sector Masterplan of the nation, Islamic banking and *takaful* is projected to capture 20 per cent of the market share by the year 2010.

1. Interest-Free Banking

> The setting-up of the Islamic Bank is not just symbolic, but an effort to ensure that the Islamic banking system could play a role in the modern economy.
>
> (Dr. Mahathir Mohamad, 1983, on the opening of Bank Islam)

The establishment of Bank Islam Malaysia Berhad in 1983 was seen as a major leap forward in providing the Muslims (and non-Muslims) with an alternative to conventional banking practices. Based on *shari'a* principles, and under the supervision of *Shari'a* Regulatory Council the bank replaced all interest-based transactions with Islamic alternatives. After almost 20 years, the bank is still receiving good response from the Muslims (and non-Muslims). The government in the beginning basically funded the bank, although it now owns only 13 per cent of the bank which was listed on the main board of the Kuala Lumpur Stock Exchange in 1992. In terms of performance, it has maintained an average standing among its competitors. It has opened up numerous branches all over the country and has had a monopoly as far as Islamic banking is concerned. Only in 1993 did the government allow other commercial banks to open up "interest-free counters" practising what is known as *Skim Perbankan Tanpa Faedah* (Interest-Free Banking). In 1997, a National *Shari'a* Advisory Council on Islamic Banking and Takaful was established by the Central Bank of Malaysia and in October 1999, the second Islamic bank, Bank Muamalat Malaysia Berhad, was established (with forty branches nationwide).

It is important to note that these developments in the banking sector have generally been welcomed by Muslims and have also been accepted by non-Muslims. As long as no attempt was made to force anyone to patronize the Islamic bank or the counters, non-Muslims seem to be rather open. The government has been very cautious in its efforts so as not to offend anyone. Also it may be noted that the gradual "dual banking" approach adopted by the Malaysian Government was not like the "revolutionary" approach adopted in Iran, Pakistan and Sudan. The former seems to have proven to be a more sustainable approach.

2. Tabung Haji (Pilgrims Savings Fund)

Based on a paper by Royal Professor Ungku Aziz in 1959, the Perbadanan Wang Simpanan Bakal-Bakal Haji (Pilgrims Savings Fund Corporation) was established in November 1962. Operations officially began in September 1963, focusing on providing an avenue for Muslims wanting to perform the *haj*, to save their money without having to be involved with the interest based system. The functions were widened to include the administration and organization of *haj* activities for Malaysian pilgrims under the Lembaga Urusan dan Tabung Haji (LUTH) Act of 1969 and by August 1997, an amended act saw the Tabung Haji take up a more "corporate" image involved in three core "businesses", that is, savings, investment, and *haj*. Besides the Employees Provident Fund (EPF) and the Permodalan National Berhad (a national level equity fund), Tabung Haji is one of the biggest savings/ investment institutions in the country, but one that has from its inception, been "*shari'a* compliant". Its success earned it the Faisal Award for Islamic Economics in the late 1990s.[12]

3. Yayasan Pembangunan Ekonomi Islam Malaysia (YPEIM, or Islamic Economic Development Foundation of Malaysia)

YPEIM was established in 1976 but was reorganized and reactivated in 1984 under the initiative of the federal government. The main objective of the foundation was to collect voluntary funds from various (permitted) sources and to invest these funds into (permitted) projects and activities to provide economic assistance (employment and monetary) to Muslims and to promote human welfare in general. YPEIM combines the practice of *amal jariah* (donations/ charity) with that of investment and efficient management under the guidelines of the *shari'a*. The welfare activities are intended to promote brotherhood, altruism and cooperation while the investment activities would provide employment and generate economic activity to cater for the material needs of society. It has since 1993 undertaken many projects dealing with "Islamic pawnshops" and the rural development scheme *Amanah Ikhtiar* modelled after the Grameen Bank in Bangladesh.

4. Takaful Malaysia Berhad (Islamic Insurance)

Under the auspices of the ICB, Takaful Malaysia Berhad was set up in 1984 as a subsidiary of Bank Islam Malaysia Berhad (BIMB) through the passing of the Takaful Act. As an alternative to conventional insurance companies, Takaful did not deal with the fixed "no claims bonus" system. Instead, they introduced a similar type of arrangement as in the Islamic bank, that is, returns on one's contribution to the Takaful fund, based on the principles of voluntary contribution, joint protection and profit-sharing. Together with the Islamic bank, the Takaful company invested the contributions made by the participants in "permitted" areas, while the returns were paid back to the participants in the form of yearly profit. Since 31 July 2002, Takaful Malaysia has been listed on the Kuala Lumpur Stock Exchange. Besides the BIMB which owns about 75 per cent of shares, other owners include the State Religious Councils/*Baitul Mal* of Terengganu, Pahang and Negeri Sembilan. Based on the success of Takaful Malaysia, the government allowed the setting up of the second company, Takaful National Berhad in 1999.

5. Zakat and the Restructuring of the Baitul Mal

Zakat — which is a fundamental tenet in Islam- basically requires those who have more than a stipulated amount of wealth to give to those who are entitled. Being one of the pillars of the religion, *zakat* collection and disbursement have been a regular feature of Malay society and culture since the times of the Melaka Sultanate in the fifteenth century. Studies on the institution of *zakat* in Malaysia have shown that various aspects including the collection, disbursement, coordination and management of *zakat* funds were in need of reorganization.

Under the auspices of the ICB/Prime Minister's department, a committee to study the *zakat* institution in Malaysia was formed comprising scholars, administrators and others who were directly involved with the aim of reorganizing and upgrading the relevant bodies in charge. Since 1990, *zakat* collection centres have been in operation. Similarly, the institution of *Baitul Mal* has been under scrutiny. Since in Malaysia, all matters relating to Islam come under the jurisdiction of the state authorities and the sultan or state ruler, there has been a very uneven development of this institution from state to state. In some states like the federal territory of Kuala Lumpur, there has been a major reorganization of management, utilizing modern management practices and knowledge of finance and investment to create more "professionally" run organizations.

Other institutions established include Islamic Cooperatives and Islamic alternatives to pawnshops. In early 1992, two states introduced Islamic alternatives to pawnshops. The federal-led Terengganu and the PAS-led Kelantan, both predominantly Malay states and economically less developed. In addition, there is also a *shari'a* compliant stock index called the Kuala Lumpur *Shari'a* Index representing "approved" stocks according to criteria set by the *Shari'a* Panel of the Securities Commission.

B. Non-Economic/Financial Institutions

While economic/financial institutions are a very large component of the Islamic reforms undertaken in the last twenty-five years, there have also been very important developments in supporting areas, especially in the education and legal spheres.

1. Educational/Research Institutions

The first was the establishment of the International Islamic University in 1983. Although originally envisioned as an institution being funded by the international Islamic community, the Government of Malaysia has almost exclusively backed the IIUM. To date, the IIUM offers an integrated curriculum in courses such as economics, law, Islamic revealed knowledge, education, human/social sciences, engineering, architecture, medicine and basic sciences, taught in English (with some courses in Arabic). The underlying mission of the university is to produce graduates who are not only professionally competent, but imbued with good values, from an Islamic perspective. Since its first graduates in 1987, the IIUM has so far produced about 20,000 graduates who have joined both the public and private sectors. In addition, the university is involved in providing diplomas and other short courses to *Qadis* (*shari'a* court judges), lawyers, businessmen and members of the public on various aspects of Islam related to their own fields. In 1999, the government set up the Kolej Universiti Islam Malaysia (KUIM), also focusing on integrating Islamic Studies with professional degrees, but using the Malay and Arabic languages and with greater relationship with some Middle Eastern institutions like al-Azhar in Egypt.

In 1987, through the IIUM, the government set up the International Institute of Islamic Thought and Civilization (ISTAC) with the objectives of promoting and undertaking more serious research in the fields of Islamic thought and civilization.[13] In 1992, the Institute of Islamic Understanding (IKIM) was set up under the auspices of the Prime Minister's Department with the objective of providing a proper understanding of Islam, its principles and values to all Malaysians, especially the non-Muslims.

2. Legal Reforms

While Malaysia was interpreted to be a secular state in the time of the previous three prime ministers, it is clear that Dr. Mahathir saw a very positive role for Islam in Malaysia, especially for the Malays. Numerous scholars have put forward their views regarding the status of Islam and its applicability in state affairs. Besides the IIV policy and the institutions discussed earlier, there have been serious attempts to "upgrade" the status and scope of Islamic law in Malaysia. From a constitutional perspective, there have been scholars who have tried to put forward the view that nothing in the constitution precludes Islamic law as a valid element in the Malaysian legal system.

Ahmad Ibrahim argued that since the federal constitution states that "Islam is the religion of the Federation" (Art. 3 (1)), reforms should be carried out to enable Muslims to follow Islamic law in its entirety, albeit gradually.[14] To those who argue that this would contradict the federal constitution (Art. 4), which puts the constitution as the supreme law of the country and any law that contradicts the constitution is null and void, he interprets this to mean only "written law and laws after independence". Since Islamic law was not written but applied, and since it was the law of the land before independence (even before colonial rule), then Islamic law is not bound by Art. 4, except in matters pertaining to its administration and codification. Seen in this perspective, Art. 12 (2), which states that the government can establish and maintain Islamic institutions (financially as well), is an indication that Islamic reforms are possible and within the power of the government of the day.

In this light, various acts and legislations of the country have been amended to enable the Islamic institutions to function legally. For example the Banking Act had to be amended to enable the Islamic bank to operate. Although these may seem to be simple matters, the fact that a large number of Members of Parliament are non-Muslim indicates the political will and agreement and support from non-Muslims are needed to get these amendments passed. The status of *shari'a* courts have also been upgraded and are being reorganized with better qualified personnel. Attempts are being made to widen the jurisdiction of the *shari'a* courts but this is being done very cautiously.

ISLAMIC ECONOMIC INSTITUTIONS IN MALAYSIA: RELATIONSHIP WITH THE MIDDLE EAST, IMPACT AND FUTURE

Economic interaction between Southeast Asia and the Middle East has been minimal in the past and remains so today. There was historically "religious" and intellectual interaction and a minimal political influence, especially in the early part of the twentieth century as mentioned by von der Mehden (1993).[15] Even where there was financial/economic aid, it was related more to religious activities and the building of mosques, schools and other organizations involved in *dakwah* (call to faith) activities. According to von der Mehden (1993, pp. 17–23), Saudi Arabia and Libya were the most active in the 1970s and 1980s.

As far as trade and economic institutions are concerned, the interaction is very minimal. Even the hopes of an increased Middle East investment climate after the oil crisis in 1973 did not really see any sustained and significant increases in Middle East-Southeast Asian Trade. While international trade with the Middle East has increased, as a percentage of total trade it is almost insignificant. For example, in the case of Malaysia, total exports of manufactured products to "West Asia" (including the Middle East) for the year 2001 was only 2.4 per cent of total exports, while the figures were 25.3 per cent (ASEAN), 23.1 per cent (US), 14.3 per cent (EU) and 11.4 per cent (Japan) (Central Bank of Malaysia, 2001 Report).

As far as the Islamic economic institutions established in Malaysia are concerned, they have generally been Malaysian owned and managed. The BIMB, YPEIM, Takaful Companies, Finance Companies are "local" in ownership and management. Due to its relatively good economic performance, Malaysia has not been dependent on foreign funding for its Islamic economic institutions. As far as management is concerned, Malaysia, due to its human resource planning since the 1970s, has probably one of the most well educated and trained workforce in the Muslim world. In fact, Malaysian management expertise is sought by other Muslim countries. Hence in this area, Malaysia has been a net exporter to other Muslim countries.

Despite the Islamic economic reform efforts in Malaysia, the impact of Islam in development policymaking has been marginal. If we take statistics like the percentage of Islamic finance as a percentage of total finance (about 8.5 per cent in 2001), one can conclude as Wilson did, that it has been the economic success of Malaysia that has contributed to the development of Islamic economics and not *vice-versa*. However, if we look at the contribution of Islam to the development of "social capital" in Malaysia, that is, inculcating "right" values, attitudes, creating incentives and motivation, then we may have to undertake more research before we can make any conclusions. One point however cannot be denied; the Malaysian Government has given significant emphasis on education and training in its development plans.

In many other parts of the Muslim world, modernization has been seen as a form of Westernization and has been viewed as being inconsistent with religion and beliefs. While the masses resist, the governments of many Muslim countries also adopt a "confrontation" stance towards Islamic groups and reforms rather than the "accommodation and cooption" alternatives seen in

Malaysia in the 1980s. One only has to look at any World Bank or even Islamic Development Bank report to see the economic backwardness of Muslim countries. Malaysia is clearly the most economically advanced "non-oil exporting" Muslim country.[16] Malaysia (since the 1980s), and to a lesser extent Indonesia (since the 1990s) seem to have shown, at least until the crisis of 1997–98, that Islam was not a hindrance to economic growth and development and that Islam could play a positive role.

One writer has called the Malaysian experience "Malaysia's corporate Islam model," where "economic *jihad*" was seen as being a very important requirement for Muslims.[17]

This idea of "economic *jihad*" is quite unique to Malaysia and has manifested itself in the establishment of Islamic economic institutions, human resource management and management practices. The government has always been stressing the need for the people to change negative attitudes and cultural traits. For Muslims, this was done via the IIV policy, while for the non-Muslims, other value policies such as Look East policy and the Clean, Efficient and Trustworthy campaigns were emphasized. Presently, the long term goal of *Vision 2020* is to make Malaysia a "developed" nation according to its own mould, one that does not only stress material well-being but intellectual and spiritual dimensions as well.[18]

Due to historical reasons, Southeast Asia has been the meeting point of the major civilizations of Asia, that is, the Chinese, Indian and Malay. Nowhere better than Malaysia to see this confluence of civilizations. History, the nature of the Malays (and the Malaysian Chinese and Indians), social, cultural and political reasons have created a plural environment that can be proud of its relatively peaceful and harmonious record. National unity has been the overall objective of the country and Islam has been adopted in a positive way to serve this goal. Denying Islam or trying to neglect it would not be acceptable to the Muslims. Hence the state has tried to channel the Islamic resurgence along a modernization path, that is, its corporate Islam model. In addition, instead of talking about Islamic economics *per se*, the tone and message has been about corporate culture and Muslim participation in the global economy. In the process, it has "de-radicalized" (Shukri, 1999) the Islamic fervour which has gripped some parts of the Muslim world.

Other Muslim countries, some even in the Middle East, while possibly frowning on some manifestations of Islamic reforms in Malaysia, such as the practice of the "sale of debts" through the creation of Islamic private debt securities, are also eager to learn from Malaysia's economic, social and political experience. Malaysia has been trying to portray itself as an example of "moderate and progressive" Islam in a plural setting. "Civilizational Dialogue", has been a key project in Malaysia since the early1990s, not only between Islam and the West, but equally important between Islam and Chinese civilization. The economic success of Southeast Asia, and of Malaysia and Indonesia in the early 1990s was a great boost to the confidence of Muslims in Southeast Asia and was clearly creating more "independent" views about Islam. Some like Kishore Mahbubani even put forward the position that Malaysia and Indonesia may even be able to "take over" the leadership of Islam from the Middle East:

> So far, no Islamic nation has successfully modernized. But if Malaysia and Indonesia, two Muslim countries far from the birthplace of Islam, can be swept along by the rising Asia Pacific economic tide....the winds of the Islamic world will no longer move west to east but in the reverse direction, a major historical change.[19]

In this respect, the post-*merdeka* generation of Malays, especially those in their thirties and below, not only have a greater understanding of modern sciences but, through the Islamic resurgence of the last two decades and policies implemented, are more confident with their own traditions so that they are able to selectively accept or resist aspects of "Westernization". A look at the practices of the Islamic economic institutions in Malaysia clearly shows an integration of modern (Western) and traditional approaches to knowledge, science and policy formulation and implementation. Modern management practices are combined with Islamic values and ethics in a process of "Islamization" acceptable to Muslims and non-Muslims alike. In fact, we would not be wrong to say that Malaysia's Islamic economic reforms have taken equally from both tradition and modern sciences, maybe even more from the latter. This may also partially explain why non-Muslim are generally able to "relate" to the Islamic economic reforms in Malaysia.

Unfortunately, 11 September 2001 has changed the entire scenario. Once hailed as the bastion of moderate and progressive Islam, Southeast Asia is being increasingly seen as being "no different" from other more aggressive and volatile parts of the Muslim world. It is as if the decades of relative peace were mere illusions. Numerous articles in major papers and magazines now prefer to point out the "exceptions rather than the rule".[20] If this trend is allowed to continue, it would be a great loss not only to Muslims in Southeast Asia, but to Muslims all over the world, and one could argue to all humanity, since this would mean Huntington's thesis is being forced on the world, and "Islamophobia" and the views of its proponents are given the prominence it does not deserve.[21]

CONCLUSION

This chapter has given an overview of the development of Islamic economic institutions and related reforms in Malaysia for the last two decades. Notwithstanding the absence of studies to evaluate the success or failure of these institutions and reforms, this chapter has tried to argue that the Malaysian experience offers many lessons. Firstly, religion can be a source of modernization. Secondly, a gradual/evolutionary approach which offers alternatives to Muslims is much more sustainable than revolutionary attempts which usually end up with strife and instability. Thirdly, Islam can be applied in a plural setting. Fourthly, Muslim countries need to present Islamic alternatives that are "indigenous" rather than import models from the West and even from other Muslim countries and regions. What has been argued in Malaysia is that modernization, development advancement and progress, being legitimate goals that are sought, cannot be attained by overlooking, or at the expense of, religion. On the contrary, religion, in this case Islam, can provide, and has provided, the basis for effective development policies. The following quotes underscore the main arguments in this chapter.

> We see absolutely no contradiction between Islam and modernization. Indeed, the Islam of the 21st century must be an element of our modernization programme'. (Musa Hitam, Former Deputy Prime Minister of Malaysia, 1987)

> …Religion and spirituality run deep in the Asian psyche….the challenge before us is to cultivate moderation in religious life and to promote universal perspectives….suggests a confidence in our own heritage to retrieve shared ideals wherever they are found, East or West. (Anwar Ibrahim, Former Deputy Prime Minister of Malaysia, 1995)

> Malaysia has been at the forefront in promoting the Muslim world….What we have tried to do in Malaysia, by placing greater import on substance than form, is to demonstrate that Islam is a dynamic, tolerant and progressive religion that is relevant for all ages. (Abdullah Ahmad Badawi, Deputy Prime Minister of Malaysia, 2002).

Notes

*   The author acknowledges the comments of Dr. Mohammed Arif of the Malaysian Institute of Economic Research for his comments and suggestions.

1   For this section, I have used von der Mehden, Fred (1986), *Religion and Modernization in Southeast Asia*, Syracuse University Press.

2   The other characteristics mentioned were self-sustaining growth, political participation, a high degree of geographical and social mobility.

3   Jeff Haynes, *Religion, Globalization and Political Culture in the Third World,* London: Macmillan, 1999.

4   Samuel Huntington, "Clash of Civilizations?", *Foreign Affairs* 72.

5   Foreword in Akbar S. Ahmed and Hastings Donnan, eds., *Islam, Globalization and Postmodernity,* London: Routledge, 1994.

6   Material for this section is taken mainly from Mohamed Aslam Haneef. "Intellectual Parameters of Contemporary Islamic Economic Thought and Policy: A Malaysian Case Study", Ph.D. thesis submitted to University of East Anglia, UK, 1994; ibid. (2001), "Islam and Economic Development in Malaysia — A Reappraisal", *Journal of Islamic Studies* 12, no. 3 (2001); refer also to Muhammad Hussin Mutalib (1990), *Islam and Ethnicity in Malay Politics,* Oxford University Press, 1990.

7   For greater analysis into this aspect of Islamic resurgence in Malaysia, see Chandra Muzaffar, *Islamic Resurgence in Malaysia,* Fajar Bakti, Kuala Lumpur, 1987; Mutalib op. cit., 1990; David Camroux, "State Responses to Islamic Resurgence in Malaysia: Accommodation, Co-option and Confrontation", *Asian Survey* 36, no. 9 (1996) and M. Shukri Salleh, "Recent Trends in Islamic Revivalism in Malaysia", *Studia Islamika* 6, no. 2 (1999).

8   Unfortunately, the parting of ways between Mahathir and Anwar, leading to the sacking and subsequent imprisonment of Anwar in 1998 proved disastrous for Malaysia and the Federal government, as far as its Islamic credentials were concerned. There was a huge backlash against the federal government and especially in the UMNO. Results in the 1999 election showed that more than 50 per cent of the Malay Muslim voters voted for the opposition and not UMNO. Even from the perspective of total popular vote, the ruling coalition only managed to garner about 53 per cent of support, although they retained more than a two thirds majority in parliament. Since then, the UMNO led government has managed to win back some support among the Malays but mostly from the non-Malays/Muslims since the events of September 11.

9   See *Panduan Penerapan Nilai-Nilai Islam* (Inculcation of Islamic Values Guide), Prime Minister's Department, 1986 and *Dasar-Dasar Baru kerajaan* (Government's New Policies), Ministry of Information, 1986.

10 Francis Fukuyama, *Trust — The Social Virtues and the Creation of Prosperity,* Penguin, 1995.

11 Bank Negara Report, 2001, pp. 148–54.

12 Unfortunately, in the last couple of years, the performance of Tabung Haji has deteriorated, not only in terms of profitability but also in questions relating to its investments and management. Although it is not possible at this moment to make any conclusions, it seems as if even "Islamic" institutions are not free from human weaknesses.

13 For both the IIUM and ISTAC, former Deputy Prime Minister, Anwar Ibrahim played a pivotal role as President from 1988–98. In the aftermath of his sacking and subsequent arrest and imprisonment, both these institutions, as well as all other institutions of higher learning, have been targetted by the government as they were seen to be too "anti-establishment". Stricter controls and even a "signed declaration" of loyalty by staff and students were demanded by the government to curb any perceived (opposition) political biases. On the surface, these actions seem to have produced the desired results.

14 Ahmad Ibrahim, "The Principles of an Islamic Constitution and the Constitution of Malaysia: A Comparative Analysis". Paper presented at symposium Towards A Better Understanding of the *Shari'ah*, IIUM, Kuala Lumpur, 1989.

15 Fred. Von der Mehden, *Two Worlds of Islam — Interaction Between Southeast Asia and the Middle East*, University Press of Florida, 1993.

16 See Nabil Md. Dabour, "Annual report on the OIC Countries: 2001", *Journal of Economic Cooperation Among Muslim Countries* 23, no. 1 (2002).

17 See Bruce Lawrence, *Shattering the Myth: Islam Beyond Violence*, Princeton University Press, 1998.

18 With the numerous corporate scandals slowly being revealed in the West, one cannot but agree with this approach of holistic development. Ethics must be reunited with economics if modernization is to be meaningful. Having said that, the rise in instances of corporate/public scandals in Malaysia does not seem to show that efforts here have necessarily borne the desired results.

19 "The West and the Rest", *The National Interest*, Summer 1992.

20 See for example, Seth Mydans, "In Indonesia, Once Tolerant Islam Grows Rigid", NYT, December 2001; Rajiv Chandrasekaran, "Concerned by Indonesia's Voice of Caution", *Washington Post*, 14 May 2002; "The Challenge for Moderate Islam", *Economist*, 20 June 2002. Also see the Economist's "Survey of Islam", 6 August 1994.

21 To explain why this distorted view exists, see J. Hippler and A. Lueg, *The Next Threat: Western Perceptions of Islam*, trans. Laila Friese, London: Pluto Press, and Bobby Sayyid, *The Fundamental Fear: Eurocentrism and the Emergence of Islamism*, London: Zed Books, 1997.

PART TWO

Politics, Governance, Civil Society and Gender Issues in Southeast Asian Islam

6

ISLAM EMBEDDED: 'MODERATE' POLITICAL ISLAM AND GOVERNANCE IN THE MALAY WORLD

Shamsul A.B.

INTRODUCTION

The "Malay world" is a riverine-maritime complex of contemporary Southeast Asia, a geo-body often compared to the Mediterranean because of their many similarities, especially, as historical and civilizational "sites" where many great world civilizations, both from the East and West, interacted and cross-fertilized. Physically, the Malay world is located at the centre of the region known as Southeast Asia, where 90 per cent of over 250 million of its population are Muslims who speak the Malay language and its various dialects. They inhabit present-day Malaysia, Indonesia, Brunei, Singapore, Southern Thailand, Southern Philippines and Southern Cambodia. Therefore, it is the largest single linguistic group of Muslims, with Malay as the *lingua franca*, and even larger than the Arab-speaking Muslims of the Middle East and North Africa put together. This fact is rarely highlighted nor publicly known to the majority of Muslims around the world. With such a huge population of Muslims residing in this vibrant region, it is not unexpected that many Western countries fear it may become a new "nest of global terrorists". The fear is largely unfounded because historically the majority of them have been law-abiding and democracy-respecting citizens, in short, practising a moderate Islam. This chapter examines the origin and construction of the "moderateness".

The first part of the chapter will focus on past and present discourse amongst social scientists, specializing on Southeast Asia, on the ontological nature of the Malay world Islam. The discussion revolves around two major conceptualizations-cum-analyses put forward by two world famous scholars, namely, Clifford Geertz, the cultural anthropologist from Princeton University, and William Roff, the historian from Columbia University, both of the United States. We will offer an alternative conceptualization upon which our subsequent discussion in this chapter shall be based. The second part will briefly deal with a central theme that has dominated analyses on global Islam in the last three decades, namely, "political Islam". Indeed, the theme has become the framework within which the phenomenon labelled as "the revival of Islam" and the character of Muslim communities implicated in the movement, have been located, rigorously analyzed and have become the subject of numerous animated discussions and concerns worldwide. The third part is an empirical description of the Malaysian experience. It aims at giving substance to the preceding conceptual discussions and at the same time it is an attempt to present a description and, to a limited extent, an argument of how Malaysian Islam has been viewed as a "moderate Islam".

ISLAM EMBEDDED: THE ONTOLOGY AND THE ANALYTICAL

The discourse and analysis on the ontology of Islam in the Malay world has been informed by an interesting argument within scientific discourse within Southeast Asian studies (read "Malay world studies"), particularly, the one initiated in the 1960s by Clifford Geertz, an American cultural anthropologist, to which, in the 1970s, William Roff, a historian of the Malay world of Scottish origin, reacted. Both have created their own niche in the production of knowledge on Southeast Asian societies, and, in particularly, on Islam and the Muslims in the Malay world region.

Geertz made famous the phrase "Islam observed", the idea and ethnography of which is articulated in his book of the same title, that compares Islam and Muslims of Indonesia with that of Morocco (Geertz 1968). Ontologically, his emphasis is on "Islamic praxis" or "Islam as a lived reality amongst Javanese Muslims", hence his famous cultural reading and observation on the *abangan-priyayi-santri* continuum, a typology of Indonesia Muslims. His many writings on Islam as a cultural practice in the Sukarno era of Indonesia have been read widely and have indeed been influential beyond the academy.

Roff, in an article in the French journal, *Archipel*, introduces the phrase "Islam obscured" (Roff 1985). Although the article is not a direct reaction to Geertz's "Islam observed", it nonetheless serves as a general response to an analytical trend popular amongst Southeast Asianists, both within and outside the region, that privileges a "culturalist" perspective in their representation of Islam in the region. He suggests that one must not emphasize too much on the cultural face of Islam at the expense of obscuring its significant political role in shaping the social life of Muslims, both at the structure and agency levels. In his elaboration on the political role of Islam in the Malay world, Roff describes the nature of "political Islam", or "Islam as a political system", in the form of Malay *KERAJAAN,* a pre-colonial Malay feudal polity, thus providing us an alternative meaning and form of "political Islam" to that of the contemporary one.

It is argued that, correct as they are in their analyses of Islam in the Malay world, Geertz and Roff provide only part of the ontological story. Like Hinduism and Buddhism, Islam's original home is not the Malay world. So, when Islam came to this region, they were brought by foreign persons, who were merchants and Sufis. When it arrived in the Malay world, it entered into an enormously rich and vibrant Malay civilization that had a history of at least a thousand years, with indigenous animistic beliefs providing the anchor. Thus, anthropologically, it is unthinkable that Islam transformed this civilization overnight. It took Islam a few centuries after its arrival to find a home in the Malay world (Hooker 1983, Harper 1999).

That sociological process of settling in this new home, so to speak, involves a complicated, indeed a dialectical, interaction between the foreigners, who brought Islam, and the locals, who eventually embraced the faith. Even amongst the locals the "Islamic spread" was evidently uneven. This was the experience of Hinduism and Buddhism too. If Hinduism and Buddhism had to contend with indigenous beliefs and cultural practices, accepting and accommodating the latter as part of their ontological existence, when Islam came it had to contend with all that existed previously. Whether we want to label this whole diffusionistic process as "syncretism" (if we are structuralists) or "hybridization" (if we are post-structuralists), one rather deceptively simple fact remains, Hinduism, Buddhism and Islam had to go through, for want of a better term, a process of "embedization".

The Islam that Geertz "observed" and the Islam that Roff felt "obscured" is the Islam that has been truly embedded into pre-existing historical and sociological contours of the Malay world "civilizationalscape". That is not the end of the ontological story. We would argue further that the Islam that the foreigners brought to the Malay world, be it from the Arabian Peninsula, India or China, each one of them had previously went through a complicated process of "embedization" in the respective regions. In other words, ontologically, the Islam that came to this region was definitely the "embedded form" and not the "pristine form". Otherwise, how could we explain the many shapes and patterns of the mosques found in the Malay world? How do we account for the dominance of white-coloured garments donned by Muslims from the Malay world and black from other parts of the world, in Mecca, during the *haj* season?

In other words, although there existed a set of Islamic theological universals accepted by all Muslims, such as the five articles of faith, that promise to bind all Muslims as brothers and sisters, the material and non-material renditions of these universals into a lived reality have been mostly reconfigured to local ontologies, or sociological moulds. The "embedization" process does not end there. A continuous process of "de-embedization" and "re-embedization" takes place when new social forces arrived, after Islam, to the Malay world, the most significant of which was European colonialism. Both Islam and European colonialism, as practised in the region, became reconfigured in a redefined social, political and economic scenario.

In the context of European rationalist epistemology, that informed the colonial process, Islam and other religions, like Christianity in Europe, were perceived as non-rationalist and even anti-rationalist social entities. In the British Empire, the latter became "traditionalized", "marginalized" or taken out of the mainstream, through the application of the technology of rule and official procedures called modern bureaucracy. As a result, Hindus were separated from Hinduism and Muslims were separated from Islam. The separation was supported and legitimized through the construction of "colonial forms of knowledge", such as "Malay studies" that focuses on the Malay *ethnie* as a unit of analysis and consists of a corpus of material that detailed and elaborated exotic, non-scientific and yet aesthetically-laden "traditional" Malay cultural practices and material culture. This is just an example of what we could call the process of "de-embedization" and "re-embedization" that has affected Islam in the Malay world.

Therefore, the Islam that Geertz observed and the Islam that Roff felt obscured has undergone, in the last six centuries, a series of embedization process within sociological contexts and historical circumstances that prevailed before and after Islam came. We would then argue that it is necessary for analysts, before characterizing or labelling Islam in the Malay world, to take a closer second look at the "embedded Islam" and the complex process that contributes to that "embeddedness". Perhaps in our attempt to understand and explain the ontology of Islam in the Malay world, be it in terms of "Islam observed" or "Islam obscured", it would be enormously helpful if we take cognizance of "Islam embedded" more seriously and not in a perfunctory fashion as a historical given. This is the approach we wish to take in trying to understand and offer our tentative explanation on and in trying to make sense of the ontology of Islam in the Malay world — the "home of Islam" within the larger Southeast Asian region.

ISLAM IN THE MALAY WORLD: A "POLITICAL ISLAM" PERSPECTIVE

The main intention of this part of the chapter is to present an argument that if we wish to begin to understand the different dimensions of the complex relationship between Islam and governance in the Malay world, whether in the past or at present, and other issues related to that relationship, such as the debate on Islamic state and the demand for the reintroduction of *hudud* laws, we have to recognize the fact that, ontologically, there are two forms of political Islam that have existed in the region. They are, namely, the new "global imagination" version and the other is the old "embedded practice" form. Both have affected that complex relationship between Islam and governance in the Malay world. We need to have a second look at this extremely dynamic and sometimes contentious relationship. It must be noted that the terms "global imagination" and "embedded practice" political Islam are both heuristic analytical labels of our choice. Others may want to label them differently.

The term "political Islam" as understood today, and its articulation will be examined, followed by a description of the indigenous "embedded practice" version. The term "political Islam" has been coined to describe and characterize, both in popular and academic terms, contemporary Islamist movements, that is, the activist groups who see in Islam as much a political ideology as a religion, and who are therefore perceived sometimes as breaking with certain aspects of Islamic tradition themselves. The movements introduced a new thought orientation that endeavoured to define Islam primarily as a "political system", in keeping with the major Western-derived ideologies of the twentieth century. But they brought legitimacy to this new vision of "political Islam" by the theme of a "return" — a return to the texts and to the original inspiration of the first community of believers. The term and its current usage has to be located in the larger global context, namely, in the presence of modern nation-states.

Although the conception of Islam as a political system is not new, introduced in the 1930s by prominent Muslim scholars such as Hassan Al-Bana, in Sudan, and Abul-Ala Maududi, in Pakistan, its widespread influence as a global "political imagination" that since the 1970s motivated worldwide Islamic revival and renewal, is relevant to the present discussion. Based on the growing literature on contemporary political Islam, the present form of political Islam can be characterized as a "global imagination", one that proposes as its ultimate aim the creation of a "borderless space" of global Islamic brotherhood, free of nation-state boundaries. This ultimate aim is, in many ways, still a hope, an expectation and an ambition, if an elusive one.

The second version of political Islam, indeed an indigenous one in the context of Malay world, we refer to as the "embedded practice" version. This version is based not an imagination, hope or an illusion. It is based on something real and empirical and has existed for centuries. Indeed, many parts of it, in a redefined social scenario, still exist today. This version is a familiar one to many of us, namely, the pre-colonial Malay-Muslim *KERAJAAN* (literally polity of the raja/sultan). Perhaps others may want to call it a "feudal" political Islam.

This version of political Islam resides in the concept of *KERAJAAN*, which is both a polity as well a system of governance based on partial (such as in *KERAJAAN* Malacca) or full implementation (such as in *KERAJAAN* Aceh) of *shari'a*. It has its pre-Islamic origins though. The partial *shari'a*-based *KERAJAAN* is more dominant and common in the Malay world than the full-fledged one. In the numerous *KERAJAAN* that proclaimed itself as an Islamic *KERAJAAN*, but only partially implement the *shari'a*, they survive functionally within the pre-Islamic Hinduistic "Brahmanic" political structure. It means that the raja or sultan, though at the centre or apex of power, is not himself a well known Islamic clergy, or *ulama*, with the stature of, say, Ayatollah Khomeini of the Iranian Government in the contemporary political Islam sense. The *raja* is usually dependent on his religious advisers or specialists, called *mufti*, who commands and controls Islamic religious knowledge, to provide wisdom, interpretation on matters related to the *shari'a*, especially in the promulgation of *fatwa* (religious decree), and on other mundane Islamic practices. Based on such advice the *raja* makes a final ruling on a particular Islamic matter thus turning it into the law of the land.

In other words, the raja and his *KERAJAAN* derives his religious legitimacy not through his own expertise on Islam or because he is the absolutist Muslim monarch, but instead from his circle of "Brahmin-like" *ulama*. As such, whether the *shari'a* is implemented fully or partially, whether it fits or not the definition of political Islam that of Hassan Al-Bana or Maududi or Ayatollah

Khomeini, these pre-colonial system of *KERAJAAN*, by definition is a form of political Islam, too, and certainly not an object of some future political hope and ambition for a social movement. The rich historiography on Southeast Asia, hence the Malay world, has provided us with such detailed evidence about the existence of this form of political Islam (Hooker 1983). But social scientists, particularly political scientists, who are "experts" on Southeast Asian or Malay world Islam, in their discussion on contemporary political Islam, have chosen to ignore or remain silent on *KERAJAAN*, the indigenous form and an "embedded practice" of political Islam. The exception in this case is of course the significant contribution of the Australian historian, Anthony Milner, whose work on pre-colonial *KERAJAAN* (1982) and post-colonial *kerajaan* (1995), remains unsurpassed in analytical breadth and depth and has become the benchmark for the general analyses on the making, consolidation and transformation of Malay polity in Malaysian historiography.

This selective forgetting by scholars of the human sciences specializing in Malay world studies has disadvantaged a more holistic analysis of political Islam in the Malay world, thus rendering contemporary analysis and discourse on the said phenomenon — and its structural influence and impact on contemporary modern nation-state in the Malay world, in general, and in Malaysia, in particular — rather limited and unsatisfactory. For instance, because we have been focusing mainly on the impact of contemporary "global imagination" version of political Islam, say, on the post-September 11 debate between UMNO (United Malays National Organization, the Malay/Muslim-dominated dominant political party in the National Front coalition government of Malaysia) and PAS (Malay/ Muslim Islamic Party, once a member of the National Front) on "Islamic state" in Malaysia, we have failed to see it as a contestation between two epistemologies of a historically and sociologically restructured practice of Islamic governance; one based on the concept of a modern nation-state constituted in the Western rationalist framework organized within a constitutional arrangement (the UMNO version) and the other on the "return to the first community of believers" approach (the PAS version). Nonetheless, both are reactions to the old "political Islam", or *KERAJAAN*, which has been greatly transformed as a result of colonialism.

The analytical absence of a discussion on *KERAJAAN* in Southeast Asian discourse on contemporary Islam and governance in the Malay world — the feudal political Islam and how it got transformed structurally and, subsequently, became embedded through colonialism into a new European epistemology of official procedures and technology of rule — needs to be redressed rather urgently. This chapter is a modest attempt towards that goal.

FROM *KERAJAAN* TO *kerajaan:* POLITICS AND
GOVERNANCE IN THE MALAY WORLD

The pre-colonial Malay *KERAJAAN[1]* is a form of governance in which the "church" (read Hinduism, Buddhism and Islam) and the state (the social organization) is not separated. As such, it is not unlike the situation in Europe before the Enlightenment era. However, there is a fundamental difference between these two experiences.

In Europe, it is Christianity that dominates the state and its organization and functioning. However, in the Malay world, the situation is rather pluralistic and perhaps more complex. Islam is not the only religion that provides Malay *KERAJAAN* its "church". Before Islam, it was Hinduism and then Buddhism. But not all *KERAJAAN*, after the arrival of Islam, became Islamic simultaneously. Some remained Hinduistic, some partially Hinduistic and partially Islamic, others more Islamic, and very few could be called totally Islamic. The "church"-based and absolutist feudal nature of these *KERAJAAN,* in terms of governance, gave them, depending on which historical period, the "political Hindu", or "political Buddhist" or "political Islam" character. Of course, the majority of them were Malay-Muslim or Islamic-based *KERAJAAN* before the European came to trade and colonize them for centuries after. The use of capital letters, in some places, and lower case, in some others, to spell the word *kerajaan* is deliberate to differentiate the fact that before European colonialism, *KERAJAAN* was a holisitic one, or the state, which is the fusion of "church" and "state", but in the colonial era and beyond, *kerajaan* was reduced and became only a component of the modern nation-state constructed by the colonial ruler.

How Islam came and Islamized the pre-Islamic *KERAJAAN* has been a subject of lively academic discourse for decades. Sometimes, the discourse amongst the scholars of various ethnic origins becomes rather ethnicized: scholars of Arab descent would like to claim that it was brought by the Arabs *sufis* and those of Indian descent would then claim that the Indian traders did and not the Arabs. We were made to understand that they all managed to produce much evidence to support their theories, apparently, enough to create for each, groups of student-scholar followers.

However, the political and socio-cultural impact of Islam on the pre-Islamic Malay *KERAJAAN* in pre-colonial Southeast has been tremendous, especially in terms of spirituality, intellectual contribution and the establishment of new ground rules for social order through the adoption of the *shari'a*. We shall now turn to each briefly.

'KERAJAAN' AS ISLAMIC GOVERNANCE

In terms of spirituality, the impact of Islam in the Malay world is not simply a veneer over the structure of the Malay-Indonesia society, argued some scholars, for it has played an enormous role in transforming both the "body" and the "soul" of the different societies in the Malay world. In particular, Islamic mysticism of *tasawwuf* has functioned as the strongest means of purifying the heart and intellect of the members of the Malay world societies. Through the efforts of Sufis, who acted as preachers (*mubaligh*) to the king as well as the masses, the nature of Malay spirituality, as some Muslim scholars have claimed, has been elevated to a higher state. The foremost amongst the scholars was Naguib Al-Attas (1967). He argued that the highly intellectual and rationalistic Islamic religious spirit entered the receptive minds of the Malays of the archipelago and turned them away from all forms of mythology. Besides, he argued the doctrine of One God, and man as essentially His creation, together with the equality of spirituality between man and man, gave the ordinary man in the Malay world a sense of worth and nobility denied him in pre-Islamic times.

He further argued that Islam brought spiritual refinement and knowledge to the people of the Malay world through an intellectual and rational impetus, not only to the courts, but also to the people in general, as evidenced by the fact that not all philosophical treatises were written solely for the pleasure of kings. The elevation of spirituality among the Malaysian society led to the growth and proliferation of the Sufi orders (*tariqah*) which stressed the importance of practicing mystical teachings in an organized manner.

The intellectual contribution of Islam from the fifteenth to seventeenth century to Malay civilization has been most significant in providing the epistemological change, hence the establishment of a stronger Islamic-based social order in the Malay *KERAJAAN*. During that period, the Malay Islamic literati, especially mystical poets and writers, undertook both missionary and intellectual works to spread Islam. One of them was 'Abd al-Ra'uf al-Sinkli (d. 1693) who is recorded as the first Malay translator of the Qur'an together with al-Baydawi's commentary on it. However, prominent among these missionaries was Hamzah al-Fansuri (h. 1589/1604) a Sufi poet and writer who belonged to the Qadariyyah Order. He was followed by another Malay Sufi, Shams al-Din al-Sumatrani, Shikh al-Islam of Acheh, who was intellectually involved in the mystic doctrine of *wujudiyyah*. His theosophical concerns were shared by another controversial Malaysian Sufi theologian, historian and missionary par excellence, Nur al-Din al-Raniri (d. 1666).

Al-'Attas explained that Nur al-Din al-Raniri's thought had a tremendous impact in the Malay world because, firstly, he was the first man in the region to clarify the distinction between the true and false interpretation of Sufi theosophy and metaphysics; secondly, al-Raniri was known as the first scholar to prepare a Malay translation of best commentary on the creed by al-Nasafi; thirdly, al-Raniri's *Sirat al-Mustaqim* is considered a classic, dealing with the essentials of Islam, and, finally, al-Raniri was also a highly celebrated Malay writer because of his book *Bustan al-Salatin*.

Without doubt, the most significant and central element in governance in the Malay-Muslim *KERAJAAN* was the *shari'a*. One could say that Islamic civilization in the Malay world manifested itself by way of enacting the Islamic *shari'a* holistically, that is, by applying *shari'a* in all aspects of social life. For example, the Malacca Sultanate in the fifteenth century applied officially two forms of *shari'a*-based law: first, the Malacca Digest (*Hukum Kanun Melaka*) and second, the Maritime Laws of Malacca (*Undang-undang Laut Melaka*). These two legal codes were complementary in providing solutions to all legal disputes. While the Malacca Digest embodied all matters of criminal and civil laws, family law, the legal power of the ruler, rules relating to proper conduct, particularly with regard to sexual matters, laws regarding slavery, and penalties for all offences, the Maritime Laws consisted entirely of rules, regulations, procedures and codes of conduct which were to be used at sea.

Studies by Malaysian historians reveal the tremendous impact of Islam in the Malacca legal system by looking into both of these two legal codes (Hooker 1983, Harper 1999). For instance, in the Maritime Laws of Malacca, the captain of a ship (*maalim*) was considered an *imam* (leader) and his subjects as *ma'mum* (followers). Similarly, the Malacca Digest contained many provisions based in the *shari'a* in order "to follow injunctions in the Qur'an and enjoin good and forbid evil (*amr bi al-ma'ruf wa-nahy 'an al-munkar*)". It has been observed as well that the Islamic influence was clearly felt throughout the legal texts and that many terms and concepts have been absorbed and widely used, such as *imam, mu'allim, taksir fufuli, amanah, hak ta'ala, thayyib, ta'zir* and *mithqal*.

It must be mentioned that in spite the Islamic dominance in governance and social life of Muslims under the Malay-Muslim *KERAJAAN* there have been conflicting opinions about Islam and its relationship with pre-Islamic customs or *adat*. The continued practice of both the matrilineal-based *Adat Perpateh* and the patrilineal-based *Adat Temenggong* by the Malay-Muslims have created a measure of tension and conflict with *shari'a*. Proponents of the *adat* tend to justify the position of *adat* as something not contradictory to the *shari'a*. Indeed *adat* and other forms of pre-Islamic rituals (many of which are considered non-Islamic) such as magic, superstition, spirit worship, taboos, consultation of shamans (variously called, *pawang, dukun* and/or *bomoh*), and belief in *jin* and *iblis* (supernatural beings) still persist and permeate the life of many Malays, particularly in the villages. However, theologically, Islam has always recognized the existence of *jin* and *iblis*.

One can conclude that the coming of Islam to the Malay world constituted a new era in its history. Undoubtedly, Islam transformed many aspects of the pre-Islamic cultural practices and beliefs of the people and imbued it with an Islamic worldview, but it is an embedded version not in the pristine form practised by the first community of believers in Mecca and Medina. Islam also brought progress in the sphere of Islamic knowledge, with Malacca exercising its special role as the centre of Islamic learning throughout the Malay world. Some have also argued that it was Islam that unified the Malay sultans in confronting the encroachment of Western imperialism.

'kerajaan' AS SECULAR BUREAUCRACY

Scholars have argued elsewhere that colonialism involves more than just the conquering of physical space (Cohn 1966, Shamsul 1999, 2001). More importantly, it involves the conquest of the indigenous "epistemological space", or put simply, the dismantling of indigenous thought system, hence the disempowering it of its ability to define things and subsequently replacing it with a foreign one, through a systematic application of a series of colonial "investigative modalities". According to Cohn, an American anthropologist who has spent his whole life studying the anthropological history of India,

> "an investigative modality includes the definition of a body of information that is needed, the procedures by which appropriate knowledge is gathered, its ordering and classification, and then how it is transformed into usable forms such as published reports, statistical returns, histories, gazetteers, legal codes, and encyclopedias" (Cohn 1996, p. 5).

The empirical evidence presented here is based on the more familiar Malaysian case.

The colonial conquest of the epistemological space, through the use of various forms of investigative modalities, has resulted in the reconfiguration and reconstitution of the concept *KERAJAAN*, one in which the "church" (read Islam) and the state are fused, to another version of *kerajaan* that separates the "church" (read Islam) from the state. The colonial and post-colonial use of the concept *kerajaan* is divorced from the Islamic content. This is not unexpected because when the British took over Malaysia, for instance, the whole exercise was informed by a notion of state and governance that was already divorced from the church, as it was the case in Britain. As a result, the indigenous church (read Islamic) component of pre-colonial *KERAJAAN*, has been systematically "traditionalized" and perceived as a non-rational system, hence its position recasted into a peripheral role in a larger modern-rationalist complex of a secular colonial state. The process of the transformation from *KERAJAAN* to *kerajaan* occurs in at least three critical spheres of influence, namely, the general bureaucracy, judiciary, and education. The Malaysian case will be examined as an example.

British colonialism in Malaysia has had a far-reaching impact on its society. Despite the fact that the British did contribute to the improvement of Malaysian life, many criticize them for being responsible for whittling away the domination of Islam in Malaysian society. Syed Naguib al-'Attas, for instance, criticized the presence of western imperialism, including the British colonialists, as "attempting a consistent policy of separating Muslims from their religion" (1967, p. 2)

The impact of British bureaucratic presence and policies can be clearly discerned in the following events. First, the British began establishing itself through an indirect intervention in 1786 when Penang was acquired from Kedah, which later led to a widening of its direct involvement upon areas traditionally the domain of the Malay sultans. British residents were stationed first in the Federated Malay States (FMS) and later in the Unfederated Malaysian States (UFMS). The Pangkor Treaty (1874), which was signed by the Malay sultans, gave full authority for the British to control Malaysia, stipulating that the sultans receive and provide a suitable residence for a British officer to be called resident, who are accredited to his court, and whose advice must be asked and acted upon on all questions other than those touching Malay religion and *adat* (custom). It simply means that religion (read Islam) is clearly separated from secular matters such as politics, administration, law, economics, education and so forth. Islamic and Malay customs are under the jurisdiction of the sultans, the rest came under the British. Later, the British administration even violated the so-called "non-interference" policy in Islamic and Malay *adat*. On this particular point, Moshe Yegar noted that under the treaty, matters affecting the religion and custom were under the jurisdiction of the rulers and their chiefs, yet even they in the end were controlled and regulated by the British (Yegar 1979).

The bureaucratic changes flow into the realm of religious administration hence religious judicial matters. Despite the fact that the British introduced some reforms in the religious aspects of the Malay-Muslim society through the Council of Islamic Affairs and Malaysian Customs (*Majlis Hal Ehwal Islam dan 'Adat Melayu*), this newly established institution excludes the role of Islam from all aspects of life except in limited religious affairs. H.B. Hooker, a well known British scholar on Malaysian Muslim laws, argued that the British motivation was to limit the sphere of Islamic law to family law and to introduce their own secular legal system (1983). The British policy for seclusion of *shari'a* became evident, for instance, in a court decision in the case of Ainan vs. Syed Bakar (1939). In this particular case, the issue was raised whether a baby, delivered by Ainan after a marriage of only three months, may be considered legitimate or not. The *Shari'a* Court considers the baby illegitimate. Nevertheless, as a result of the implementation of the Evidence Enactment Law in the Malaya Court, the court ruled that the law which should be followed is the Evidence Enactment Law not the *shari'a*. Therefore, the disputed baby was considered legitimate by the civil law (Ibrahim 1978).

The religious administrative reform restricts the independence and jurisdictions of the Islamic judges, or *qadis*. Their power is limited compared to the civil judges. They are denied the power to arrest and punish offenders. The British administrators only permitted the *qadis* to become prosecutors in magistrate courts for criminal offences. This, in fact, is in striking contrast to the powerful position of *qadis* in the pre-colonial period of the Malay sultanates. This is not surprising because all the laws and regulations introduced during the colonial period aree taken almost completely from the British laws. The late Professor Ahmad Ibrahim (1978) pointed out that the deteriorating position of the *shari'a* is mainly caused by the British misunderstanding of Islam as a religion, since the term *ugama Islam* has been equated with the Christian understanding of religion. In addition, all the senior judges were appointed by the resident general with the approval of the high commissioner and were trained in the British system of law, thereby making it natural for them to refer to and apply English law. As a result, the power wielded by the British in implementing legal policies led to the Malaysian view of the *shari'a* as a legal code which is confined to personal law.

In the sphere of education, Islamic education suffers the same fate of being peripheralized or transformed into a modern form. Before the British educational policy was introduced, Islamic education had been an extremely important homogenizing socialization tool because it provided the means by which Islam continued to flourish among the Malays. The introduction of the Arabic script, popularly known as *tulisan jawi*, has been the oldest Islamic traditional education in this country. Traditionally, Malaysian children began to learn the Qur'an at home (*mengaji* Qur'an) by way of recitation (*membaca*) and memorization (*menghafal*). Later, these children were sent to specific houses where religious teachers, known as *Tok Lebai*, taught the Qur'an and personal duties (*fardu 'ain*). For more advanced studies in religion, Malaysian parents sent their children to educational institution such as *pondok* and *madrasah*. Malaysian students used *kitab jawi*, a popular religious book written in the Malaysian language using the Arabic alphabet, as their textbook on different subjects, ranging from Islamic law (*fiqh*), kalam (*usul al-din*), Qur'anic exegesis (*tafsir*), and the prophetic tradition (*hadith*) among others.

Both *pondok* and *madrasah* play important roles in preserving the Islamic identity of Malays and providing them with the core of Islamic education. Some scholars hold the view that the essence of the *pondok* institution for Malay society can be described as "template" for the cultural view of education in Malay-Muslim society." Beginning in the nineteenth century, Malay society witnessed the growth of *madrasah*, a differentiated version of the *pondok* system. It is more formal and organized in terms of administration and some school even combined theological subjects and that of secular academic and vocational ones. Important among these schools was Madrasah al-Hamidiyyah in Limbong Kapal, Alor Star, Kedah, founded in 1906. In this school, the curriculum included the study of *fiqh, tasawwuf, tafsir, hadith* and a comparative study of the four *fiqh al-mazahib* (for schools of *shari'a*) at a more advanced level. It is interesting to note that in Sekolah al-Diniah, which was established in 1924 in Kampong Lalang, Padang Rengas, Perak, the school's curriculum included mathematics, history, English and commercial subjects. More importantly, the students were also taught business, the techniques of padi planting, and of making ketchup and soap. Because of its advanced curriculum, Sekolah al-Diniah became popular. With sixteen students enrolled in 1924, it had no less than 500 pupils in 1941 and opened at least eight branches of the school in the surrounding areas.

The strength of Islamic education, as illustrated above, began to deteriorate gradually with the direct involvement of the British in educational policy. Several noted Malaysian scholars have admitted that during the British regime an element of secularism was introduced into Malay society, mainly through the establishment of secular schools. The first attempt made by the British administrators in the sphere of education was to set up English medium schools in urban areas. Only a limited number of Malays were admitted and thereby assured of employment and high posts in the administration. Meanwhile, it is interesting to observe that the British also established Malay medium and Islamic religious schools in the rural areas. The purpose of these two types of schools, according to George Maxwell, the chief secretary, was to train "the sons of Malay fishermen to become better fishermen and the sons of Malay farmers, better farmers" (Roff 1994, p. 28). It is clear that the British preferred the English medium school and it became their policy that Malay and Islamic education remain of lower quality than English education. Even O.T. Dussek, a famous British educator who became the first principal of the Sultan Idris Teacher Training College (SITC) in Tanjong Malim, Perak, criticized the system of English education for failing to cater to "the needs of the country or the state of intellectual development, or to the social culture attained by the inhabitants" (ibid).

Apart from the secularization process incurred by the English medium school, the British administrators implemented the same policy in the Malay schools (*Sekolah Melayu*) by initiating the following actions. First, the Qur'an could be taught in schools but had to be separated from the teaching of the Malay language. Second, education in the morning was concentrated on the teaching of the Malay language. The teaching of the Qur'anic lessons could be done only informally in the afternoon. Third, teachers' allowances from the government were meant only for the teaching of the Malay language, while parents were obliged to pay for the allowances of those teaching Qur'an lessons.

In 1905, the British administration established for the children of the aristocracy the elite Malay College Kuala Kangsar (MCKK), located in Kuala Kangsar, Perak. The formation of this prestigious college strengthened the British policy toward secular education in Malay society. MCKK was formed to educate "Malays of good families" and to train them to fill subordinate post in government services. Quite apart from its excellent academic achievements, it enhanced the separation of Malay traditional leadership from the masses (Roff 1994, p. 30).

The process of secularization among the Malaysian students became more complex with the entry of English missionary schools. Although the British officially forbade Christian missionaries from operating missions in British Malaya, the administration allowed these same Christian preachers to establish missionary schools in towns and cities. Malay children were encouraged by the British to attend these missionary schools even though some did enrol against the wishes of their parents. It could be argued therefore, as elsewhere in the Muslim world, with the deepening influence of secular education in Malaysia, the value of a secular education had more appeal. Thus with the consolidation of British colonial rule we witness the rise of both religious and secular schools, which dichotomized the dissemination of knowledge within the Malay society.

It is hoped that the brief account above has helped to put into context the evolution of the Malay-Muslim *KERAJAAN* to a colonial-constituted *kerajaan*, in which the latter became only a component of a larger complex of modern state bureaucracy, based on a rationalist European knowledge structure. Sociologically, it involves the "disembedding" of *KERAJAAN* as a form of political Islam and governance. It was then reconstituted and re-embedded into a new and different epistemological mould in the form of *kerajaan*.

CONCLUSION

The embedding of Islam into the social life of the Malay-speaking inhabitants of the Malay world involved a number of other versions of "embedded Islam", namely, the Arabic, Indian and Chinese. The articulation of the impact affected the ruling class and the *rakyat* (the ruled or the ordinary folks) rather differently, with the former strong on written/textual tradition while the latter survived on the oral tradition. It thus pluralized the understanding and the practice of Islam in the Malay world. The pluralized Islam was embedded and set into a non-Islamic mould that constitutes an admixture of indigenous belief, Hinduism and Buddhism. The layering and the bundling process between the previous non-Islamic beliefs and faiths and the Islamic one has somewhat deradicalized the general practice of Islam in the Malay world, giving it characteristics quite different to those found in the Middle East, India and China.

The onset of European colonialism, with its strong non-rationalist or anti-rationalist position and its powerful bureaucratic influence, redefined the position of Islam within the Malay world communities. The embedded Islam and other religions became not only peripheralized but also fragmented under the dominance of a pro-state and anti-church colonial stance. This fragmentation became consolidated with the establishment of modern nation-states, thus breaking-up the "psychic unity" of the Malay world, transforming Malay-speaking Muslims into components and citizens of different nation-states. In some nation-states, they are dominant, like in Indonesia, Brunei and Malaysia, but in others they have become minorities, such as in Thailand, Singapore, the Philippines and Cambodia. In a redefined political, economic and cultural scenario, Islam's ever progressive character became the source for creative dissent for the locals against the colonizers in each of the nascent modern-nation states — hence the emergence of Islam-oriented nationalist movement throughout the Malay world, a minority of which has resorted to violent methods to further their cause. The majority remains democratic in their approach, for they have been conditioned so by the secular-oriented colonial government and later the post-colonial ones.

The arrival of a new version of political Islam, one that is often referred to as "global Islam", did not diminish the support or dilute the practice of the "old" political Islam of the *KERAJAAN* as well as the *kerajaan* type. It remains at the core of politics and governance in the Malay world, as shown in the Malaysian case. This makes the Malay world Islam quite different from those in other parts of the world, in the sense that, resorting to "revolutionary approach", such as we have witnessed in Iran, is never really an option. Furthermore, the Islam in the Malay world is informed by a more conservative Sunni school while in Iran its Islamic axis is the Shia school doctrines. Therefore, the "moderateness" of Islam, or political Islam, in the Malay world, has been the result of its embedded diversity that accommodates and, at the same time, restricts any extremist tendencies.

References

Al-'Attas, Sayyid al-Naguib. *Preliminary Statement on a General Thoery of the Islamization of the Malay-Indonesian Archipelago.* Kuala Lumpur: Dewan Bahasa & Pustaka, 1967.

Cohn, Bernard. *Colonialism and its Form of Knowledge.* New Jersey: Princeton University Press, 1996.

Geertz, Clifford. *Islam Observed: Religious Development in Morocco and Indonesia.* New Haven, Conn.: Yale University Press, 1968.

Harper, T.N. *The End of Empire and the Making of Malaya*, Cambridge: Cambridge University Press, 1999.

Hooker, B., ed. *Islam in Southeast Asia.* Leiden: Brill, 1983.

Ibrahim, Ahmad. "The Position of Islam in the Constitution". In *The Constitution of Malaysia: Its Development 1957–1977*, edited by Muhammad Suffian, H.P. Lee and F.A. Trindade. Kuala Lumpur: Oxford University Press, 1978.

Milner, Anthony. *Kerajaan: Malay Political Culture on the Eve of Colonial Rule.* Tuscon: Asian Studies Association, 1982.

Milner, Anthony. *The Invention of Politics in Colonial Malaya.* Cambridge: Cambridge University Press, 1995.

Shamsul A.B. "A History of Identity, an Identity of History: The Idea and Practice of Malayness in Malaysia Reconsidered". *Journal of Southeast Asian Studies* 32, no. 3 (2001): 355–66.

Shamsul A.B. "Colonial Knowledge and the Construction of Malayness: Exploring the Literary Component". *Sari* 17 (1999): 3–17.

Roff, William. "Islam Obscured? Some Reflections on Studies of Islam and Society in Southeast Asia". *Archipel* 29 (1985): 7–34.

Roff, William. *The Origins of Malay Nationalism*. Second Edition. Kuala Lumpur: Oxford University Press, 1994.

Yegar, Moshe. *Islam and Islamic Institutions in British Malaya*. Jerusalem: The Magness Press, 1979.

7

LAW-MAKING IN THE NAME OF ISLAM: IMPLICATIONS FOR DEMOCRATIC GOVERNANCE

Zainah Anwar

INTRODUCTION: ISLAM AS A POLITICAL IDEOLOGY

The rise of political Islam in countries throughout the Muslim world has posed particular challenges to democratic principles of governance, human rights and women's rights.most Muslim states are in crisis today, politically, economically, socially. Many remain under authoritarian rule of well-entrenched monarchs, despots, and autocratic elected leaders. The fact that the modern Muslim state is conceptualized and organized within the framework of modern political institutions which are regarded as western and secular, the state failure to deliver on the aspirations of the people is seen as the failure of these Western political models and processes. As they become delegitimized in the eyes of the discontented, disenfranchised and marginalized groups of society, the reactive search for an alternative governing ideology in Muslim countries often takes the form of religiosity. In these societies, Islamist activists have become the most vocal and effective opponents to the ruling elite as they successfully construct and package religion into an ideology for political struggle against the oppressive state.

The political ideals of Islamism (Islam used as a political ideology) have found widespread appeal among disparate social forces in Muslim societies — young urbanites, upwardly mobile professionals adrift from tradition and culture, the underclass left behind by the new prosperity and modernization agenda, and socially conscious citizens outraged by the corruption, mismanagement, and authoritarianism of the ruling elite and see no hope for change. Harnessing these discontentments, political Islamists whose objective is to topple the existing political order and replace it with an Islamic order, have crafted and packaged religion into an appealing political ideology of protest and resistance. The complexity and depth of religion is reduced to one fixed ideological worldview to determine and direct public behaviour.[1] This worldview is constructed in opposite to an ideological enemy and the world is then interpreted based on these opposites.[2]

The ideology is moulded into a set of dichotomies, presented as the:
Divine order vs. secular order
Islamic state (no separation between religion and politics) vs secular nation-state (separation between religion and politics)
Consultation (*shura*) vs. secular democracy
Divine law vs. human legislation
Sovereignty of God's rule on earth vs. sovereignty of the people

This packaged ideology made up of clear and unambiguous messages is then presented as the true authentic face of faith and piety where there is no separation between religion and politics. The objective is clear: to delegitimize the existing political order and political elites and replace them with an Islamic order. The ideology is then sold to societies undergoing massive transformations and dislocations from traditional to modern, from rural to urban, and from agricultural to industrial. It becomes appealing, either as an idiom of protest or as a source of faith and tradition to a people torn away from their own religious and cultural roots and are seeking refuge in absolute truths under modern conditions of uncertainty in their lives.

THE ISLAMIZATION RACE IN MALAYSIA

While Islamic based political parties in Malaysia, in particular PAS (Islamic Party of Malaysia), had called for the establishment of an Islamic state and *shari'a* rule in the 1940s and 1950s, this demand for an Islamic social order had always gone in tandem with Malay sovereignty and Malay nationalism. In fact PAS leaders in the first three decades of the party's existence were better known as Malay nationalists, seen as no more Islamic than their rivals in UMNO. The ouster of the last PAS nationalist leader, Muhammad Asri Muda, in 1982 and the takeover of the party by a group of religious Young Turks educated in Islamic jurisprudence and theology from Middle Eastern universities saw PAS discarding its Malay nationalist identity to remake itself into a party led by *ulama* pushing for the establishment of a theocratic state. It became unequivocal and strident in its call for an Islamic state with a constitution based on the Qur'an and Traditions of the Prophet, and the imposition of *shari'a* law. It declared the existing federal constitution a secular constitution designed by the infidel colonials and that the UMNO-led government was therefore a secular government, un-Islamic and illegitimate. This challenge posed to the UMNO-led National Front government led to the launching of Malaysia's Islamization policy in 1982. Thus, a government that since independence in 1957 had made a conscious effort to separate religion from politics, made a watershed decision twenty-five years later that for its own political survival, it had to co-opt its critics and opponents and gain support from a more religiously conscious electorate by appealing to Islam for legitimacy.

Since then, UMNO and PAS have engaged in an escalating holier-than-thou battle for the hearts and minds of the Malay electorate, each desperate to out-do the other to prove their religious credentials within a society engulfed by the forces of Islamic revivalism. This chapter will focus on the area of law-making in the name of Islam and the implications of both this process and its contents on democratic governance in multi-ethnic Malaysia, and on women's rights and human rights.

In the 1990s, a slew of Islamic laws were introduced or existing laws were amended as part of the government's effort to upgrade the status of Islam in Malaysia and also to prove its Islamic credentials *vis-à-vis* PAS. *Shari'a* criminal laws were passed, designed to ensure that the Muslim lifestyle does not transgress Islamic teachings. New offences were created, and moral surveillance, enforcement and more severe punitive punishment of Muslims were introduced. Eating in public during the month of Ramadan, consuming alcoholic beverages in public, women or men indulging in cross-dressing, homosexuality, lesbianism, indecent behaviour became punishable *shari'a* crimes. The Islamic family law, one of the most enlightened personal status laws in the Muslim world, was amended to make divorce and polygamy easier for men and to reduce men's financial responsibilities towards women. The Administration of Islamic Law was amended to ensure that *fatwas* issued by the state *mufti* would be given the automatic force of law, once they are gazetted, without going through the legislative process. Only the Mufti has the sole power to revoke or amend a *fatwa*. This was accompanied by new amendments to the *Shari'a* Criminal Offences Act which provided that any violation of the *fatwa*, any effort to dispute or to give an opinion contrary to the *fatwa* constitutes a criminal offence. To even possess books on Islam that are contrary to a *fatwa* that is currently in force is also an offence.

In Kelantan and Terengganu, the *hudud* laws passed by the state governments under PAS control, contain contentious provisions for punishments such as flogging, amputation of limbs, stoning to death and crucifixion, and which discriminates against Muslim women and non-Muslims. This race to measure one's piety and Islamic credentials based on one's dressing, the status and control of women in one's society, the severity of punishment one imposes on those who transgress the teachings of the religion, is a reflection of the reality in Muslim societies today when religion is transformed into an ideology for political struggle and a source of legitimacy.

IMPLICATIONS FOR DEMOCRATIC GOVERNANCE

1. Shroud of Silence

Until recently, what has been remarkable about the making of Islamic laws in Malaysia is the silence that shrouds the whole process, both at the drafting and legislative levels. First, is the absence of any kind of consultation and public debate in the law making process even though such personal laws have widespread impact on the private and public lives of some sixty per cent of the Malaysian population, and their implications to society at large. This means that very often laws are made and passed without any public knowledge that they even exist — until there is a public outcry when they are enforced by the religious authorities. For example, most Malaysians did not know that the Administration of Islamic Law provides that upon publication in the Government Gazette, a *fatwa* is binding on all Muslims as a dictate of their religion. Most Malaysians were also not aware that the *Shari'a* Criminal Offences Law was amended to provide that it is an offence to violate or dispute a *fatwa* and to dress indecently — until this law was enforced in 1997 when three Muslim girls were arrested and charged for taking part in a beauty contest and for indecent dressing. There was a public outcry; no one knew it was a crime for Muslim women to take part in beauty contests and that there existed a gazetted *fatwa* on the matter; and the public was critical of the way the girls were publicly humiliated when they were arrested and taken off the stage in full glare of the audience and photographers.

Second is the lack of any substantive debate in the legislative bodies when Islamic laws are tabled. Most elected representatives are too fearful to speak out, question or debate, let alone criticize Islamic bills. The non-Muslim opposition MPs, especially from the Democratic Action Party, have often been silenced whenever they raised questions about Islamic matters. They were usually drowned by the jeering and thumping by the UMNO Muslim backbenchers who claim that the Chinese MPs as non-Muslims do not have a right to talk about Islam. Thus they are prevented from playing their law-making role when it comes to Islamic matters. It is significant to note in the recent furore over the *hudud* law passed by the Terengganu state assembly, the four UMNO assemblymen could not summon the political courage to vote against the bill, as instructed by the federal government. In fact, they felt that given the political realities on the ground, they had to defy federal instructions and the best they could do was to abstain from voting. One assemblyman absented himself. When the Kelantan state assembly passed the *hudud* law in 1993, the two UMNO state assemblymen deemed it necessary, for their political survival, to join in the unanimous support for the bill, even though their party was against it. Their action reflects the fear of most Muslim politicians to criticize or oppose anything done in the name of Islam. In states controlled by PAS, any attempt to oppose any Islamic law can be seen as an act of apostasy, as the PAS chief ideologue, Hadi Awang, declared in 1993 on those opposing the *hudud* law. What are the implications to the process of law-making and democratic governance if lawmakers are too scared to debate any law made on the basis of religion and political ideologues use religion to declare those who challenge their ideological conception of Islam as apostates?

Third, when there is no debate in the legislative assemblies, there is no press coverage. At the most, a straightforward news story — if at all — that such and such a law has been passed by the legislative body. It is then up to concerned NGOs to scramble to find copies of the bill and scrutinize it and then take the initiative to generate a public debate on the issue. Or if there has been a total silence, then civil society will only find out about the existence of such a law only when it is enforced.

2. Fear and Ignorance

A major reason for the silence that surrounds law-making in the name of Islam is fear and ignorance. The bifurcations of the modern education system mean that those trained in secular schools have little knowledge of religion and those trained in religion have little understanding of the world outside. As Islam increasingly shapes and redefines our lives today, many Muslims who are concerned about the intolerant and extremist trends are too fearful to speak out and express their concerns because they feel they don't know enough about Islam. Their tentative attempts to raise questions and express concern are often silenced by the pronouncement that they should desist, lest their faith be undermined. Second, those who are knowledgeable about Islam are often reluctant to speak out if their views do not coincide with the mainstream orthodox view. They fear that they will get into a controversy, or fear that they will be labelled as anti-Islam, and accused of questioning the word of God by the conservatives. It is not that they do not have the knowledge to defend themselves, but that they would rather hide in the safety of their ivory tower than be embroiled in any kind of controversy, especially when they exist in a working and social environment dominated by orthodoxy.

For example, a renowned Islamic scholar recently expressed his deep concern about how increasingly mosques in Malaysia are disturbing the public peace by using loud speakers not only for the *adhan* (call to prayer), but for Qur'an-reading and religious talks. This could go on for hours, to the chagrin of not just non-Muslims in the community, but also to Muslims. This is un-Islamic, he says, as the Qur'an teaches one to pray quietly. The *fuqaha* (Islamic jurists) have said that loud speakers are needed only for the congregation in the mosque to hear the *imam* who leads the prayers and the *khatib* who delivers the sermon, not for the neighbourhood and beyond. He was concerned that this practice was building resentment against Islam from among non-Muslims. When it was suggested to him that a man of his stature would be the right person to initiate a public debate on this issue which has long been a source of so much murmuring discontent, he immediately said no as he did not wish to get into any controversy, and that this was a sensitive issue.

3. The Authority to Speak on Islam

The issue of who has a right to speak on Islam is a major contentious issue in Malaysia today. Traditionally, most Muslims believe that only the *ulama* have the right to speak on Islam. Those not traditionally educated in religion do not have the right to engage publicly with religion. Therefore, very few Muslims have the courage to question, or challenge or even discuss matters of religion, even when they doubt the teachings that appear unjust or inappropriate to the realities of their lives today. They have been socialized to accept that those in religious authority know best what is Islamic and what is not. Thus, when groups like Sisters in Islam and lay intellectuals like Chandra Muzaffar and Farish Noor speak about Islam, their credentials, and their right and authority to speak publicly are questioned. To me, the attempt earlier this year by the Ulama Association of Malaysia to charge six writers for insulting Islam, is nothing more than an attempt to monopolize the meaning and content of Islam to serve the political agenda of those who use Islam to mobilize popular support. The real issue is not about who has the right to talk about Islam. It is about one's position on various issues in Islam. If one supports the death penalty for apostasy, the *hudud* law, and the Islamic state, then one will enjoy the freedom and space to speak on Islam, even if one is only a third class engineering graduate from a third rate American university.

Sisters in Islam takes the position that when Islam in Malaysia is used as a source of law and public policy, with widespread impact on the lives of the citizens of a democratic country, then any attempt to limit writing, talking, and debating about Islam to only the *ulama* or those with supposedly "in-depth knowledge" of Islam really tantamounts to rule by a theocratic dictatorship. Why is it that all citizens have the right to speak on political, economic and social issues that impinge on their well-being and rights, but when it comes to matters of religion, we have to defer to the *ulama*? The Islamists argue smugly that religion is like medicine. It needs an expert to dispense opinion. This is really a misguided analogy for many reasons, but most importantly, if the client does not like the opinion and treatment of one doctor he is free to go to another and will not be declared an apostate or accused of insulting the profession and the expertise of the doctor and be incarcerated at best, or sentenced to death at worst. To earn the respect and continued patronage of their patients, top doctors keep abreast with latest developments in their specialization, but the top *mullahs* remain dazzled by facts and prescriptions that are a thousand years old, ignoring the changing realities on the ground.

4. The Misogynistic Bent

Muslim countries today remain patriarchal and unjust to women. While civil laws are being repealed or amended to recognize equality between men and women, Islamic laws remain discriminatory against women. In the 1990s in Malaysia, a slew of laws were introduced or amended that discriminated against Muslim women. This happened at the same time when the government, in response to long-standing demands from women's groups, was taking steps to amend laws that discriminated against women. In the name of Islam, Muslim women were denied the privilege of enjoying the same legal rights and protection granted to women of other faith. For example, in early 1999, the Guardianship of Infants Act was amended to give non-Muslim mothers the equal right to guardianship of their children, but no similar amendment was made to the Islamic family law to accord the same right to Muslim mothers. This reflects the propensity among many in government to declare any matter which touches on religion as sensitive and therefore untouchable. Are Muslim women expected to turn over and play dead while their non-Muslim sisters are accorded greater spheres of rights to be treated as equal to men?

The negotiations for a Domestic Violence Act in the early 1990s also saw attempts to exclude Muslims from the jurisdiction of the act because of the belief that Muslim men have a right to beat their wives. Again, the women's groups had to lobby the government hard for many years, to make domestic violence a crime whether it is committed by a Malay, a Chinese or an Indian man. Even after the law was passed by Parliament, we had to go through two more years of pressure and lobbying to get it implemented because of objections that it should not apply to Muslims because domestic violence was a family matter and therefore should come under *Shari'a* jurisdiction of the states, rather than a criminal matter under federal jurisdiction. The *hudud* law of Kelantan and Terengganu grossly discriminates against women by disqualifying women (and all non-Muslims — which means three-fourths of the population) as eyewitnesses in *hudud* crimes and by assuming that an unmarried woman who is pregnant or has delivered a baby has committed *zina* (adultery/illicit sex). If she claims she has been raped, the burden of proof lies on her to substantiate her claim. The original draft of the Terengganu law which provided that a woman who reports rape would be charged for *qazaf* (slanderous accusation) and flogged eighty lashes if she was unable to prove the rape (through four Muslim male eyewitnesses) caused such an outrage that the PAS government was forced to amend the law to allow for circumstantial evidence.

The obsession with introducing the *hudud* law by the Islamist party in control of the two states displays a mindset frozen in seventh century Arabia and medieval jurisprudence without the ability or willingness to consider that the application of Islamic teachings in the twenty-first century has necessarily to change given the changing times and circumstances. Amendments to the Islamic family law since the early 1990s are another major area of discrimination against Muslim women. The amendments include:

(a) allowing polygamous marriages contracted without the permission of the court, to be registered upon payment of a fine or jail sentence. This has led to a proliferation of illegal polygamous marriages contracted in southern Thailand or by illegal marriage syndicates operating in Malaysia.
(b) deleting the fifth condition before permission for polygamy can be granted. The fifth condition requires that the proposed polygamous marriage should not directly or indirectly lower the standard of living enjoyed by the existing wife and dependants. Its deletion makes it easier for a man to be given permission to take a second wife.
(c) registration of divorces pronounced outside court. It now provides for the court to approve divorces pronounced by a man without permission

of the court if it is satisfied that the *talaq* (repudiation) is valid. As a result of this amendment, research shows that in some states, the number of men who unilaterally divorce their wives outside the court is almost three times those who applied for divorce through the courts.

All these new laws and amendments to existing laws reflect the misogynistic bent of those in religious authority, be they in government or in PAS. At a time when the Malaysian Government, at least at the leadership level, recognizes equality between men and women in this country and are responding to calls by women's groups to amend all laws that discriminate against women, other arms of that very same government do not share this egalitarian vision or have no courage, nor are enlightened enough to see the necessity for *ijtihad* (reinterpretation) to ensure that fellow Muslim women who are supposed to be equal citizens of this country benefit equally from the efforts at law reform. The recent amendment to Article 8 of the Federal Constitution to prohibit discrimination on the basis of gender poses a special challenge to the *shari'a* court and the Islamic religious authorities in Malaysia to take steps to end all forms of discrimination against Muslim women in law and in practice, committed in the name of Islam.

5. The Tendency to Codify the Most Conservative Opinion

Be it in the area of fundamental liberties or women's rights, the tendency displayed by the religious authorities is often to codify the most conservative opinion into law. For example, traditionally there are three juristic positions on apostasy. First is the orthodox view of death to all apostates. The second view prescribes the death penalty only if apostasy is accompanied by rebellion against the community and its legitimate leadership. The third view holds that even though apostasy is a great sin, it is not a capital offence in Islam. Therefore a personal change of faith merits no punishment. This is the position of al-Azhar University under its current Grand Sheikh, Dr. Mohammed Sayed Tantawi. However, PAS in its vision of Islam has chosen the most extremist juristic opinion to codify into law. The approach by the government's religious authorities in dealing with apostasy is a compromise position: one-year compulsory rehabilitation instead of death. If at the end of the detention period, the person still refuses to repent, then the judge will declare that the person is no longer a Muslim and order his release. One-year mandatory detention is no consolation to freedom of religion. The person's rights and fundamental liberties have been violated. If he is married, his marriage will be dissolved and the judge will determine his obligations or liabilities under Islamic family law. And yet, the Qur'an is explicit in its recognition of freedom of religion and there exists within the Islamic juristic heritage a position that supports freedom of religion.

And yet when the religious authorities codify Islamic teachings into law, it is seldom that they would choose the most enlightened opinion. All the more in the area of women's rights. For example, the provision that women cannot be witnesses in the PAS *hudud* law is only a juristic opinion with no explicit support in the Qur'an or Traditions of the Prophet Muhammad. Pregnancy as evidence for *zina* is a minority position of the Maliki school of law. The majority *shari'a* opinion is that pregnancy is not admissible as proof of *zina* because circumstantial evidence cannot be accepted to secure a *hudud* punishment. And yet the PAS ideologues who belong to the Shafie school chose to ignore the more enlightened Shafie opinion and instead codify a harsher Maliki opinion.

In effect, what PAS did was to simply reproduce wholesale into statute format the chapter on criminal punishments from an eleventh century classical book on the laws of Islamic governance by a famous Shafie jurist, al-Mawardi, with no effort at *ijtihad*, nor a consideration for the realities of Malaysian society today.[3] In classical Islamic jurisprudential texts, gender inequality is taken for granted, *a priori*, as a principle.[4] Women are depicted as "sexual beings" not as "social beings" and their rights are discussed only in the context of family law. The classical jurists' construction of women's rights reflected the world in which they lived where inequality between women and men was the natural order of things and women had little role to play in public life. But the conservative *ulama* that dominate the religious authorities and Islamist activists of today seem unable or unwilling to see Islamic laws from a historical perspective as rules that were socially constructed to deal with the socio-economic and political context of the time and that given a different context, these laws have to change to ensure that the eternal principles of justice are served. Even though the source of the law is divine, the human understanding of God's message and human effort at codifying God's message into positive law are not infallible or divine. They can be changed, criticized, refined and redefined. Unfortunately, in the traditional Islamic education most of our *ulama* have gone through, the belief in *taqlid* (blind imitation) and that the doors of *ijtihad* are closed is so strong. This rationale is based on the belief that the great scholars of the classical period who lived closer to the time of the Prophet were unsurpassed in their knowledge and interpretative skills.

6. A Holier-Than-Thou Competition

In the battle for the hearts and minds of the Muslim voters, PAS and UMNO are engaged in a one-upmanship game to prove each other's religious credentials. This is dangerous to democratic governance. In giving in to the demands of the religious ideologues, the government continually legitimizes them and becomes hostage to the PAS agenda and framework of Islam. For example, in 2000, attempts were made to introduce the Islamic *Aqidah* (Faith) Protection Bill which provides for a one-year mandatory detention in a Faith Rehabilitation Centre for those who attempt to leave Islam. This is in response to the pressure to provide for a specific punishment for apostasy. The pressure was not just from PAS and its supporters, but also from UMNO members and leaders as they found no answer to the PAS charge in the Malay villages that this government could not be regarded as Islamic as it provided no punishment for those who leave Islam, and yet would fine a citizen RM500 just for throwing a cigarette butt on the market floor. PAS, as the true Islamic party, had already introduced the death penalty for apostasy in its *hudud* law in Kelantan, and at the federal level, its chief ideologue, Hadi Awang, had for years been trying to introduce a private member's bill in Parliament to impose the death penalty for apostasy as a federal law.

In yet another example of competitive one-upmanship, in late 2001, the Prime Minister, Dr. Mahathir Mohamad, declared Malaysia an Islamic state. This was clearly a politically motivated move to blunt the challenge from PAS and its demand for an Islamic state to be established. Malaysia was already an Islamic state, so why the call for one, Dr. Mahathir seemed to taunt. If in playing this one-upmanship game, the government hopes to win over PAS supporters, then it is engaged in a futile exercise. Nothing less than an Islamic state ruled by *shari'a* and *hudud* laws would be enough to win over the diehard Islamists. It could be that Dr. Mahathir intended this for UMNO members at the grassroots to give them the confidence to confront the PAS challenge that this is a government of infidels for not establishing an Islamic state. Still, while the government clarifies that its declaration of Malaysia as an Islamic state is a statement of fact rather than a statement of intent, it is treading on dangerous grounds. First, it legitimizes the demand for an Islamic state. Second, it raises expectations and provides a justification for overzealous civil servants to define their own public policy based on their own personal piety.

First to feel the impact of these pronouncements are of course women and minorities. Thus, you get security guards and government clerks refusing entry or service to women in sleeveless or tight outfits. In the name of promoting and protecting Islam, circulars are issued to prevent the setting up of societies to promote other religions, decisions are made to stop rock bands from performing, rules are established on campuses to closely regulate the dress and conduct of students and interaction between boys and girls, guidelines are set strictly limiting the construction of temples and churches. These are not new incidents, but they tend to escalate if no firm action is taken to put a stop to them.

ISLAM IN A DEMOCRATIC SOCIETY

If Islam is to be used as a source of law and public policy to govern the public and private lives of citizens, then the question of who decides what is Islamic and what is not is of paramount importance. What are the implications for democratic governance when only a small exclusive group of people have the right to interpret the Text, and codify it in a manner that very often (a) isolates the Text from the socio-historical context in which it was revealed, (b) isolates classical juristic opinion from the socio-historical context of the lives of the founding jurists of Islam, and (c) isolates the Text from the context of the contemporary society we live in today?

Increasingly in Malaysia today, women's groups, human rights NGOs, political parties, the media, concerned professionals are beginning to engage publicly on issues of fundamental political importance to the future of the country:

(a) What is the role of religion in politics?
(b) Is Islam compatible with democracy?
(c) How do we deal with the conflict between our constitutional provisions of fundamental liberties and equality with religious laws and policies that violate these provisions?
(d) Should the state legislate on morality? Is it the duty of the state in order to bring about a moral society to turn all sins into crimes against the state?
(e) Can there be one TRUTH and one final interpretation of Islam that must govern the lives of every Muslim citizen of this country?
(f) How do we deal with the new universal morality of democracy, human rights and women's rights and where is the place of Islam in this dominant ethical paradigm of the modern world?

The reality and implications of Islamic governance in a multi-ethnic modernizing country like Malaysia are just beginning to sink in as issues such as the Islamic state, the *hudud* law, discrimination against women, freedom of expression, freedom of religion spill into the public sphere as the contestation for power between UMNO and PAS escalates. More than any other Muslim country in the world, Malaysia has the fundamentals — economic, social and religious — to lead the way in creating a model for how a society can be developed, modern and democratic and at the same time remain authentic to Islamic values and principles. Malaysia is at an advantage for several reasons. At the leadership level, the government is committed to reform and reconstruction of Islamic thought, culture and society in order to deal with the challenges of modernization and change. We have adopted parliamentary democracy as our political system, its many flaws notwithstanding. We live in a country whose people historically had been open to change and to outside influences and fertilization of cultures and religions, and who today can confidently embrace the challenge of change, diversity and pluralism. We have a tradition of an Islam that is progressive and open until just about fifteen to twenty years ago when the global forces of Islamic revivalism engulfed us. We can reclaim the Islam of our forbearers that have stood us in good stead for hundreds of years. We have a government that at the policy level believes in equality between men and women. We live in a multi-ethnic and multi-religious society and therefore the kind of Islam that evolves must necessarily take into consideration the rights of other citizens in a democratic state. We have a mainstream mass media that supports the push for a more enlightened Islam and provide women's groups the public space to articulate their grievances and alternative views.

However, these democratizing structures and progressive voices are up against very powerful forces that in the name of religion, whether in an effort to remain in power or in an effort to gain power, deny the plurality and diversity of the Malaysian heritage and the democratic principles and fundamental liberties most Malaysians believe in. If an Islamic state, as conceptualized by such forces, (they exist both in government and in the opposition) asserts different rights for Muslim men, Muslim women and non-Muslims and minorities, rather than equal rights for all, why would those whose equal status and rights are recognized by a democratic system support the creation of an Islamic state? If an Islamic state means an authoritarian theocratic political system committed to enforcing gender-biased doctrinal and legal rulings, and silencing or even eliminating those who challenge its authority and its interpretation of Islam, then why would those whose fundamental liberties are protected by a democratic state support such an Islamic state?

Just as the failure of modern Muslim states today is seen as the failure of western secular institutions and laws, the failure of a government that rules in the name of Islam and claims its legitimacy from God can only be seen as the failure of Islam. This is already happening in Iran where the tensions between democracy and theocracy gave rise to the reformist movement, albeit one that is still working from within the Islamic framework. However, one is hard pressed to find people in the streets of Tehran today who still support the Islamic revolution. The myth that clerical rule would bring paradise on earth has been shattered by the failure of the Iranian Government to deliver on its promises of justice, freedom and prosperity. The dictatorship of an absolute monarch was replaced by the dictatorship of the clerics. Iran's foremost reformist thinker, Abdolkarim Soroush, sees the danger in ideologizing Islam as it promotes a dogmatic understanding of religion that results in intellectual rigidity and exclusivism.[5] The place of religion in politics is as a guiding source of ethical principles and values. Islam's eternal commitment to justice, equality, freedom and dignity are universal principles that are valid for all times. It is these ethical principles that should form the framework within which we seek to reconstruct society. To successfully do this, however, Muslims need the intellectual vigour, moral courage and political will to open the doors of *ijtihad* and strive for a more enlightened interpretation of the Qur'an and *hadith* (Traditions of the Prophet), in our search for answers to deal with our ever changing times and circumstances. This is not heretical, but an imperative if religion is to remain relevant to our lives today.

Notes

[1]   See Soroush, Abolkarim, *Reason, Freedom and Democracy in Islam*, Oxford University Press, 2000.

[2]   See Bassam Tibi, *The Challenge of Fundamentalism, Political Islam and the New World Disorder*, Berkeley: University of California Press, 1998.

[3]   Kamali, Mohammad Hashim, *Punishment in Islamic Law — An Enquiry into the Hudud Bill of Kelantan*, Kuala Lumpur, Ilmiah Publishers, 2000, p. 40.

[4]   Mir-Hosseini, Ziba: "The Construction of Gender in Islamic Legal Thought and Strategies for Reform". Paper presented at the Sisters in Islam Regional Workshop on Islamic Family Law and Justice for Muslim Women, Kuala Lumpur, 8–10 June 2001.

[5]   See Soroush, op. cit., 2000.

8

IS IT ALWAYS ISLAM VERSUS CIVIL SOCIETY?

Patricia A. Martinez

INTRODUCTION

This chapter will explore the issue of whether Islam — especially the agendas of political Islam — is antithetical to the democracy that defines a Civil Society. Among the many vital aspects one could explore in terms of civil society and Islam, I am choosing to address a core element of concern in Southeast Asia: are civil society and Islam antithetical to each other? This concern is about relatively new states and democracies — especially those with Muslim majorities — which are either appropriating, struggling against or juggling Islamists, political Islam and a fidelity to being Muslim countries, together with being configured as democratic, modern nation-states with heterogeneous populations. Among the questions raised by those who live with Islam and modernity, especially the nation-state, are: how can the universalism of Islam be reconciled with the reality of the nation-state, the embodiment of difference and pluralism beyond Islam encapsulated within national boundaries? Are the defining elements of a nation, premised on fundamental freedoms and an individual's rights, resonant with a theocracy and/or the objectives of political Islam which are often to establish an Islamic legal and social order defined by the *shari'a*? This chapter deals with aspects of these questions, exploring whether the democracy inherent in the notion of civil society is cohesive with Islam, especially political Islam. These questions are especially acute in the context of the calls for and declarations about an

Islamic state in Malaysia and to a lesser extent, Indonesia; as well as the plan by Jemaah Islamiyya militants to forge a *dawla islamiyya* or Islamic nation in *nusantara* or Southeast Asia. The chapter explores what has been articulated theoretically about Islam and civil Society in both the Middle East and in Southeast Asia, while offering some reflections on a specific example, Malaysia.

I am using the term "political Islam" to indicate a defining element of groups who proclaim an Islamic agenda — such as the primacy of the *shari'a* or the implementation of an Islamic state — to achieve power through political participation and democratically-constituted elections. As such, the coherence of "political Islam" is with groups that are essentially fundamentalist-oriented, applying text and historical tradition literally to evolve a polity for the present. I struggle with using and finding terms that do not generalize all of Islam and all Muslims into orthodoxy's extremists and/or terrorists — an especially acute problem since the attack on the United States in September 2001. I am sometimes even more uncomfortable with using "Islamists" and "political Islam" than I am with the term "fundamentalist", because at least with the latter, Islam is removed from the immediate etymology although one has to qualify that these are Muslim fundamentalists because there are Christian, Jewish and Hindu fundamentalists. At various meetings, I have heard Indonesian academics too struggling with semantics: "cultural Islam" as opposed to "formal Islam" and "substantive Islam" as the antithesis of "political Islam", to demarcate contextual and interpretive positions from those that demand literal applications of text and history.

Civil society is a useful prism with which to explore whether Islam is contiguous with modern, democratic states. John Kean argued in the late 1990s that the emerging consensus that civil society is a realm of freedom highlights its basic value as a condition of democracy. He wrote, "where there is no civil society there cannot be citizens with capacities to choose their identities, entitlements and duties within a political-legal framework".[1] In its most general sense then, the term "civil society" when invoked generically, refers to autonomous, self-organized public and multiple forms of civic initiative. These are often defined in contra-distinction to the state, existing in a modern, industrial society with the pillars of liberal democracy, market economy and a scientific outlook. I choose not to hold theoretical detailed definitions from the substantial literature available on civil society as normative in measuring Islam and its embedded contexts against these definitions. I have chosen instead to surface what has been articulated by individuals reflecting about civil society in the Middle East and in Southeast Asia, thus privileging context and exemplification over theoretical definition, without making context and theory mutually exclusive from each other.[2]

Since I am defining the parameters of the main terms and their assumptions it is also important to point out that I do not posit democracy unproblematically. Democracy appears to be the most viable system in the world after the collapse of communism, although it is a flawed system premised on a "winner takes all" zero sum equation. This is what Lani Guinier argues citing James Madison: that democracy is a tyranny of the majority, warning that consensus must be more than manoeuvring to avoid controversy — it has to be built, not just located.[3] The majority may not always represent the minority especially in a heterogeneous community with competing interests.

ISLAM AND THE CORE-PERIPHERY SYNDROME OF SOUTHEAST ASIAN MUSLIMS

Much of the writing about civil society and Islam is premised mostly on the Middle East. Although contexts differ considerably, it is imperative to explore this corpus of work as the Middle East is held as authoritative. The significance of Islam as it evolves in the Middle East is not only because of its coherence as authority for the rest of the Muslim world. I suggest that what happens with Islam in the Middle East is important because in the Muslim countries of Southeast Asia, especially after twenty years of Islamic revivalism and Islamization of state and identity that have grown exponentially, the Islam of the Middle East defines South East Asian Muslims more than it ever did before. This core-periphery dynamic — with the heartland of Islam as core and Southeast Asian Muslims as periphery — gives rise to an infantalized religiosity among many ordinary Southeast Asian Muslims. In over 800 interviews conducted during 2001 — early 2003 in Malaysia, many Muslims spoke to me about their feelings of being "inadequate" Muslims and how they would defer to those trained in Islam or with knowledge of Arabic. The most frequent statements were, "We don't have enough knowledge of Islam, we need to be guided"; "even though I am well educated, I am poor in religious knowledge and I cannot argue"; and "I feel ashamed that I don't know enough about my religion, and I welcome anyone who can teach me". Sometimes, such statements would be the first made by Muslims I interviewed when I explained that I wanted to ask them about their religious identity or how they perceived and practised Islam.

It is also significant that the Muslim middle class in Malaysia includes those who feel they have no problem with increasing Islamization because for the majority of them, "being more Muslim" resonates with their own concerns as described above. In addition, many are caught up in more overt manifestations of piety and religious conformity as this is what constitutes a great deal of public discourse and what comes under the rubric of "Islamic teaching" by religious teachers in government and religious schools. These concerns are therefore more about ritual, behaviour that enhances not only Muslim identity but the way it demarcates Malay difference over the approximately 40 per cent non-Malay and non-Muslim Malaysian population, and conformity to notions ranging from piety to peer pressure, and less about philosophical or ideological issues. In answer to my question "How is Islam defined for you?" the majority of Muslims interviewed described it as "rules and laws and fines" and some added, "always telling us what to do". However it is significant that many of such responses were said without rancour, but in a matter-of-fact tone. Many Muslim men and women are comfortable with more conservative interpretations of Islam simply because it is couched as their duty, as right behaviour by religious teachers and by those who speak and write with authority on Islam. Since most Muslims I interviewed stated that they "do not know enough about Islam and need to be guided by those who are knowledgeable", this infantalization-cum-wanting to do the right thing often results in a lack of resistance to those who define narrow orthodoxy or even extreme interpretations of Islam.

This deference to the *ulama* and the abdication of their right to enable the evolution of Islam in Malaysia by many Muslims is also due to their conservatism. An example of this is the public response to the successful outcome of a long campaign by women activists, academics and the government's Ministry for Women and Family Affairs, for the appointment of women as judges in the *shari'a* courts. There has been a great deal of publicity in Malay and English newspapers about the injustice meted out to women by the *shari'a* court system. The result of an on-line poll conducted by the Malay newspaper Berita Harian in April 2003 showed the disjuncture between such initiatives for egalitarianism, and the actual sentiments about such issues by the masses. In response to the question "The measure appointing women as *shari'a* court judges enhances the prestige of the system of Islamic law in the nation. Do you agree or disagree?" (*"Langkah melantik wanita sebagai haim mahkamah syariah akan memartabatkan lagi system perundangan Islam negara. Adakah anda setuju atau tidak?"*). Sixty one percent of 13,427 respondents disagreed.

The inability to read and understand the Qur'an in Arabic (although many Southeast Asian Muslims can recite it), as well as read the huge corpus of theology, philosophy, exegesis and jurisprudence that is the rich heritage of a Muslim, as most of it is in Arabic, engenders a sense of being second class Muslims. This then facilitates deferring to the heartland of Islam — the Middle East — and those who represent it. Therefore, more than in the

Middle East, many Muslims in the periphery rely on the mediators of Islam such as those who are *ustaz* (religious teacher) and *alim* ("knowledgeable", loosely translated as clergy, plural *ulama*), to interpret and guide. What transpires then is an abdication by many ordinary Muslims of their right and ability to decide and define how Islam will evolve in their particular milieu, giving power instead to the guardians of tradition and the final arbiters of law and life — the *ulama* and those who claim to be in authority. The *ulama* invoke authority by a fidelity to not only (selective) applications of text and tradition, but also by exhorting and even policing how Southeast Asian Muslims cohere with their source of legitimacy, the heartland of Islam or the Middle East.

There is a significant but silent segment of Muslims in Malaysia who are concerned about increasing implementation of policies and laws that curtail the individual freedom of Muslims (for example, legislation in many states that criminalizes opposition to a *fatwa* or legal opinion by a *mufti*; the proposal in February 2003 by the Malaysian *Shari'a* Lawyers' Association that will render any party — except court officials and lawyers it recognizes — in contempt, for issuing statements about the *shari'a* system and its courts). This much smaller group of respondents said that they couldn't speak up or speak up in limited ways because the discourse on Islam is so polemical that many feel they have to conform or be silent, or be damned. Some of these such as the Muslim women's NGO Sisters in Islam who criticize aspects of Islamization have been labelled *murtad* (apostate) or *munafiq* (hypocrite) — a serious charge which appears in the Qur'an, applied to those in Medina whose fidelity and zeal the Prophet Muhammad felt he could not trust. The intensity of the policing and punitive action that some Muslims are willing to take was evident when five Muslims (who ranged from a political cartoonist to academics) and a non-Muslim (the author of this paper) were accused of "insulting Islam" by the Ulama Association of Malaysia who lodged a complaint against them with the highest authority for Islam in the country, the Conference of Rulers. Most of the accusations were simply taken from newspaper reports of what was purported to have been said by those accused at a seminar on Human Rights and Islam organized by the Bar Council of Malaysia in December 2000. The Conference of Rulers found no case against all of the accused.

CIVIL SOCIETY, ISLAM AND THE MIDDLE EAST

This section's analysis of civil society's compatibility with Islam will begin with a quick survey of what has been written about the Middle East, before moving on to Southeast Asia, especially Malaysia. In the work of those who write about the Middle East and the nation, the protagonists of what constitutes that large term "political Islam" are often excluded from definitions of civil society. It is significant that even before 9/11, theorists almost totally neglected to acknowledge "the forces that struggle against Islamic conformism and state hegemony"[4] such as the many attempts at reform, anti-conformism and interpretive thinking, because of the attention focused on the struggle for orthodoxy within militant Islam. Muslims themselves persist the dynamic. Jamal al-Suwaidi bemoans the fact that "Muslims have continued to assume that only a 'religious leader' can provide good government for the Muslim community — as if all Muslims were of one mind on such matters. Islamic thinkers apply the Qur'an variously to the challenges of modern life, and their efforts are usually lost on analysts".[5]

A perception of Islam's incompatibility with civil society is also largely on the grounds that — as with most religions — Islam and Islamism are part of traditional and primordial formations, whereas a civil society emerges from the evolution of a culture of rational thought in civilization. The incompatibility of a religious-based society sought, for example, by Islamism, is also partly argued on its perceived incompatibility with a pluralist democracy. This latter idea has particular relevance for Southeast Asia's ethnic, cultural and religious diversity. Perceptions of Islam's incompatibility with democracy is reinforced by the totalitarian and authoritarian manifestations of many Islamic movements, especially in the Middle East, but in analyses that often elude the totalitarian and authoritarian governments these movements oppose.

One of the earliest advocates of civil society in the Middle East, Saad Eddin Ibrahim, defines civil society as a basis for democracy in the region, describing it in terms of "volitional, organized collective participation in public space between individuals and the state".[6] He insists that a condition of civil society is "civility" — the acceptance of differences and commitment to peaceful procedures for managing conflict. Faced with denials of the possibility of civil society and democracy in the Muslim world, many Arab writers including Ibrahim defensively define civil society as resilient Arab civil formation which include the social formations of pre-modern Arab and Middle Eastern cities: guilds, *awqaf* (trusts and foundations), the *ulama* who played a leadership role in the urban communities and Sufi orders. Ibrahim writes that the leaders and notables of these civil associations also acted as advisors to the rulers and as mediators between them and the populace, and in this capacity they reduced the absolutist nature of the pre-modern Arab Islamic state.

These "traditional" civil society social formations differed widely over time and in different parts of the Muslim world, argues Sami Zubaida, but "it would be fair to say that they were almost uniformly patriarchal and authoritarian and often coercive...all stressed authority, loyalty and obedience".[7] Zubaida insists that these patriarchal associations and attitudes have persisted or been reconstituted under modern associations, mosques, charities and Islamist organizations, stating that the latter have sought to control and colonize many civil society formations in the Middle East. He concludes that "Arbitrary and oppressive government on the one hand, and a civil society increasingly controlled by Islamists with tenuous claims to pluralist democracy on the other, do not appear hopeful for a civil society based on civility and tolerance."[8]

Gellner (often described as the orientalist in this debate) does not agree. He characterizes Muslim urban society as a strong culture facing a weak state. The culture is built, he argues, on the strength and immutability of the sacred law, the *shari'a*, and the communal leadership of the *ulama* who upheld and continue to uphold it. The state is weak because it lacks legitimacy as arbiters and dispensers of the *shari'a*, and was subject to regular cycles of disintegration and conquest. It should be pointed out that Gellner's definition of civil society, like that of most other Western writers, rests on the field of autonomy and security of the economic sphere, which then generate powers and institutions which bind the state and shape it.[9] Zubaida points out that although there is no necessary or direct connection between capitalism and democracy, an autonomous capitalism can be an important condition for democracy, but that "this line of thought does not seem to come naturally to many Egyptian and other Middle Eastern intellectuals, secular or Islamist, who seem to retain an implicit statist nationalism when it comes to the economy".[10] Zubaida states that Middle Eastern intellectuals seem to focus on associations because they regard them as expressions of democratic practice, and reminds again that this is an assumption which is not always justified in Muslim history.

With the end of the Cold War, the disintegration of the USSR and the declining appeal of left-wing ideas in the past ten years, the hopes of a further expansion of representative democracy have, without a doubt, increased. Events in the Arab-Islamic region have meanwhile reinforced a contrary but widespread idea according to which that part of the world has been slow in adjusting to this trend, somewhat resistant to a rapid democratization process — or in the aftermath of 9/11, as incapable of it at all. The idea of an Arab and/or Islamic "exceptionalism" has thus re-emerged among both Western proponents of universal democracy and established orientalists. Unfortunately, this in turn has encouraged many Muslim apologists of "cultural authenticity" in their rejection of Western models of government, which in turn reinforces rejection of democracy and constitutionalism as "Western" or even "Christian". For example, when justifying the introduction of the *hudud* (prescribed punishment) in the Malaysian state of Terenggannu, the Chief Minister of the state and acting President of Parti Islam SeMalaysia (PAS) described the Malaysian constitution as being devised by "the Christian, Lord Reid". I have heard him at two rallies in June 2002 describe the Malaysian constitution as "Christian" in order to diminish it in comparison to what is defined by PAS as incumbent upon a Muslim — the *shari'a* and its ultimate legislation, the *hudud*. This is a powerful if misleading strategy of foregrounding Islam against another religion with its history of conflict with Muslims, instead of the real issue, which is Islam's compatibility with the constitutional structure of a secular state.

However, there is a more complex picture to Islamic exceptionalism than Western proponents of universal democracy or Muslim apologists are willing to admit. Ghassan Salame, for example, argues for a more nuanced understanding of democracy. He first agrees that there are often no compelling unifying factors triggering a unilateral political evolution towards democracy, and that calls for democratization may indeed be muted. He states, however, that while the political discourse dealing with democratization may be only partly convincing, forms of political opening are increasingly viewed by the leaders themselves, if not by society, as a precious instrument through which a rapid deterioration of law and order, if not of the collapse of the whole state apparatus, might be avoided or at least delayed. "Pacts" on limited forms of political participation are, in these situations, negotiated between the ruling group and significant sectors of civil society.[11]

Salame and his co-authors argue that such pacts could prove to be crucial to the survival not only of nascent experimentations with democracy but also of the state itself. They argue that in this sense, democracy could be judged less by the attachment to its principles by some actor or the other, than by its common use as a means to avoid civil war or institutional chaos. Thus, forms of political participation are being sought by regimes which have come to believe that their old-style authoritarianism may be difficult to maintain or is becoming counter-productive. Others states have arrived at the same conclusion because of their inability to adopt an IMF-inspired austerity program without help from representative sectors of civil society. Still others have concluded that this is, after all, the only way to make a segmented society live together. Those who have engaged in the process may well be intolerant, repressive, and dictatorial. The programme of some opposition groups may well be simply to replace an existing authoritarianism by one of their own. In all such cases, forms of democracy are better defined and judged less by the identity of those who made them happen, than by their efficacy in phases of transition. Salame and his co-authors concede that democrats may not exist at all, or they may not exist in great numbers. Yet democracy can still be sought as an instrument of civil peace and hopefully, gradually, even inadvertently, produce its own defenders.

Saad Eddin Ibrahim describes a three-way race to maintain or seize power among autocratic regimes, Islamic activists, and civil society organizations. In some Arab countries one variant of the race has been the squeezing of civil society out of the public arena by autocratic regimes on one hand and by Islamic activists on the other hand. In another variant, both the autocratic regimes and Islamic activists have attempted to win over or appropriate civil society organizations. Ibrahim sees the second variant as containing the greatest promise for civil society and the democratization process in Muslim societies. Importantly, it has provided ample bargaining power for civil society organizations when they deal with the state in attempts to gain concessions of a socio-political reformative nature. Attempting to win over or appropriate civil society organizations have had a moderating effect on several Islamic activists groups: in Jordan, Kuwait, Yemen and Lebanon, this promise has actually been unfolding, Ibrahim claims. In each, Islamists have accepted the principle of political pluralism, participating alongside other secular forces in national elections and are currently represented in those countries parliaments.

Ibrahim proposes that as long as religious-based parties and associations accept the principle of pluralism and observe a modicum of civility in behaviour toward the different Other, then they can expect to be integral parts of civil society (and Nazih Ayoubi makes a similar argument in "Rethinking the Public/Private Dichotomy: Radical Islam and Civil Society in the Middle East").[12] Ibrahim suggests that even Islamists may evolve into something akin to Christian Democrats in the West. He is emphatic that there is nothing intrinsically Islamic that contradicts with the codes of civil society or democratic principles, and warns "that when the middle classes and other socio-economic formations that have a legitimate quest for participation in the public affairs of their societies are not allowed to do so peacefully, they force their way into the system, or against it — violently. Islam, in this case, provides a mere culturally legitimate idiom permitting this."[13]

Others who work on Islam and civil society in the Middle East would find the claim that Islam is only a cultural idiom, too simplistic a conjecture. Social and political Islam is the most active and vital force in modern societies in the Middle East: any account of civil society that ignores or even diminishes this fact is unrealistic. As described earlier in this chapter,

Sami Zubaida argues that the strongest and most durable associations outside the government are precisely new Islamic and Islamist social and political formations that are "neo-traditional" and "primordial" groupings excluded from civil society by most definitions, and that are patriarchal.[14] (While Zubaida uses the term "patriarchal" only, his explanations are beyond the androcentricity of 'patriarchy' to intimate the paternalist paradigm of dominance and/or authoritarianism.)

What becomes obvious is that by unpacking "civil society" by using the broadest definitions provided at the beginning of this chapter, there are varying interpretations of what enables the plurality of voices that constitute a democracy; as well as more nuanced understandings of how to discern such pluralism. I do not offer this perspective along the lines of cultural relativism or exceptionalism — that Islam is different, or that whatever is Western-engendered is not applicable to a non-Western context, so as to conclude unproblematically that civil society flourishes in the Middle East. Indeed, it is relevant to point out how the examples proffered of embedded possibilities can also be understood as limitations that can also stymie. The point is only that more detailed investigation and exploration of what could come under the rubric of enabling civil society and democracy, evinces the existence of civil society formations and democratic institutions in even the most unlikely places.

For example, I have heard Iranian women activists describe their nation as a "religious democracy", indicating their understanding of the coherence of a Muslim theocracy with democracy. If one understands that in classical doctrines about the state such as Al Mawardi's *Al Ahkam Al-Sultaniyya* (which is held as normative by Sunni Muslims)[15] and the examples of the Rightly-Guided Caliphs as well as those of the Umayyad, Abbasid and Fatimid dynasties, that there were no elections, no elected ruler and no parliament, then Iran can be defined as a "religious democracy". Although Iran's Khomeinist doctrine of clerical dictatorship by the Vilayat-e-faqih or Regency of Jurists requires elderly theologians to approve or reject candidates for elections, the point is that there are elections and that this system offers potential for further democratic reform. What is significant is that although there are no elections and parliaments mandated in Islam or historical Muslim states and empires, a self-proclaimed Islamic nation such as Iran has embraced, however liminally, these fundamental premises of democracy and civil society formation. This in turn seems to refute Mawdudi's decree that has influenced generations of political Islamists: "Wherever this order [democracy] exists, we do not consider Islam to exist, and wherever Islam exists, there is no room for this order."[16]

However, the cultural and historical contexts into which Islam is embedded elsewhere in the world differ considerably, and provide new understandings of whether Islam and civil society are only antithetical to each other or if in fact they also enable the democracy that is the ultimate objective.

CIVIL SOCIETY, ISLAM AND SOUTHEAST ASIA

A survey of literature on Islam and civil society in Southeast Asia shows that it is relatively limited compared to what is available in terms of the Middle East. In a project over the period 1998–2000, multidisciplinary teams of researchers in Indonesia, Malaysia and Singapore used interviews and ethnographic methods to assess the quality of civil society by focusing on participation in associations. Robert Hefner, who directed the project, concludes that civil forces in society require the support and protection of the state in order to prosper and that in all three countries, civil society and the public sphere "have matured considerably more than has the state".[17] Hefner is careful not to presume that democratic participation and a vibrant public sphere are contiguous "givens", and the reflections by his co-authors reveal continuing, uncertain and sometimes countervailing processes of change which include Islamic resurgence, urbanization and the growth of a middle class, electronic information flows and nationalism, and where the state struggles to contain the pressures for and arguments about change.

Hefner also points to "the dearth of statements of civil society analysts and activists in Southeast Asia who do not identify how civic associations may be cross-cut by deep ethnic, religious or ideological divides… civic associations can be organized in a manner consistent with existing ethno-religious divisions in society."[18] In other words, Hefner is pointing out that civil society activists and analysts are not self-critical about their own uncivil limitations. He concludes that history has shown how rather than serving as social capital for democracy, at times these divisions can engender debilitating social rivalries that diminish rather than enhance the prospects for civic decency. "To put the matter bluntly, then, civil society is not always 'democracy-good'."[19] This perspective, together with Sami Zubaida's argument that civil society groups in the Middle East are patriarchal and not egalitarian, provide a vital perspective that disrupts the assumption that conflates civil society with democracy, when reflecting on the question posed in this chapter: whether Islam and civil society are antithetical to each other.

In *Civil Islam*,[20] which is a definitive text about Islam and civil society in Indonesia, Hefner engages directly with the fundamental questions of this chapter: Are Islam and democracy compatible? Do Islamic states or states that are predominantly Muslim have the ability to foster and tolerate civil societies? Writing in the period before the unravelling and subsequent resignation of President Abdurrahman Wahid, Hefner argues that Islamic states and civil society are compatible, and that the intellectual and political foundations for a civil Islam were in place and in practice in Indonesia, albeit in contestations that hindered a full achievement of a national Islamic civil polity. In subsequent conversations and lectures, in the aftermath of Abdurrahman Wahid's tenure, Hefner has since problematized his optimistic account while maintaining his fundamental thesis.

In a brief but significant article entitled, "The Challenge of Democracy in the Muslim World: Traditional Politics and Democratic Political Culture", Azyumardi Azra of Indonesia points out that there is no single Muslim politics, and directs our gaze to the increasingly complex contest and rivalry among a variety of Islamic political traditions in contemporary and ongoing Islamic revivalism. He concludes that it is difficult to imagine that Indonesia would and could be transformed into an Islamic state, which he juxtaposes against a secular, democratic order. He describes three main factors inhibiting democracy in the Muslim world. The first factor is weaknesses in the prerequisites that are instrumental in the development of democracy when patrimony, corruption, cronyism and nepotism inhibit economic progress and distort socio-cultural development. The second problematic factor Azra identifies is the tendency among Muslims who "believe in the unity and merge of politics"[21] and the third is the state's practice of undemocratic politics when Muslim states use violent approaches against those who oppose regimes, causing Muslims to lose their faith in democracy while turning to an Islamic alternative.

Besides those whose works are summarized in the next section of this chapter, Malaysians who have reflected on civil society include Johan Saravanamuttu, Mustafa K. Anuar, Maznah Mohamed and Saliha Hassan. They provide insights into components of what constitutes civil society in Malaysia, but there is little in their work that engages specifically with Islam and civil society. National University of Singapore lecturer Syed Farid Alatas addresses issues of civil society and Islam theoretically in terms of the epistemology of the social sciences. In the article entitled "*Islam, Ilmu-Ilmu Sosial, dan Masyarakat Sipil*" (Islam, the social sciences and civil society), he discusses the concepts of Civil Society and the term often used in Malay and Indonesian — *masyarakat madani* — which he claims is often mistranslated and misunderstood as representing the English meaning of civil society. In demarcating the difference between the two terms because of the way the social sciences impact upon our cognition, Syed Farid explains the relevance of Islam in the context of the need for a moral public as an integral element of a *masyarakat madani*.

Malaysia's former deputy Prime Minister Anwar Ibrahim's thesis on democracy and civil society resonates with Alatas' delineation of a different way of conceptualizing civil society. Anwar Ibrahim writes of an "Asian vision" of civil society which departs in a fundamental respect from the model(s) articulated by the social philosophy of the Enlightenment. Arguing that because religion and spirituality run deep in the Asian psyche, he states that religion is a source of strength and a bulwark against moral and social decay. "More fundamentally, the Asian world view and its intellectual resources will shape its civil society in its own direction. Foremost among them is the concept of man as a moral being with a transcendent dimension, endowed not only with inalienable rights but also with unshirkable responsibilities: to God, to family, to fellow humans and to nature."[22] It can be argued that Syed Farid Alatas and Anwar Ibrahim make Islam incumbent upon the evolution of a civil society.

Malaysian academic Francis Loh deals tangentially with the term "civil society" but gives fundamental insights into the evolution of its values in Malaysia. He inscribes the psychology of economic development — the consuming project of the Malaysian state — into understanding the limits of democratic discourse. In *Democracy in Malaysia* Loh defines the term "developmentalism" as "the cultural consequence of the *dirigiste* developmentalist state, where citizens begin to enjoy improved living conditions as a result of the economic growth the state brought about."[23] He describes how "driving a particular fancy car, residing in a luxury condominium, wearing designer-brand apparel, or engaging in certain leisure activities can become emblems of achievement, identity and even 'freedom'".[24] Loh's conclusion is that mass consumerism disaggregates the members of an ethnic group and of Malaysian society generally into individuals and not as groups or communities. This conclusion is significant for an understanding of civil society in Malaysia. "Developmentalism" informs the frustration or even contempt that activists for social justice and fundamental freedoms often express over the lack of broad or popular support for their trenchant critiques of an authoritarian state and diminishing freedom.

In the introduction to *Southeast Asian Middle Classes: Prospects for Social Change and Democratization*, Abdul Rahman Embong describes two schools of thought in terms of the role of the state in economic development that inflect the problems and possibilities of civil society in Malaysia. He proposes that "precisely because states do not allow or encourage the flowering of democracy, good governance practices, empowerment and growth of a vibrant civil society that can act as checks and balances on the excesses of the state and market that have caused their eclipse",[25] hard-earned economic achievements are undermined.

As one of those who writes consistently to surface the subaltern voice and provide an alternative to what he would call "authority-defined" statements, Shamsul A.B.'s analyses are also significant, if not directly addressed to the issue of Civil Society in Malaysia.[26] He uses the concept of 'Nations-of-Intent' as an "inclusive construct, open to others, and which is employed as the basis for a political platform voicing dissent or a challenge to the established notion of a nation"[27] and an alternative way of formulating political intentions "even though, mostly, it remains at the discourse level."[28] Shamsul has expanded these ideas, more recently describing the significance of the "everyday-defined" perspectives since 1998 as a new political movement in Malaysia, one not concerned simply with winning votes and general elections but more with openly articulating differences, plurality, and dissent. He describes the numerous, largely informal groups including ABIM that are linked to the notion of the *reformasi* launched by Anwar Ibrahim in 1998 as "a nationwide 'politics of resistance', a struggle for social justice and therefore an attempt to transform 'Civil Society' to 'democratic civility' ".[29]

In *Islam and Civil Society in Southeast Asia* published in 2001, the following are identified as significant for the recognition of the congruence of the concept of "civil society" with Islam:

- Rising concern for civil society in Europe and the United States since the late 1980s;
- Growing awareness in Japan of the importance of NGOs, NPOs and philanthropy in public life
- Rapid emergence of civil society in the Asia-Pacific region;
- "Discovery" of Islamic civil society in the Middle East and North Africa
- Increasing assertiveness of Islamic civil society as an important actor in the recent trends of democratization in Southeast Asia.[30]

The introduction by Nakamura Mitsuo reminds us, in tandem with Omar Farouk Bajunid in 1995[31] and Robert Hefner in 1997,[32] that Muslim communities in the region differ greatly from each other in many respects in terms of indigenous or pre-Islamic context, but these Muslim communities are nevertheless most profoundly influenced by the differences in their experiences of colonization and de-colonization.

The two Malaysian contributors in *Islam and Civil Society in Southeast Asia* are Mohamad Abu Bakar and Sharifah Zaleha Syed Hassan. Mohamad Abu Bakar focuses his chapter on the way Islam shapes ethnic relations in

Malaysia, describing it as an important ethnic boundary marker, and — like Hussin Mutalib and Muhammad Ikmal Said wrote many years earlier — as a premise for Malay unity across the many schisms that divide them. He writes about how "Muslim Malays were partly accountable for keeping the non-Malays in perpetual ignorance of their religion"[33] and attributes this reason for non-Malays interacting freely with Malays over almost any issue except the religious dimension. He concludes, "no matter what certain Islamic books had been saying about the universalistic character of Islam, the Malays generally upheld the view that it was co-terminous with Malayness. This synonymity had registered well in the minds of all, notably the Chinese and Indians".[34] I explore this point — about Islam being co-terminous with Malay ethnicity — in a chapter of a book evaluating the administration of Malaysian Prime Minister Mahathir Mohamad. In discussing the exigency of Islam for political and national agendas, I argue that Islam is racialized to the extent that "Muslim" and "Malay" are used in mainstream discourse and academia as a strategic inverse of each other.[35]

Despite writing about Malay ethnicity and Islam, neither Mohamad Abu Bakar nor I engage with whether Malay culture itself is enabling of surfacing a plurality of voices which is paramount in democracy. In this context, it is relevant to understand much of Malay cultural tradition as legitimating feudal absolutism. For example, Kassim Ahmad's introduction to the 1968 edition of the *Hikayat Hang Tuah* contains a critical analysis revealing the extent to which *Hikayat Hang Tuah* was a pro-establishment courtly narrative that concealed the class differentials and power relations within the Malaccan sultanate via recourse to a cult of absolute leadership (sanctified and justified on Islamic grounds) and the culture of blind loyalty to the ruler.[36] However, as Meredith Weiss points out, the political culture of the Malays is changing. "Malays are responding politically far more openly than usual…demanding a higher level of accountability and transparency than before…."[37]

Sharifah Zaleha Syed Hassan focuses on the urbanization of Islam and its ramifications for civil society. She analyzes Bandar Baru Bangi, a new township outside Universiti Kebangsaan and extrapolates this Muslim community — in what is perhaps a too generalized assumption — to indicate the mobilization of urban Muslims into formal and informal associations. She defines these groups as concerned with promoting charity work, mutual assistance and missionary work, which in turn have opened up opportunities for a large number of men and women from all levels in urban areas to become involved in the organization of Islam. The implications of such mobilization for civil society in a nation where the state exercises considerable control over Islamic matters must be appreciated she asks, because urban Muslims are now "concerned with harmonizing religious beliefs with the urban economy and urbanism rather than one which is biased towards existing political parties".[38] This is a useful insight into the evolution of Islam beyond the dichotomies of politicized Islam versus Islam as private practice.

Malaysian newspaper columnist and activist Farish Noor writes a great deal about Islam, and tangentially about elements of its engagement with what constitutes civil society. He consistently exhorts an Islam that is contiguous with universal notions of Human Rights, gender and racial egalitarianism, and democracy. Since 2001, he has written increasingly in polemical diatribes about Islam as the antithesis of "the West" and in particular the foreign policies of the USA to which he takes great exception. He writes, "Islam can and must be a vehicle for social transformation, democratization and justice on both the local and global levels. But most of all it has to be an effort initiated and sustained by conscientious Muslims themselves, and not Western technocrats and Cold War Warriors who can only see Muslim states and peoples as pawns on a global battlefront."[39]

The most recent exploration of civil society in Malaysia is perhaps the most comprehensive to date. It is Vidhu Verma's *Malaysia: State and Civil Society in Transition.* Verma deals significantly with Islam, and among her conclusions is that Islamic resurgence in Malaysia is not only an expression of spiritual dissatisfaction but is also linked to the drive toward building civil society organizations for greater political participation in the political process. She writes, "An important point is that besides being an expression of political opposition and social discontent, Islam is being used to acquire and sustain political legitimacy and to mobilize masses. The way these two stories of Islam are combined in the future will be a testing point for Malaysia."[40]

Verma distinguishes four levels of the role that Islam plays in Malaysia. The first is functional — to mobilize believers against colonialism, for political protest or political support. The second is cultural, and she defines this as configured by Muslim NGOs and other religious groups with domestic agendas but international links with Islam beyond Malaysia. The third is spiritual, in which the specific norms and values of Islam are asserted to protest against whatever is defined as religious deprivation. And the fourth is the ideological power of Islam for instrumental or political purposes by the state and political leaders in seeking legitimacy.[41] She argues that Islamic resurgence in Malaysia is more than religious ideology, that it is articulated at all the levels described above and in terms of civil society. She argues also that Islam performs an integrative function by laying down a bond of unity among different classes in the Malay community while she concedes (less trenchantly) elsewhere that political Islam is also divisive. Verma concludes, "the effort to accommodate the concepts of Islam to those of democracy is a challenging, complex and incomplete task because it involves a rethinking of the major ethical and legal precepts of Islam."[42]

Although Verma's important contribution to analyses of civil society in Malaysia does not follow entirely the paradigm of using political science theoretical models and measuring the Malaysian context against them, she nevertheless delineates clear boundaries between antithetical constituents of civil society in Malaysia — especially in terms of Islam. Since September 2001, the confusion if not at least the messiness of the state of Islam in Malaysia since the Prime Minister's announcement on 29 September that Malaysia is an Islamic state, eludes demarcating Islam as largely enabling or disabling of the democracy inherent in a civil society.

The overwhelming reason for the Prime Minister's announcement of Malaysia as an Islamic state was as another salvo in the battle for the legitimacy of Islam between his party in the ruling coalition, and the Islamic opposition party, PAS. Dr. Mahathir Mohamad's statement that Malaysia is already an Islamic state, and the booklet that was issued, include articulations that in Malaysia, the responsibilities which are an obligation of an Islamic state have been implemented despite a few weakness and shortcomings that are unavoidable because of a system of government inherited from colonialists.[43] In cognizance of this fact, the text *Malaysia adalah sebuah Negara Islam* (Malaysia is an Islamic nation) describes how the government has launched a policy *"Penerapan Nilai-nilai Islam"* ("Application of Islamic Values") into the administration of the country. Through this policy, the text states, everything that conflicts with Islam will be brought in line with the requirements of Islam in stages and in a way that is wise. The text further states that this policy is in fact large and open, covering all values as well as Islamic law that are the obligation of the government to implement, and that this policy will proceed continually until the aim of upholding an Islamic nation in the national system is fully implemented (*"Ia juga adalah satu dasar yang akan dijalankan secara berterusan sehinggalah matlamat untuk menegakkan negara Islam dalam sistem negara terlaksana sepenuhnya"*).[44] Although the English-language version of the booklet has since been withdrawn, the Bahasa Melayu version continues to be circulated, and there are many statements by the Prime Minister and his cabinet that continue the objective and rhetoric about Malaysia as an Islamic state, most recently by the next Prime Minister, Abdullah Badawi in the first session of Parliament for 2003.

Before this watershed moment in the evolution of Islam in Malaysia, the administration of Prime Minister Mahathir Mohamad had, since 1982, defined and enabled an Islam that engendered his vision of Malaysia as a developed nation on par with the First World, by the year 2020. As such, Muslims in Malaysia appeared to have two different choices about the kind of Islam that they endorsed: the Islam of the government which embraced modernity, and especially economic progress and development, or the Islam of the opposition political party PAS which was theocratic, defined by a fidelity to establishing an Islamic state with the *shari'a* as the law of the land. After Mahathir's Islamic state announcement, the rhetoric of the government, its politicians and its religious functionaries became conflated with that of its Islamist opposition. What has ensued is that the discourse on Islam is enjoined, but it is now defined by the terms of the *ulama* who lead PAS. The exclusive strictures of establishing a state premised on the religious laws of one community does not enhance the evolution of the pluralism and egalitarianism inherent in a civil society, and that are imperative for a multi-religious, multi-racial nation.

THE CIVIL SOCIETY AND ISLAM CHECKLIST

In a summary of the points explored thus far in this chapter, the possibilities for Islam and civil society as enabling and not antithetical to each other are:

- In a departure from Enlightenment notions of religion as private and civil society as the public domain, Islam is integral to an Asian — especially Southeast Asian — civil society that prioritizes ethics and values;
- Muslims who argue about the coherence of Islam and civil society point to the concept of *shura* or consultation as indicative of incipient democracy in Muslim society; others to even pre-modern civil formations that indicate early civil society;
- Islam is the idiom to mobilize for a civil society, to enable reform, anti-conformism and interpretative thinking which enhance democracy;
- If one broadens what qualifies as incipient civil society, leaders and notables who acted and act as advisors to rulers and as mediators for the people are indicative of a plurality of voices and opinions;
- Even an autocratic ruler and state may employ democracy or at least limited forms of political participation to maintain power in the face of resistance — therefore the possibilities are always present if only as a glimmer;
- If democracy is defined and judged also by its efficacy in phases of transition and less by the identity of those who made it happen — such as Islamists who seek election — one is able to discern the possibilities of Islam and civil society.

- The ethos of Islam can unite a people riven by schisms, for example over issues of social justice.
- Islam can provide the resources to overcome the Arab region's three deficits identified in the UNDP's first Arab Human Development Report: freedom, women's empowerment and human capabilities and knowledge relative to income. (The United Nations Development Programme — UNDP — and the Arab Fund for Economic and Social Development released in June 2002 the "Arab Human Development Report 2002" or AHDR. The AHDR is authored by a team of Arab scholars and policymakers with an advisory committee of well-known Arabs in international public life.)
- Islam is just the idiom used for positions against democracy, civil society, etc. — so the conundrum posed: "Is it always Islam versus civil society?" is a false dichotomy.

However, also from the points explored thus far in this chapter, many of the problems which reinforce the argument about the incompatibility of Islam and civil society (almost always at the cost of democracy) are:

- Muslims wanting to conflate religion and politics which are two distinctly different systems, can either undermine each entity or reinforce each in less constructive ways. In this context, as Azyurmardi Azra points out, there are Muslims who believe that only Islamic law, a religious leader or *ulama* can provide good government for Muslims;
- Authoritarian or totalitarian elected Muslim governments whose cruelty and lack of ethics are the cause of many Muslims deciding that Islamists and their agendas (such as the Islamic state, or the rejection of civil law for the *shari'a*) may be a viable alternative, although even political Islam can use the democratic process to gain power but may not necessarily be democratic itself once it forms the government;
- The "incivility" of civil society groups that reflect rather than bridge ethno-religious schisms and/or their rhetoric and discourse because of the polemics that religious exclusivism and righteousness inevitably evoke;
- Leaders and notables who act as advisers to rulers and mediators for the people are almost always the elite who work more to justify the ruler than the ruled;
- When Islam (or for that matter any religiosity) is the yardstick, then Islamists who invariably claim a "true" or generic Islam leave the state and everyone else scrambling to justify their version of Islam even though what is claimed as "true" is itself an eclectic selection from text and tradition;

- Democracy and civil society are not contiguous givens. Civil society groups are not always civil: they can reflect acrimony and divisiveness that disable or defeat democracy;
- "Developmentalism": the religion of the market holds sway while the language of Muslim religiosity continues on the surface. The faithful of materialism and consumerism can choose economics over fundamental rights and freedoms;
- Like most religious traditions, Islam can create the deepest schisms of all including among Muslims;
- Islam is invoked as part of the cause of the Arab region's three deficits identified in UNDP's first Arab Human Development Report: freedom, women's empowerment and human capabilities, and knowledge relative to income.

CONCLUSION

It becomes obvious that some of the problems summarized above negate some of the points in the earlier list of how Islam and civil society are enabling of each other. One could substitute any religion — even one as plural as Hinduism — for some of the points above, and come to the conclusion that the dynamic of conformity to religion and religiosity is contrary to that of a pluralist democracy. In large measure, this is because most religions — especially those that are monotheistic — make exclusive claims. The religious strictures and religious adherents of one group are privileged over other religions. On the other hand, as the experience of Liberation Theology in Latin America has shown, religion can be very powerful in uniting for and legitimating the call for civil society and the democracy inherent to it.

Political Islam must enter these deliberations as a unique force. It is unique in that at its very heart lies its sacred text. For the present, there does not seem to be much room, in practical political terms, for interpreting and relativizing those texts insofar as they bear on the organization of government and the definition of political rights. Perhaps this re-interpretation of the texts on a scale large enough to be significant and accepted will come soon, or perhaps not for a generation or more. Therefore advocating democracy at all costs may not be the best route. Perhaps with political Islam, a period of confrontation and bargaining may be what is needed to hasten the process of reinterpretation so that a pacted transition to full democracy can begin, in which all parties accept the logic if not the spirit of the rules.

Therefore other perspectives relevant to these reflections on civil society and Islam are: How should we think about the relationship of "religion" to the concept of "civil society"? Is religion part of the "civil"? In much of the theoretical literature, NGOs are seen as occupying public space, while religions reside — or ought to reside — in private. The modern sociological imagination premised on Enlightenment rationalizations objects to the idea that religious formations are components of civil society. A common assumption is that religious affiliations are assigned by ascription, that they are inherited identities rather than chosen ones and thus religiosity does not necessarily resource the fundamental of an individual's assertion of his or her rights.

Some of the authors whose work has been quoted in this chapter show Islam blurs this distinction between the private and public. But is it only Islam that does so? In Southeast Asia, it often seems obvious that any religiosity and public religious ritual show that religion resides in both private and public spheres. It has been argued that Asian state doctrines and practice do not necessarily recognize a separate and distinct space for religion. "There was no word for religion as a separate and distinct sphere of life and religions were not seen as inherently different from other forms of communal activity", states Don Baker about East Asia. He argues that the little autonomy religious communities did enjoy, they enjoyed only because of neglect or indifference by the state, and that this autonomy could be violated by the state at any time the state chose to do so.[45]

In terms of networks and organizations, religion and its communities straddle the space between private and public. These networks and organizations are significant for the evolution of a civil society: religious formations may squeeze the state. Or they may be used by the state for its own purpose. Civil society and its actors may be uncivil: the same forces that make for democracy can make for dictatorship. In resonance with Hefner, Don Emmerson points out that "the rise of NGOs that insist on transparency in government while themselves remaining organizationally opaque and electorally unaccountable would constitute an uncivil society".[46]

Religion is no master variable that will determine the political cleavages that lead to authoritarianism or the solidarities that promote democracy. Religions are themselves internally contested, and even more so with Islam because it has no central authority like the Vatican. So religion provides one division among the many social cleavages that will influence the patterns of alliance that civic and state actors will choose. There is always the temptation to hypothesize in generalizations. But perhaps we should not give up the tedium of investigating particulars for the comfort of totalizing hypotheses such as those that throughout history have proven to be ephemeral.

Notes

1   John Kean, *Civil Society: Old Images, New Visions*, Stanford: Stanford University Press, 1998, p. 114.
2   I explore the academic ramifications of such a paradigm as enabling work in post-colonial space in "A Reflection on Theory in Malaysian Studies" in *New Perspectives in Malaysian Studies*, edited by Mohd. Hazim Shah, Jomo K.S. and Phuah Kai Lit. Kuala Lumpur: Vin Lin Press, 2002.
3   Lani Guinier, *The Tyranny of the Majority: Fundamental Fairness in Representative Democracy*, New York: The Free Press, 1994, p. 20.
4   Charles E. Butterworth and I. William Zartman, "Introduction" in *Between the State and Islam*, edited by Charles E. Butterworth and I William Zartman. Cambridge: Cambridge University Press, 2001, p. 1.
5   Jamal al-Suwaidi, "Arab and Western Conceptions of Democracy" in *Democracy, War and Peace in the Middle East*, edited by David Garnham and Mark Tessler. Bloomington: Indiana University Press, 1995, p. 87. See also Nazih Ayubi's chapter on reformists in his excellent book, *Political Islam*, London: Routledge, 1991.
6   Saad Eddin Ibrahim, "Civil Society and Prospects for Democratization in the Arab World" in *Civil Society in the Middle East*, edited by Augustus Richard Norton, Leiden: E.J. Brill, 1995, p. 28.
7   Sami Zubaida, "Community and Democracy in the Middle East" in *Civil Society: History and Possibilities*, edited by Sudipta Kaviraj and Sunil Khilnani. Cambridge: Cambridge University Press, 2001, p. 234.
8   Ibid., p. 242.
9   Ernest Gellner, *Conditions of Liberty: Civil Society and Its Rivals*, London: Hamish Hamilton, 1994, pp. 61–80.
10 Sami Zubaida, op. cit., p. 249.
11 Ghassan Salame, "Introduction" in *Democracy Without Democrats? The Renewal of Politics in the Muslim World*, edited by Ghassan Salame. London: I.B. Taurus, 1996, p. 2.
12 Nazih Ayoubi, "Rethinking the Public/Private Dichotomy: Radical Islam and Civil Society in the Middle East" in *Contention* 4, no. 3 (Spring 1995): 79– 105.
13 Saad Eddin Ibrahim, "The Troubled Triangle: Populism, Islam and Civil Society in the Arab World", in *Islam in a Changing World: Europe and the Middle East*, edited by Anders Jerichow and Jorgen Baek Simonsen. London: Curzon Press, 1997, p. 26.
14 Sami Zubaida, "Community and Democracy in the Middle East", pp. 234–35; and "Islam, the State and Democracy: Contrasting Conceptions of Civil Society in Egypt", *Middle East Report* (1992), p. 979.
15 I explore the issue of the Islamic state in classical doctrine, especially *Al Ahkam*

Al-Sultaniyya in "The Islamic State or the State of Islam in Malaysia", *Contemporary Southeast Asia* 23, no. 3 (December 2001).

16   Abu al-A'la Mawdudi, as cited in Shukri B. Abed, "Islam and Democracy", in *Democracy, War and Peace in the Middle East*, edited by David Garnham and Mark Tessler. Bloomington, Indiana University Press, 1995, p. 123.

17   Robert W. Hefner, ed., *The Politics of Multiculturalism: Pluralism and Citizenship in Malaysia, Singapore and Indonesia*, Honolulu: University of Hawaii Press, 2001, p. 43.

18   Ibid, p. 9.

19   Ibid.

20   Robert, W. Hefner, *Civil Islam: Muslims and Democratization in Indonesia*, Princeton, New Jersey: Princeton University Press, 2000.

21   Azyurmardi Azra, "The Challenge of Democracy in the Muslim World: Traditional Politics and Democratic Political Culture", *WARITAKITA*, publication of the Majlis Ugama Islam Singapore (MUIS), no. 139 (May–June 2002).

22   Anwar Ibrahim, *The Asian Renaissance*, Singapore: Times Books International, 1996, p. 51.

23   Francis Loh, "Developmentalism and the Limits of Democratic Discourse", in *Democracy in Malaysia: Discourse and Practices*, edited by Francis Loh Kok Wah and Khoo Boo Teik. London: Curzon Press, 2001, p. 21.

24   Ibid., p. 48.

25   Abdul Rahman Embong, *Southeast Asian Middle Classes: Prospects for Social Change and Democratisation*, Bangi: Penerbit Universiti Kebangsaan Malaysia, 2001, p. 15.

26   See Shamsul A.B., *From British to Bumiputera Rule; Local Politics and Rural Development in Peninsular Malaysia*, Singapore: ISEAS, 1982. Others include Donald M. Nonini's *British Colonial Rule and the Resistance of the Malay Peasantry 1900–1957*, New Haven: Monograph Series 38/Yale University Southeast Asia Studies, 1992, and Patrick Sullivan "A Critical Appraisal of Historians of Malaysia: the Theory of Society Implicit in their Work", in *Southeast Asia. Essays in the Political Economy of Structural Change*, edited by R. Higgot and R. Robison. London: Routledge and Kegan Paul, 1985.

27   Shamsul A.B. explains that the term "Nations-of Intent" was introduced by Robert I. Rotberg in 1966 and also employed in the work of Malaysian social scientist Rastam A. Sani. See Shamsul A.B., "Nations-of-Intent in Malaysia" in *Asian Forms of the Nation*, edited by Stein Tonnesson and Hans Antol. London: Curzon Press, 1996, p. 328.

28   Ibid., p. 329.

29   Shamsul A.B. "'Asian Values', moral communities and resistance in Malaysia" in *Malaysian Business in the New Era*, edited by Chris Nyland, Wendy Smith. Cheltenham, UK: Edward Elgar, 2001, p. 254.

30   Nakamura Mitsuo, Sharon Siddique and Omar Farouk Bajunid, eds., *Islam and Civil Society in Southeast Asia*, Singapore: ISEAS, 2001, p. 2.

31   Omar Farouk Bajunid, "Islam and the State in Southeast Asia," in *State and Islam*, edited by C. van Dijk and A.H. de Groot. Leiden: Research School, CNWS, 1995.

32   Robert W. Hefner, "Introduction" in *Islam in an Era of Nation-States: Politics and Religious Renewal in Muslim Southeast Asia*, edited by Robert W. Hefner and Patricia Horvatich. Honolulu: University of Hawaii Press, 1997.

33   Mohamad Abu Bakar, "Islam, Civil Society, and Ethnic Relations in Malaysia", in *Islam and Civil Society in Southeast Asia*, edited by Nakamura Mitsuo, Sharon Siddique and Omar Farouk Bajunid. Singapore: ISEAS, 2001, p. 63.

34   Ibid.

35   Patricia Martinez, "Islam, Mahathir and the New Malay Dilemma" in *Mahathir's Administration: Performance and Crisis in Governance*, edited by Ho Khai Leong and James Chin. Singapore: Times Books International, 2001.

36   Kassim Ahmad, *Hikayat Hang Tuah*, Kuala Lumpur: Dewan Bahasa dan Pustaka, 1968.

37   Meredith L. Weiss, "What Will Become of *Reformasi*? Ethnicity and Changing Political Norms in Malaysia", *Contemporary Southeast Asia* 21, no. 3 (December 1999): 425.

38   Sharifah Zaleha Syed Hassan, "Islamization and the Emerging Civil Society in Malaysia", in *Islam and Civil Society in Southeast Asia*, edited by Nakamura Mitsuo, Sharon Siddique and Omar Farouk Bajunid. Singapore: ISEAS, 2001, p. 86.

39   Farish A. Noor, "Towards a Progressive Islam on Our Own Terms", <http://www.just-international.org/Farish-Iraq.htm>.

40   Vidhu Verma, *Malaysia: State and Civil Society in Transition*, Boulder and London: Lynne Rienner Publishers, 2002, p. 94.

41   Ibid, p. 117.

42   Ibid., p. 214.

43   Dato Wan Zahidi Wan Teh, *Malaysia adalah sebuah Negara Islam*, Kuala Lumpur: Jabatan Hal Ehwal Khas, Kementerian Penerangan Malaysia, 2001, p. 8. For a more detailed analysis of the text and the Malaysia as an Islamic state issue, see my article "The Islamic State or the State of Islam in Malaysia", *Contemporary Southeast Asia* 23, no. 3 (December 2001).

44   Ibid.

45   Don Baker, "World Religions and National States: Competing Claims in East Asia," in *Transnational Religion and Fading States*, edited by Susanne Hoeber Rudolph and James Piscatori. Boulder, Colorado: Westview Press, 1997, p. 168.

46   Donald Emmerson, "Reforms Needed for Democratic Transitions in Asia: Some Thoughts Outside the Box" in *Democratic Transitions in Asia*, edited by Uwe Johannen and James Gomez. Singapore: Select Books, 2001, p. 98.

References

Abdul Rahman Embong. *Southeast Asian Middle Classes: Prospects for Social Change and Democratisation*. Bangi: Penerbit Universiti Kebangsaan Malaysia, 2001.

Anwar Ibrahim. *The Asian Renaissance*. Singapore: Times Books International, 1996.

Arab Human Development Report, The. UNDP. 2002. <http://www.undp.org/rbas/ahdr/>.

Azyurmardi Azra. "The Challenge of Democracy in the Muslim World: Traditional Politics and Democratic Political Culture," *WARITAKITA*, publication of the Majlis Ugama Islam Singapore (MUIS), no. 139 (May–June 2002), Singapore.

Baker, Don. "World Religions and National States: Competing Claims in East Asia". In *Transnational Religion and Fading States*, edited by Susanne Hoeber Rudolph and James Piscatori. Boulder, Colorado: Westview Press, 1997.

Butterworth, Charles E. and I. William Zartman, eds. *Between the State and Islam*. Cambridge: Cambridge University Press, 2001.

Emmerson, Donald. "Reforms Needed for Democratic Transitions in Asia: Some Thoughts Outside the Box." Uwe Johannen and James Gomez, eds., *Democratic Transitions in Asia*. Singapore: Select Books, 2001.

Farish A. Noor. "Towards a Progressive Islam on Our Own Terms", <http://www.just-international.org/Farish-Iraq.htm>.

Francis Loh. "Developmentalism and the Limits of Democratic Discourse", in *Democracy in Malaysia: Discourse and Practices*, edited by Francis Loh Kok Wah and Khoo Boo Teik. London: Curzon Press, 2001.

Gellner, Earnest. *Conditions of Liberty: Civil Society and Its Rivals*. London: Hamish Hamilton, 1994.

Ghassan Salame. "Introduction" in Ghassan Salame, ed. *Democracy Without Democrats? The Renewal of Politics in the Muslim World*. London: I.B. Taurus, 1996.

Guinier, Lani. *The Tyranny of the Majority: Fundamental Fairness in Representative Democracy*. New York: The Free Press, 1994.

Hefner, Robert W. and Patricia Horvatich, eds., *Islam in an Era of Nation-States: Politics and Religious Renewal in Muslim Southeast Asia*. Honolulu: University of Hawaii Press, 1997.

Hefner, Robert W. *The Politics of Multiculturalism: Pluralism and Citizenship in Malaysia, Singapore and Indonesia*. Honolulu: University of Hawaii Press, 2001.

Jamal al-Suwaidi. "Arab and Western Conceptions of Democracy". In *Democracy, War and Peace in the Middle East*, edited by David Garnham and Mark Tessler. Bloomington: Indiana University Press, 1995.

Kassim Ahmad. *Hikayat Hang Tuah*. Kuala Lumpur: Dewan Bahasa dan Pustaka, 1968.

Keane, John. *Civil Society: Old Images, New Visions*. Stanford: Stanford University Press, 1998.

Martinez, Patricia. "The Islamic State or the State of Islam in Malaysia". *Contemporary Southeast Asia* 23, no. 3 (December 2001).

_____. "Islam, Mahathir and the New Malay Dilemma". In *Mahathir's Administration: Performance and Crisis in Governance*, edited by Ho Khai Leong and James Chin. Singapore: Times Books International, 2001.

_____. "A Reflection on Theory in Malaysian Studies". In *New Perspectives in Malaysian Studies*, edited by Mohd. Hazim Shah, Jomo K.S. and Phuah Kai Lit. Kuala Lumpur: Vin Lin Press, 2002.

Mitsuo, Nakamura, Sharon Siddique and Omar Farouk Bajunid, eds. *Islam and Civil Society in Southeast Asia*. Singapore: ISEAS, 2001.

Mohamad Abu Bakar. "Islam, Civil Society, and Ethnic Relations in Malaysia". In *Islam and Civil Society in Southeast Asia*, edited by Nakamura Mitsuo, Sharon Siddique and Omar Farouk Bajunid. Singapore: ISEAS, 2001.

Nazih Ayubi. *Political Islam*. London: Routledge, 1991.

_____. "Rethinking the Public/Private Dichotomy: Radical Islam and Civil Society in the Middle East" in *Contention* 4, no. 3 (Spring 1995).

Nonini, Donald M. *British Colonial Rule and the Resistance of the Malay Peasantry 1900–1957*. New Haven: Monograph Series 38/Yale University Southeast Asia Studies, 1992.

Omar Farouk Bajunid. "Islam and the State in Southeast Asia". In *State and Islam*, edited by C. van Dijk and A.H. de Groot. Leiden: Research School, CNWS, 1995.

Saad Eddin Ibrahim. "The Troubled Triangle: Populism, Islam and Civil Society in the Arab World". In *Islam in a Changing World: Europe and the Middle East*, edited by Anders Jerichow and Jorgen Baek Simonsen. London: Curzon Press, 1997.

_____. "Civil Society and Prospects for Democratization in the Arab World". In *Civil Society in the Middle East*, edited by Augustus Richard Norton. Leiden: E.J. Brill, 1995.

Sami Zubaida. "Community and Democracy in the Middle East"and "Islam, the State and Democracy: Contrasting Conceptions of Civil Society in Egypt". *Middle East Report*, 1992.

_____. "Community and Democracy in the Middle East". In *Civil Society: History and Possibilities*, edited by Sudipta Kaviraj and Sunil Khilnani. Cambridge: Cambridge University Press, 2001.

Shamsul A.B. *From British to Bumiputera Rule; Local Politics and Rural Development in Peninsular Malaysia*. Singapore: ISEAS, 1982.

_____. "Nations-of-Intent in Malaysia". In *Asian Forms of the Nation*, edited by Stein Tonnesson and Hans Antol. London: Curzon Press, 1996.

_____. " 'Asian Values', Moral Communities and Resistance in Malaysia". In *Malaysian Business in the New Era*, edited by Chris Nyland, Wendy Smith. Cheltenham, UK: Edward Elgar, 2001.

Sharifah Zaleha Syed Hassan. "Islamization and the Emerging Civil Society in Malaysia". In *Islam and Civil Society in Southeast Asia*, edited by Nakamura Mitsuo, Sharon Siddique and Omar Farouk Bajunid. Singapore: ISEAS, 2001.

Shukri B. Abed. "Islam and Democracy". In *Democracy, War and Peace in the Middle East*, edited by David Garnham and Mark Tessler. Bloomington, Indiana University Press, 1995.

Syed Farid Alatas."Islam, Ilmu-Ilmu Sosial dan Masyarakat Sipil". In *Antropologi Indonesia*, 66 (2001): 13–22.

Sullivan, Patrick. "A Critical Appraisal of Historians of Malaysia: the Theory of Society Implicit in their Work". In *Southeast Asia. Essays in the Political Economy of Structural Change*, edited by R. Higgot and R. Robison. London: Routledge and Kegan Paul, 1985.

Verma, Vidhu. *Malaysia: State and Civil Society in Transition*. Boulder and London: Lynne Rienner Publishers, 2002.

Weiss, Meredith L. "What Will Become of *Reformasi*? Ethnicity and Changing Political Norms in Malaysia". *Contemporary Southeast Asia* 21, no. 3 (December 1999).

9

ISLAMIZATION, CIVIL SOCIETY, AND RELIGIOUS MINORITIES IN MALAYSIA

Peter G. Riddell

INTRODUCTION

The last three decades of the twentieth century witnessed a fundamental shift in Islamic politics in Malaysia. Islamic resurgence throughout society produced a discernible response at the level of the state directed towards conscious and concerted Islamization through the organs of state. This went hand in hand with a power struggle between the main Muslim political actors in Malaysia. This intra-Muslim struggle concerning the shape of Islamization in Malaysia has had a series of dramatic knock-on effects on religious minority communities in that country.

In this chapter the impact of Islamization in Malaysia, with particular reference to religious minorities will be considered. The various themes addressed will be seen through the eyes of the minorities, as it were.

PERCEPTIONS OF ISLAMIZATION THROUGH NON-MUSLIM EYES

What are the hallmarks of Malaysian Islamization according to the perception of the religious minorities? Several features are key.

1. Demographics

Recent decades have witnessed verifiable demographic changes in Malaysia which are significant to the Islamization process from the perspective of the religious minorities. The national census taken in the year 2000 showed that the Muslim proportion of Malaysia's population had increased from 58.6 per cent to 60.4 per cent over a ten-year period.[1] The Muslim percentage had been counted as 53 per cent according to the 1980 census,[2] so there had been a rise of 7 per cent in 20 years. In 2000 figures for other religions stood at 19.2 per cent for Buddhism, a significant reduction from the 28 per cent recorded in the census of 1970; 9.1 per cent for Christianity, up from 6.4 per cent in 1980;[3] and 6.3 per cent for Hinduism, down from 7 per cent in 1980.[4]

Though conversion to Islam accounted for some of this change,[5] a greater cause was the changing ethnic composition of Malaysia's population. The 2000 census recorded that Bumiputera — Malays and indigenous tribes in Sarawak and Sabah — constituted 65.1 per cent of the population, up by 4.5 per cent in 10 years, while Chinese represented 26 per cent, down from 28.1 per cent in 1990 and 37 per cent in 1957. As the vast majority of the Bumiputera are Muslim, and the majority of the Chinese are non-Muslims, especially Buddhists, such changes in ethnic composition of the population had a telling effect on the religious mosaic of Malaysia.

2. Statements by Political Leaders

While the society around the religious minorities is perceived to be becoming more Islamic through demographic changes, another factor which adds fuel to this perception relates to a changing emphasis in statements made by political leaders. Tunku Abdul Rahman, the first Prime Minister of Malaya (1957–63) and of Malaysia (1963–70), made the following statement in Parliament in May 1958: "I would like to make it clear that this country is not an Islamic State as it is generally understood; we merely provide that Islam shall be the official religion of the State."[6] He was rejecting a statement by Dato' Haji Yahya bin Haji Wan Mohamed in Parliament that "We have been officially recognised as an Islamic State."[7] On another occasion Tunku Abdul Rahman affirmed his opposition to the concept of an Islamic state for Malaysia in the following terms:

> "There is no way we should have an Islamic State here … we cannot force the non-Malays and non-Muslims to follow our way of life. Our

slogan 'live and let live' must be maintained because it is the only practical solution in a multi-racial society like ours."[8]

However, in October 2001 Dr. Mahathir Mohamad, Prime Minister from 1981-2003, declared Malaysia was already an Islamic state, and that the kind of constitutional change called for by the opposition Islamic Party of Malaysia (PAS) was not necessary.[9] In mid-June 2002, Dr. Mahathir affirmed his earlier statement, adding that Malaysia was "an Islamic fundamentalist state" because his Barisan Nasional government adhered to the fundamental teachings of Islam.[10] These statements were essentially reactive, as observed by Father Lawrence Andrew, Editor of the Catholic *Herald*: "Dr. Mahathir's statement about Malaysia being an Islamic state is politically motivated, driven by the need to confront PAS. He is trying to win back votes lost in the 1999 elections."[11]

However, this perceived shift in federal prime ministerial view between 1958 and 2001 caused profound disquiet among Malaysia's religious minorities. Their sense of concern was exacerbated by statements and actions around the same time from the chief ministers of two of Malaysia's states which had elected PAS to power. In 2001 Kelantan Chief Minister, Nik Abdul Aziz Nik Mat, criticizing what he saw as the ineffectual Islamizing policies of the Mahathir government, called for the federal Ministry of Education to return the national education system to an Islamic basis more clearly grounded in the Qur'an.[12] On March 25, 2002 Chief Minister of Terengganu, Abdul Hadi Awang, said the state constitution would be amended to "project the supreme law in Islam", adding that although the federal Barisan Nasional government led by the United Malays National Organization (UMNO) claimed to be Islamic, existing *shari'a* laws were "too simplified and very light".[13] In fulfilment of this call, the Terengganu *Shari'a* Criminal (*Hudud*) Bill was presented at the State Legislative Assembly on 7 July 2002.

3. Islamizing Measures Taken by Governments

A dispassionate examination of the Islamizing policies and practices of the UMNO-led Barisan Nasional federal government and the PAS-led state governments of Kelantan and Terengganu reveals profound differences in approach and ideology, with the former being essentially modernist in thinking, and the latter being conservative and traditionalist. However, religious minorities do not necessarily focus on such differences, often considering instead that a federal government emphasis on inculcation of Islamic values and a PAS state government emphasis on implementation of Islamic law are two sides of the same coin.

(a) Federal Government

Islamization under the influence of federal government policies has had a range of manifestations. Since Dr. Mahathir assumed the prime ministership in 1981, there has been an observable increase in programmes with Islamic content on the government-controlled television and radio stations. Political speeches gradually became more embellished with Qur'anic quotations. But such subtle measures were accompanied by more tangible decisions.

The Barisan Nasional government prioritized reforms to the educational system as part of the Islamization programme. Dr. Mahatir had initiated this process as Minister of Education in 1974. Under his guidance the Ministry of Education approved a substantial funding allocation for training of teachers of Islamic Studies in 1975. After his assumption of the post as Prime Minister, the government introduced a compulsory course at university in "Islamic Civilization" (*Tamadun Islam*) for all Muslim students. In 1997 this course was made compulsory for all students of all religions.[14] Moreover, religious minority schools witnessed a slow but steady Islamizing of their staff and student body as a result of being absorbed into the government education system, which empowered the federal Ministry of Education to take responsibility for both appointment of school teaching staff and admission of students.[15]

Institution building was also a priority in the federal government's Islamization drive. In 1983 the International Islamic University was established outside Kuala Lumpur. That year also saw the establishment of PERKIM, an Islamic group which became active in mission, especially targetting the Chinese.[16] Simultaneously, Bank Islam and *Syarikat Takaful* were established, as alternative Islamic banks and insurance bodies respectively. During the 1980s the Islamic Economic Foundation and an Islamic foundation for social welfare were also established. Then on 3 July 1992 the Institute of Islamic Understanding (IKIM) was inaugurated by Dr. Mahathir to design and implement the Islamic input into the vision for nation-building of the Mahathir government.

(b) State Governments

Mohamad Hashim Kamali points out that "PAS opposes the government's description of Islamization as a commitment to the promotion of 'Islamic values'."[17] In short, PAS considers that such an approach to Islamization represents a sell-out of core Islamic principles. In contrast, PAS is committed to the implementation of Islamic law as the central legal system by which the Malaysian nation operates, at both state and federal levels.

Since regaining power in Kelantan in 1990,[18] the PAS government has passed Islamic legislation relating to the banning of gambling, discotheques, karaoke lounges and unisex hair salons, prohibiting the sale of alcohol to Muslims, and requiring official permission to organize carnivals, theatre performances, dances, beauty pageants and song festivals. In addition, the PAS state government legislated for gender-based checkout counters in supermarkets.[19]

In November 1993, the PAS Government in Kelantan passed the *Shari'a* Criminal Code (II) Bill providing for *hudud*, or Islamic penal codes, in that state. However, they could not come into force without approval from the federal government, as under the Malaysian Constitution, crime is a federal matter. The Barisan Nasional government of Dr. Mahathir blocked PAS moves to bring their Islamic penal codes into operation. It was the original intention of the PAS government of Kelantan that this bill should apply to Muslims and non-Muslims alike.[20]

In late 1999, PAS won power in the Malaysian state of Terengganu for the first time. From 1 January 2000, hotels in Terengganu were prohibited from selling alcohol.[21] In March 2000, a dress code for women was announced; it was to commence with government office staff and workers in business premises. This would not apply to non-Terengganu women visiting the state.[22] Pressure was placed on local supermarkets by government officials to separate males and females into different queues at cash registers.[23]

In August 2001, six *shari'a* enactments were passed by the Terengganu State Legislative Assembly, and came into force on 1 August 2002. They were the *Shari'a* Criminal Procedure Enactment (Terengganu) 2001; *Shari'a* Court Evidence Enactment (Terengganu) 2001; *Shari'a* Criminal Offence Enactment (*Takzir*) (Terengganu) 2001; Islamic Religious Affairs Administration Enactment (Terengganu) 1422H/2001M; *Shari'a* Court Enactment (Terengganu) 2001 and *Shari'a* Court Mal Procedure Enactment (Terengganu) 2001.[24]

As mentioned earlier, in July 2002 the PAS government in Terengganu introduced its Shari'a Criminal Offences (*Hudud and Qisas*) Bill. Terengganu Chief Minister Abdul Hadi Awang was reported to say: "For now, it will apply to only Muslims, but when the time comes, the *hudud* and *qisas* laws will be extended to all non-Muslims."[25]

New Islamic rulings at the state level do not only occur where PAS is in power. A series of new Islamic measures were introduced in UMNO-ruled Johor state in recent years, and the religious adviser to Prime Minister Mahathir, Dr. Abdul Hamid Othman, indicated in an interview that Selangor, Kedah and Kuala Lumpur would probably take similar measures. Such a flood of Islamic legislation at the state level was a cause of considerable concern to religious minorities throughout Malaysia.

(c) Measures Perceived as Discriminating Against Religious Minorities

In addition to such a range of measures taken by federal and state governments which religious minorities viewed as strengthening the position of Islam in Malaysia, there were specific developments seen as active discrimination against the minorities themselves.

In 1981, legislation was passed at the federal level forbidding ownership of the Bible by any Malaysians except Christians. Restrictions were also placed upon the importation of non-Islamic religious literature. Obstacles to the construction of new houses of worship for religious minorities meant that Muslims were clearly favoured in this regard. By 1992, the ratio of mosques to Muslim worshippers was 1:800 in Johor and Perak, whereas the ratio of non-Muslim places of worship to worshippers was 1:4000 in Johor and 1:5000 in Perak.[26] In September 1998, this situation seemed to be set in cement by a new document attributed to the federal Ministry of Housing and Local Government, entitled *Guidelines for Planning Places of Worship for non-Muslims*, which kicked up a storm among the religious minorities.[27] A prominent Christian publication reflected religious minority discontent in commenting that "the Guidelines are oppressive, unfair, unjust and unconstitutional".[28]

Federal legislation passed in 1989 forbade the use by non-Muslims of forty-two terms deemed Islamic. In 1991, this list was reduced to four terms: *Allah, Kaabah, Baitullah,* and *Solat.*[29] This was particularly significant for Christians, as *Allah* had hitherto been the standard term of reference for God in Christian worship and literature. In a connected development in early 1997, some 230 Christian books imported into Malaysia from Singapore and Indonesia were confiscated by the Johor state government authorities under the 1991 law.[30] Brother Anthony Rogers of the Catholic Church of Malaysia commented that "these measures banning use of Allah and the Indonesian Bible reflect a culture of insecurity on the part of the Malays rather than a direct preoccupation with Christian doctrine".[31] Nevertheless, many Christians perceived these developments as hostile acts against their minority faith.

The knock-on effects of government-driven Islamization and measures discriminating against religious minorities are felt by non-Muslims in many areas of daily life. There are reports of increasing tendencies towards exclusiveness among Muslim students in Malaysia's universities. Farish

Noor described an incident where, at the beginning of one of his lectures at the University of Malaya, a Muslim student asked him to delay the lecture to allow for prayer, saying "This is just for the Muslims. The rest of you must not take part."[32] Such a culture of exclusion has also penetrated the commercial sector. For example, Christian videos and DVDs concerning the life of Christ attracted complaints from the Malay language tabloid *Harian Metro*, as they were on sale in public shopping malls and, according to this newspaper, this could "adversely affect the faith of Muslims that are weak in their religion's teachings".[33]

MOVES BY THE RELIGIOUS MINORITY TO ORGANIZE

Mohamad Abu Bakar writes as follows:

> One aspect of this Islamization drive, which was to have a significant impact on race relations, was the central and state governments' attempts to bring their administrations in line with religious requirements... [Non-Muslims] entered the fray by activating their own organizations, mobilizing their members, or forming their own societies in order to champion the cause of their co-religionists in the face of the Islamists' challenge.[34]

Such has been the religious minority contribution to civil society in Malaysia. Under a feeling of threat, religious minorities moved during the last quarter of the twentieth century to organise themselves in order to shore up their position in Malaysian society and to make a positive contribution to the building of a multi-cultural, multi-religious and tolerant nation. We will now examine how they have gone about this, drawing links with specific aspects of Islamization, where possible, with the primary focus on the Malaysian Christian community to ensure sufficient focus in a paper of this size.

1. Existing Structures

Christianity has deep roots in Malaysia. The earliest Christian community has been traced back to around 650CE, probably located in Kedah.[35] However, this early community did not survive. It was not until the Portuguese period that a lasting Christian community was established, leading to the emergence of many different church groups.

Churches were quickly established by the Portuguese after their capture of Malacca in 1511. By 1641, the Catholic community stood at 20,000 with twenty churches present.[36] At the end of 1995, there were 637,000 Catholics in Malaysia, constituting three per cent of the population, and at least one third of the overall Christian minority.[37]

Following the momentous change in direction brought about by the Second Vatican Council (1963–65), the Catholic Church of Malaysia instituted ten yearly meetings to plan the way ahead as a response. The Aggiornamento, held in 1976 in Penang, included 123 bishops and clergy, and identified the building of basic ecclesial communities as the core need, with four related needs: unity formation, ecumenical and inter-religious dialogue and integral human development.[38] Ten years later, the First Peninsular Malaysia Pastoral Convention (PMPC I) was held in Kuala Lumpur and was attended by 183 bishops, clergy and laity. PMPC II, held in Johor in 1996, gathered together 390 bishops, clergy and laity, and made a commitment to "A New Way of Being Church" in the Malaysian context. Among the priorities identified by PMPC II were inter-religious and ecumenical dialogue, and inculturation,[39] both key to the Catholic Church's response to Islamization around them.

Dutch and British colonization brought a wide range of Protestant denominations from 1641 onwards, adding to the Catholic presence remaining from the Portuguese period. In January 1948 the Malayan Christian Council (MCC) was founded and it assembled local Anglicans, Methodists, Presbyterians, the Orthodox Syrian Church, the Lutheran Church, the Salvation Army and the YMCA. With the establishment of Malaysia in 1963, the MCC metamorphosed into the Council of Churches of Malaysia and Singapore in 1967, and then the Council of Churches of Malaysia (Majlis Gereja-Gereja Malaysia) in 1975.

2. The Problem of Internal Disunity

Christians in Malaysia have long suffered from internal disunity, due to historical, ethnic and denominational factors. Many churches continue to be ethnically based, so the language of worship has often been the language of the predominant group in a given congregation. In order to overcome this problem, the "CCM has consistently promoted the use of the Malay language at all levels of church life."[40] In fact, in identifying its objectives, the CCM took account of the challenges faced by the church in terms of internal disunity by setting itself the following goals:

• To offer itself as an instrument or agency to the Churches in Malaysia whereby they can more and more do together everything except what irreconcilable differences of the sincere conviction compel them to do separately.

- To show forth among its members that Christian unity which is God's gift to his people.
- To promote discussion and action among churches in Malaysia towards Church union.[41]

However, such aspirations needed outside factors to bring about moves towards the hoped-for unity. As Albert Walters says: "The real integration of ecumenism into the life of Malaysian churches had to wait until there were Malaysian issues which proved beyond doubt the value of this sort of co-operation."[42]

3. New Initiatives

The "issues" about which Walters speaks relate to Islamization. Christian writer Ng Kam Weng comments that:

> "Ethnic divisions within the church are diminishing as a factor in church life. For example, many Indians from the minority within the Christian community hold leadership positions. This is never a topic of discussion. Islamisation has brought Christians together."[43]

The emergence of the Barisan Nasional Islamization policies in the 1980s, themselves representing partly a response to PAS' more strident Islamization rhetoric, created an environment where non-Muslims saw a clear need to voluntarily come together and to seek safety in numbers, as it were.

(a) Interfaith Initiatives: the MCCBCHS

In an important move towards interfaith co-operation, Buddhists, Christians, Hindus and Sikhs came together in 1983 to found the Malaysian Consultative Council of Buddhism, Christianity, Hinduism and Sikhism (MCCBCHS). Its website explains what triggered this initiative:

> In August [1981], statements were made by the governing authorities and others regarding Malaysia's ultimate status as an Islamic State. These statements gave rise for concern to the leaders of the non-Muslim religions and they saw that as a positive opportunity to come together to promote matters of mutual interests [and] defend against common threats, to build a nation where religious and racial harmony reigns.[44]

Its establishment was welcomed by Tunku Abdul Rahman, who promised it his support.[45] However, the invitation by the founders to Muslim groups to join was not taken up. MCCBCHS set about defining specific objectives, including the promotion of the call for racial and religious harmony enunciated in the *Rukun Negara* (State Pillars) of 1969, the holding of conferences and seminars, and the publishing of journals, periodicals, leaflets and books in fulfilment of its objectives.[46]

In recognition of its multi-religious make-up, the MCCBCHS chairmanship follows a two-year rotation between the different religious groups represented, and it champions the causes and articulates the grievances of the different groups. The MCCBCHS has established branches in seven of Malaysia's thirteen states. Speaking of the MCCBCHS track record since its establishment, Father Philip Thomas and Dr. John Gurusamy of the Council of Churches of Malaysia commented that:

> MCCBCHS lobbying has prevented the situation of non-Muslims from deteriorating, and it has brought other faiths together to some degree. However, it is only a consultative council, and it doesn't include some groups which should be present, such as the independent churches outside the NECF, and certain other faiths such as the Taoists and Bahais.[47]

(b) Christian Initiatives

The move to bring non-Muslim minority faiths together into the MCCBCHS was mirrored in two initiatives taken by the Malaysian Christian community. First, Malaysian evangelical Protestant churches formed the National Evangelical Christian Fellowship (NECF) Malaysia in May 1983. It brought together churches from the Assemblies of God, Baptist, Lutheran, Methodist, Presbyterian and Brethren traditions, as well as Full Gospel Churches, the Evangelical Free Church, the Full Gospel Assembly, Bible Seminaries and a host of other churches across the Malaysian Federation. As a mark of its commitment to interfaith co-operation in the face of a perceived challenge from the Islamization programme, NECF became a member of the MCCBCHS.

Second, an even more ambitious enterprise, the Christian Federation of Malaysia (Persekutuan Kristian Malaysia — CFM) was founded in 1986 as the government-driven Islamization programme picked up steam. This is a broad-based Christian alliance, and includes almost all Christian denominations through its founder members: the Catholic Church, the CCM, and the NECF. In December 2001, the CFM represented around 5,000 member churches,[48] and spoke for about ninety per cent of the Christian population of Malaysia. The CFM holds a general conference in April every two years.

The third of the stated aims and objectives identified in the CFM constitution highlights the body's concern to address perceived marginalization of Malaysian religious minorities under the Islamization policies of the federal and state governments: "To look after the interests of the Christian community as a whole with particular reference to religious freedom and rights as enshrined in the Federal Constitution".[49]

The CFM is itself a member of the MCCBCHS. Brother Augustine Julian of the Catholic Church commented that "The CFM has served as a vehicle for Christian unity, and has generated mutual respect between the various member groups."[50] However, its design somewhat circumscribes its impact. CCM spokespeople commented that,

> in certain respects, the CFM has contributed to Christian unity. However, it is a federation without rules, and therefore it lacks teeth. It produces no regular publication, and it has no state branches. The statements of one CFM member group tend to become generalised to the CFM as a whole.[51]

In another creative method of response to the pressures of Islamization, Christian groups have moved to set up centres designed to conduct research and publishing with a focus on community concerns. An example is the Catholic Research Centre (Pusat Penyelidikan Katholik — CRC), which publishes a monthly magazine, *Catholic Asian News*, as well as *Information and Formation*, a volume appearing periodically and containing articles of interest to Christians. The CRC also operates a public library that has a collection of books, periodicals and publications on religion and inter-related topics. The CRC has also served as the secretariat for the MCCBCHS.

In a similar initiative, Malaysian evangelical Christians established the Kairos Research Centre (KRC) in 1993. This centre has two main objectives: first, to encourage and facilitate Christian research and scholarship on issues relevant to Malaysian Christianity, and second to contribute towards the intellectual development of Christian leaders and thinkers. In fulfilment of these objectives, KRC set up specialized study groups in areas such as religion and society, a Christian approach to inter-religious encounters, and Christian faith and modern science. KRC actively publishes on its priority topics. Its publications have included a practical guide on legal matters for churches in Malaysia, addressing church building, propagation of the faith, and language issues; "Freedom of Religion in Malaysia"; and "Modernity in Malaysia: Christian Faithfulness".

NON-MUSLIMS SPEAK OUT

It is beneficial to listen to non-Muslim voices at this juncture and to understand how they are addressing what they see as the need for greater concern for issues of civil society. This section will consider how non-Muslims have responded to specific aspects of the Islamization efforts of both the UMNO-led federal government and the PAS state governments in Kelantan and Terengganu.

(a) Concerns Expressed

A key concern articulated by non-Muslim writers is marginalization of their communities under the impact of Islamization, and lack of official interest in their views. Robert Hunt speaks for Malaysian Christians in saying:

> Christians have felt systematically excluded from discussion and debate on Islamisation and its implications. Non-Muslim criticism, or even comment, on government policies promoting Islamisation has been regarded as highly offensive by Muslims, despite the fact that such policies impact the entire Malaysian society.[52]

The more conservative nature of the PAS approach does not mean that non-Muslims are necessarily pre-disposed towards the federal government's approach of inculcating Islamic values. Many non-Muslims see this policy as undermining non-Muslim faiths, and potentially laying the groundwork for a greater appeal of PAS rhetoric among Muslim voters in the future. Ng Kam Weng comments:

> Non-Muslims ... have for some years experienced painful restrictions on their own religious rights even under an UMNO led government. ... Is it any surprise that non-Muslims fearfully anticipate that PAS — with an even more narrow interpretation of Islam — can only make matters worse?[53]

A pervasive concern expressed by non-Muslims is that they are the victims of unfair policies which disadvantage religious minorities. This view is linked with specific policies. For instance, Paul Tan, former Director of the Catholic Research Centre and Past Secretary of MCCBCHS, argues that the insistence that all university students study the Islamic Civilization subject is unfair and discriminatory:

> If the intention of introducing the subject of Islamic Civilization was that the non-Muslims would come to understand Muslims better through

it, then for the same noble reason the Government should introduce a subject of other major religious civilizations so as to help the Muslims to understand the non-Muslims.[54]

Another key concern of non-Muslim writers is the polarization of the Malaysian community under the effect of Islamization and Islamic revivalism. Sadayandy Batumalai calls on the Barisan Nasional government to focus its concern for inculcating spiritual values on promoting all religions, not just Islam, in order to avoid creating "two types of communities in Malaysia; one spiritually oriented and the other materially oriented."[55] In a similar vein, Ng Kiok Nam warns:

> At the grassroots level, Islamic revivalism tends to make the Muslim community more and more self-contained. As a reaction, also non-Muslims place more emphasis on their identity and religion. As a result, a dangerous polarization along religious lines is occurring. Social interaction between Muslims and people of other religions, Christians included, is becoming more and more limited.[56]

Yet another concern expressed by Malaysian Christians was that their faith was seen as being a Western faith by Malaysian Muslims.[57] This is illustrated by Ahmad Yousif who comments on religious conversion in the following terms: "Many Malaysians who convert to Christianity readily give up their own culture, language and traditions in favour of Western culture, language and traditions".[58] Albert Walters says such a perception is curious, as "today the Christian Church in Malaysia is largely local in leadership, membership and finance".[59] A related problem arises from this, in that because of being perceived as adherents of an alien faith, Christians have tended to retreat into a ghetto mentality, resulting in lack of commitment towards engaging through their faith with the world around them.

A further matter of concern expressed is encapsulated by Brother Anthony Rogers who says:

> PAS Islamisation is definitely seen as more threatening for Christians than Barisan Nasional Islamisation. However I consider materialism and secularism to be even more threatening to the soul and the spirit. Many Christians only focus on the perceived threat of Islamisation and ignore the latter threat.[60]

(b) Solutions Proposed

Non-Muslims have not been content merely to point out areas of marginalization and discrimination felt by their communities. As part of the minority moves by religious minorities to become increasingly organized, community leaders have proposed specific solutions in order to address their concerns of the religious minorities.

Lobbying Government

Firstly, non-Muslims have become increasingly adept at lobbying government. For example, in response to the federal government prohibition on Christian use of terms deemed Islamic, CFM brought bishops from its member churches together in 1989 to draw up a letter to Prime Minister Mahathir which stated the following:

> It is inconceivable to us that the Bible in any translation can be regarded as a threat to national security in any country ... Nowhere else in the world, as we know, have people been forbidden to use words which are part of their National Language.[61]

Since its establishment, the CFM has actively lobbied the federal government, choosing appropriate times and contexts. On Malaysia's forty-fifth National Day, on 31 August 2002, a CFM press statement called on the government:

> to continue to act against attempts by some to misuse religion for domination and to assert apartness which has profoundly affected the delicate fabric of harmony in a multi-ethnic and multi-religious society.[62]

While many instances of lobbying the government have not produced the desired effect, there are areas where non-Muslim lobbying of government authorities has produced successful results. In January 1993 MCCBCHS representatives lobbied authorities in the state of Perak about plans to demolish forty-five houses of non-Muslim worship. The plans were stopped as a result of this meeting.[63] In another example of successful MCCBCHS lobbying, the group made strong representations to the authorities after the polemical South African Islamic preacher, Ahmed Deedat, was accused of ridiculing the Bible in a broadcast of "Islam Today" on the government-run state television in 1992. The programme was subsequently taken off the air as a result.[64]

The MCCBCHS is particularly well equipped to exert lobbying pressure, as it notionally speaks for a significant proportion of the 40 per cent non-Muslim minority of Malaysia's population. The group has not hesitated to exert such pressure. On 22 June 1988, the MCCBCHS issued the "Declaration on Freedom of Religion or Belief and on the Elimination of Intolerance and of Discrimination based on Religion and Belief",[65] as a response to increasing

Islamization in Malaysia. This six-page document includes a large number of specific requests relating to all the main areas of grievance of the religious minorities, with a summary in Article 1 paragraph 1:

> Everyone shall have the right to freedom of thought, conscience and religion. This right shall include freedom to have or to adopt or to change one's religion or belief of one's choice, and freedom, either individually or in community with others and in public or private, to manifest one's religion or belief in worship, observance, practice and teaching.[66]

On 10 April 1990, MCCBCHS leaders met with Dr. Mahathir and presented a memo listing non-Muslim grievances in detail.[67] In December of the same year, the MCCBCHS challenged the government over the arrest of non-Muslims in Sabah under the Internal Security Act (ISA).[68] Shortly after that the group challenged the Selangor Islamic Act permitting children under the age of eighteen to convert to Islam, even against the will of their parents.[69]

In January 2002, MCCBCHS issued an updated version of the *Declaration on Freedom of Religion or Belief and on the Elimination of Intolerance and of Discrimination based on Religion and Belief*, in response to Dr. Mahathir's statement that Malaysia was already an Islamic state.[70] This is a substantial statement, basing itself firmly on the United Nations declaration of freedom of religion, and providing a detailed list of where MCCBCHS considers UN guidelines should apply in Malaysia (implying that they are being contravened).

In fact, MCCBCHS lobbying of government has covered virtually all areas of grievance expressed by the religious minorities:

a. the hasty amendments to state constitutions on Islamic law affecting non-Muslims,

b. the plight of wives who are automatically divorced on conversion to Islam by their husbands and left stranded without maintenance,

c. the ban on using certain Islamic terms by non-Muslims,

d. the problems experienced by non-Muslims with the Immigration Department regarding visits for foreign priests and temple musicians, and

e. the question of religious education not given to non-Muslim school children in their school curriculum.[71]

Participation in the Political Process

Calls for increased participation in the political process have been issued by religious minority representative bodies and spokespeople. The MCCBCHS issued a press statement prior to the 1999 elections saying:

As citizens, it is our duty to vote. But we must vote wisely so that we will have leaders of integrity who can stand up for Truth and Justice. Only then will we have lasting peace and harmony. Hence we, citizens, must make sure that our representatives chosen by us in a democratic election process are persons who genuinely love Malaysia in all its variety of traditions and cultures. They must be leaders who will not try to force our people to conform, to one homogeneous culture, rejecting ... specific cultures, and to accept one religious system of Laws. They must be persons of integrity so that they are strong enough to denounce all corrupt practices.[72]

Similarly, the Christian Federation of Malaysia issued a press release prior to the 1999 national elections, urging Christians to vote on the basis of "how far views expressed and political programmes espoused meet with God's standards and Christian values". In a thinly veiled criticism of those candidates campaigning on a specifically Islamist platform, the CFM press statement expressed the hope that "the coming election campaign will be fair and that there will be no attempt by politicians to publicly misrepresent or miscast any particular religion, or, subject any particular religious community to unfair and adverse publicity for the purpose of political gain".[73]

Former politician Dato' Lew Sip Hon urged Christians to participate in politics in more specific terms. He called on Christians to do that through forming pressure groups; joining political parties; standing for parliament, especially for a party likely to win government; and forming a Christian political party.[74]

Such calls for greater Christian involvement in the political process mask the extent to which the Christian community operates as a ghetto. The NECF Malaysia Survey of Churches (2001) found that less than two per cent of Christians surveyed contacted a member of parliament or took some action on a public issue during the previous twelve-month period.

Engaging with Muslims

The degree to which Malaysian Christians exist within a ghetto was underlined by the NECF Malaysia Survey of Churches (2001), which found that 48 per cent of Christians surveyed rarely interacted with Muslims and 36 per cent of churches did not organize any activities that involved interaction with non-Christians in their neighbourhoods. On the average, churches surveyed spent only 8 per cent of budgets on social concern and community involvement, compared within 32 per cent on salaries and 23 per cent on building maintenance.[75]

This problem does not only exist for evangelical Christians in Malaysia. Catholic Archbishop Anthony Soter Fernandez, in his keynote address to the PMPC II in August 1996, pointed to a similar problem existing within the Catholic community:

> Why is there so much participation in sacrament and worship with so little commitment to living out the Gospel in our lives? … Has our Catholicism been one that observes certain religious practices and ceremonies without adequately understanding them, experiencing their reality, and living them out in daily life? We need to find out if our tepidity and our indifference and a lack of proper understanding of our evangelising mission has promoted an incoherent Christian life.[76]

Christian leaders point to inter-civilizational dialogue as a key instrument in engaging with the Muslim majority around them. The Catholic Church of Malaysia's Aggiornamento meeting in 1976 in Penang identified one of the pressing needs of the church as ecumenical and inter-religious dialogue. This was reinforced by PMPC I and II. The thrust of such calls was directed towards practical issues: "Inter-religious dialogue has no meaning if it is purely a theoretical or academic exercise … Primarily a dialogue of life stems from the shared values taught by the different religions and not from theological positions which can be both technical and divisive".[77]

In response to the Catholic Church's evolving policy, St. Francis Xavier Parish in Kuala Lumpur launched the "Movement for Interfaith Enhancement" in 1999, with meetings with other faiths devoted to topics such as "Islam and Buddhism's attitude towards other religions" (April 1999), and "Islam and Hinduism's Attitude towards Justice and Peace" (August 1999). A course on "Understanding World Religions" was organized as a joint dialogue initiative by St. Francis Xavier Church and the Interfaith Spiritual Fellowship from 13 February–10 April 2002. It was attended by eighty-three participants from various faiths: Muslim, Buddhist, Christian, Hindu, Confucianist, Taoist, and Sikh. The group studied dialogue and listening skills and methods, enjoyed fellowship together, and visited different worship houses. St Francis Xavier Parish is acting as a catalyst to involve other parishes in such inter-civilizational dialogue.

To enhance this rapidly developing dialogue process, the Catholic Archdiocese of Kuala Lumpur established an Archdiocesan Ecumenical and Inter-Religious Department (AEID) in order to create an awareness among Catholics of the world of ecumenism and inter-religious dialogue, recognizing that "Catholics at large need to be aware of the need to know and to understand another's religion so that whatever biases, misconceptions or fears one has when talking of another religion will be put on rest".[78]

The Malaysian churches' commitment to inter-civilizational dialogue with other faiths is also expressed on the website of the Council of Churches of Malaysia in the following terms: "Being a Christian community in a multi-religious Malaysia demands that the churches keep all channels of communication open and through dialogue with the government and others, to resolve issues and build religious harmony".[79]

Some Christian writers express concerns about Muslim willingness to dialogue. Ng Kam Weng writes that: "Muslim scholars are only interest in pursuing a dialogue with Western Christians rather than local Christians… because Dialogue with local Christians… confers legitimacy on local Christian Movements".[80]

The Anglican scholar Sadayandy Batumalai questions government commitment to dialogue, noting that "Despite lack of much encouragement from the government, dialogue has continued informally".[81] Similarly, Catholic Archbishop Emeritus in Kuala Lumpur Tan Sri Vendargon, writing in the mid-1990s, commented that "there is very little dialogue with Muslims. The Christian churches are working only among non-Muslims in Malaysia".[82]

However, there are instances where Muslims take the initiative to interact with non-Muslims. For example, the International Islamic University of Malaysia (IIUM) requested that a group of forty of its students from the Department of Comparative Religions visit the Assumption Catholic Church in Petaling Jaya, Kuala Lumpur, on 19 May 2002. The visitors attended a full mass in the morning, mingled with Assumption Church worshippers during refreshments, and then joined in a question and answer session. A Muslim spokesperson expressed a hope that this would become a regular semester event for IIUM students.[83]

Some Christians indicate that Muslim interest in interfaith dialogue has noticeably increased since the terrorist attacks in America on 11 September 2001 and the prime minister's statement regarding the Islamic state.[84] However, the general consensus among Christians is well expressed by the following NECF statement: "Though dialogues at local and national levels have been convened, much remains to be done to create a more permanent and stable climate that is conducive to religious harmony."[85] For such dialogue activities to be effective, Ng Kam Weng warns against a selective approach in seeking dialogue partners, and calls on Christians to "dialogue with social and political activists who differ with us, whether they come from UMNO or PAS".[86]

Contextualizing the Faith

Church leaders articulate another urgent need facing the Church in Malaysia in overcoming its being perceived as an alien implant. Council of Churches leaders comment that "the Church has great difficulty knowing how to portray its identity in a way which is Malaysian, especially in West Malaysia where Christians are non-Bumiputera".[87] Brother Anthony Rogers of the Catholic Church suggests that "The Church needs to rediscover the Asian roots of Christianity. This is key to incarnation and inculturation."[88] Albert Walters says that "the challenge remains for the churches to relate themselves more fully to the soil of [Southeast Asia] — to get down to the rice-roots level of Asian civilization".[89]

The Jesuit Priest Jojo M. Fung demonstrates this concern to contextualize Christianity into the Malaysian context. In an article in the *East Asian Pastoral Review*, Fung discusses four everyday Malaysian practices: *tea tarik*, *gotong royong*, *pakai tangan*, *kaki ayam*, and explains the symbolism of each of these terms. He then reinterprets them into a Christian context, and proceeds to link the symbolism of these Malaysian terms with the symbolism of the Christian faith; for example, *gotong royong* is seen as "a symbol which points to an ever-creative God who continues to collaborate with humankind in the ongoing process of co-creation".[90]

In another article, Fung presents suggestions for interfaith worship which take account of local custom and culture:

> Light emitting from the different kind of lamps and candles, the different sacred texts as normative guides for the different believers, waters for cleansing and blessing, even incense can be used as religious symbols in a common worship. Adherents can come in cultural and national costumes to express our ethnic and cultural diversity. This worship can culminate in a fellowship where a variety of cakes and dishes can be served so that believers mingle freely to enhance and deepen the spirit of solidarity.[91]

Albert Walters takes up the challenge which he himself levelled at the church. He presents a case for Christian liturgy having been "transported to but not transplanted in" Malaysia; in other words, he considers the liturgy of Malaysian churches as largely a left-over of the colonial era. He calls for the Christian doctrine of the Trinity to be reconsidered, arguing that while central Trinitarian tenets should not be discarded, the presence of a neighbouring Muslim majority should encourage Christians to contextualize their understanding and methods of articulation of the Trinity in their dealings with Muslims. He argues that this will facilitate greater multi-faith harmony and better Christian-Muslim relations, and will also assist Christians to better grasp the import of the Trinitarian doctrine themselves. Walters works towards a "Trinity from below" formula. He draws on two images which are integral to the Malaysian cultural environment: hospitality and friendship — which he relates to God's friendship with humankind through Jesus[92] — and the fruit-bearing banana tree, which he sees as symbolizing "a fruit-bearing and self-giving Christian in the community".[93]

Christian representative bodies are also addressing this challenge to contextualize. In an effort to break down linguistic barriers within the Christian community and between Christians and others, NECF has developed a specialized Bahasa Malaysia Ministry in order "to encourage English speaking churches to start at least 200 BM speaking congregations in Peninsular Malaysia by the year 2000".[94] Similarly, the Catholic Church organized a meeting on ministering in Bahasa Malaysia on 21 July 2002. The church aims for more masses in Malay, as well as retreats and faith formation programmes in Malay for those Catholic worshippers lacking fluency in English.[95]

Undertaking Advocacy and Apologetics

Finally, Christian writers are increasingly engaging in advocacy and apologetics in multiple forums, to more assertively defend what they see as threats to the faith of the Christian minority.

There have been increasing calls in recent years for the establishment of a government-sponsored and recognized Interfaith Council. Bishop Antony Selvanayagam, head of the Commission for Ecumenism and Interreligious Affairs of the Catholic Church, said such a council would "pave the way for a 'civilized dialogue' between different religions and cultures".[96] In similar fashion, MCCBCHS Past President Anthony Soter Fernandez presented a Memorandum to the Commission on Human Rights (SUHAKAM) on 8 April 2002, entitled "Problems faced by Non-Muslims in Freely Professing and Practising their Respective Religions". This memorandum called for Inter-religious Councils to be established by statute at both state and federal levels. The meeting was also attended by the Malaysian Department of Islamic Development (JAKIM) and the Association of Muslim Scholars of Malaysia.[97]

Robert Hunt observes that "anti-Christian polemical works are commonly found in Muslim bookstores and anti-Christian comment is allowed in the context of larger presentations of Muslim theological concerns". This situation has produced a felt need among some Christians to respond. Ng Kam Weng and Paul Tan have each developed a specifically Malaysian apologetic for

Christianity to respond to Muslim theological criticisms, the former from an evangelical perspective, and the latter from a liberal perspective.[98] In a related incident, the Council of Churches of Malaysia issued a press statement condemning misuse of Christian symbols in the 2002 by-election campaigning in Pendang and Anak Bukit: "To depict the Prime Minister as '*paderi besar gereja*' is not only distasteful but also hurtful to Christians, as it not only shows insensitiveness on the part of those who have resorted to such election tactics, but also politicizes religious differences".[99]

In an attempt to translate words into action, Ng Kam Weng called on Christians "to join organizations that call for transparency in political and corporate governance. In particular set up educational institutions that help Christians develop a public philosophy that supports pluralistic democracy. I call upon Christian lawyers and journalists to be more socially engaged".[100]

THE ISLAMIC STATE DEBATE

The most active area of advocacy among non-Muslim circles in 2001–02 related to the Islamic state debate which was triggered by two factors: PAS Islamic legislation in Kelantan and Terengganu, and Prime Minister Mahathir's October 2001 declaration, in response to PAS calls for Malaysia to be an Islamic state, that it was already one.

Non-Muslim writers articulated the sense of alarm within their communities. An editorial in the Christian periodical *Berita NECF* picked up on this:

> PAS' public declaration of its intent to set up an Islamic state should it come into power has once again sent jitters through the non-Muslim community... The resurgence, consolidation and expansion of Islam is expected to continue irrespective of whichever party is in control, an alarming trend to communities of other religious faiths. Generally, the Government is of the view that religious freedom — as enshrined in our federal constitution — is a pre-requisite for national harmony and integration. In reality, however, the practice is not consistent with this view.[101]

On 31 January 2002, Anthony Soter Fernandez, Archbishop of the Catholic Diocese of Kuala Lumpur, issued a press statement as President of MCCBCHS in response to the prime minister's statement. He too based his arguments upon the Malaysian Constitution:

> ... the [Constitutional] position of Islam being the religion of the Federation shall not imply that Malaya and Malaysia is not a secular

state. In other words, Malaya and Malaysia is a secular state... The Constitution of our country provides that the Constitution is the supreme law of the country and any law passed which is inconsistent with the Constitution shall to the extent of the inconsistency be void. In 1988, we deemed it necessary to come out with a declaration. More than thirteen years later, we are of the view the situation has become worse and therefore find it appropriate to reiterate our stand and urge the federal and all State governments to respect the rights of every person to freedom of religion and recognise that Malaysia is constitutionally a secular state.[102]

The Christian Federation of Malaysia issued a press statement on the prime minister's statement regarding the Islamic state, stating in clear terms that "the assurances by the Prime Minister and Barisan Nasional leaders that the constitution will not be tampered with do not offer sufficient guarantee that Malaysia will not degenerate into something of the Islamic model which PAS is promoting. Rhetoric may lead to reality".[103]

In this statement, the CFM offered a seven-point proposal for government consideration, calling for a government instrument to monitor misrepresentation of Islamic policy, a parliamentary commission and officer to check and report on abuse of religious rights, introduction of a Religious Liberty Law, establishment of a Religious Harmony Commission, a Declaration of Religious Freedom (also to be included in the National Education Curriculum), appointment of a cabinet minister responsible for non-Muslim affairs and rights, and the achievement of a more representative civil service.

The *Catholic Asian News* called for a national referendum to decide whether an Islamic state or secular state was the preferred model among Malaysians.[104] A meeting of Catholic archbishops and bishops in Johor in July 2002 issued a statement clearly linking the effects of the prime minister's statement and PAS policies:

> We ... view with alarm and grave concern the recent developments in the country with the statement [by Dr. Mahathir] that Malaysia is already a model Islamic State and [PAS] passing of the *Shari'a* Criminal Offences (*Hudud* and *Qisas*) Bill ... and the increasing trend of politicising Islam in the political arena.[105]

The peak representative body for Malaysian non-Muslims, MCCBCHS, was similarly far from silent on the Islamic state debate. It issued a press release on 20 July 2002 following the passing of the Shari'a Criminal Offences (*Hudud* and *Qisas*) Bill by the Terengganu Legislative Assembly, stating that "the bill is an alarming attempt by the state to change the character of our country, which is multi-racial, multi-religious and constitutionally secular".

Christian responses have also included the holding of meetings and seminars to discuss their concerns, a sign of developing civil society among Malaysian non-Muslims. In July 2001 NECF organized a forum of fifty leading Christians, who issued a unanimous call for the Malaysian Constitution to be upheld and defended "to ensure the continuance of religious freedom, a right which has been continually threatened by calls for an Islamic state". Universiti Malaya law lecturer Dr. Khoo Boo Teong said at this forum: "Unless orthodox *shari'a* can be reformed, the treatment of non-Muslims will always be a major stumbling block in enabling the *shari'a* to be consonant with the definitions of Rule of Law today and into the twenty-first century".[106]

The Catholic Research Centre organized a closed-door forum in late 2001, on the topic "Is Malaysia an Islamic State?"[107] Speakers included Lim Kit Siang, Chairman of the opposition Democratic Action Party, PAS Vice-President Dr. Hasan Ali, and Anuar Razak from IKIM. It was held at St. Francis Xavier's Church, and was attended by 600 people from various faiths. Kairos Research Centre organized a public forum on 10 January 2002 at which Philip Koh, Kairos Director, argued that the prime minister's statement had no foundation. He based himself on the Malaysian Constitution, unpacking in great detail constitutional provisions that supported his case; legal precedent, quoting several cases in support of his arguments; and official memoranda, indicating a widespread view that the state should be seen as a secular state, notwithstanding the definition of Islam as the official religion.[108]

In parallel with activities organized by other Christian groups, the Council of Churches of Malaysia organized a panel discussion on "Islamic State — Where Do We Go From Here?" at Luther House in Petaling Jaya on 19 March 2002. Speakers included Dr. Chandra Muzaffar, the Muslim Director of JUST World Trust, who urged non-Muslims to speak out on the issue "as it involves the fundamental human right of freedom of expression" but recommended against "projecting the secular state concept" as Muslims were uneasy with the idea of secularism.[109] In concert with such events organized by the national body, regional committees of CCM moved to respond to the Islamic state debate. For example, the Perak Regional Committee planned a forum for late October 2002 to discuss the Islamic state issue.[110]

CONCLUSION

Our exploration of the Malaysian scene in previous pages suggests that Malaysian religious minorities tend to regard Islamization as a continuum.

The federal government's emphasis on inculcation of Islamic values and the PAS opposition's more strident campaigning for the implementation of a literalist understanding of Islamic Law are seen by religious minorities as two parts of the same process. The statements by Prime Minister Mahathir about Malaysia already being an Islamic state have sent shock waves through religious minority communities. These concerns are amplified by continuing moves by PAS state governments to pass Islamic legislation. The religious minorities are increasingly doubting the federal government's stated commitment to a religiously pluralist and secular state.

This environment of Islamization has resulted in a dramatic contribution by the minorities themselves to civil society. All major religious minority groups have voluntarily come together to shore up their position in society. They are doing this through both the formation of non-government advocacy groups and a much more outspoken, activist contribution to public debate. Within the Christian community, government Islamization policies in their various forms have triggered a process whereby Christians are finally making progress in their long-state aim of overcoming internal disunity. These effects, unanticipated on the part of government, will likely continue if the struggle to define the form of Islamization within the Malaysian Muslim community causes an increasing spiralization in Islamization policies.

Notes

1   "Malaysia Census Shows Minorities Dwindling", *The Straits Times Interactive*, 8 November 2001.
2   Quoted in Ng Kiok Nam, "Islam in Malaysia", in *Islam in Asia: Perspectives for Christian-Muslim Encounter*, edited by J.P. Rajashekar and H.S. Wilson, Geneva: Lutheran World Federation, 1992, p. 97.
3   Ahmad F. Yousif, *Religious Freedom, Minorities and Islam. An Inquiry into the Malaysian Experience*, Selangor: Thinker's Library, 1998, p. 83.
4   Ibid., p. 109.
5   There are reports that between 1994 and mid-1997, over 11,000 Malaysian non-Muslims converted to Islam. Cf. "Anti-Conversion Bill in Final Stages", <www.pbi.ab.ca/servant/Archive/1999Win/anti.conversionbillinfinalstages.htm>, copied July 2002.
6   Mohammad Hashim Kamali, *Islamic Law in Malaysia. Issues and Developments*, Kuala Lumpur: Ilmiah Publishers, 2000, p. 30.
7   Philip Koh, "Does the Federal Constitution Support an Islamic or Secular State?", paper presented at Kairos Public Forum, Kairos Research Centre, Kuala Lumpur, 10 January 2002, p. 7.
8   Cited in Foong, Lim Siew "What Makes an Islamic State", *Berita NECF* November/December 2001, p. 3.

9   "Malaysia Seeks Views from Cairo on Islamic State", MSNBC News/Reuters, 24 October 2001.

10 "Mahathir: Malaysia is 'Fundamentalist State' ", <CNN.com>, 18 June 2002.

11 Father Laurence Andrew in interview with the author, Xavier Hall, Petaling Jaya, 29 August 2002.

12 Salmah Mat Hussin, *"Jadikan Al-Quran asas Kemajuan Sains — Nik Aziz"*, <HarakahDaily.com>, 27 July 2001.

13 "Hardline Islamic Opposition Presents New Challenge to Mahathir", AFP, 25 March 2002.

14 Murray Hiebert, "Required Lessons", *Far Eastern Economic Review*, 160/29, 17 July 1997, p. 22.

15 "Christian Mission Schools in Sarawak Concerned about Their Future", *Herald, the Catholic Weekly*, 25August 2002, p. 3; Ahmad F. Yousif, *Religious Freedom, Minorities and Islam. An Inquiry into the Malaysian Experience*, Selangor: Thinker's Library, 1998, pp. 94–95, 178–79.

16 M. Nash, "Islamic Resurgence in Malaysia and Indonesia", in *Fundamentalism Observed*, edited by M.E. Marty, Chicago: Univ. of Chicago, 1991, p. 714.

17 Mohammad Hashim Kamali, *Islamic Law in Malaysia. Issues and Developments*, Kuala Lumpur: Ilmiah Publishers, 2000, p. 9.

18 PAS had previously held power in Kelantan from 1959 to 1978.

19 Roger Mitton, "Inside Story Malaysia. Return to Islam", *Asiaweek*, 7 June 1996.

20 PAS authorities in Kelantan announced at the time that non-Muslims could choose whether the *Hudud* Bill should apply to them or not. M.H. Kamali points out that such a choice itself runs counter to the *Shari'a*, and would potentially prove discriminatory *vis-à-vis* Muslims. Mohammad Hashim Kamali, *Punishment in Islamic Law. An Enquiry into the Hudud Bill of Kelantan*, Petaling Jaya: Ilmiah Publishers, 1995, pp. 18–21.

21 Eight liquor shops were left open to cater to non-Muslims.

22 *Bernama*, 20 March 2000.

23 Francis Harrison, "Malaysian State Swaps Tourism for Morality", *The Guardian*, 21 April 2000.

24 "Hadi Tables *Shari'a* Criminal (*Hudud*) Bill", *Utusan Online*, 8 July 2001.

25 *The Star*, 9 July 2002, p. 5.

26 Quoted in Ng Kiok Nam, op. cit., p. 100.

27 Documents relating to the debate surrounding this issue are available on the website of the *Pahlawan.com* advocacy group. Cf. "Why Guidelines Will Destroy Harmony" and "MCCBCHS' Alternative Guidelines", *Harmoni* 2000, <http://www.pahlawan.com.my/harmoni/>, copied 1 August 2002. However, at a meeting between MCCBCHS and the Minister of Housing and Local Government on 15 February 2000, the Minister said that this document was never approved by his Ministry. Cf. *Harmoni 2/2*, March 2000, p. 6.

28 "Editorial. Let's Dialogue", *Catholic Asian News*, September 1999, p. 1.

29 S. Batumalai, *Islamic Resurgence and Islamization in Malaysia*, Ipoh: Charles Grenier, 1996, pp. 262, 270.

30 *The New Christian Herald*, 15 March 1997; Mohammad Hashim Kamali, *Islamic Law in Malaysia. Issues and Developments*, Kuala Lumpur: Ilmiah Publishers, 2000, pp. 185–86.

31 Brother Anthony Rogers in interview with the author, National Office for Human Development, Kuala Lumpur, 29 August 2002.

32 "Islamization on Campus", *Asiaweek*, 16 June 2000.

33 "Objections to Image of Jesus", *Catholic Asian News*, March 2002, p. 5.

34 Mohamad Abu Bakar, "Islam, Civil Society, and Ethnic Relations in Malaysia", in *Islam & Civil Society in Southeast Asia*, edited by Nakamura Mitsuo, Sharon Siddique and Omar Farouk Bajunid, Singapore: Institute of Southeast Asian Studies, 2001, pp. 69–70.

35 John C. England, "The Earliest Christian Communities in South East Asia and North East Asia", *East Asian Pastoral Review* 25, no. 2 (1988): 145.

36 Anne Ruck, *Sejarah Gereja Asia*, Jakarta: Gunung Mulia, 1997, p. 216.

37 *1998 Catholic Almanac: Our Sunday Visitor*, USA (1997), pp. 333–67, cited at <http://www.adherents.com/adhloc/Wh_192.html#463>, copied 9 August 2002. These figures are disputed, with some writers arguing that Catholics constitute over half of the Malaysian Christian community. Cf. Ahmad F. Yousif, *Religious Freedom, Minorities and Islam. An Inquiry into the Malaysian Experience*, Selangor: Thinker's Library, 1998, p. 84.

38 "Our Journey as Church in Peninsular Malaysia", <http://www.catholic.org.sg/web_links/AVE/pmpc/pmpc1.html>, copied 22 May 2002.

39 <http://www.archway.org.my/>, copied 1 August 2002.

40 A.S. Walters, *We Believe in One God? Reflections on the Trinity in the Malaysian Context*, Delhi: ISPCK, 2002, p. 54.

41 <http://www.newwomen.net/affiliates/ccm/CCMALAYSIA/ccm/objectives_of_ccm.htm>, copied 24 July 2002.

42 A.S. Walters, op. cit., p. 40.

43 Ng Kam Weng in interview with the author, Kairos Research Centre, Petaling Jaya, 6 September 2002.

44 "Introduction to MCCBCHS", <http://www.mybuddhist.com/public_html/Chi/FourReligion/FourReligion_C-10%20Introduction.htm>, copied 1 August 2002.

45 Olaf Schumann, Christians and Muslims in Search of Common Ground in Malaysia", *Islam and Christian-Muslim Relations*, 2, no. 2 (December 1991): 256.

46 "Introduction to MCCBCHS", <http://www.mybuddhist.com/public_html/Chi/FourReligion/FourReligion_C-10%20Introduction.htm>, 1 August 2002.

47 Fr. Philip Thomas and Dr. John Gurusamy in interview with the author, Syrian Orthodox Church, Kuala Lumpur, 30 August 2002.

48 *Berita NECF* January/February 2002, p. 1.

49 "Constitution of Persekutuan Kristen Malaysia/ The Christian Federation of Malaysia", Selangor, January 1986, p. 2.
50 Brother Augustine Julian in interview with the author, Xavier Hall, Petaling Jaya, 30 August 2002.
51 Fr. Philip Thomas and Dr. John Gurusamy in interview with the author, Syrian Orthodox Church, Kuala Lumpur, 30 August 2002.
52 Robert Hunt, "Christian Theological Reflection and Education in the Muslim Societies of Malaysia and Indonesia", *Studies in World Christianity* 3, no. 2 (1997): 215.
53 Ng Kam Weng, "A Christian Case for Pluralist Democracy", paper presented at Kairos Public Forum, Kairos Research Centre, Kuala Lumpur, 10 January 2002, p. 2.
54 Ghazali Basri, *Christian Mission and Islamic Dakwah in Malaysia*, Kuala Lumpur, Nurin Enterprise, 1990, p. 32.
55 S. Batumalai, op. cit., p. 134.
56 Ng Kiok Nam, op. cit., p. 103.
57 Y. Hwa, "Vision 2020 and Theological Education in Malaysia", in *Christian Response to Vision 2020*, edited by Hwa, S.W., Persatuan Penulis-Penulis Kristian Malaysia, 1993, p. 26.
58 Ahmad F. Yousif, op. cit., p. 84.
59 A.S. Walters, op. cit., p. 41.
60 Brother Anthony Rogers in interview with the author, National Office for Human Development, Kuala Lumpur, 29 August 2002.
61 Olaf Schumann, "Christians and Muslims in Search of Common Ground in Malaysia", *Islam and Christian-Muslim Relations* 2, no. 2 (December 1991): 258.
62 "National Day message of the Christian Federation of Malaysia", *Herald, the Catholic Weekly*, 1 September 2002, p. 10.
63 "Report on the Meeting with the Perak Menteri Besar", MCCBCHS Press Statement, <http://www.mybuddhist.com/public_html/Chi/FourReligion/FourReligion_C-10-C%20Report.htm>, copied 1 August 2002.
64 Cf. *Harmoni* 1/5 (May 1992); "Introduction to MCCBCHS", <http://www.mybuddhist.com/public_html/Chi/FourReligion/FourReligion_C-10%20Introduction.htm>, copied 1 August 2002.
65 Resulting from a seminar at Cardijn House, Kuala Lumpur, 22 June 1988.
66 *Declaration on Freedom of Religion or Belief and on the Elimination of Intolerance and of Discrimination based on Religion and Belief*, 1988, p. 2.
67 "Our Meeting with the Prime Minister", MCCBCHS Press Statement, <http://www.mybuddhist.com/public_html/Chi/FourReligion/FourReligion_C-10-C%20Our.htm>, copied 1 August 2002.
68 Olaf Schumann, op. cit., p. 256; S. Batumalai, op. cit., pp. 139–40.
69 Olaf Schumann, ibid.; "Religious Leaders Protest Over Conversion of Minors to Islam", MCCBCHS Press Statement, <http://www.mybuddhist.com/public_html/Chi/FourReligion/FourReligion_C-10-B%20Religious.htm>, copied 1 August 2002.

70 "A Declaration on Freedom of Religion or Belief & Elimination of Intolerance and of Discrimination Based on Religion or Belief (January 2002)", <http://www.mybuddhist.com/public_html/Chi/FourReligion/FourReligion_Declaration-2002.htm>, copied 1 August 2002.

71 "Introduction to MCCBCHS", <http://www.mybuddhist.com/public_html/Chi/FourReligion/FourReligion_C-10%20Introduction.htm>, copied 1 August 2002.

72 "General Elections Message", <http://www.mybuddhist.com/public_html/Chi/FourReligion/FourReligion_C-10-A%20General.htm>, copied 1 August 2002.

73 Christian Federation of Malaysia Press Release, <http://www.ccmalaysia.org/netscape/press/press2.htm>, copied 20 May 2002. I have corrected linguistic flaws in the English language of the internet version of the press release, without making any change to meaning.

74 Hon Lew Sip, "Christians and Political Realities", *Berita NECF* September/October 2001, pp. 4–5, 14.

75 Edmund Ng, "A Post-Survey Analysis: Towards Greater Community Involvement", *Berita NECF* March/April 2002, p. 11.

76 Anthony Soter Fernandez, "Our Journey as Church in Peninsular Malaysia toward the Third Millennium", <http://www.catholic.org.sg/web_links/AVE/pmpc/key.html>, copied 22 May 2002.

77 Rufus Bruno Pereira, "What is the Dialogue of Life?", *Catholic Asian News*, August 2002, p. 5.

78 <http://www.archway.org.my/dir/depart.htm>, copied 29 July 2002.

79 <http://www.ccmalaysia.org/netscape/events/past1.htm>, copied 20 May 2002.

80 Ng Kam Weng, "Dialogue and Constructive Social Engagement: Problems and Prospects for the Malaysian Church", *Trinity Theological Journal* 5 (1995): 32.

81 S. Batumalai, op. cit., p. 145.

82 Ibid., p. 144.

83 "Announcements — 19 May 2002", The Assumption Church, Petaling Jaya, <http://www.rc.net/kualalumpur/assumption/bulletin/bulletin.htm>, copied 24 May 2002. Linda Archibald, "Muslim students attend Pentecost Mass", *Herald, the Catholic Weekly*, 2 June 2002, p. 3.

84 Ng Kam Weng in interview with the author, Kairos Research Centre, Petaling Jaya, 6 September 2002; Fr. Philip Thomas and Dr. John Gurusamy in interview with the author, Syrian Orthodox Church, Kuala Lumpur, 30 August 2002.

85 "Rising Religious Activism. Ready to Respond", *Berita NECF* September/October 2001, p. 1.

86 Ng Kam Weng, op. cit., p. 3.

87 Fr. Philip Thomas and Dr. John Gurusamy in interview with the author, Syrian Orthodox Church, Kuala Lumpur, 30 August 2002.

88 Brother Anthony Rogers in interview with the author, National Office for Human Development, Kuala Lumpur, 29 August 2002.

89 A.S. Walters, op. cit., p. 57.

90 Jojo M. Fung, S.J. "Faith: A Malaysian Perspective", *East Asian Pastoral Review* 38, no. 1 (2001): 90.

91 Jojo M. Fung S.J., "Many Faiths, One Family", *Catholic Asian News*, August 2001, p. 8

92 A.S. Walters, op. cit., 267ff.

93 Ibid., 275ff.

94 <http://www.necf.org.my/html/ministry_f.htm>, copied 20 May 2002.

95 "Ministering to Bumis and Others Who Speak Malay", *Herald, the Catholic Weekly*, 4 August 2002, p. 3.

96 "Call to Establish Interfaith Council in Malaysia", *Herald, the Catholic Weekly*, 23 June 2002, p. 1.

97 Herman Shastri, "Suhakam Initiates Dialogue between Islam and MCCBCHS", *Herald, the Catholic Weekly*, 28 April 2002, p. 1.

98 Robert Hunt, "Christian Theological Reflection and Education in the Muslim Societies of Malaysia and Indonesia", *Studies in World Christianity* 3, no. 2 (1997): 217; cf. also Ng Kiok Nam, op. cit., p. 103.

99 *CCM Newslink*, July 2002.

100 Ng Kam Weng, "A Christian Case for Pluralist Democracy", op. cit., p. 3.

101 "Rising Religious Activism. Ready to Respond", *Berita NECF* September/October 2001, p. 1.

102 "Declaration on Freedom of Religion", Press Statement, <http://www.archway.org.my/>, copied 1 August 2002.

103 "Christian Federation of Malaysia's (CFM) Stand and Proposal", *Catholic Asian News*, March 2002, p. 14. This statement represents an excerpt from the MCCBCHS Memo to the Deputy Prime Minister of 10 December 2001.

104 "Editorial", *Catholic Asian News*, March 2002, p. 2.

105 "Declaration of Catholic Bishops of Malaysia on the Freedom of Religion", *Herald, the Catholic Weekly*, 11 August 2002, p. 9.

106 "Defend Constitution to Protect Religious Freedom", *Berita NECF* September/October 2001, pp. 3–4.

107 It was reported in detail in the March 2002 issue of *Catholic Asian News*.

108 Philip Koh, "Does the Federal Constitution Support an Islamic or Secular State?", paper presented at Kairos Public Forum, Kairos Research Centre, Kuala Lumpur, 10 January 2002, p. 6.

109 Terrence Netto, "Participate in debate on Islamic State", *Herald, the Catholic Weekly*, 31 March 2002, p. 24.

110 *CCM Newslink*, August 2002.

10

ISLAM AND GENDER: READING EQUALITY AND PATRIARCHY

Lily Zakiyah Munir

"Women have always been the best friends of religion,
but religion has generally not been a friend of women."
(Moriz Winternitz, a German Indologist)

INTRODUCTION

The above remark is cited by Annemarie Schimmel in her foreword to *The Tao of Islam* (Murata 1992, vii). Winternitz's observation is particularly evident when put in the context of Islam, as Schimmel contends that "it is certainly easier to look only at the surface ... of polygamy and easy divorce and ... *purdah* ... than to try to see the more positive sides of Islam". Muslims have been exposed with various gender-biased discourses and stereotypes, such as women not having equal rights as men or not allowed to be involved in their own religious matters, that negative images of Islam will more immediately capture people's attention than otherwise when talking about Islam and women.

WOMEN IN PRE-ISLAMIC ARABIAN PENINSULA

Two verses which can be cited to explain the mission of God in revealing the Qur'an and in creating human beings are Surah al-Anbiya' (21:107).[1] "We sent thee not, but as a mercy for all creatures", and Surah al-Hujurat (49:13)

"O mankind! We created you from a single (pair) of a male and female, and made you into nations and tribes, that you may know each other (not that you may despise each other). Verily the most honoured of you in the sight of Allah is (one who is) the most righteous of you."[2]

To appropriately understand the Qur'an's treatment of women and gender, and therefore to appreciate its revolutionary breakthrough for women's liberation and empowerment, it is important that one observe the socio-cultural and historical context of its revelation. The reason is obvious, as noted by Engineer (1992, p. 20), that "no revolution, political or religious (and Islam was indeed a socio-religious revolution), can remove all traces of the past". Continuity is always there and it is this continuity which maintains relationship with the past. A total breaking from the past, however hard it is attempted, may not be possible. Similarly, the history of Islam also reveals that whatever was reformed or prohibited by the Prophet Muhammad that prevailed during the period of *jahiliyya* (ignorance) in the advent of Islam, crept back into Islamic *shari'a* through *adat* (that is, pre-Islamic traditional practices). In fact, in many cases, the *shari'a* provisions were based on the *adat* in the absence of other provisions (Engineer 1992, p. 20).

What was the status of women in pre-Islamic society? Was it better or worse than in the Islamic period? History notes that during the period of ignorance (*jahiliyya*) at the Arabian Peninsula, women enjoyed no rights whatsoever and were treated no better than a commodity. Women were enslaved and could be inherited as a possession. The Qur'an prohibited this practice as depicted in Surah al-Nisa' (4:19): "O ye who believe! Ye are forbidden to inherit women against their will, nor should ye treat them with harshness".

The Qur'an also mentions that to the Arabs in *jahiliyya* the birth of a baby girl was a shame to them (Surah al-Nahl, 16:58–59). Condemning the evil practice of the killing of female children by pre-Islamic Bedouin Arabs, the Qur'an reminds the perpetrators of female infanticide that on the Day of Judgement, when "the female (in fact) buried alive, is questioned for what crimes she was killed" (Surah al-Takwir, 81:8–9), they will have to answer to God for their heinous crime. The motive of this barbaric practice of burying baby girls alive seemed to be twofold (Asad in Engineer 1992, p. 21): the fear that an increase in female offspring would result in economic burdens, as well as the fear of the humiliation caused by girls captured by a hostile tribe and subsequently preferring their captors to their parents and brothers. The Prophet shows his defence for the baby girls and greatly improves the status of women by saying that one to whom a daughter is born and who does not bury her alive, does not humiliate her, nor prefers a son to a daughter, will be sent by Allah to paradise.³ The Prophet also says that hell-fire is prohibited to one who has to go through trials and tribulation due to a daughter and yet does not hate her and behaves well to her.⁴

During *jahiliyya* there was no restriction on the number of wives a man could have. Tribal chiefs and leaders had many wives in order to establish familial relationships for political alliances to minimize tribal competition and attacks. The noted commentator of the Qur'an, Imam Al-Tabari (in Engineer 1992, p. 21) mentions that a person belonging to the tribe of Quraysh on average married ten wives. There were people who married four, five, six, or even ten women and asked who could stop him from marrying more than the others. There were instances from pre-Islamic period of the then trend of men marrying hundreds or tens of women. The Qur'an ended this practice in its verse:

> And if you have reason to fear that you might not act equitably towards orphans, then marry from among (other) women such as are lawful to you—two, or three, or four; but if you have reason to fear that you might not be able to treat them with equal fairness, then (only) one. (Surah al-Nisa', 4:3)

Thus the permission to marry more than one and up to four wives must be seen in this context. It was a drastic reduction of the number of wives one could take. However, this is just one possible justification — there are other justifications related to widowhood and orphans due to wars, which will be discussed later in this paper in the part on polygamy. But they are all contextual justifications and not a normative one and, hence, its applicability must be seen as contextual and not universal. When the verse was revealed the Prophet advised many who had more than four wives to opt for the four and divorce the rest. Thus it could be inferred that Islam did not encourage the marrying of more than one wife. On the contrary, Islam discouraged it, restricted it and conditionally allows up to four wives in the then prevailing situation.

THE QUR'AN AND EQUALITY

That God's creation as a whole is "for just ends" (Surah al-Hijr, 15:85) and not "for idle sport" (Surah al-Anbiya', 21:16) is one of the major themes of the Qur'an. A special favour God has blessed the humanity who has been shaped "in the best of moulds" (Surah al-Tin, 95:4) is that God has created mates for men and women and these mates are intended as a source of mutual love, peace and fulfilment (Surah al-A'raf, 7:189; Q.S. al-Rum, 21:21).

The most revolutionary of the Qur'an's teachings, which constitutes the basic nature of sexual equality in Islam and which undermines the notions of radical differences and hierarchy between the sexes, is related with the origin and nature of human creation. As the Qur'an describes it, man and woman, although biologically different, are "ontologically and ethically-morally the same/similar inasmuch as both women and men originated in single Self, have been endowed with the same natures, and make up two halves of a single pair" (Barlas 2002, p. 133). Man and woman are two categories of the human species given the same or equal potential. There are no indications, whatsoever, that women have more or fewer limitations than men. Neither is excluded in the principal purpose of the Qur'an, which is to guide humankind towards recognition of and belief in God's truths.

Hence, the idea that woman is a secondary creation deriving from the rib of man which is part of the Biblical tradition illustrated in Genesis 2: 18–24 (in Lerner 1986, p. 181) finds no support in the Qur'an. There is no single verse in the Qur'an which states that man and woman were created from different substances, or that woman was created of Man's rib, or even that woman was created *after* man, claims which have, for over two millennia, been cited as proof of divine sanction for the subordination of women. According to the Qur'an, all human beings derive from a single source described as "*nafsin wahidatin*". In the Qur'an, argues Riffat Hassan (in Barlas 2002, p. 135):

> none of the thirty or so passages which describe the creation of humanity … is there any statement which could be interpreted as asserting or suggesting that man was created prior to woman or that woman was created from man. In fact there are some passages which could — from a purely grammatical/linguistic point of view — be interpreted as stating that the first creation ("*nafsin wahidatin*") was feminine, not masculine![5]

In relation to the absolute, woman is equal to man in all essential rights and duties. God makes no distinction between man and woman; they are to be equally rewarded or punished for their deeds. The Qur'an says: "Never will I suffer to be lost the work of any of you, be he male or female; ye are members, one of another" (Surah Ali Imran, 3:195). The following verse is equally instructive:

> For Muslim men and women — for believing men and women, for devout men and women, for true men and women, for men and women who are patient and constant, for men and women who humble themselves, for men and women who give in charity, for men and

women who fast (and deny themselves), for men and women who guard
their chastity, and for men and women who engage much in Allah's
praise—for them has Allah prepared forgiveness and great reward. (Surah
al-Ahzab, 22:35)

Commenting on this verse, Maulana Mohammad Ali (in Engineer 1992,
p. 44) contends that the verse "repeats ten times that women can attain every
good quality to which men can have access and settles it conclusively that
according to the Qur'an women stand on the same spiritual level as men."
Thus unlike in other religions in Islam there is absolutely no distinction
between man and woman in religious matters either.

Regarding gender relationship in the marriage, a Qur'anic verse that
perfectly symbolizes equality and reciprocity is Surah al-Baqarah (2:187):
"Your wives are a garment for you and you are a garment for them." This
verse beautifully illustrates the nature of women and men, who need,
complement, and support each other. Schimmel (in Murata 1992, p. ix)
posits that the term "garment", according to ancient religious ideas, is a
reference to the alter ego of a human being. The garment can function as a
substitute for the person, and with a new garment one gains as if it were a new
personality. Furthermore, it hides the body, blocks the looking at the private
parts, and protects the wearer. Husband and wife are, according to this
interpretation, so to speak each other's ego, a sample of perfect togetherness.

PATRIARCHAL READING OF THE QUR'AN

While advocating sexual equality and reciprocity, the Qur'an, however, at the
same time does speak of man having a slight edge and social superiority over
women. This, as Engineer (1992, p. 45) contends, must be seen in its proper
social context. He says that:

> The social structure in the Prophet's time was not such as to admit of
> complete sexual equality. One cannot take a purely theological view in
> such matters. One has to adopt a socio-theological view. Even a revealed
> scripture comprises both the contextual and the normative. No scripture,
> in order to be effective, can totally ignore the context.

A pivotal verse in the Qur'an on gender which is frequently cited as a
foundation for justifying gender hierarchies is Surah al-Nisa' (4:34). The
verse, in classical exegeses, is interpreted as illustrating sexual hierarchy, with
women as sexual objects at the service of men. The verse in question, in
Al-Tabari and al-Baydawi's reading (Stowasser 1998, p. 33), says:

Men are in charge of/are guardians of/are superior to/have authority over/women (*al-rijalu qawwamuuna 'ala l-nisa'*) because God has endowed one with more/because God has preferred some of them over others (*bi-ma faddala Allahu ba'duhum 'ala ba'din*) and they support them from their means (*wa-bi-ma anfaqu min amwalihim*). Therefore the righteous women are obedient, guarding in secret that which God has guarded. And for those whom you fear may rebel (*nusyuz*), admonish them and banish them to separate beds, and beat them. Then if they obey you, seek not a way against them. For God is Exalted, Great.

The verse legislates men's authority over their women, conferring on them the right to discipline their women in order to ensure obedience. *Nusyuz* or rebellion, according to Tabari, refers to female appropriation of superiority over the husband, undue freedom of movement, objection of sexual contact when desired by the husband, and other acts of defiance. Meanwhile, men's "superiority over" women, according to Baydawi (Stowasser 1998, p. 33) refers to the fact that men have been endowed with "a perfect mind, good management skills, and superb strength with which to perform practical work and pious deeds. To men (alone) were allotted the prophethood … and the monopoly in the decision to divorce".

The above quotations are examples of how the Qur'an was read and interpreted by classical exegetes and documented in classical books that have remained immutable as a source of Islamic family law to the present time. A human product, nevertheless viewed as "sacred" and unchangeable, such work, undeniably has impacted greatly on Muslim societies, exacerbating the already existing patriarchal attitudes. Prophet Muhammad and the Qur'an had initiated the process of transformation into just and egalitarian societies. However, history notes that Islam's achievement during the Prophet's period in liberating the oppressed groups, particularly women, was at stake when Islamic societies fell back into feudalism. Under feudalistic system of the Abbasid dynasty, women's status was set back to the periphery. Women had no political rights and responsibilities; and the court culture had given rise to sexual objectification of women. The social context during this period was far more negative to women than that sanctioned during the Prophet Muhammad. The seventh to the tenth century was the period when classical books with classical exegeses were documented. Muslim law, the *shari'a*, was codified and the doors of *ijtihad* (logical reasoning) were closed, as *shari'a* was considered fully and exhaustively elaborated by that time.

This rigidity was probably necessary, as An-Na'im (2002, p. 7) points out, for maintaining stability of the system during the decline of the social and political institutions of Islamic societies. The diminishing possibility for *ijtihad* was questioned by more recent scholarship (Hallaq 1994; Gerber 1999: "Introduction", in An-Na'im 2002, p. 7) as it pushed Islam into "the era of sterility" which has lasted to the present time (Mahmasani 1961, in Esposito 1982, p. 104). Islamic laws codified during this period are documented in classical books which remain in use until now as important references for developing legal opinions (*fatwa*) by jurists. These *fatwa* are developed and adapted from *shari'a* to address upcoming issues which may not be addressed in the classical books. But these developments and adaptations apparently take place firmly within the framework of already established broader principles and methodology. An-Na'im (7), along with other scholars, claims that there has been hardly any change in the basic structure and methodology of *shari'a* and it has remained immutable over the last thousand years or so. The core content of *shari'a* has continued to reflect the social, political, economic conditions of the eighth to tenth centuries, thereby more and more out of touch with subsequent developments and realities of society and state, especially in the modern context (Schacht 1974, pp. 394–95). The androcentric and misogynist traditions prevailing during the period of the codification have, undoubtedly, been sustained by *shari'a* till the present time, producing a face of Islam which is oppressive to, rather than liberating, women. Unless a fundamental change is made in understanding religious texts, Islam will fail to achieve its liberating mission (Surah al-Hujurat, 49:13) and as a blessing to the whole universe (Surah al-Anbiya', 21:107), and that will lead us to the discussion of methodology.

METHODOLOGICAL DEBATE: A HERMENEUTICS APPROACH

Controversies regarding gender issues in Islam arise out of different methodologies in approaching and paradigms in viewing the issues. The Qur'an is laden with messages on justice and equality including sexual equality; however, these messages are hardly captured by Muslims. Muslim societies have apparently contributed to the realities of Muslim women's backward status and their being deprived from basic women's rights. In response to women's detrimental situation, the Egyptian theologian and jurist Muhammad Abduh (d. 1905) called for the education of men "in the true meaning of Islam", which would make them give up all selfishness, material greed, power hunger, and love of tyranny, so they would begin to deal with their wives in the spirit of love, compassion, equality that the Qur'an enjoins (Muhammad Abduh, n.d., p. 117).

Fazlur Rahman (1965) brought into light a new epistemology by taking into consideration the historical sociological contexts when the Islamic traditions were formed. Muslims, he argues in his later book (1982) have yet to resolve "basic questions of method and hermeneutics".[6] No method of Qur'anic exegesis is fully objective as each exegete makes some subjective interpretation which is not necessarily the intent of the text. It is, therefore, crucial to distinguish between the text and its interpretation. A similar view was expressed by Barlas (2002, p. 6), who contends that Qur'anic texts, like other texts, are polysemic; they are open to variant readings. The Qur'an can be read in multiple modes, patriarchal as well as egalitarian ones. We cannot look to a text alone to explain why people have read it in a particular mode or why they tend to favour one reading of it over another. This is especially true of the Qur'an, as it "has been ripped from its historical, linguistic, literary, and psychological contexts and then been continually recontextualized in various cultures and according to the ideological needs of various actors" (Arkoun 1994, p. 5).

Wadud (1999, pp. 1–3) identifies three categories by which the Qur'an has been interpreted in terms of woman. First, the so-called "traditional", uses atomistic methodology which interprets verse by verse from the beginning to the end. Little or no effort is made to recognize themes and to discuss the relationship of the Qur'an to itself thematically. Most of the exegeses were done by males which means that "men and men's experiences were included while women and women's experiences were either excluded or interpreted through the male vision, perspective, desire, or needs of woman" (p. 2). Second, the reactive method consists primarily of modern scholars' reactions to severe handicaps for women which have been attributed to the text. This method, in spite of its concerns for valid issues, lacks a comprehensive analysis of the Qur'an. The third category, which is relatively new, reconsiders the whole method of Qur'anic exegesis with regard to various modern social, moral, economic, and political concerns — including the issue of woman. This final method, the hermeneutics, is proposed by contemporary Islamic scholars (Rahman 1982; Wadud 1999; Barlas 2002) to yield a creative synthesis of Qur'anic principles by recognizing the connections between different themes of the Qur'an. This means that in interpreting a certain text, consideration is to be given to three aspects of the text: 1) the context in which the text was revealed, 2) the grammatical composition of the text, and 3) the whole text, that is, the worldview.

Concerns for the misogynist tradition among Muslim societies were expressed by a prominent Muslim feminist, Fetima Mernissi (1985, 1987), who convincingly argues that neither the Prophet Muhammad nor Allah as a source of the holy law desired anything other than equality between the sexes; but these teachings are reversed in reality. Muslim societies, in general, appear to be more concerned with trying to control women's bodies and sexuality than with supporting them in achieving their rights. Another Muslim feminist, Riffat Hasan (1995, p. 25), makes a similar observation. While the Qur'an, because of its protective attitudes toward all oppressed classes, appears to be weighted in many ways in favour of women, many of its women-related teachings have been used in patriarchal Muslim societies against, rather than for, women. She criticizes Muslim scholars for "either not speaking of women's rights at all or are mainly concerned with how a woman's chastity may be protected". Afkhami (1995, p. 1) shares a similar concern, that for Muslim fundamentalists "every domestic issue is negotiable except women's rights and their position in society".

In sum, as argued by al-Durra (in Haddad 1998, p. 4), religion can be seen as a double-edged sword. On one side, it can "bring mercy to the whole universe" (Surah al-Anbiya', 21:107) and to "free human beings from any oppression and discrimination …" (Surah al-Hujurat, 49:13). However, it can also bring detriments to women when read in a patriarchal way.

TREATMENT OF GENDER ISSUES IN ISLAM

Several issues in family life such as polygamy, inheritance, sexual health, husband-wife relations, divorce, and child custody remain controversial. Similarly, religious discourses on women's issues in public sphere such as women's leadership, women's seclusion or domestication, women's veiling and women's rights issues in general appear to place more favour on men than on women. The following part will briefly discuss two most controversial subjects of debates for centuries, polygamy and veiling.

Polygamy: The Misunderstood Phenomenon

Polygamy was widely practised in pre-Islamic society. There was no limit for the number of wives a man could take. Early commentators of the Qur'an recorded cases of some Arabs having up to ten wives. The notion of justice towards these wives was not there in this society. The husband had unilateral privilege to determine whom he would love most and whom he would shower with his unlimited favours. The wives had to accept their fate without any recourse to the process of justice.

Islam does not accept this state of the affairs. Along with its basic project, empowerment of women, though within certain limitations of the given society, the Qur'an accepts the fact that women are victims of injustices in the society. However, abolishing polygamy completely and giving women equal status with men in every respect was not a practical proposition in that type of society. Thus, the Qur'an applied the middle-way solution, in what is termed "pragmatic-ideological" course (Engineer n.d., p. 87). While it hinted at equality directly as well inferentially, it sought solutions more acceptable to the society that was dominated by men.

It is clear from the Qur'an's statements that polygamy was not a very happy solution as far as the Qur'an was concerned, and yet it had to advocate it in a very restricted manner. The Qur'anic verse that refers to polygamy is Surah al-Nisa' (4:3), which translates as follows: "If you fear that you will not be able to deal justly with orphans, marry of your choice, two or three or four; but if you fear that you will not be able to deal justly with them, then only one." This rule on polygamy was introduced conditionally; the verse especially refers to the justice to be done to orphans. The verse was revealed immediately after the Battle of Uhud when Muslim community was left with many orphans and widows and captives of war. Their treatment was to be governed by principles of the greatest humanity and equity. As argued by Ali (1989, p. 184), the occasion is past but the principles remain. He reads the verse as a possibility for a man to marry the orphans if he is sure that it is the way to protect their interests and their property with perfect justice to them and to his own dependence, if he has any.

The verse is not merely limited to orphans, but has a general application with regard to the marriage laws in Islam. Muslim jurists, as pointed out by Doi (1992, p. 51) lay down the following conditions for a polygamous man: i) he must have sufficient financial resources to look after the needs of the additional wives; ii) he must do equal justice to them all. The wives are to be treated equally as far as the fulfilment of their conjugal and other rights are concerned. The condition of being just and fair is hardly possible to realize due to humanly limitations. The Qur'an is explicit about this, which makes it even clearer in its attitude for not advocating polygamy. The verse (Surah al-Nisa', 4:129) is translated by Ali (227) as follows: "You are never able to be fair and just as between women; even if it is your ardent desire; but turn not away (from a woman) altogether, so as to leave her (as it were) hanging (in the air)." This verse even affirms the Qur'an's attitude against polygamy. It is quite categorical that it is not within the power of human beings to treat wives, more than one, with equal fairness. There is a big gap between desire and its fulfilment, and as far as polygamy is concerned, the Qur'an is clear: in spite of good intentions, men cannot deal justly between their wives. This may be because, as the Qur'an says, "God has not made for any man two hearts (Surah Al-Ahzab, 33:4), implying that a man cannot love two women equally. These verses, then, can be read together as presenting a case against generalized polygamy, which Muslims derive from reading half a line of Surah al-Nisa' (4:1).

The core issue of polygamy in current Muslim societies is that it has been taken as a general attitude of Islam, ignoring the social justice reason of the revelation of the verse. Polygamy, which was common in pre-Islamic society, apparently has a new meaning in Islam. Islam intended to change it from a male right into a female privilege in limited circumstances beneficial to women and children, not in circumstances detrimental to women. If it is acceptable to women, polygamy may be a way to protect them and give them sexual access to men at a time when women outnumber men. However, the Qur'an itself does not refer to the sexual nature or needs of women or men in dealing with polygamy; it refers only to the need to ensure social justice for orphaned girls, in a time when unprotected women were open to all kinds of abuse. Even so, polygamy is not the Qur'an's ideal; otherwise, "its admonition to marry only one, its assertion that men cannot do justice between wives, and its reference to the oneness of the human heart would hold no meaning" (Barlas 2002, p. 192). And since for believers the Qur'an's teachings cannot be meaningless, as Barlas argued further, it is we who must be willing to re-read the verses cumulatively as an argument against a generalized mode of polygamy.

Veiling (*hijab, jilbab*)

There are two words that are currently used in Indonesia to refer to the same meaning: *hijab* and *jilbab*. The term *hijab*, which literally means "curtain" — in appearing seven times in the Qur'an, indicating metaphorical meaning, a concrete object, and an eschatological reference — has been interpreted as a mixture of the two. Semantically, the general meaning of *hijab* refers to the concept of "separation", which can be literal, metaphorical, or abstract. *Hijab*, in its concrete meaning, segregates individuals or groups of individuals from the society in general, and also the abstract institution of such segregation. In medieval royal circles, the *hijab* was the curtain behind which the ruler was hidden from the eyes of the courtiers and commoners alike. This practice, first documented for the Umayyads and the Abbasids, later became part of an elaborate system of court ceremonials (Stowasser 1994, p. 168). While the custom of screening-off was not practised by the Prophet and the four rightly guided *(rashidun)* successors themselves, it is here divinely legislated for the female elite of the first Medinan community, the Prophet's wives.

The descent of the *hijab* is an event dating back to Surah al-Ahzab, 33:53 (Ali 1989, pp. 1074–75), which was revealed in the fifth year after the *hijra* (AD 627).

> Oh ye who believe! Enter not the Prophet's houses, until leave is given you for a meal, not to wait for its preparation; but when you are invited, enter; and when ye have taken your meal, disperse without seeking familiar talk. Such (behavior) annoys the Prophet: he is ashamed to dismiss you, but Allah is not ashamed (to tell you) the truth. And when you ask (his ladies) for anything you want, ask them from before a screen; that makes for greater purity for your hearts and for theirs.

The wedding of Zainab bint Jahsy to the Prophet is identified in the majority of *hadith* and *tafsir* accounts as the occasion for God's legislation of the *hijab,* imposed by God to shield the Prophet's women from the eyes of visitors to his dwellings. As pointed out by a number of great exegets (Ibn Sa'd; Tabari; Zamakhshari; Ibn Kathir, in Mernissi 1991, p. 100; Stowasser 1994, p. 90), the *hijab* "came down" in a double sense: Firstly, it was, literally, a "curtain" the Prophet loosened while standing on the threshold to Zaynab's chamber, in order to bar his servant Anas Ibn Malik from entering; secondly, the *hijab* also "came down" by way of God's revelation of the verse, which the Prophet recited to Anas. Other traditions report that the *hijab* was decreed after the Prophet saw some men loitering in the vicinity of Zaynab's house on the morning after the wedding night. Another strand of traditions mention that Umar ibn al-Khattab, urged the Prophet to conceal and segregate his wives, because both the righteous and the wicked entered into the Prophet's house.

Muslim interpreters stipulate that the Prophet's wives participated fully in the communal affairs of Medina until the revelation of the *hijab* verse. Their exclusion from public life was due to several factors, among others to provide domestic comfort and privacy for the female elite of Islam (the Prophet's wives). This notion, in turn, connotes an element of "privilege". Indeed, the medieval *hadith* informs that the *hijab* was imposed upon the Prophet's wives as criterion of their elite status. In addition, the *hijab* is also seen as a protective device, especially during periods of civic tension when the hypocrites were instigating disorder and stirring up inter-communal fears. Because of this social condition, the Prophet felt compelled to heed Umar Ibn Khattab's council and seclude his wives (Stowasser 1994, p. 91).

Soon after the revelation of the *hijab* verse, the self-protection of "the Prophet's wives, his daughters, and the women of the believers" was enjoined in the Qur'an (Surah al-Ahzab, 33:59–60) by way of God's command that Muslim women cover themselves in their "mantles", or "cloaks" (*jalabib,* singular: *jilbab)* (when abroad), "so that they be known (as free women, not slaves) and not molested (in the streets) by the hypocrites, and those in whose hearts is a disease". (Stowasser 1994, p. 91). This legislation differs from the previous verse in two ways: firstly, it concerned individual female appearance when outside the home, not seclusion within; secondly, it applied to all Muslim women, not just the Prophet's wives. Once again, classical exegesis has identified Umar Ibn Khattab as the main spokesman in favour of this clothing law.

Given the multiple meanings of the *hijab* and the context of its revelation, it is hard to understand how this phenomenon was made obligatory for Muslim women at large. Stowasser (1984, p. 93) relates it to the period after the expansion of Islam beyond the borders of Arabia, and later in the Islamicized societies still ruled by pre-existing (Sasanian and Byzantine) traditions. Rules on women's dress and space were formulated in the mid eighth century in an absolute and categorical way, reflecting the practices and cultures of that time. Meanwhile, Mernissi (1987, p. 97) points out that the *hijab,* also meaning a veil that hides God from men, takes on an eminently negative significance. She further questions, how the *hijab,* with such a negative meaning, is claimed in our day as a symbol of Muslim identity and manna for the Muslim woman. Mernissi (101) concludes that the Prophet, during a troubled period at the beginning of Islam, introduced a breach in space separating the public from the private, or indeed the profane from the sacred, but which was to turn into a segregation of the sexes. The veil that descended from Heaven was going to cover up women, separate them from men, from the Prophet, and so from God. Is this the intended intepretation of the term?

CONCLUSION

Controversies regarding the issues of gender in Islam basically arise from the methods of reading the Qur'an. Since all texts, including Qur'anic texts, can be read in multiple modes, patriarchal as well as liberating, it is crucial that a proper method be applied so as to produce liberating interpretations of the Qur'an. In this regard, it is necessary to look into the realm of hermeneutics, of epistemology, and the extra-textual contexts of gender politics, that shape religious knowledge and authority in ways that enabled patriarchal readings of the Qur'an. Arguments for and against polygamy and women's veiling, two

204 Lily Zakiyah Munir

most hotly debated subjects, have been presented in order to illustrate how the same scriptures may be interpreted differently: to support justice and liberation for women or to perpetuate the oppression of women.

Notes

1   This means that it is a quotation from the Qur'an in *surah* (chapter) number 21, that is, al-Anbiya' verse 107.
2   Translation of the verses quoted in this chapter, unless otherwise stated, is adopted from Abdullah Yusuf Ali (1989).
3   See Sunan Abi Dawud, *Kitab al Adab*, Bab *Fadl man 'ala Yatama.*
4   See Sahih Bukhari, *Kitab al-Adab*, Bab *Rahmat al-walad wa taqbilihi.*
5   Verses illustrating that man and woman were created from a single source described as "nafs-in wahidatin" or the unitary "nafs" or "being" are among others Q.S. al-Nisa'/4:1, Q.S. al-An'am/6:98, Q.S. al-A'raf/7:189, and Q.S. al-Zumar/39:6.
6   Hermeneutics derives from Greek *"hermeneutikos"*, a branch of philosophy which deals with the origin of language and texts. It seeks to explicate alien speech, words and texts deriving from God who speaks in a heavenly language or from previous generations who lived and spoke an alien language (Hidayat 1995, p. 126). Initially used for biblical studies, hermeneutics is also familiar in Islamic tradition as *tafsir* (exegesis).

References

Abduh, Muhammad. *Al-Islam wa-al-Mar'ah fi Ra'y al-Imam Muhammad Abduh* (Islam and Women in the View of Imam Muhammad Abduh). Cairo: Muhammad 'Imara.n.d.

Afkhami, Mahnaz. *Faith and Freedom: Women's Human Rights in the Muslim World.* London: I.B. Tauris & Co. Ltd., 1995.

Ahmed, Leila. *Women and Gender in Islam.* New Haven and London: Yale University Press, 1992.

An-Na'im, Abdullahi A. *Islamic Family Law in a Changing World: A Global Resource Book.* London: Zed Books Ltd., 2002.

Arkoun, Mohammed. *Rethinking Islam: Common Questions, Uncommon Answers.* Translated by Robert D. Lee. Boulder, Colorado: Westview Press, 1994.

Ali, Yusuf. *The Holy Qur'an: Text, Translation and Commentary.* Washington D.C.: Amana Corporation, 1989.

Barlas, Asma. *Believing Women in Islam: Unreading Patriarchal Interpretations of the Qur'an.* Austin: University of Texas Press, 2002.

Engineer, Asghar Ali. *The Rights of Women in Islam.* New York: St. Martin's Press, Inc., 1992.

_____. *The Qur'an, Women & Modern Society*. Kuala Lumpur: Synergy Books International, n.d.

Esposito, John L. *Women in Muslim Family Law*. Syracuse, N.Y.: Syracuse University Press, 1982.

Figes, Eva. *Patriarchal Attitudes: Women in Society*. New York: Persea Book, 1970.

Haddad, Yvonne Yazbeck and John L. Esposito. *Islam, Gender, and Social Change*. New York: Oxford University Press, 1998.

Hassan, Riffat. *Women's Rights in Islam: From I.C.P.D. to Beijing*. Compilation of unpublished papers, 1995.

Hidayat, Komaruddin. *Memahami Bahasa Agama (Understanding the Language of Religion)*. Jakarta: Paramadina, 1995.

Howland, Courtney W. *Religious Fundamentalisms and the Human Rights of Women*. New York: Palgrave, 1999.

Lerner, Gerda. *The Creation of Patriarchy*. Oxford: Oxford University Press, 1986.

Mernissi, Fetima. *The Veil and the Male Elite: A Feminist Interpretation of Women's Rights in Islam*. Massachusetts: Perseus Books, 1985.

_____. *Beyond the Veil: Male-Female Dynamics in a Modern Muslim Society*. New York: Halstead Press Book, 1986.

Murata, Sachiko. *The Tao of Islam: A Sourcebook on Gender Relations in Islamic Thought*. New York: State University of New York Press, 1992.

Peach, Lucinda Joy. *Women and World Religions*. New Jersey: Pearson Education, Inc., 2002.

Rahman, Fazlur. *Islamic Methodology and History*. Karachi: Central Institute of Islamic Research, 1995.

_____. *Islam*. Chicago: The University of Chicago Press, 1997.

_____. *Islam and Modernity: Transformation of an Intellectual Tradition*. Chicago: The University of Chicago Press, 1982.

Rich, Adrienne. *Of Woman Born: Motherhood as Experience and Institution*. New York: Norton, 1986.

Schacht, J. "Law and State". In *The Legacy of Islam*, edited by J. Schacht and C.E. Bosworth. Oxford: Oxford University Press, 1974, pp. 392–423.

Stowasser, Barbara Freyer. *Women in the Qur'an's Tradition and Interpretation*. New York: Oxford University Press, 1994.

Wadud, Amina. *Qur'an and Women: Rereading the Sacred Text from a Woman's Perspective*. New York: Oxford University Press, 1998.

Wolterstorff, Nicholas. *Divine Discourse: Philosophical Reflections on the Claim that God Speaks*. Cambridge: Cambridge University Press, 1995.

PART THREE

Modernization, Globalization and the 'Islamic State' Debate in Southeast Asia

11

ISLAM AND MODERNIZATION

Syed Farid Alatas

INTRODUCTION

Modernity refers to the end result of the process of modernization. It is the condition that a society attains after having gone through specific patterns of social and economic change which began in Western Europe in the eighteenth century and which has been spreading throughout the rest of the world. The process of modernization refers to the introduction of modern scientific knowledge to increasing aspects of human life, first of all in Western civilization, then to non-Western societies, by different means and groups, with the final aim of achieving a better life as defined by the society concerned (Alatas, S.H. 1972, p. 22). The traits of modernization include the rationalization of economic and political life, rapid urbanization, industrialization, differentiation in the social structure, and greater popular involvement in public affairs. If we understand these traits as constituting the modern condition, then modernism would refer to the ideology, attitude or mentality that subordinates the traditional to the modern.

This chapter begins with a brief introduction to development studies as a modernist discourse. This is followed by a concise overview of the Islamic ideal of development which is juxtaposed to the economic realities of Muslim societies. It then proceeds to theoretically assess attempts in Muslim countries such as Malaysia, Pakistan, and Saudi Arabia to create an alternative discourse on development that draws on Islamic law and an Islamic philosophical anthropology. The next sections move on to a consideration of the role of the

209

state in development and the questions of democracy and civil society. The concluding section makes some remarks on the problematic state of discourse in the Muslim world on modernization.

DEVELOPMENT STUDIES AS MODERNIST DISCOURSE

The vast majority of Muslims around the world live in economically under-developed countries, with high rates of inflation, low rates of economic growth, low life expectancy, and a high level of adult illiteracy. There are also severe problems in the health and nutritional status of Muslims worldwide, which have serious implications for the quality of human resources. Muslim countries also lag behind industrialized nations in educational attainment, especially where access to tertiary education is concerned (Hassan 1992).

Such is the relative economic state of affairs of the Muslim world. It is also a fair description of the Muslim world in the 1930s, 1940s and 1950s, when economists and social scientists in the West first began to draw their attention to the economic problems of the Third World. It was also during this period that development theory started to be uncritically adopted in a wholesale manner throughout the Third World. The type of scholarship along these lines later came to be known by reference to the phenomenon of the captive mind, as conceptualized by Syed Hussein Alatas (1972; 1974). Mental captivity connotes a mode of thinking that is characterized by the uncritical imitation of external ideas and techniques. There is a lack of capacity to be creative and raise original problems, to forge original methods. There is also a general alienation from the main issues of the local society, and the unquestioning imitation of the Occident (Alatas 1972, 1974; Dube 1982, pp. 497–500; Sardar 1987, p. 56).

The structural context of mental captivity can be understood in terms of the idea of academic dependency. The structure of academic dependency links social scientists in advanced industrialized nations to their counterparts in the Third World. The nature of these links is such that scholars in the Third World are dependent on colleagues and contacts in the industrialized West and, to some extent, Japan for research funds and opportunities, gaining recognition and other types of rewards from such relationships (Dube 1982, p. 499).[1]

In addition to the problems of mental captivity and academic dependency is the state of development theory itself (Booth 1985; Edwards 1989; Manzo 1991; Sheth 1987; Smith 1985; Vandergeest and Buttel 1988; Wiarda 1989). It was primarily the disciplines of sociology, economics, and political science that dealt with the modernization of Asia, Africa, and Latin America in the 1950s and 1960s. Modernization theory can be understood in terms of its structural and psychological components.

The structural version of modernization theory is founded on an evolutionary vision of social, political, and economic development. It derives its inspiration from classical theory, that is, the belief in progress and increasing complexities in the social, economic, and political spheres (Portes 1976, p. 55). It was perhaps Rostow who gave modernization theory its best known form (Rostow 1960), suggesting that there are five stages which all societies would go through in order to industrialize. Despite the fact that these five stages were derived from the experience of industrialized nations and are, therefore, questionable in this light, Rostow's stages of economic growth were applied to under-developed countries as well.

The psychological version of modernization theory views Western society as possessing those psychological traits, such as a high need for achievement and economic rationality, that are prerequisites for economic success (Hagen 1962; McClelland 1967; Inkeles and Smith 1974). By now it is well understood that the trajectory of development experienced by advanced industrialized nations in both its structural or psychological terms, is not necessarily an experience that is available to under-developed countries. According to Marxist and neo-Marxist theories under-developed countries would never be able to catch up with developed countries because of the historical evolution of a highly unequal capitalist system of relations between rich and poor countries. Unequal power relationships between advanced industrialized and under-developed countries do not enable the latter to experience independent and sustainable development.

To a great extent, under-development is attributed to the policies of industrialized countries and their extensions in the form of elite groups in the periphery. World-system theory sees the world as constituting a single division of labour, this division of labour being hierarchical. These approaches are correct to criticize modernization theory for its lack of attention to the structure of the world economy and its hierarchical relationships. Nevertheless, their inadequacies are not to be denied, particularly those they share with modernization theory. Both modernization and Marxist-inspired theories can be said to fall within the orbit of a modernist discourse which is informed by the principles of nineteenth-century liberal philosophy and which confines its understanding of development to Westernization (Alatas 1972, ch. 2), democratization, economic growth, and other technical aspects of economic development (Manzo 1991, p. 6).

DEVELOPMENT IN THE MUSLIM WORLD:
BETWEEN IDEALS AND REALITY

The Islamic ideal of development can be adequately captured by referring to the Arabic term, *iqtisad*, which is conventionally translated as economy. The term *iqtisad* is derived from the root, *qasada*, which together with the derivation, *iqtasada*, convey the notion of economizing and being moderate, frugal, thrifty and provident. However, this is only one of the meanings. The verb *iqtasada* also connotes adopting a middle course or a mediatory position. We could understand *iqtisad*, therefore, not simply as economy in the technical sense of the term, but as economy in the context of thrift, frugality and providence and, above all, moderation. Indeed, the Qur'an stresses moderation in economic affairs: Make not thy hand tied to thy neck, nor stretch it forth to its utmost reach, so that thou become blameworthy and destitute (17:29).

Here Muslims are exhorted to be neither niggardly nor extravagant. Such moderation in economic as well as other behaviour defines Muslims as constituting a median community (*ummatan wasatan*, Qur'an, 2:143). The median path is, therefore, the right path (*al-sirat al-mustaqim*), that is, the path that leads to God (Qur'an, 11:56). The ideal of the economy in Islam, therefore, is not divorced from the notion of human beings as moral creatures with obligations to God as well as to each other.

At the philosophical level, the foundations of development from an Islamic point of view can be understood in terms of four concepts (Ahmad 1980, pp. 178–79; Aidit 1990, pp. 22–23).[2] *Tauhid* or the principle of the unity of God establishes the nature of the relationship between God and man as well as that between men. *Rububiyyah* refers to the belief that it is God who determines the sustenance and nourishment of man and it is He who will guide believers to success. It follows that successful development is a result of man's work as well as the workings of the divine order. *Khilafah* is the concept of man as God's vicegerent on earth. This defines man as a trustee of God's resources on earth. *Tazkiyah* refers to the growth and purification of man in terms of his relationship with God, his fellow men, and with the natural environment. The putting into practice of these principles results in *falah*, that is, prosperity in this world as well as the hereafter (Ahmad 1980, p. 179). The Islamic concept of development is, therefore, *tazkiyah* or purification combined with growth (Ahmad 1980, p. 179). This concept encompasses the spiritual, moral, and material aspects of development and the ultimate aim is to maximise welfare both in this life and in the hereafter. At the more practical level, the organization and functioning of the economy, apart from being based on the above philosophy of development, are also guided by three economic principles (Sadr 1991). In the principle of double ownership neither private nor public or state ownership are fundamental principles of the economy. Both forms of ownership are acceptable in Islam, but only in their respective areas of the economy. In the principle of limited economic freedom economic activities must take place within the boundaries of a both self-imposed and socially-enforced normative order, which is, of course, defined by Islam. Finally, the principle of social justice refers to the Islamic theory of distribution of produced as well as natural wealth, and is based on the notion of mutual responsibility and equity.

Arising from this philosophy of development are a number of policy goals (Ahmad 1980, pp. 180–84):

(i) Human resource development should be concentrated on the development of the right attitudes, aspirations, character, personality, physical and moral well-being, and efficiency (Afzal-ur-Rahman 1980a, pp. 189–99), and would call for the Islamization of education (Al-Attas 1980).

(ii) Production and consumption would be restricted to those goods and services which are deemed as useful for man in light of the value constellations of Islam. This refers to the adoption of a middle way between crass materialism and other-wordly asceticism (Afzal-ur-Rahman 1980b, p. 11)

(iii) Efforts to improve the quality of life include employment creation, the institutionalization of zakah (poor tax), and the equitable distribution of income and wealth through tax policies, charity, inheritance laws, the prohibition of usury, speculation, an so on (Afzal-ur-Rahman 1980b, pp. 55–105, 268–72).

(iv) Development should be along the lines of regional and sectoral equality to achieve balanced development for the Muslim world (Sardar 1987, pp. 107–12).

(v) Technology must be indigenized to suite the conditions of Muslim society and must, therefore, be in harmony with the goals and aspirations of the community without, at the same time, causing serious social disruption (Sardar 1987, p. 146).

(vi) Economic dependency on the non-Muslim world must be reduced and integration within the Muslim world must be brought about (Alatas 1987b).

THE MUSLIM RESPONSE TO MODERNIZATION:
THE CASE OF ISLAMIC ECONOMICS

The Islamic ideal of development, as described above, has far from been realized in the empirical world. Muslim responses to the problems of modernization have taken the form of the articulation of broad ideological orientations such as modernism, neo-modernism and traditionalism. But some Muslims have attempted to respond to the problems of modernization and under-development by developing a new discipline, that of Islamic economics. This is in line with other calls within specific disciplines to revamp theoretical perspectives and create visions of a new Islamic order along social, economic and political lines. Hence, the notions of Islamic sociology, Islamic political science and Islamic economics. Here, the focus is on the economic dimension.

Due to both the problems associated with modernist discourse as well as the state of development in Muslim countries, there were demands for alternative discourses to both modernization and Marxist theories (Anisur Rahman 1991). The perceived crisis in development studies had resulted in efforts in the Muslim world to ground development theory in Islamic law and philosophical anthropology, resulting in what is referred to as Islamic economics (Siddiqi 1989; Abu Saud 1989). The question of whether Islamic social science in general is possible on philosophical and epistemological grounds has been dealt with elsewhere (Fazlur Rahman 1988; Alatas 1987a, 1993a, 1995). In what follows, I attempt to layout in broad outline the fundamental premises of what is presented as Islamic economics (Afzal-ur-Rahman 1980a, 1980b; Choudhury 1983; Gilani 1980; Khan 1989; Philipp 1990; Pryor 1985; as-Sadr 1982–84, 1984; Siddiqi 1981; Taleqani 1983).

The notion of Islamic economics did not arise from within the classical tradition in Islamic thought. In the classical Islamic tradition, there were discussions and works on economic institutions and practices in the Muslim world, but the notion of an Islamic science of economics and a specifically Islamic economy did not exist (Abdullah 1989; Masters 1988; Udovitch 1962, 1970a, 1970b). Islamic economics, therefore, is a modern creation. It emerged as a result of dissatisfaction with capitalist and socialist models and theories of development in the 1950s (Abdul Rauf 1984; Nasr 1987; As-Sadr 1984; Shari'ati 1980). It is mainly in Pakistan and Saudi Arabia that Islamic economic research is being carried out, although there has also been a great deal of interest in this field in Egypt, India, Iran, Malaysia, and Sudan. Interest in Islamic economics predates the rise of the modern Islamic states of Iran, Libya, Pakistan, Saudi Arabia, and Sudan. Islamic economics rejects the ideology of "catching up" with the West and is committed to discerning the nature and ethos of economic development from an Islamic point of view (Alatas 1995, p. 92; 1997, p. 70). The need is, therefore, to identify the Islamic ideal of economic development (Ahmad 1980, p. 171).

Islamic economics rejects various ethnocentric misconceptions to be found in modernization theory with regard to Muslim society such as its alleged fatalism and the lack of the achievement motive (Ahmad 1980, p. 173). They maintain that the prerequisites of development are to be found in Islam but that development within an Islamic framework is based on the constellation of values that are found in the Qur'an and the *Sunnah* (the Traditions of the Prophet of Islam) (Alhabshi 1990). Western development theory and policy, on the other hand, are based on the peculiar characteristics, problems, and value constellations that are found in Western society.

The Islamic economic critique of development studies is not directed only at modernization theory but more generally at the entire body of modernist development thought encompassing perspectives from the left to the right. The modernist call is to promote development by recasting Islam in a modern light, by tempering its traditionalist tendencies, by accepting Western notions of economic and political development — in short, by recasting itself in a Western mold (Tibi 1988; Nasr 1993). Islam, on the other hand, has a different outlook on life and the nature of social change, and implies a unique set of policy options for the solution of the problems of development. Muslim scholars have attempted to articulate an alternative concept of development, refusing to evaluate the backwardness and progress of Muslim societies in terms of Western theoretical perspectives and values. In this way it is counter-modernist in tone and can be added to the list of those other critiques of developmentalism such as liberation theology and feminist ecology (Manzo 1991). Nevertheless, Islamic economics suffers from a number of problems, some of which have been dealt with by others (Kuran 1983, 1986, 1989; Fazlur Rahman 1964, 1974). The following remarks on Islamic economics, however, are centred on the distinction between ethical and empirical forms of theory.

Ethical theories express preference or distaste about reality in accordance with certain standards of evaluation. In addition to this, they specify the ideal goal toward which changes should be made. In contrast, empirical theories are generalizations about observable reality and require the process of abstraction and conceptualization (Alatas 1995, p. 93; 1997, p. 72).[3]

Islamic economics presents an ideal of development that is based on an Islamic philosophy of life. Arising from this alternative vision of development, various policy options have been suggested such as the introduction of interest-free banking and *zakah* (poor tax) (Ahmad 1987; Ariff 1982; Faridi 1980; Iqbal and Mirakhor 1987; Karsten 1982; Khan 1986; Khan and Mirakhor 1987, 1990; Sadr 1982; Uzair 1980). What is presented as Islamic economics are in fact ethical theories of production, distribution, price, and so on. When Islamic economists discuss the traditional categories of economics such as income, consumption, government expenditure, investment, and savings they do so in terms of ethical statements and not in terms of analyses and empirical theory. Contrary to what is often claimed, it would be difficult to refer to an Islamic science of economics, although we do have the scientific study of economies in Muslim countries, as well as the study of Muslim economic institutions and commercial techniques.

When Islamic economists are doing empirical theory, what is presented as Islamic economics turns out not to be an alternative to modernist discourse as far as empirical theory is concerned. The foci and method that have been selected by Muslim economists for economic analysis is essentially that of neo-classical, Keynesian or monetarist economics. The foci are the traditional questions that come under the purview of theories of price, production, distribution, trade cycle, growth, and welfare economics with Islamic themes and topics involved such as *zakah*, interest-free banking, and profit-sharing. There are at least three problems associated with this:

First of all, the techniques of analysis that have been selected, that is, the building up of abstract models of the economic system, have not been translated by Islamic economists into empirical work. For example, works on interest tend to construct models of how an interest-free economy would work. There is no empirical work on existing economic systems and the nature, functions, and effects of interest in these systems, in a manner that could be regarded in theoretical and methodological terms as specifically Islamic.

Secondly, these attempts at Islamic economics have sought to ground the discourse in a theory of wealth and distribution in very much the manner that Western economic science does, as a glance at some of their works will reveal (Kahf 1982; Khan 1984; Khan 1986; Abdul Mannan 1982; Siddiqui and Zaman 1989*a*, 1989*b*; Zarqa 1983). When it is engaged in the sort of discourse that one could understand as constituting empirical theory, it is not doing so from a specifically Islamic economic approach, and "despite their repeated references to *tawheed, akran* and other fundamental Islamic concepts, Islamic economics is little more than one huge attempt to cast Islamic institutions and dictates, like *zakah* and prohibition of interest into Western economic mould" (Sardar 1985, pp. 42–43). The point here is that attempts to create a "faithful" economic science have not yielded policy options for the problems that are being addressed because what "Islamic economics" amounts to is neo-classical, Keynesian or monetarist economics dressed and made up in Islamic terminology. Islamic economics is very much embedded in the tradition of British and American economics in terms of its near exclusive concern with technical factors such as growth, interest, tax, profits, and so on. According to Sardar (1985, p. 43), over eighty per cent of the Islamic economic literature is on monetarism.

A host of issues relating to political economy such as uneven development, unequal exchange, bureaucratic capitalism, corruption, and the role of the state that have been addressed by structuralist, neo-Marxist, dependency, and new institutional economic theorists, are not dealt with at the theoretical and empirical levels by Islamic economists. This is not to suggest that Islamic economists should uncritically adopt these other perspectives to replace neo-classical or monetarist economics. The successful indigenization of development economics and the claim to scientific status depend on the degree to which indigenization efforts retain what is of utility in neo-classical and other theories of development.

The main problem with this state of affairs is that under the guise of "Islamic economics" the policies generated in industrialized capitalist centers are implemented in the Muslim world and are legitimated, thereby undermining the very project that Islamic economics is committed to.

In attempting to ground itself in a theory of rational man and a hypothetical-deductive methodology it has merely substituted Islamic terms for neo-classical ones, retaining the latter's assumptions, procedures and modes of analysis. As such, it has failed to engage in the analysis and critique of a highly unequal world economic order in which the gaps are ever widening. That this supposedly anti-Western economics was co-opted and made to serve those very trends that it outwardly opposes must be considered.

Thirdly, not very different from neo-classical economics it extends a technical-economic rationality over a wide range of problems which presupposes viewing different ends as comparable outcomes, which in turn, entails the elimination of cultural hindrances to the comparability of outcomes. In this sense, neo-classical economics, Islamic economics, Marxist as well as other alternative theories of development are similar in that they are based on narrow assumptions about human action.

THE STATE AND DEVELOPMENT IN MUSLIM SOCIETIES

The problems that beset Islamic economics in terms of its theoretical perspectives, methodology and practical results are not disconnected from the political contexts of Muslim societies. As noted above, Islamic economics has generally neglected those areas of interest that have become the trademarks of neo-Marxism, dependency and world-systems theories. Islamic economics, therefore, has been rather innocent of political economy, which is ironic considering the ominous role that the state plays in the Muslim world. Indeed, the neglect of the state in Islamic economics is in stark contrast to the all-encompassing presence of the state in Muslim societies.

Political economy, that is, the study of the interactions of the state and economy, is virtually non-existent among Islamic development scholars. Whenever the subject of the state is broached, it is done so in terms of ethical statements and not in terms of analyses and empirical theory. While it is necessary to understand the political ideals of Islam, it is equally important to examine the realities. Statements to the effect that the Islamic state is an instrument of Allah and a symbol of divine power on earth (Nyang 1976) are true and generally acceptable to Muslims. The problem lies elsewhere, that is, in the nature and functioning of contemporary states in Muslim countries. For this reason, the study of economic development in the Muslim world must lie within the field of political economy. Let us consider what some of the concerns of such a political economy might be.

The state in the Muslim as well as the rest of the world is an important determinant of what men and women wish to and can achieve. This is nonetheless true in the economic arena. While many are uninterested in the activities of the state, nobody remains unaffected by it. State power is unceasingly wielded in the name of economic development and there are various roles that the state plays in this area, which include the provision of infrastructure, the regulation of the economy, the transfer of income, research and development, the formation of state-owned enterprises, and the advancement of the private interests of state officials and politicians.

The provision of social and economic infrastructure such as electricity, water, sanitation, roads, and communications help to facilitate economic activities and is a basic function of any state. But beyond the provisioning of infrastructure, the state can play a more involved role in the process of economic development through the regulation of the economy by means of various monetary and fiscal policies as well as a host of other development policies that involve exchange rate and wage controls, industrial licensing, investment incentives, and immigration quotas. The state may step in to redress the problem of income inequality through the instrumentality of transfer payments which include subsidies, grants, and welfare payments. The state may also fund basic scientific and technological research. However, the economies of Muslim countries have yet to benefit from the fruits of research and development as less than four per cent of all world research and development expenditures originate in the Muslim world. For various reasons, states in the Muslim world, as elsewhere, have found it necessary to be directly involved in the process of capital accumulation through the formation of state-owned enterprises which are public corporations owned and operated by the government. Clearly, the state has a positive role to play in the process of economic development. These various roles of the state outlined above are clearly vital. But what is the nature of the state in Muslim and other Third World societies that may function as a brake on development?

The political economy of most Muslim countries is such that the state intervenes directly in the relations of production making surplus-extraction and capital accumulation a major political issue. Rather than the market or social classes it is the state that is the main driving force in the political economy of these countries. This is due to the autonomy of the state from the dominant classes. But what is important is the manner in which this autonomy in manifested. The notion of the autonomy of the state from dominant class interests implies that the state has interests of its own.

In Malaysia and Indonesia we have the *ersatz* form of capitalism, due to the peculiar nature of state involvement in development (Kunio 1988). *Ersatz* capitalism is capitalism that is based on state patronage, and the investment of transnational corporations and their technology. Muslim countries outside of Southeast Asia are not even blessed with this less than dynamic form of capitalism for a variety of geopolitical reasons. The focus on *ersatz* capitalism leads to a consideration of patronage and related phenomena such as rent-seeking and corruption. Capitalists are dependent on the state for assistance in order to be successful. Kleptocrats (Andreski 1968) or corruptors extend various forms of favours to private capitalists, that encompass incentives, licensing, protectionism, low interest loans from state banks, concessions, and joint-ventures. The relationship between kleptocrat and capitalist is one of patron and client. This is a special relation between a politically powerful patron and client who needs his/her protection due to the inadequacies of formal economic institutions. Therefore, the role that state officials play in advancing their private material interests takes its toll on economic development. Here we are referring to the activities of corrupt state officials. Their presence in various Muslim countries is sufficiently felt and has generated some research (Alatas, Syed Hussein 1990; Gillespie and Okruhlik 1988; Kameir and Kursany 1985; Waterbury 1976).

The kleptocratic state is one that is dominated by state officials who subordinate the interests of the public to their private interests. But the kleptocratic state refers to more than just a state in which corruption is present.[4] It refers to a state in which the dominant means of capital accumulation are via corruption. Much of the debate in Asia on democracy and authoritarianism tends to overlook the fact that corruption is what Syed Hussein Alatas calls transystemic (1990). In other words, it is found in all political and economic systems, whether feudal or capitalist, democratic or authoritarian. Nevertheless, to the extent that democracies demand greater accountability and allow for a greater role of the public in the affairs of government, the push for democracy and the rise of civil society in the Muslim world are important developments. But what are the prospects of democracy in the Muslim world?

CIVIL SOCIETY AND DEMOCRATIZATION: IDEOLOGY AND UTOPIA

A distinctive feature of democracies is citizenship. While all types of political systems have rulers and the ruled, it is only democracies that have citizens. The concept of citizenship dates back to classical Greece but acquired its modern meaning after the French and American revolutions. A citizen is one who has civil, political and social rights. Therefore, a society has citizens only to the extent that it is democratic. A central feature of a democracy is the prominence of civil society, the intermediate sphere of society between the private realm of the family and the political relations of the state. Civil society consists of a variety of organizations and individuals engaged in various activities as interest and pressure groups seeking to influence public policy as well as the free-floating intellectuals that Karl Mannheim spoke of.

If we understand the role of intellectuals in terms of agitation for change and consciousness raising of the masses, the question, as far as Indonesia and Malaysia are concerned, becomes whether the intellectuals and other civil society actors here can play such a role effectively. Whatever the structural constraints and objective conditions might be, there is always potential for the opening up of democratic space, as the last three years have shown. So, as I see it, a central issue is the role that intellectuals can play in this process of expanding democratic space.

Here, it is useful to approach the question in terms of Mannheim's concept of utopia. In a paper entitled "Religion and Utopian Thinking Among the Muslims of Southeast Asia", Shaharuddin Maaruf (2000/01) applies this concept to the study of the social and political thought of Muslims in the region. Utopian thinking refers to that which "is incapable of correctly diagnosing an existing condition of society" because those doing the thinking "are not at all concerned with what really exists; rather, in their thinking they already seek to change the situation that exists. Their thought is never a diagnosis of the situation; it can only be used as a direction for action" (Mannheim 1976, p. 36). Individuals or groups guided by utopian thinking are so keen on the transformation or destruction of the existing situation that they only see those aspects of that situation that tend to negate it. Utopias are, therefore, different from ideologies that focus on those elements of a given condition that tend to preserve it.

Utopian thinking "lends a millenarian, populist, eschatological and orthodox character to the religious life of many Muslims in Southeast Asia" and "underlies the demands for the establishment of the Islamic states and the implementation of Islamic laws" (Shaharuddin Maaruf 2000/01, p. 2). Shaharuddin lists the following as traits of utopian thinking as they apply to Muslims in Southeast Asia: (1) the rejection and denial of the existing order, (2) the posing of a radical alternative to the existing order, (3) distortion of certain aspects of current realities which challenge their ideas, (4) the role of ideas in mobilization rather than for the purpose of diagnosis, and (5) its populist rather than intellectual nature.

An example of utopian thought that Shaharuddin gives is the totality of the claim that Islam is a complete way of life, which thereby denies the necessity of debate with rival ideas such as capitalism, socialism, democracy, and humanism, and ensures "the integrity of their own system of thought..." (Shaharuddin Maaruf 2000/01, p. 5).

This being the case, what can we say of the role of Muslim revivalist and orthodox *ulama*. If we accept the idea that their thinking is dominated by utopias of one variety or another, what will be their impact on civil society? We can think of at least the following:

1) The lack of a common agenda for political and social transformation among the Muslim intelligentsia;
2) The lack of cohesion in civil society, in that there is little engagement or co-operation with the so-called secular elements of civil society owing to their lack of Islamicity;
3) The lack of engagement with modern knowledge and ideas, especially those pertaining to capitalism as an economic system, democracy, liberalism, and others;
4) Little diagnosis of the existing situation.

What this spells is an under-developed Muslim social thought in theory and practice, and an intellectually impoverished Muslim civil society, and therefore the inability to engage in those activities that contribute to the opening up of democratic space. This translates into little change as far as the regimes of Malaysia and Indonesia today are concerned.

Finally, the point needs to be made about Islam in relation to the idea of civil society. Many suggest that the Islamic notion of *mujtama' madani* (*masyarakat madani*) in Malay/ Indonesian corresponds to the idea of civil society as it is understood in the social sciences. This is not the case. Those calling for a more vibrant civil society seek greater political space and participation. Those calling for the establishment of *mujtama' madani* have in mind something quite different. Syed Muhammad al-Naquib Al-Attas (1976) has pointed out that the concept of *masyarakat madani* does not refer to civil society but rather to a religion-based society founded upon the ethical and moral system of Islam. The terms *madani*, *madinah* (city), and *din* (usually translated as religion) are all derived from the same root, d-y-n. According to al-Attas, the fact that the name of Yathrib was changed to al-Madinah means that it was there that the real *din* was established (Al-Attas 1976, ch. 3). The term *madaniyah* refers to a religious community. In Islam, civilized life is life in a *masyarakat madani*, and it is the *madinah* where a *madani*-type existence is established, informed by the ethical system and moral order of Islam.

Rather than use civil society and *masyarakat madani* interchangeably, we should have a correct understanding of their different meanings and realize that the struggle for the democracy of Islam is in fact a struggle for both civil society and *masyarakat madani*, that is, for democratic space as well as an Islamic moral order. To acknowledge that democracy is a term and institution that originated in the West is not to say there is no notion of democracy in Islam or that democracy cannot be Islamized, as Syed Hussein Alatas pointed out in an early work, *The Democracy of Islam*. According to Alatas, two fundamental features of the democracy of Islam are concerned with the unity of the human race and the freedom of belief. Mutual benefit and understanding are to be derived from differences among people. Because these differences are natural, it follows that people should be free in expressing their different ways of life (Alatas, Syed Hussein 1956, p. 37). We may conclude, therefore, that the public realm of freedom and action sought is part of the notion of *masyarakat madani*.

CONCLUSION

This brief assessment of the response of Islamic economists to the general issue of modernization yields a number of conclusions about this discourse that can be itemized as follows:

1. While economists have generally maintained the rigorous separation between positive and normative economics, in the Muslim world, however, concerted attempts have been made to relate moral conduct to economic institutions and practices. This is a result of dissatisfaction with both modernization and Marxist-inspired theories that are understood by Islamic economists as being located within the orbit of ideological orientations that are at odds with Islam. Demands for an alternative theory and practice of development to both modernization and Marxist theories had led to the rise of Islamic economics.

But while Islamic economic thinking presents an ideal of development that is based on an Islamic philosophy of life, it is beset by a number of problems which make it difficult to be considered as an alternative to modernist discourse as far as empirical theory is concerned. As such, so-called Islamic economics cannot be considered as presenting an indigenous and alternative development theory. As an ethical theory of development Islam offers an alternative to modernization, dependency and neo-Marxist theories. However, as an empirical theory, so-called Islamic economic theory remains within the fold of Western modernist discourse in terms of its theoretical concerns and methodology.

2. As a result, no conceptual vocabulary within the Islamic tradition developed to deal with modernization at a philosophical and social scientific level. While many Muslim scholars are against a number of labels that have become popular in the media as a well as "scientific" discourse on Islam, they generally failed to construct alternatives terms that would have arrived from new conceptualization. An example is the term Islam itself. There has been much talk of different "brands" or "versions" or "strains" of Islam in the media of late. Muslims are against such labelling as it implies that there are many Islams when in fact there is only one. How then may we discuss the problem of variation within Islam? Is there a pristine, pure Islam with the others being pretenders or aberrations? The only way out is to have the correct conceptual vocabulary that would enable social scientists to talk about Islam in a way that captures its unity as well as its diversity without falling into the trap of the labels mentioned above. For example, a distinction could be made between Islam at the abstract level (*din*) and concrete translations of this in the sense of different kinds of social groupings such as *tariqah* (ways of life), *ahl* (people, relations) and so on. The variations among Muslims can be captured by such terms. From the point of view of Islam, it would not be erroneous to speak of a backward *tariqah* or *ahl*.

This would imply not only an Islamic ideal of development but also serious investigations into the practice of Islamic economic institutions in history. While there are such studies (for example, Udovitch 1962, 1970*a*, 1970*b*; Abdullah 1989; Orman 1997, 1998), proponents of Islamic economics have generally not taken these into account in their theoretical work.

3. Another problem concerns that of legalistic thinking among many Muslim scholars and community leaders. Islam is not conceived of as a way of life but rather a set of rules and regulations. Therefore, other aspects of life that are encompassed by the process of modernization such as the rational outlook on life, order, system, rights and good governance are not covered by what has been labelled as Islamic discourses on development, although these issues are tied to Islamic concepts such as *'ilm* (knowledge), *'amal* (practice), *'adl* (justice), *akhlaq* (character), *kamal* (perfection), and others.

4. I have already referred to the problem of the lack of concepts from within the Islamic tradition that may serve as a basis for speaking about the development of Muslim societies. A related problem is the relative neglect of the social sciences when it comes to the provision of rational justifications for rules and laws in Islam. I am referring to the provision of social scientific bases for rules and laws in Islam. A case in point would be Ibn Khaldun's sociological justification for not following the Prophetic tradition to the effect that the leadership of the *ummah* must always be in the hands of the *Quraysh*. Ibn Khaldun's argument was that this ruling only applied to times when the group feeling (*'asabiyyah*) of the *Quraysh* was sufficiently strong so as to command the allegiance of other groups (Ibn Khaldun 1967, pp. 396f). Social scientific reasoning would be a great asset as far as the rethinking of *hudud* and other laws are concerned.

5. Yet another problem has to do with corrupt leadership, a weak civil society and the lack of will to implement good laws and to build sound executive, legislative and legal institutions.

6. That any theory of development must take into account the role of the state as well as civil society is obvious. Islamic economics, however, tends to shun a political economy approach. This is despite the fact that there is a tradition akin to the political economy approach in Islam. An exemplar for this approach would be Ibn Khaldun.

7. There is also the problem of worldview in which Muslims of the modern period tend not to take this world seriously and not regard as obligatory (*wajib*) the study and mastery of reality in all of its dimensions.

A more creative approach among Muslim economists would result neither in the uncritical adoption Western models and theories of development with the customary terminological adornments, nor in the wholesale rejection of the Western contribution to economic thought, but in a system that is cognizant of the realities of economic life in the Muslim world and that is not innocent of political economy. Thus far, calls for a *masyarakat madani* have not been made in this context and there appears to be a disjuncture between pro-democracy proponents on the one hand and those seeking an Islamic order on the other.

Notes

1 Various aspects of academic dependency have been discussed elsewhere. See Ake (1979); Altbach (1977); Garreau 1988; Said (1993); Weeks (1990); Alatas (2000).
2 The following account draws from previous sketches of the Islamic view of development (Alatas 1995, p. 93; Alatas 1997*a*, pp. 71–72).
3 The discussion here is founded on the distinction between ethical and empirical theories, draws from Alatas (1995, pp. 93–95; 1997*a*, pp. 72–74).
4 On the need for a theory of the kleptocratic state see Alatas (1993*b*, pp. 382–83; 1997*b*). I initially raised the question of the relationship between Islam and civil society in the context of the concepts of ideology and utopia in Alatas (2001). For an exposition of this see Al-Attas (1976). In this work Al-Attas elaborates on the conceptual connections between *din* and related terms such as *madinah*, *tamaddun* and others. Personal communication with Syed Muhammad al-Naquib Al-Attas, 20 May 2000.

References

Abdul Mannan, Muhammad. "Allocative Efficiency, Decision and Welfare Criteria in an Interest-Free Islamic Economy: A Comparative Policy Approach". *Monetary and Fiscal Economics of Islam*, edited by Mohammad Ariff. Jeddah: ICRIE, 1982.

Abdul Rauf, *A Muslim's Reflections on Democratic Capitalism*. Washington, D.C.: American Enterprise Institute, 1984.

Abdullah Alwi bin Haji Hassan. "Al-Mudarabah (Dormant Partnership) and its Identical Islamic Partnerships in Early Islam". *Hamdard Islamicus* 12, no. 2 (1989): 11–38.

Abu Saud, Mahmoud. "Toward Islamic Economics". In *Toward Islamization of Disciplines*. Herndon, Virginia: International Institute of Islamic Thought, 1989.

Afzal-ur-Rahman. *Economic Doctrines of Islam* 1. Lahore: Islamic Publications, 1980*a*.

Afzal-ur-Rahman. *Economic Doctrines of Islam* 2. Lahore: Islamic Publications, 1980*b*.

Ahmad, Kurshid. "Economic Development in an Islamic Framework". *Studies in Islamic Development*, edited by Kurshid Ahmad. Jeddah: International Centre for Research in Islamic Economics, King Abdul Aziz University, 1980.

Ahmad, Ziauddin. "Interest-Free Banking in Pakistan". *Journal of Islamic Banking and Finance* 4 (1987): 8–30.

Aidit Ghazali. *Development: An Islamic Perspective*. Petaling Jaya: Pelanduk Publications, 1990.

Ake, C. *Social Science as Imperialism: The Theory of Political Development*. Ibadan: University of Ibadan Press, 1979.

Alatas, Syed Farid. "Reflections on the Idea of Islamic Social Science". *Comparative Civilizations Review* no. 17 (1987*a*): 60–86.

_____. "An Islamic Common Market and Economic Development". *Islamic Culture* 61, no. 1 (1987*b*): 28–38.

_____. "Agama dan Ilmu Kemasyarakatan: Masalah Teoretis" [Religion and Social Science: Theoretical Problems]. *Journal Antropologi dan Sosiologi* 21 (1993*a*).

_____. "Theoretical Perspectives on the Role of State Elites in Southeast Asian Development". *Contemporary Southeast Asia* 14, no. 4 (1993*b*): 368–95.

_____. "The Sacralization of the Social Sciences: A Critique of an Emerging Theme in Academic Discourse". *Archives de Sciences Sociales des Religions* 91 (1995): 89–111.

_____. "Islam and Counter Modernism: Towards Alternative Development Paradigms". In *Islamic Political Economy in Capitalist-Globalization: An Agenda for Change*, edited by Masudul Alam Choudhury, Abdad M.Z. and Muhammad Syukri Salleh. Kuala Lumpur: Utusan, 1997*a*, pp. 67–89.

_____. "The Post-Colonial State: Dual Functions in the Public Sphere". *Humboldt Journal of Social Relations* 23, nos. 1–2 (1997*b*): 285–307.

_____. "Islam, Ilmu-Ilmu Sosial, dan Masyarakat Sipil". *Antropologi Indonesia* 25, no. 66 (2001): 13–22.

_____. "Academic Dependency in the Social Sciences: Reflections on India and Malaysia". *American Studies International* 38, no. 2 (2000): 80–96.

Alatas, Hussein [Syed Hussein Alatas], *The Democracy of Islam: A Concise Exposition with Comparative Reference to Western Political Thought*, Bandung and The Hague: W. Van Hoeve, 1956.

Alatas, Syed Hussein. *Modernization and Social Change: Studies in Modernization, Religion, Social Change and Development in South-East Asia*. Sydney: Angus and Robertson, 1972.

_____. "The Captive Mind in Development Studies" *International Social Science Journal* 34, no. 1 (1972): 9–25.

_____. "The Captive Mind and Creative Development". *International Social Science Journal* 36, no. 4 (1974): 691–99.

_____. *Corruption: Its Nature, Causes and Functions*. Aldershot: Avebury, 1990.

Al-Attas, Syed Muhammad al-Naquib. *Islam: The Concept of Religion and the Foundation of Ethics and Morality*, Kuala Lumpur: ABIM, 1976.

_____. *The Concept of Education in Islam: A Framework for an Islamic Philosophy of Education*. Kuala Lumpur: ABIM, 1980.

Alhabshi, Syed Othman. "Peranan Akhlak dalam Pengurusan Ekonomi dan Kewangan" [The Role of Morality in Economic and Financial Management]. In *Kecemerlangan Pentadbiran: Dasar dan Amalan dalam Islam* (*Administrative Excellence: Policy and Practice in Islam*), edited by Shafie Hj. Mohd. Salleh and Mohd. Affandi Hassan. Kuala Lumpur: INTAN, 1990.

Altbach, Philip G. "Servitude of the Mind? Education, Dependency, and Neocolonialism" Teachers' College Record 79, 2 (1977): 187–204.

Andreski, Stanislav. "Kleptocracy or Corruption as a System of Government". The African Predicamant. New York: Atherton, 1968.

Anisur Rahman, Md. "Towards an Alternative Development Paradigm", IFDA Dossier 81 (1991): 18–27.

Ariff, Mohammad, ed. Money and Banking in Islam. Jeddah: ICRIE, 1982.

As-Sadr, Muhammad Baqir. Iqtisaduna: Our Economics, 2 vols. Tehran: World Organization for Islamic Services, 1982–84.

_____. Towards an Islamic Economy. Tehran: Bonyad Be'that, 1984.

_____. Islam and Schools of Economics, Tehran: Bonyad Be'that, 1984.

Booth, David. "Marxism and Development Sociology: Interpreting the Impasse" World Development 13, 7 (1985): 761–87.

Choudhury, Masudul Alam. "Principles of Islamic Economics", Middle Eastern Studies 19, 1 (1983): 93–103.

Dube, S.C. "Social Sciences for the 1980s: From Rhetoric to Reality". International Social Science Journal 34, no. 3 (1982): 495–502.

Edwards, Michael. "The Irrelevance of Development Studies". Third World Quarterly 11, 1 (1989): 116–35.

Faridi, F.R. "Zakat and Fiscal Policy". In Studies in Islamic Development, edited by Kurshid Ahmad. Jeddah: International Centre for Research in Islamic Economics, King Abdul Aziz University, 1980.

Fazlur Rahman. "Riba and Interest" Islamic Studies 3 (1964): 1–43.

_____. "Islam and the Problem of Economic Justice". Pakistan Economist 14 (1974): 14–39.

_____. "Islamization of Knowledge: A Response". American Journal of Islamic Social Science 5, no. 1 (1988):

Garreau, Frederick H. "Another Type of Third World Dependency: The Social Sciences" International Sociology 3, no. 2 (1988): 171–78.

Gilani, Ijas Shafi. "The Political Context of Islamic Economics". In Studies in Islamic Development, edited by Kurshid Ahmad. Jeddah: International Centre for Research in Islamic Economics, King Abdul Aziz University, 1980.

Gillespie, Kate and Gwenn Okruhlik. "Cleaning Up Corruption in the Middle East". Middle East Journal 42, no. 1 (1988): 59–82.

Hagen, E.E. On the Theory of Social Change: How Economic Growth Begins. Homewood, Il: Dorsey, 1962.

Hassan, Riaz. "The Muslim World in the International Economic System — An Overview". Journal: Institute of Muslim Minority Affairs 13, no. 2 (1992).

Ibn Khaldun. The Muqaddimah: An Introduction to History. 3 vols. London and Henley: Routledge & Kegan Paul, 1967.

Inkeles, A. and D. Smith. Becoming Modern: Individual Change in Six Developing Countries. Cambridge: Harvard University Press, 1974.

Iqbal, Zubair and Abbas Mirakhor. *Islamic Banking.* Occasional Paper no. 49, Washington, D.C.: International Monetary Fund, 1987.

Kahf, Monzer. "Savings and Investment Functions in a Two- Sector Islamic Economy". In *Monetary and Fiscal Economics of Islam,* edited by Mohammad Ariff. Jeddah: ICRIE, 1982.

Kameir, El-Wathig and Ibrahim Kursany. "Corruption as the 'Fifth' Factor of Production in the Sudan". Scandinavian Institute of African Studies, research report no. 72, Uppsala, 1985.

_____. "The Economic System in Contemporary Islamic Thought". *International Journal of Middle East Studies* 18, no. 2 (1986): 135–64.

_____. "On the Notion of Economic Justice in Contemporary Islamic Thought". *International Journal of Middle East Studies* 21, no. 2 (1989): 171–91.

Karsten, Ingo. "Islam and Financial Intermediation". *IMF Staff Papers* 29, no. 1 (1982): 108–42.

Khan, Fahim. "A Macro Consumption Function in an Islamic Framework". *Journal of Research in Islamic Economics* 1, no. 2 (1984): 1–24.

Khan, Mohsin S. "Islamic Interest-Free Banking: A Theoretical Analysis". *IMF Staff Papers* 33, no. 1 (1986): 1–27.

Khan, Mohsin S. and Abbas Mirakhor, eds. *Theoretical Studies in Islamic Banking and Finance.* Houston: Institute for Research and Islamic Studies, 1987.

_____. "Islamic Banking: Experiences in the Islamic Republic of Iran and in Pakistan". *Economic Development and Cultural Change* 38, no. 2 (1990): 353–75.

Khan, Muhammad Akram. "Islamic Economics: The State of the Art". In *Toward Islamization of Disciplines.* Herndon, Virginia: International Institute of Islamic Thought, 1989.

Kunio, Yoshihara. *The Rise of Ersatz Capitalism in Southeast Asia.* Singapore: Oxford University Press, 1988.

Kuran, Timur. "Behavioral Norms in the Islamic Doctrine of Economics: A Critique". *Journal of Economic Behavior and Organization* 4 (1983): 353–79.

Manzo, Kate. "Modernist Discourse and the Crisis of Development Theory". *Studies in Comparative International Development* 26, no. 2 (1991): 3–36.

Masters, Bruce. *The Origins of Western Economic Dominance: Mercantilism and the Islamic Economy in Aleppo, 1600-1700.* New York: New York University Press, 1988.

McClelland, D.C. *The Achieving Society.* New York: Free Press, 1967.

Mehmet, Ozay. *Islamic Identity and Development: Studies of the Islamic Periphery.* Kuala Lumpur: Forum, 1990.

Muhaimin, Yahya. *Bisnis dan Politik: Kebijaksanaan Ekonomi Indonesia 1950–1980.* Jakarta: LP3ES, 1990.

Nasr, Seyyed Vali Reza. "Towards a Philosophy of Islamic Economics". *Muslim World* 77, nos. 3–4 (1987): 175–96.

_____. "Religious Modernism in the Arab World, India and Iran: The Perils and Prospects of a Discourse". *Muslim World* 83, no. 1 (1993): 20–47.

Nyang, Sulayman S. "The Islamic State and Economic Development: A Theoretical Analysis". *Islamic Culture* 50, no. 2 (1976): 1–23.

Orman, Sabri. "Sources of the History of Islamic Economic Thought". *Al-Shajarah* 2, no. 1 (1997): 21–62.

_____. "Sources of the History of Islamic Economic Thought II". *Al-Shajarah* 3, no. 1 (1998): 1–17.

Philipp, Thomas. "The Idea of Islamic Economics". *Die Welt des Islams* 30 (1990): 117–39.

Portes, A. "On the Sociology of National Development". *American Journal of Sociology* 82, no. 1 (1976): 55–85.

Pryor, Frederic L. "The Islamic Economic System". *Journal of Comparative Economics* 9 (1985): 197–223.

Rostow, W.W. *The Stages of Economic Growth: A Non-Communist Manifesto.* Cambridge: Cambridge University Press, 1960.

Sadr, Sayyid Muhammad Baqir. *An Introduction to Principles of Islamic Banking.* Tehran: Bonyad Be'that, 1982.

Sadr, Muhammad Baqer (Sayyid Muhammad Baqir). "General Edifice of the Islamic Economy". In *Islamic Economics: Contemporary Ulama Perspectives*, edited by Muhammad Baqer Sadr and Ayatullah Sayyid Mahmud Taleghani. Kuala Lumpur: Iqra', 1991.

Said, Edward. *Culture and Imperialism.* London: Chatto and Windus, 1993.

Sardar, Ziauddin. "Islamic Economics: Breaking Free From the Dominant Paradigm". *Afkar Inquiry* 2, no. 4 (1985): 40–47.

_____. *The Future of Muslim Civilization.* London: Mansell Publishing, 1987.

Shaharuddin Maaruf. "Religion and Utopian Thinking Among the Muslims of Southeast Asia". Seminar Papers, Department of Malay Studies, National University of Singapore, 2000/01.

Shari'ati, Ali. *Marxism and Other Western Fallacies: An Islamic Critique.* Berkeley: Mizan Press, 1980.

Sheth, D.L. "Alternative Development as Political Practice," *Alternatives* 12 (1987): 155–71.

Siddiqi, Muhammad Nejatullah. *Some Aspects of the Islamic Economy.* Delhi: Markazi Maktaba Islami, 1981.

_____. "An Islamic Approach to Economics". In *Islam: Source and Purpose of Knowledge.* Herndon, Virginia: International Institute of Islamic Thought, 1988.

_____. "Islamizing Economics". In *Toward Islamization of Disciplines.* Herndon, Virginia: International Institute of Islamic Thought, 1989.

Siddiqui, Shamim Ahmad and Asad Zaman. "Investment and Income Distribution Pattern under Musharka Finance: A Certainty Case". *Pakistan Journal of Applied Economics* 8, no. 1 (1989*a*): 1–30.

_____. "Investment and Income Distribution Pattern under Musharka Finance: The Uncertainty Case". *Pakistan Journal of Applied Economics* 8, no. 1 (1989*b*): 31–71.

Smith, T. "Requiem or New Agenda for Third World Studies". *World Politics* 37, no. 4 (1985): 532–61.

Taleqani, Seyyed Mahmood. *Islam and Ownership*. Lexington, Kentucky: Mazda Publishers, 1983.

Tibi, Bassam. *The Crisis of Modern Islam: A Preindustrial Culture in a Scientific-Technological Age*. Salt Lake City: University of Utah Press, 1988.

Udovitch, A.L. "At the Origins of the Western Commenda: Islam, Israel, Byzantium?" *Speculum* 37 (1962): 198–207.

_____. *Partnership and Profit in Medieval Islam*. Princeton: Princeton University Press, 1970*a*.

_____. "Commercial Techniques in Early Medieval Islamic Trade". In *Islam and the Trade of Asia*, edited by D.S. Richards. Oxford: Bruno Cassirer, 1970*b*.

Uzair, Muhammad. "Some Conceptual and Practical Aspects of Interest-Free Banking". In *Studies in Islamic Development*, edited by Kurshid Ahmad. Jeddah: International Centre for Research in Islamic Economics, King Abdul Aziz University, 1980.

Vandergeest, P. and Buttel, F.H. "Marx, Weber and Development Sociology: Beyond the Impasse". *World Development* 16, no. 6 (1988): 683–95.

Waterbury, John. "Corruption, Political Stability and Development: Comparative Evidence from Egypt and Morocco". *Government and Opposition* 2 (1976).

Weeks, Priscilla. "Post-Colonial Challenges to Grand Theory". *Human Organization* 49, no. 3 (1990): 236–44.

Weiss, Dieter. "Ibn Khaldun on Economic Transformation". *International Journal of Middle East Studies* 27 (1995): 29–37.

Wiarda, H. "Rethinking Political Development: A Look Back over Thirty Years, and a Look Ahead". *Studies in Comparative International Development* 24, no. 4 (1989): 65–82.

Zarqa, Mohammed Anas. "Stability in an Interest-Free Islamic Economy: A Note". *Journal of Applied Economics* (published in Pakistan) 2 (1983): 181–88.

12

MODERNIZATION AND THE PROCESS OF GLOBALIZATION: THE MUSLIM EXPERIENCE AND RESPONSES

Abdul Rashid Moten

INTRODUCTION

This chapter analyzes Muslim responses to the various challenges and opportunities associated with modernization, and processes of globalization. These two processes have aroused anxiety, suspicion, and opposition, especially in the Muslim world. Muslims regard modernity and globalism as a Western, particularly American, project for world domination. They believe that America's attempt to homogenize the world would degrade all other countries into servants. When members believe their core faith is being corrupted, many are angered and some organize to rectify matters. The Western media, barring few exceptions, have mainly taken note of "Islamic fundamentalism" in its most violent manifestations — blowing up apartment blocks, kidnapping geologists and razing the WTC towers in New York to the ground. The West deploys "Islamic fundamentalism" as a pejorative term to disparage and discredit Muslims "as irrational, irresponsible and extremist forces, dedicated, actually or potentially, to the goal of international terrorism."[1] It is unfortunate that Muslim concerns about the global system and the globalization process have been sorely neglected by the dominant forces in the West. Is modernization and globalization compatible with Islam? How do Muslims perceive this process of globalization? What is the nature of their response and what alternatives do they provide to the ongoing process of modernization and globalization?

MODERNIZATION, GLOBALIZATION AND ISLAM

Modernization refers to the processes whereby society becomes modern. It implies industrialization, economic growth, increasing social mobility, and political participation. At the level of values, the process of change has sometimes been described as one of cultural "secularization" — a decline in the influence of religion and of traditional ideas as to the "naturalness" of social inequality, and correspondingly the spread of materialistic, this-worldly values and the ideals of universal equality and liberty. At the ideological level, this found expression, firstly, in nationalism and then in various formulations of democracy, whether the liberal parliamentary democracy of Western states or the more radical communist version.

In the past two decades, modernization has been accelerated and accentuated by globalization. Modern institutions like the nation-state and liberal economics, with its emphasis on the creation of markets, have become the means through which the world is being made one. Giddens defines globalization as "the intensification of worldwide social relation which link distant localities in such a way that local happenings are shaped by events occurring many miles away and *vice versa*."[2] It is a technologically-driven process that increases commercial and political relations between people of different countries. A globalized system is characterized largely by capitalistic competition where goods, services, capital, ideas and even values cross national boundaries and acquire a transnational character. In short, globalization refers to the process of growing inter-connectedness by which the world is made into a single place economically, politically and culturally. It aims at creating a world system that shifts many former national concerns to the world geopolitical stage. Globalist ideology comes in many forms. Bill Gates wants to tie the entire world together through Internet and Microsoft. Greenpeace wants to save the world by fighting environmental degradation everywhere. A huge human rights network forced the United States and Britain to fight a war in Kosovo. However, it is the United States that has championed globalization. It has done so by systematically pressing to remove any national barriers to the free movement of capital, goods, and services. It has done so through international, now global, financial institutions, especially the International Monetary Fund (IMF), the World Bank, and the World Trade Organization (WTO).

Although most Muslim societies have not yet experienced an industrial revolution, they have, as a consequence of colonization, witnessed an increase in commercialization and, perhaps equally important, in the influence of Western institutions, values, beliefs and ideologies. These factors, it has been argued by many, have generally worked to undermine traditional or pre-colonial values, beliefs and political institutions. While initially there was resistance to the intrusion of the West, gradually the Muslims realized that most of these values are not incompatible with Islam. From a historical perspective it would seem that of all the non-Western civilizations in the world, Islam offers the best prospects for modernization and democracy. As President Clinton puts it, Islam's "traditional values are in harmony with the best of Western ideals."[3]

Islam is not merely a religion. It is a complete, comprehensive civilization. Muslims all over the world are inspired by their religion with pride and self-respect, and a desire for freedom. This spirit underlies this century's continuous revolts against foreign rule. Islam is rooted in divine revelation. However, the truth of revelation was always appreciated in the light of reason. From the very beginning, revelation's relation to reason continued to be of central importance in all philosophical and theological debates. It is well known that great Muslim jurists like Imam Abu Hanifah, al-Tahawi, al-Maturidi and al-Ghazali adopted the principles and methods of reasoning as an avenue to knowledge. This is in accordance with the Qur'an's repeated exhortations to reason out and rationally weigh all matters to enable one to follow the "right way" (see *Surat al-Hashar*, 59:2; *Surat al-A'raf*, 7:86, etc.).

Islam instructs its followers to believe in this world and the world to come in such a way as not to have one overpower the other. The Muslim has the right to enjoy the pleasures of this world, because it was created for him: "But seek with the (wealth) which Allah has bestowed on you, the Home of the Hereafter, nor forget your portion in this world." (*Surat al-Qasas*, 28:77).

Thus, contrary to widespread belief, there is not much disagreement between Islamic principles and values espoused by modernization. However, Islam is not secular. The fundamental principle of Islam is *tawhid*, meaning unity and sovereignty of Allah. Consequently, there is no separation between religion and the state.[4] However, if secularism is defined as belief in pluralism and respect for all religions, then Islam may also be called secular. Islam is categorical: "Let there be no compulsion in religion" (*Surat al-Baqarah*, 2:256) and "To you be your Way and to me mine" (*Surat al-Kafirun*, 109:6).[5] The Qur'an also reminds humankind that society, by divine design, is plural that is, multi-ethnic, multi-racial, and multi-religious. The definite purpose to this diversity and pluralism is "to know one another" (*Surat al-Hujurat*, 49:13). Thus, unlike the West, "modernity" in Islam is mediated by religion as a spiritual force and as a self-transforming technique.

Like modernization, many of the major ideas associated with globalization are in harmony with Islamic thought. Islam is a force of global proportions; it is universalistic. Islam has pronounced all mankind as one and it compared it to a single organic entity in which the individual cannot do without the entire human society and *vice versa*. As an absolute that includes everything in the universe, Islam is based on the nature of things, particularly on the Divine nature itself. Hence the idea of unity (*tawhid*) is seen as a means of becoming whole and realizing the inherent oneness of all existence. The oneness of Allah necessarily implies the unity of the human race. According to the global Qur'an, "Mankind was one single nation" (*Surat al-Baqarah*, 2:213). From a Muslim point of view, the principle of unity (*tawhid*) applies to spirit and matter, soul and body, science and religion, and also to Muslims as social beings; their aim is always to unite as a community (*ummah*). This unity rejects any world order that perpetuates the dominance and control of an oligarchy over the rest of humanity. Domination diminishes human dignity and splits humankind into the powerful few and the powerless many. The human being surrenders only to Allah who is the Creator of the universe. Before Allah human beings are equal. Unity of mankind is predicated upon the equality of mankind. All human beings must have equal access to the mental, moral and material resources that will enable them to contribute meaningfully to the overall development of humankind. The egalitarianism in Islam is genuine and pronounced. This is confirmed by the daily prayers facing the *qiblah*, and the very formation in which they are said.

Unity also implies toleration. The Qur'an repeatedly maintains that differences between men, in terms of colour, wealth, race and language, are natural (*Surat al-Rum*, 30:22). It even describes ideological and religious pluralism as given by Allah (*Surat al-Ma'idah*, 5:48) and reminds that these differences are meant for greater facility of inter-connectedness.[6] This attitude compels tolerance and is corroborated in many verses of the Qur'an (*Surat al-Kahf*, 18:29). At the heart of this attitude of comprehensive intellectual and practical tolerance is the fundamental statement in *Surat al-Baqarah* (2:256), a statement both factual and normative: "There is no compulsion in matters of faith." Some people tend to view Islam as if it were a monolithic or uni-dimensional entity. Islam is undoubtedly the faith of transcendental monotheism, the belief in the one and only Allah, who transcends both man and nature. But monotheism does not lead to monism; on the contrary, it leads to plurality and diversity. From a strictly Islamic point of view, except for Allah, everything else exists in variety.

Equally important, human beings should remain actively conscious of their roles as vicegerents or trustees (*khalīfah*) of Allah. As bearers of Allah's trust, human beings exercise rights and shoulder responsibilities for the good of the whole of the human race. Everybody has a right to participate in the process of production and no section of the society will be ignored in the process of distribution. Islam encourages all types of economic activities and recognizes the right of lawful possession, enjoyment and transfer of property. It permits the holding of what is known as functional property and encourages the productive and beneficial use of capital. It discourages hoarding by a few self-seeking rich individuals and stimulates spending. Islam emphasizes equitable distribution of wealth and looks with disdain at those who profiteer at the cost of suffering millions.

The Qur'an, the *haj*, and the *Qiblah* are among the Islamic symbols that relate to globalism. These are living testimonies to the fact that Islam considers the whole world as one object and the whole of humankind as one object and they are subject to moral striving. This moral imperative requires all individuals to co-operate and work closely to build a cohesive human society for unity and common prosperity. The eternal Islamic message is concerned with the public interest of humanity at large, which cannot be superseded by any interest claimed by a particular class or nation for itself. It has enjoined all nations to refrain from acting on the supposition of their supremacy and assuming that the interests of any one nation take precedence over those of another (see *Surat al-Nahl*, 16:92).

Doctrinally, Islam incorporates Judaism and Christianity. There is a lot about the Torah and of the Old Testament in the Qur'an and the substantial recognition of the Jewish prophets. There is a lot from the New Testament in the Qur'an, from the virgin birth of Jesus, to his sacred miracles. Islam as a civilization began as a creative synthesis. Between the ninth and fourteenth centuries Islamic civilization also demonstrated a high capacity for scientific and technological syntheses. Just as Islam had been receptive to Judaism and Christianity in the sphere of religious doctrine it demonstrated receptivity to ancient Greece in the secular field. Abu Nasr al-Farabi (259–339AH/870–950 CE) gave an "authoritative beginning to the integration of Greek-Hellenic philosophy in all its branches with Islam."[7] Abul Walid Ibn Rushd (520–592AH/1126–1198 CE) was a confirmed Muslim and an Aristotelian who concluded that the world was round. Likewise, Abu Ali Ibn Sina (379–428AH/980–1037 CE) wrote extensive commentaries on Greek philosophers. He also wrote an important medical work of medieval times, *The Canon of*

Medicine, which became a standard medical reference book at European universities until well into the seventeenth century.

The globalization of Islam began not with converting a ready made empire but with building an empire almost from scratch. The Ummayads and the Abbbasids put together bits of other people's empires — former Byzantium, Egypt and Persia and created a whole new civilization — all of which contributed to globalization in the comprehensive sense.

MUSLIM EXPERIENCES OF MODERNIZATION AND GLOBALIZATION

Islam, as stated, bore the dignity and accomplishment of centuries of cultural sophistication. Indeed, it held sway across a vast region of the globe where a multiplicity of ethnic and regional cultures flourished. It created a world civilization which was poly-ethnic, multi-racial and international. In commerce, in the arts and sciences, in mathematics, in military strength, Islam in the Middle Ages was supreme over Europe and China. Since then, however, this once mighty civilization has fallen low. During the nineteenth century, European armies and enterprises overran the Muslim world and reduced all Muslim territories to a colonial or semi-colonial status. The civilizational mission to "win the world for the Christ" came to be waged by the secular adherents of modernization.

The task of the colonialists, as suggested in 1901 by Baron Carra de Vaux of Catholic Institute, was "to split the Muslim world, to break its moral unity, using to this effect the ethnic and political divisions to accentuate these differences."[8] Eugene de Roberty, the Russian free-thinker and sociologist suggested that Europe should "work on the Muslim elite ... and to proceed with a secular colonization of land and industry (and) to segment the principal Muslim power, the Ottoman Empire."[9] The major victim of the colonial domination was the Muslim's self-image and cultural identity. This was due to the colonial policy of progress and enlightenment which was interpreted to mean education. Lord Macaulay's insistence that "a single shelf of a good European library was worth the whole native literature of India and Arabia" marked the onset of an educational policy which replaced the Oriental with English learning.[10] The educational policy was geared at transmitting the European cultural values to the natives and to make available to the British Raj a class of clerks, collaborators and cronies to continue the cultural onslaught of the West. Lord Macaulay summed up the goal as that of forming "a class who may be interpreters between us and the millions whom we govern; a class of persons Indian in blood and colour but English in taste, in opinions, in morals and intellect."[11]

The policy was pursued with the full force of colonial might and economic pressure. With the resources of Western imperialism at the disposal of English language educational institutions, attempts were made to suppress Islamic education and to phase *shari'ah* out of existence. If Islamic education was permitted, it was made a private affair devoid of public funds. If public funds were made available, a secular curriculum was imposed in the name of progress and enlightenment. The traditional leadership was systematically destroyed and replaced with a new class of Western educated elite. The *ulama*, who had a virtual monopoly of the legal profession, were routed out in favour of those who studied Western law and education. A foreign-oriented local leadership was thus imposed which eventually became the heir of the imperial powers. It is this class which became voluntary or involuntary instruments of intermediate domination for the Westernization of Muslim society. They imbibed and implemented liberal ideas and institutions (like nationalism, liberal democracy and a capitalist economic system) and incorporated them into their respective constitutions.

The Westernized local leadership adopted nationalism to unite, for a time, the divergent elites and to mobilize much-needed mass support for independence from colonial rule.[12] Nationalism eventually led to the structure of the modern nation-states, each replete with national frontiers, flags, anthems and its own interests in preference and at the cost of all others. These nation-states were carved out without any reference to geographical factors, the availability of economic activities or lines of communication. As Huntington points out:

> In 1919 Woodrow Wilson, Lloyd George [British Prime Minister], and Georges Clemenceau [French Prime Minister] together virtually controlled the world. Sitting in Paris, they determined what countries would exist and which would not, what new countries would be created, what their boundaries would be and who would rule them, and how the Middle East and other parts of the world would be divided up among the victorious powers.[13]

As a result, many Muslim communities were partitioned into two or more states.[14] For example, example, Hausa/Fulani Muslims of Africa were partitioned between Niger, Nigeria and Chad; the Somalis between Kenya, Ethiopia and Somalia. These have resulted in the estrangement between man from his fellow man, the outbreak of conflicts and wars between nations and the dismemberment of the political power of Islam. The centralized nation-state, growing more authoritarian and stronger, expanded and reached the most private aspects of man's life, and, through its sophisticated security and educational *apparati*, tried to guide its citizens. Maintained by internal oppression and external imperial support, none of these states have solved any of its problems or those of its people. Rather, in this age of hegemonic world order of power states, Muslim powers have become third ranking client states.

Within these nation-states, the prime concern of the ruling elites has been to perpetuate and exploit the inherited liberal democratic principles and institutions, that is, the election system, the media and the three arms of government.[15] Elections in the Muslim world, however, have been notorious for the way in which the dominant political forces have suppressed opposition parties, coerced the masses and workers into voting for the approved candidates, used goon squads to harass political rallies, and miscounted ballots or conveniently lost entire ballot boxes in hostile precincts. On numerous occasions, the army has stepped in to nullify elections after the vote showed an unacceptable party or candidate on the verge of winning. The media, another by-product of Western modernity, extensively invaded the private lives of citizens, accelerating the process of standardization and escalating the consumerist fever. In the meantime, hedonistic pursuits became very rampant leading to an increase in social problems such as high divorce and crime rates. These ills have been termed the "malaise of modernity", as they limit people's aspirations and promote erotic utopias and pornography.[16]

In economy too, the ruling elites followed the Western model. Industrialization is its firmly entrenched goal and a capacity for self-sustained growth its major characteristic. Yet, no Muslim country can be said to be fully industrialized, as the average industrial labour force is about twenty per cent with the Muslim majority states of Africa contributing a meagre ten per cent. The development strategy aimed at economic growth and material prosperity has resulted in the rising incidence of urban crime, prostitution, corruption, misuse of power and other aspects of decadence in general. They are equally the product of technical and professional education which ignores moral and spiritual values. In short, not only are Muslims generally poor, many of them are also alienated from their traditions and cultural roots.

The onset of globalization ought to have ameliorated the situation somewhat. It is certainly possible to imagine a world in which globalization could raise the standard of living for the majority of the world's people. In fact, the world economy did show signs of improvement. More products, including previously expensive items, are produced in abundance and at low cost, enabling most of the world to enjoy video cassette recorders (VCRs) and computers. Big, transnational corporations are able to design an item in one country, assemble it in a second country with components from a third, and market it in a fourth. Technological advances are not merely shrinking the world space but are driving down costs at a pace never before seen:

> The cost of transmitting a trillion bits of information from Boston to Los Angeles has fallen from US$150,000 in 1970 to 12 cents today. A three minute phone call from New York to London that in 1930 cost more than $300 (in today's prices) costs less than 20 cents today. E-mailing a 40-page document from Chile to Kenya costs less than 10 cents, faxing it about $10, sending it by courier $50.[17]

There is a rapid development of international trade and an increased flow of capital. Throughout the entire post-war period (with the exception of 1982–85), trade grew more rapidly than world production. The international capital turnover increased significantly, especially over the past two decades as its liberalization intensified. Globalization could increase the size of markets and the efficiency of production, allow countries who are short on capital to borrow from those who have a surplus, and even break down some of the barriers and prejudices that contributed to military conflicts in the past.

Although countries are directly or indirectly affected by globalization, most Muslim countries are not linked to a global economy. The forty-seven Muslim majority countries have populations of about one billion people. Africa houses 199 million Muslims. There are 258 million in the Arab states. Another 727 million Muslims live in central and east Asia. They are moderately urbanized, have relatively high rate of inflation, low rate of economic growth, low life expectancy and a very high level of adult illiteracy. According to the Human Development Report 2002, "During the 1990s the number of people in extreme poverty in Sub-Saharan Africa rose from 242 million to 300 million."[18] Within the international system of economic stratification, the majority of the Muslim population is located in the low income and poorer countries. Twenty-five of these forty-seven countries including the four most populous countries, namely Indonesia, Nigeria, Bangladesh and Pakistan are classified as low income economies (with GNP per capita of US$755 or less in 1999) and eighteen are in the middle income economies (with GNP per capita of US$756–9,265). Only four countries are included in the high income economies.[19] These four are oil-rich countries and contain only about two per cent of the total Muslim world population. In terms of the Technology Achievement Index, not a single Muslim country is included among the "leaders" with high achievements in technology creation and diffusion as well as professional skills. Of the ten Muslim countries surveyed, only one country, Malaysia, is included among "potential leaders" for having invested in high levels of human skills, and has diffused old technologies widely but innovates little. Three of these, Pakistan, Senegal, and Sudan, are termed "marginalized" meaning that technology diffusion and skill-building have a long way to go in these countries. They still use broken typewriters and preserve valuable documents on loose papers. Interestingly, Nigeria had to postpone elections because "termites have chewed up much of Nigeria's voter register."[20] The remaining six countries are termed "dynamic adopters."[21] A few of these Muslim countries, such as Malaysia, are highly integrated in the global economy. Altogether, the exports of the world's forty-seven Muslim countries amount to about 5.8 per cent of the world total. However, Malaysia, with a mere 2.8 per cent of the world's Muslim population, accounts for 25 per cent of its exports. Excluding Malaysia's contribution to that total, the Muslim world's share of the global trade stands at about 4.6 per cent. The Muslim countries' export share of GDP is also very modest especially when compared to the countries of East Asia or Latin America. Another problem facing Muslim countries is the amount of global foreign direct investment that they receive. It, too, is very modest, particularly when contrasted to other developing countries.

The fact that Muslim countries which represent about 15 per cent of the world's population now account for between 4 to 5 per cent of global trade and investment is not due to their anti-global policies. They lag far behind the industrialized countries and have proven incapable of reducing that economic gap. They have neither the opportunity nor the ability to reap the benefits promised by globalization and reduce the restrictions and losses that accompany it. Many Muslim countries feel that the world economy is not really global. As the flows of trade, foreign direct investment and finance demonstrate, the world economy is centred on the triad of Europe, Japan and North America.[22] Power has shifted to the governments and firms of the developed countries, especially the United States and other members of the G-7. Of the known 37,000 transnational corporations, 24,000 are based in only fourteen OECD (Organization for Economic Co-operation and Development) countries and 73 per cent of accumulated stock is in the United States, Japan and Western Europe.[23] There is widespread concern that this new globalization, as in the past, is inseparable from Westernization and Americanization. Brutality and mass poverty continues to dominate most Muslim lives under global capitalism. A majority of Muslim states remain loyal servants of the West and its markets, and yet, most of them cannot show growth, let alone substantial development, even in richer countries like

Nigeria. Clearly then capitalism in Muslim countries has neither been democratic nor developmental.

The reality is that America and the West control Muslim economies and exercises politico-military hegemony over the global political economy. Muslim subordination is supervised and guaranteed under the tight leash of allegedly multilateral institutions of which they are technically and theoretically equal members, such as the United Nations, the Bretton Woods institutions, the World Trade Organization and so on. As the Human Development Report 2002 indicates, "The World Trade Organization operates on a one-country, one-vote basis, but most key decisions are made by the leading economic powers in 'green room' meetings." Likewise, "the executive directors representing France, Germany, Japan, the Russian Federation Saudi Arabia, the United Kingdom and the United States account for 46 per cent of the voting rights in the World Bank and 48 per cent in the International Monetary Fund."[24]

The International Monetary Fund (IMF) and the World Bank (WB) directly control most of the Muslim-majority states and spread Western economic gospels to states who cannot afford to resist them at the same time. They advance global solutions to problems regardless of local specificities. The Structural Adjustment Programmes (SAP) proposed by these institutions call for deregulation (devaluation) of currency markets and the monetary system, privatization of public enterprises, retrenchment of public employees, liberalization of the economy, "free competition" and cutbacks in welfare programmes. Since these measures have yielded few positive results, they eventually undermine the legitimacy of the pro-Western states that submit to them. Popular resistance to austerity programmes, both SAPs and local initiatives, has been common in a number of Muslim-majority states with widely varying political ideologies (Morocco, Algeria, Egypt, Tunisia, Nigeria, Senegal, Pakistan, and Jordan). The debt crisis and neo-liberal restructuring of Muslim economies has inspired populist resistance and rallied moderates to support the more radical Islamic opposition to political programmes that reduce state subsidies, curtail state investment, and impoverish those most vulnerable in the Muslim community.

In the 1950s and 1960s, Western development experts, policymakers and planners advocated modernization (that is, import substitution, industrialization, Westernization through education and transfer of technical and non-technical knowledge) as a panacea to technological backwardness. They used the number of radio receivers per head as an index of progress, in addition to traditional indices like the rate of urbanization, number of hospitals and doctors, number of schools, percentage of people who are in "modern" industry as opposed to those in "traditional" sectors such as agriculture. Now, under structural adjustment policies, the modern sector is being steadily dismantled. The educational systems and other social services sectors have almost collapsed and there is continuing de-industrialization of the few industries that Muslim countries do have. The resultant mass retrenchment of workers is producing sprawling cities marked by high unemployment and consequent crime rates. This is wiping out the middle class and skilled labour force that only a couple of decades ago were lionized as indispensable for "third world" development by modernization theorists. The Muslim world is now experiencing a "re-colonization", not by individual European countries but under the aegis of IMF/WB and the supportive and collaborative service of Western bilateral/multilateral aid increasingly run and channelled through Western NGOs.

Globalized markets not only work against a majority of workers and peasants, even the local and indigenous capitalist classes suffer from its crushing impact. Small enterprises with a low capital base cannot compete with the big financial and industrial establishments of the West — the multinational corporations — and their enormous political influence. Understandably, the beneficiaries of privatization have been foreign business interests. According to the World Bank, the richest 200 individuals own more assets than the poorest two billion people. A recent study by Branko Milanovic, a senior World Bank economist, shows:

- The richest 1 per cent of the world's population received as much income as the poorest 57 per cent.
- The richest 10 per cent of the U.S. population had a combined income greater than that of the poorest 43 per cent of the world's people.
- Around 25 per cent of the world people received 75 per cent of the world's income.[25]

An International Herald Tribune/Pew poll suggests that much of the world views terrorist attacks as a symptom of increasingly bitter polarization between the haves and have-nots.[26]

Capital and finance, thanks to liberalization, are behaving irresponsibly. Investors pour money into a new market, make profits and when the market begins to falter, they quickly withdraw, often overnight, and escape to fresher pastures, creating a financial crisis and economic wreckage, which a now poor country is supposed to manage. A glaring example is the Asian and other financial crises. The panic selling, in the wake of the fall of the Thai baht in August of 1997, spread to other countries in the region, such as South Korea, Malaysia, the Philippines, and Indonesia. Their currencies crashed, losing as much as 75 or 80 per cent of their value within months. This caused serious economic disruption, including a sharp increase in inflation. Tens of millions of people were thrown into poverty, with many millions of Indonesians earning less than the amount necessary to purchase a subsistence quantity of rice. Decades of social progress have been undermined or reversed, as girls are pulled out of school to help their families survive. Interestingly, Malaysia refused to abide by the global rules and applied "home-made remedies" and has recovered to some extent. But Indonesia has gone down from an economic tiger to economic and political turmoil.

Globalization and modernization have had a strong impact on the world in the way of promoting a youth-based consumerism society.[27] The younger generation enjoys loud music, uses sophisticated computers, eats at McDonald's and wears T-shirts, jeans and tennis shoes. People know the faces of major international athletes, Hollywood and Bollywood celebrities and rock musicians better than the faces of their neighbours. This society is seen by some as valueless because it places importance on material goods rather than on spirituality. Although the West may be able to cope with this new dimension of society and the exponential changes that evolve from both globalization and modernization, it is the Third World and particularly the Muslim world that is mostly affected and suffocated by the changes they bring. Naturally, Muslims see these changes as a threat to their religion and traditions. Andre Gunder Frank conceptualizes modernity and the development of the Third World as going "hand-in-hand" and that the goal of the West is not to develop the Third World but, rather, to exploit it.[28] This is, therefore, seen as a valid threat to and cause for the recent Islamic resurgence.

Globalization also arguably implies calls for a respect for human rights and progress towards democratization — a call to liberalize both the economy and government. Most Muslims welcome the call for democratization. They believe that development, social progress and democracy are not possible without the fullest participation of the greatest number of their people. However, there is suspicion about both the intention and the arrogant manner in which the West is pushing its pro-democracy agenda. A study conducted by the U.S.-based Freedom House found that only 11 of 47 (or 23 per cent) countries with an Islamic majority have democratically-elected governments. As of 18 December 2001, according to the report, "within the Islamic world" there are nine countries with authoritarian presidencies, seven with dominant party states in which opposition parties are nominal, six with presidential-parliamentary systems, nine traditional monarchies, three one-party states, one military-ruled state, and, until November there was one fundamentalist theocracy, Afghanistan under the rule of Taliban.[29] Most of these Muslim despots and dictators have been enjoying Western support because of their "moderate" and "pro-West" policies. While the West is asking countries in Asia and Africa to adopt democracy and imposing human rights and democratization as conditions for aid, grants and loans, several monarchies, the Gulf states and some authoritarian regimes are excepted from such demands. It is widely believed in the Muslim world that oil was a central reason behind Operation Desert Storm and that America and the so-called Allied powers have gone to war in the Gulf in 1991 only to restore an absolute monarchy and to safeguard several other monarchies. President Ronald Reagan had openly declared that the United States would never let the Saudi monarchy be overthrown.[30] Indeed, long ago, President Eisenhower had warned that "should a crisis arise threatening to cut the Western world from Middle East oil, we would have to use force."[31]

In addition to its lack of consistency in applying the democracy and human rights test in all regions of the world, is the inconsistency in supporting the democratic process in countries where the outcome threatens to bring into power forces/interests that are seen to be anti-West. Algeria is a case in point. Throughout the Cold War era, the United States, the West and its allies put pressure on the "communist" National Liberation Front (FLN) regime by fuelling agitation among the non-Arab Berber minority and the Islamist forces. But when the Berlin Wall fell and the one-party system in Algeria converted into multi-party politics, the tune of the West changed. When it became clear that the "so-called" Islamic fundamentalists, Islamic Salvation Front (FIS) were going to win in the national parliamentary elections, a military coup with the support of the United States and France halted the process.[32] The Algerian army dismissed the Chadli government, cancelled the second round of elections for the National Assembly, declared a state of emergency (February 1992), and finally, after imprisoning its leaders, Abassi Madani and Ali Ben Hadj, outlawed the FIS in March. Not surprisingly, the FIS and like-minded Islamist groups (for example, the Armed Islamic Group) declared that if democratic alternatives were blocked by the army, they would shift their tactics and engage the army militarily. Since the closing of the democratic option by the Algerian army, Algeria has drifted toward civil war and social chaos. As a result, it seems, many Algerians turned into suicide activists. Similarly, one finds among suicide activists many Palestinians, Egyptians, and Indian Kashmiris. Osama bin Laden has been able to highlight some of the pressing problems of the Muslim world. This makes Osama a popular figure particularly among the younger generation, especially in Muslim countries.

The issue is not whether or not one likes the policies of the FIS but the efficacy of the principle of people electing those whom they wish to. It seems that the West only prefers a "democratic" outcome that does not upset the Western interest. Such an attitude can hardly promote long lasting democratic institutions or culture. The misguided short-term interests of imperialism in Algeria resulted in driving the FIS underground with extremists seeking martyrdom acquiring dominance. This strengthens anti-democratic revolts because democratization is seen as yet another Western import and imposition.

Another aspect of globalization is the prospect of creating global citizenship and governance and removing borders and barriers to trade and investment. Borders have indeed come down between Europeans. However, they have gone up in Europe against Muslims, Africans and other Third World citizens. While Europeans and Americans are truly global citizens because their passports give them unhindered entry into all parts of the world, the same is not true for Muslims and similar others. Muslim immigrants, refugees or asylum seekers in the West are the victims of all kinds of racist discrimination in medical care, housing, law and order. Whatever the economic, social or political problems facing the working people of Europe and America, the Muslim world within them suffers even more. The September 11 terrorist attacks have simply worsened their situation.

Modernization and globalization have created distrust, suspicion, anger and bitterness towards the West and whatever new or repackaged issues it now seeks to impose on the rest of the world. Surprisingly, there is an even greater distrust of America (giving rise to anti-Americanism) among those who uncritically consume CNN — most of all the American arrogance, its strutting around the world as the global policeman, and its selective use and abuse of the UN to further its narrow interests.

Anything that concerns America and its allies becomes a global issue. Anything that threatens their interest becomes by definition a "threat to world peace and security." The problem for the West is that Islam, Arab and oil seem to coincide. For as long as there is no economic alternative energy source to oil and the Middle East remains the biggest supplier, anything that threatens the friendly relationship between the feudalist aristocracies of the area and their Western "partners" will become a "global" issue. The U.S. State Department has described the Middle East as "a stupendous source of strategic power, and one of the greatest material prizes in world history." It is "probably the richest economic prize in the world in the field of foreign investment," or, in President Eisenhower's words, the most "strategically important area in the world."[33] Richard Nixon wrote that the Middle East's "oil is the lifeblood of modern industry, the Persian Gulf region is the heart that pumps it, and the sea routes around the Gulf are the jugular vein through which that lifeblood passes." In a subsequent book, Nixon argued that, because the Middle East is

likely to remain "the only source of significant exportable oil in the world for
the next twenty-five years, we have no choice but to remain engaged in the
area."[34] If a majority of Arabs were non-Muslims and they had no oil, they
would be of no interest to the West.

These ambiguities and blatant hypocrisy in the globalization processes
have fuelled distrust and suspicion in the Muslim world. Of course, the West
is not the only profiteer in this deadly game. Muslims and other Third World
despots, arms dealers and rogue regimes too are beneficiaries of the blood
industry, both materially and politically. These Muslim governing elites, as
observed by Kissinger, are linked by shared values and technologies. In the
Arab world, they form only one-tenth of one per cent of its 200 million
citizens with access to the internet. The majority of the Muslim population,
outside government and business circles, neither share this experience nor
may be prepared to accept its consequences, particularly during periods of
economic hardship. Under these circumstances, to quote Kissinger, "attacks
on globalization could evolve into a new ideological radicalism. This is
particularly true in countries where the governing elite is small and the gap
between rich and poor is vast and growing."[35]

MUSLIM RESPONSES TO MODERNIZATION
AND GLOBALIZATION

Following a period of apparent modernization and of globalization, Islam has
returned to the public sphere in most Muslim societies with vigour. Much
creative effort in the Muslim world has been directed towards the formulation
of Islamic answers to the social, political, economic and intellectual challenges
faced by these rapidly changing societies. The responses are of three kinds and
these are discussed not in any sequential order.

One response may be termed the mass response. Its source is the
overwhelming majority of the Muslims who have instinctively realized that
the processes of modernization, secularization and globalization are in essence
projects of Westernization that rob the *ummah* of its religious and cultural
heritage. These forces have only led to more colonial hegemony and to greater
class polarization within society. Adhering and clinging to Islam, the masses
encapsulated themselves within their Islamic heritage, they cry for help, and
hope for salvation from Allah. Their response is frequently expressed in the
form of spontaneous and, at times, violent acts of protest against all forms of
radical Westernization and colonial invasion. But, usually it expresses itself in
the form of philanthropy, either at the individual level (giving money to the
poor), or at the community level (building mosques, hospitals and schools).

A new fundamentalist Islamic international has emerged. Wherever Muslims live, one can see more and more covered women and bearded men. For many, if not most, that is *jihad.* For Westerners the term only means holy war, but Muslims point to the Qur'an where *jihad* means "to strive with might and main in (the cause of God)."

Part of the masses, usually the middle class professionals, academicians, students and traders perceive the need for an Islamic action that can protect this *ummah.* These people, having realized that political action is the means for achieving their objective, have set up or joined political organizations that do not resort to violence, and out of which youth and educational organizations may branch. The Muslim Brotherhood in Egypt and the Jama'at-e-Islami in Pakistan are just two examples.[36] At one time, some of these activists harboured the illusion that taking over the state machinery would be the long sought panacea. In fact, some of them did actually develop para-military organizations and tried to infiltrate the armed forces and to seize power by force. These people captured the attention of the media which gratuitously labels all Muslims as violent fanatics.[37] However, as of 1965, there has been a general inclination toward working through the existing legitimate political channels. They are generally not opposed to a degree of political pluralism, to working within the system, to democratic participation, and acknowledge the interests and rights of minorities.[38] They occupy a central place in the political sphere and have greatly influenced public policies in most of the countries of the Muslim world. Several states have declared themselves Islamic and have made efforts to develop more appropriate Islamic alternatives to, or adaptations of, institutions and legislation.[39] Other states have integrated more *shari'ah* into their secular legislation, while also intervening in the teaching and development of *fiqh* (Islamic jurisprudence), the practice of *ifta'* (issuing authoritative opinions on questions of Muslim law) or the codification of the *shari'ah.* Even secular regimes such as those of Turkey and Tunisia have to make new compromises with Islam. This response brought Islam to the forefront of world issues under the precepts of "Islamaphobia" or Islamic fundamentalism.[40]

The second response is more theoretical and intellectual. The advocates of this response recognize and emphasize the inextricable ties between Western modernity and Western imperialism. Imperialism was after all the Muslim's first encounter with modernity, and Zionist settler colonialism in Palestine is perhaps the last. They, however, try to benefit from the technological and scientific achievements of Western modernity, without adopting its worldview and without accepting the claims of scientific neutrality and value-freedom. An attempt is made to incorporate these achievements within an Islamic value system. The same applies to democracy.

The attempt to distinguish between democracy and *shura* (consultation) is
an attempt to incorporate democratic procedures within the Islamic value
system.[41] They accept cultural plurality within the framework of Islamic
values, and realize the importance of forging an alliance with the nationalist
elements in a common confrontation with the forces of hegemony and
globalization that try to eradicate autonomy, specificity, and the very idea
of absolute values and transcendence. They are perfectly aware of the
problem of the environment and the ecological crisis and persistently search
for new theories of development and new concepts of progress.[42] They
argue that Islamic theories of development should be different from the
generalist Western theories promoted by "international" organizations, for
such theories have proven to be largely a failure, and have led to an
environmental crisis and to more impoverishment of the masses.

This is linked to the continuous criticism by these intellectuals of
consumerism and its danger upon the environment, natural resources and
man's psychological and nervous systems. They realize the complex dimensions
of the question of power, the complexity of the modern state as well as its
power and ability to dominate and interfere in man's private life and the role
of bureaucracy in decision making, and in manipulating the ruler according
to its whims and purposes. Thus, taking over the state does not solve the
problems of the Muslims, as some of the advocates of mass response used to
imagine. The heart of the matter is the necessity of setting bounds to the state
and trimming its nails so that the *ummah* may play its role as vicegerents.
This explains their interest in the notion of the *ummah* and the increasing
attention to civil society and to the role of the *awqaf* (religious endowment),
and their growing interest in the new theories of the state and
administration. These intellectuals are neither puppets of governing elites nor
speakers of the unmediated voices of the subaltern, they have their own
particular voices and agendas and are very often the most significant social
group playing a crucial role as the mediators of global culture.

The third response comes from the governing elites in the Muslim
world led, among others, by former Malaysian Prime Minister Mahathir
Mohamad, the flag-bearer for Third World empowerment.[43] They believe
that globalization is an irreversible process to which Muslim will have to
adapt in order to avoid future crises. Theirs is a "structural-deterministic"
discourse arguing that there is no alternative to globalization and hence it
is imperative for Muslims to acquire modern knowledge. "Two hundred
years ago," Mahathir lamented, "we missed the industrial revolution because
we were colonized and we had little knowledge. But today in the era of
information technology revolution we are somewhat on a level playing field

and we can master information technology, even lead the way if there is a will."[44] There is no conflict between Islam and the values upheld by modernization and globalization. As Mahathir put it:

> Malaysia is an Islamic state. At the same time, and without contradiction, it is democratic, diverse, tolerant, peaceful, economically and politically stable, progressive and forward looking. There is no inherent conflict between Islam and any of these achievements.[45]

There are, however, lapses in the way globalization is steered by the West. Attempts are being made such that only "the big and rich will dominate a globalized free market world." The consequence, among others, will be high unemployment worldwide without unemployment benefits and the poor will be at the mercy of the rich. Consequently, these governing elites demand an opportunity to reinterpret and modify the rule of the game "to prevent discrimination and favouritism" and to ensure an equitable distribution of the benefits of globalization. They would like to participate fully and enjoy the beneficial fruits of the new global knowledge and information structure keeping the social cost of globalization to the barest minimum. They would like to inject human values into globalization so that it will have a human face. All these aims require active Muslim participation in the formation of globalization policies and Muslim representation at Group of Seven summit meetings and other institutions. The WTO does not allow free and frank deliberations of issues affecting millions. Certain countries have strong delegations and powerful influence over other countries simply because other countries owe them money or have been receiving aid from them. Negotiations should be fair and everybody should be given a hearing.[46]

They are, however, aware that their concerns about globalization will have no influence on the agenda of the major policy makers or corporations, who continue to strive for increasing globalization. One of the problems in making the West listen to their concerns is the lack of Muslim unity. Hence these governing elites call upon the Muslim leaders with its 1.3 billion followers to forge unity among them. They also desire a renewed interest in regional organizations, which they had earlier paralysed due to lack of political will. Thus, there is a renewed enthusiasm in regional economic and political institutions like the ASEAN, the Economic Community of West African States (ECOWAS), the Organization of African Unity (OAU), and indeed the Organization of Islamic Conference (OIC). Some of these institutions are not functioning as they should for many reasons, but mainly because most Muslim states remain neo-colonial economies under the control of both the former colonial masters and the multinational corporations.

CONCLUSION

Contrary to widespread belief, most of the principles (such as toleration, plurality, justice, unity) espoused by Islam are in harmony with those inherent in modernization and the processes of globalization. As a general rule civilizations should unite under common values, belief systems and histories. They did not. The irony of this technological advancement is that while Europeans and Americans struggle for supremacy in space, in the Muslim world, people are still trying to get to their villages. The misery for the vast majority of humanity is further circumscribed by the United States and Western domination and control over news, information and culture. Thus, the United States and others have not only fashioned the way in which goods are transported and the information is transmitted over long distances but in doing so, have helped to ensure that the lion's share of this new global market goes to the Americans and Europeans. Thus, while America and Europe are obsessed with globalization, Muslims are apprehensive about Francis Fukuyama's annihilation of history and the triumphalism about the hegemony of Western values, ideas and civilization.[47]

Samuel Huntington maintains that "it is false; it is immoral; and it is dangerous" to believe in the "universal relevance" of and the promotion of Western values, institutions and culture throughout the world. It is false, because Western values are not universal. It is immoral since values could only be effectively spread through the projection of force, suggesting some form of imperialism. It is dangerous since it posed the risk of counter-reaction.[48] The three Muslim responses are in essence a rejection of the disruptive nature of Western dominance and the suppression of their own politics and cultures, not actually against modernization and globalization. There is widespread concern that this new globalization, as in the past, is inseparable from Westernization and Americanization. From a Muslim point of view, the conduct of foreign relations and the imposition of the so-called "modernization and globalization" by the West has been both Machiavellian and coercive. There exists, throughout the Muslim world, a great sense of grievance and resentment toward the West. However, contrary to Huntington's observation, Muslims do not envy the West's "wealth, power and culture."[49] The three responses are in the nature of a reminder to the West that globalism should not serve the world by merely creating wealth, offering innovation and assuring rights. It must do so by preserving people's heritages, and incorporating moral and spiritual realms to heal wounded social structures.

Notes

1   Amin Saikal in Greg Fry and Jacinta O'Hagan, eds., *Contending Images of World Politics* (Houndmills, Basingstoke: Macmillian, 2000), p. 167. Fundamentalism, in itself, does not pose a threat until its followers believe that they have the right to impose their thoughts and beliefs on others. This imposition becomes an even greater threat when it turns into force. With the ever-increasing advancement of globalization and the West's conscious "development" of the Third world, liberal democracy has been unnaturally forced on other civilizations in this way. Hence, Western democracy can then be seen with such fundamentalist qualities as inflexibility, authoritarianism, selflessness and devotion to principle.

2   Giddens, quoted in R. Kiely and P. Marfleet, *Globalisation and the Third World*, London: Routledge, 1998, p. 65.

3   "Transcript of Remarks by President Clinton and King Hassan II of Morocco in Press Conference", *U.S. Newswire*, 15 Martch 1995, p. 2.

4   The separation of religion from the state, but not from society, has been advocated by Sheikh Ali Abdel-Raziq in his book *Islam and Principles of Rule* and by Khalid Mohammed Khalid, whose *From Here We Start* has been widely read. Most Muslims tend to endorse this line of thought. In fact, most of the Muslim world now uses secular civic law, with some modifications, rather than the *shari'ah*. Only the laws covering "personal status" — marriage, divorce, inheritance, and the like — have remained unchanged.

5   For a discussion on religious pluralism from the Qur'anic perspective see Abdulaziz Sachedina, *The Qur'an on Religious Pluralism*, Occasional Paper Series, Washington, D.C.: Centre for Muslim-Christian Understanding, Georgetown University, 1999.

6   Ibid.

7   E.I.J. Rosenthal, *Political Thought in Medieval Islam: An Introductory Outline*, Cambridge: The Cambridge University Press, 1968, p. 122.

8   S.M. Naquib Al-Attas, *Islam, Secularism and the Philosophy of the Future*, London: Mansell, 1985, p. 95.

9   *Questions Diplomatique et Colonials*, 15 May 1901, p. 588 cited in Marwan R. Bukhary, "Colonial Scholarship and Muslim Revivalism in 1900", *Arab Studies Quarterly* 4, nos. 1 & 2 (Spring 1982): 5.

10 See D.K. Hingorani, "Education in India Before and After Independence", *Education Forum* 19, no. 2 (1977): 218–19.

11 Ibid., p. 219.

12 Samuel P. Huntington, *The Clash of Civilizations and the Remaking of World Order*, New York: Simon & Schuster, 1996, p. 91.

13 Ibid., p. 93.

14 Yet, Muslims have accepted this form of political organization. Even the Organization for Islamic Conference has "non-interference in the domestic

affairs of member states" and the "respect of the sovereign, independent, and territorial integrity of each member state" as principles in Article II of its Charter.

[15] It is generally agreed that these principal institutions of secular society were an import from Europe but as implemented in the colonies, these institutions were a travesty of the Westminster model. The system of free and fair elections was not made available in the colonies. Franchise was restricted, controlled and at times coerced to obtain majority support for the government. According to Altaf Gauhar, the whole legislative arrangement was an elaborate hoax. "There was no freedom which was not suppressed by the judiciary so long as the law was not violated.... The executive objectivity which was a guarantee for the citizen at home became a justification for servility in the colonies. The press, an instrument of free expression of views at home, was used to control and influence the intelligentsia in the occupied territories. See Altaf Gauhar, "Islam and Secularism", in *The Challenge of Islam*, edited by Altaf Gauhar. London: Islamic Council of Europe, 1978, p. 303.

[16] Charles Taylor, *The Malaise of Modernity*, Concord, Ontario: Anansi Press, 1991.

[17] UNDP, *Human Development Report 2001: Making New Technologies Work for Human Development*, New York: Oxford University Press, 2001, p. 30.

[18] UNDP, *Human Development Report 2002: Deepening Democracy in a Fragmented World*, New York: Oxford University Press, 2002, p. 10.

[19] Ibid., p. 258. The report does not include Afghanistan, Iraq, Palestine and Somalia in its categorization.

[20] *New Sunday Times,* 18 August 2002.

[21] Ibid., p. 45. TAI is constructed using indicators of a country's achievement in four dimensions: creation of technology, diffusion of recent innovations, diffusion of old innovations, human skills.

[22] See P. Hirst and G. Thompson, *Globalization in Question: The International Economy and the Possibilities of Governance*, Cambridge: Polity Press, 1999.

[23] A. Green, *Education, Globalisation and the Nation State*, London: Macmillan, 1997, p. 160.

[24] UNDP, *Human Development Report 2002: Deepening Democracy in a Fragmented World*, p. 10.

[25] UNDP, *Human Development Report 2001: Making New Technologies Work for Human Development*, p. 19 and also *Guardian*, 18 January 2002.

[26] *International Herald Tribune*, 20 December 2001.

[27] A. Ahmed and H. Donnan, eds., *Islam, Globalization and Postmodernity*, London: Routledge, 1994.

[28] R. Kiely and P. Marfleet, *Globalisation and the Third World*, op. cit.

[29] The Freedom House Survey Team, "Freedom in the World 2002: The Democracy Gap", <http://www.freddomhouse.org/research/freeway/2002/essay2002/pdf>. In reality, regimes in Muslim-majority states varied in terms

of structure and social base, often recycling between military and civilian rule but in essence remaining authoritarian. Sometimes, secular regimes were based upon the military (Egypt, Libya, Mali, Niger, Nigeria, Algeria, Indonesia, Sudan), while others relied on a centralizing, secular party like the Ba'athists (Tunisia, Iraq, Syria, and Senegal); finally, some regimes institutionalized autocratic monarchical forms, combining Western technical support and claiming Islamic legitimacy for authoritarianism (Kuwait, Brunei, United Arab Emirates, Jordan, Morocco, and Saudi Arabia).

30 See "Editor's Postscript: The Regan Codicil", in *U.S. Strategy in the Gulf: Intervention against Liberation*, edited by Leila Meo, Belmont, Mass.: Association of Arab-American University Graduates, 1981, pp. 127–28.

31 Cited in Edward W. Chester, *United States Oil Policy and Diplomacy*, London: Greenwood Press, 1983, p. 29.

32 Algeria is not an isolated instance of democracy thwarted by democrats. In the persistent struggle between democratic and authoritarian principles, both London and Washington always favoured the latter. Thus, the CIA thwarted the Syrian experiment in democracy by actively supporting the coup which brought Husni al-Zaim to power in March 1949. This coup took place after the Syrian parliament refused to approve the concession to ARAMCO allowing the Trans-Arabian Pipe Line (better known as TAPLINE) to be constructed. The United States quickly recognized the new government and the TAPLINE was approved. See Douglas Little, "Cold War and Covert Action: The United States and Syria, 1945–1958", *The Middle East Journal* 44 (Winter 1990). Likewise the CIA and its British counterparts were responsible for the coup that overthrew Iranian Prime Minister Muhammad Musaddiq in 1953, replacing Iranian democracy with the dictatorship of Reza Shah Pahelvi. United States backing for the coups remained a common pattern especially when the civilian governments resisted Washington's schemes. See James A. Bill and Wm. Roger Lewis, eds., *Musaddiq, Iranian Nationalism, and Oil*, Austin: University of Texas Press, 1988.

33 Cited in Noam Chomsky, *World Orders: Old and New*, New York: Columbia University Press, 1994, p. 190.

34 Richard Nixon, *The Real War*, New York: Warner Books, 1980, p. 74; also *Seize the Moment: America's Challenge in a One-Superpower World*, New York: Simon and Schuster, 1992, p. 204.

35 Henry Kissinger, *Does America Need a Foreign Policy? Toward a Diplomacy for the 21st Century*, New York: Simon & Schuster, 2001, p. 203.

36 Abdul Rashid Moten, *Revolution to Revolution: Jama'at-e-Islami in the Politics of Pakistan*, Kuala Lumpur: The Other Press and the International Islamic University Malaysia, 2002.

37 William Millward, "The Rising Tide of Islamic Fundamentalism (1)", *Commentary*, no. 30 (April 1993): 3.

38 Ibid.

39 Samuel Huntington observes: "In the 1970s and 1980s political leaders rushed
    to identify their regimes and themselves with Islam. King Hussein of Jordan,
    convinced that secular governments had little future in the Arab world, spoke of
    the need to create "Islamic democracy" and a "modernizing Islam." King Hassan
    of Morocco emphasized his descent from the Prophet and his role as "Commander
    of the faithful." The Sultan of Brunei, not previously noted for Islamic practices,
    became "increasingly devout" and defined his regime as a "Malay Muslim
    monarchy." Ben Ali in Tunisia began regularly to invoke Allah in his speeches
    and "wrapped himself in the mantle of Islam" to check the growing appeal of
    Islamic groups. In the early 1990s Suharto explicitly adopted a policy of becoming
    "more Muslim." In Bangladesh the principle of "secularism" was dropped from
    the constitution in the mid-1970s, and by early 1990s the secular, Kemalist
    identity of Turkey was, for the first time, coming under serious challenge. To
    underline their Islamic commitment, governmental leaders — Ozal, Suharto,
    Karimov — hastened to their *hajh*." Huntington, *The Clash of Civilizations and
    the Remaking of World Order*, p. 115.

40 Religious fundamentalism is a term that seems to be the West's latest victim. It
    is often used by the media today and has become increasingly common and
    popular since the Islamic revolution in Iran. Since then, the West has conveniently
    "labelled" the new threat to a liberal democracy as "Islamic fundamentalism" or
    "Islamophobia." The West has done this clearly for self-aggrandizing political
    reasons only. In support of these reasons, there have been claims that "the
    'Islamic threat' thesis is more a myth than reality, and is designed mainly to
    promote an enemy to replace the Soviet Union, on whose enmity the US had
    staked its superpower operations for some 50 years." Although, there seems to be
    a general consensus that today's "war on terrorism" is one against religious
    fundamentalism, in actuality, it is one against political fundamentalism. "Hence
    its [the West's] deployment of 'Islamic fundamentalism' as a pejorative term to
    disparage and discredit them as irrational, irresponsible and extremist forces,
    dedicated, actually or potentially, to the goal of international terrorism." See
    Saikal in Fry and O'Hagan, eds., *Contending Images of World Politics*,
    pp. 165–67.

41 Abdul Rashid Moten, "Democratic and Shura based Systems: A Comparative
    Analysis", *Encounter: Journal of Inter-Cultural Perspectives* 3, no. 1 (March 1997).

42 Zeenath Kausar, ed., *Political Development: An Islamic Perspective*, Petaling Jaya:
    The Other Press, and International Islamic University Malaysia, 2000.

43 *New Straits Times*, 7 August 2002.

44 Ibid., 4 May 2002.

45 Ibid., 16 May 2002.

46 Ibid., 4 June 2002.

47 Francis Fukuyama, *The End of History and the Last Man*, Hammondsworth:
    Penguin, 1992.

48   Samuel P. Huntington, *The Clash of Civilizations and the Remaking of World Order*, p. 310. Although Huntington's theory aroused a lot of controversy at the time it was published, it is evident that his message was not heeded. This is perhaps due to the fact that the West did not consider Islam as a potential threat.

49   Samuel P. Huntington, "The Age of Muslim Wars", *Newsweek,* Special Davos Edition (December 2001–February 2002), p. 9.

13

THE MALAYSIAN CONSTITUTION, THE ISLAMIC STATE AND *HUDUD* LAWS

Shad Saleem Faruqi

INTRODUCTION

Malaysia has a record of racial, cultural and religious tolerance that should be the envy of all plural societies. Mosques, temples, churches and gurdwaras dot the landscape. Citizens celebrate each others' religious festivals. Unlike in some other democracies where religious/communal riots erupt with painful regularity and where holy places of minority religions are often razed to the ground, in Malaysia there is much inter-religious friendship and tolerance. Cultural and religious pluralism are not only tolerated, they are celebrated. Religious extremism and attempts to disrupt religious harmony are severely dealt with. Unlike in England where blasphemy is an offence only against the Church of England,[1] the Malaysian Penal Code in sections 295–298A punishes offences against all religions.

Legislation has been introduced to provide for Muslim and non-Muslim religious institutions. Among the laws existing are: Islamic Banking Act 1983, Islamic Development Bank Act 1975, Islamic Family Law (Federal Territories) Act 1984, *Syariah* Court Evidence (Federal Territories) Act 1997, *Syariah* Courts (Criminal Jurisdiction) Act 1965, *Syariah* Criminal Offences (Federal Territories) Act 1997, *Syariah* Criminal Procedure (Federal Territories) Act 1997 and 122 State Enactments and Ordinances on Islamic matters in the thirteen states of the Federation. In relation to non-Muslim religious affairs the prominent laws are: Daughters of Charity of the Canossian Institute (Incorporation) Ordinance 1957; Synod of the Diocese of West Malaysia (Incorporation) Act 1971 (Act 36); Muslim and Hindu Endowments Ordinance (Cap. 175); Cheng Hoong Teng Temple (Incorporation) Act 1949 (Act 519); Pure Life Society (Suddha Samajam) (Incorporation) Ordinance 1957; Superior of the Institute of the Congregation of the Brothers of Mercy (Incorporation) Act 1972 and Superior of the Institute of the Franciscan Missionaries of Mary (Incorporation) Ordinance 1957.

Financial allocations and tax exemptions are granted to all religions. Foreign priests and missionaries are allowed permits to enter and work in the country. Christian and Hindu festivals are marked by national holidays. Missionary hospitals, schools, bookshops and hostels abound. Christian missionary teachers are often retained till age sixty-five,[2] a privilege not enjoyed by other religious teachers. Hotel rooms throughout the nation carry the King James Version of the Bible. At the same time the direction of the Muslim *qiblat* (direction of prayer towards the *Ka'ba*) is required to be indicated in every hotel room. Liquor shops are allowed. Gambling casinos are permitted, though regulated. Pig-farming is widespread despite the abhorrence that Muslims have towards the swine. Shops and supermarkets are flooded with *non-halal* products.

Cultural and religious tolerance extends to the use of minority languages in trade and commerce, and the establishment of private schools using Chinese and Tamil as the medium of instruction. Unlike in a neighbouring country, minorities are not required to change their cultural identity by adopting Malay names. In primary and secondary schools religious clubs are allowed to exist. Though school uniforms are prescribed, Sikh boys wear turbans and some Muslim boys use the *songkok* or the *serban*[3] (types of headgear). Female pupils can wear pinafores or adorn the Muslim *hijab* (veil) complete with head scarves. Many Christian pupils wear crosses on chains. Hindu pupils dab their forehead with holy ash. In sum the Malaysian approach is that the state should not be indifferent to or hostile towards religions. It must promote tolerance. Tolerance comes not from the absence of faith but from its living presence.

AREAS OF CONCERN

Despite the above there is no denying that there are areas of concern to Muslims and non-Muslims alike.

(a) Planning Permission

It is alleged that local authorities often drag their feet in granting planning permissions for religious buildings if the area is heavily populated by religious communities other than the applicant's community.[4]

(b) Inter-Religious Marriages

As Muslims are not allowed to marry under the civil law of marriages, and must marry under *shari'a* law, non-Muslims seeking to marry Muslims have to convert to Islam if the marriage is to be allowed to be registered. This has caused pain to the parents of many converts. Likewise it has led to several troublesome cases of apostasy by Muslims who, for reasons of the heart, wish to marry their non-Muslim counterparts.

(c) Atheism

Does the right to believe include the right to disbelieve and to adopt atheism, agnosticism, rationalism, etc.? In most democratic countries the right not to believe is constitutionally protected. But in the light of the Rukun Negara ("*Kepercayaan kepada Tuhan*"); the language of Article 11(2) (no tax to support a religion other than one's own); Article 12(3) (no instruction in a religion other than one's own); and the existence of *shari'a* laws for Muslims, it is possible to argue that atheism is not protected by Article 11 — at least not for Muslims.

(d) Propagation of Religion to Muslims

Non-Muslims may be forbidden by state law from preaching their religion to Muslims: Article 11(4). Many non-Muslims complain that this amounts to unequal treatment under the law because Muslims are allowed to propagate their religion to non-Muslims. It is respectfully submitted that the primary purpose of this provision is to insulate Muslims against a clearly unequal and disadvantageous situation. During the colonial era, many non-indigenous religions were vigorously promoted by the merchants, the military and the missionaries of the colonial countries. Even today, the proselytizing activities of many Western-dominated religious movements that are internationally organized and funded have aroused resentment in many Asian and African societies. Some aspects of their activities, like seeking death-bed conversions, generous grant of funds to potential converts and vigorous proselytizing activities amongst minors have distinct implications for social harmony. Prof. Harding in his book, *Law, Government and the Constitution in Malaysia*, 1996, p. 201, is of the view that Article 11(4) was inserted because of public order considerations. According to him the restriction on proselytism has more to do with the preservation of public order than with religious priority. To his view one may add that Malays see an inseparable connection between their race and their religion. Any attempt to weaken a Malay's religious faith may be perceived as an indirect attempt to erode Malay power. Conversion out of Islam would automatically mean deserting the Malay community due to the legal fact that the definition of a Malay in Article 160(2) contains four ingredients. Professing the religion of Islam is one of them. A pre-Merdeka compromise was, therefore, sought and obtained that non-Muslims will not preach to Muslims.

(e) Restraints on Freedom of Religion

Under Article 11(5) the religious conduct of non-Muslims can be regulated only on the grounds of public order, public health and morality. But Muslims are subjected to many more religious restraints due to the power of the states to punish Muslims for offences against the precepts of Islam in accordance with Schedule 9, List II, Item 1. The power of the states to punish Muslims for Islamic crimes was recently confirmed by the Court of Appeal in *Kamariah bte Ali lwn Kerajaan Kelantan* [2002] 3 MLJ 657. The court held that:

> Article 11 of the Federal Constitution (in relation to Islam) cannot be interpreted so widely as to revoke all legislation requiring a person of the Muslim faith to perform a requirement under Islam or prohibit them from committing an act forbidden by Islam or that prescribes a system of committing an act related to Islam. This was because the standing of Islam in the Federal Constitution was different from that of other religions. First, only Islam, as a religion, is mentioned by name in the Federal Constitution as the religion of the Federation and secondly, the Constitution itself empowers State Legislative Bodies (for States) to codify Islamic law in matters mentioned in List II, State List, Schedule Nine of the Federal Constitution ('List II').

Persons of the Islamic faith are subject to severe restraints in relation to what are deemed to be "deviationist activities". From a constitutional law point of view laws that punish "deviationist activities" raise difficult legal issues. For example section 69 of the (Perlis) State Islamic and Malay Customs Enactment criminalizes "deviationist activities". This section may be constitutionally permissible under Item 1, List II of the Ninth Schedule. But any one punished under it may put up a vigorous challenge that the law goes far beyond the permissible restrictions of Article 11(5). Article 11(5) of the Constitution gives to every person including a Muslim a right to profess and practise his religion save to the extent that he/she does not endanger public order, public health or morality. The difficulty is that the freedom in Article 11 seems to be, in the case of Muslims, qualified by Item 1 of the State List in the Ninth Schedule. State enactments are permitted to create and punish offences by persons professing the religion of Islam against precepts of that religion. It is submitted, however, that despite the undoubted grant of power to the states to punish Muslims for offences against Islamic precepts, some limits need to be drawn on this power so that the guarantee in Article 11 is not extinguished. Further, the proper recourse against deviationist activities is to resort to excommunication and not to criminalization. Excommunication should be resorted to after the parties concerned have been given a full and fair opportunity to defend themselves and to explain their conduct.

(f) Conversions and Apostasy

The right to convert out of one's faith is not mentioned explicitly in the Malaysian Constitution though it is alluded to in Article 18 of the International Covenant on Civil and Political Rights 1966 and Article 18 of the Universal Declaration of Human Rights. For non-Muslims the right to opt out of one's faith and choose another has been regarded as an implicit part of religious liberty guaranteed by the Constitution. But because of its implications for child-parent relationships, the court in the case of *Teoh Eng Huat* [1986] 2 MLJ 228 held that a child below eighteen must conform to the wishes of his/her parents in the matter of religious faith. Thus, a Buddhist girl of seventeen had no constitutional right to abandon her religion and embrace Islam. In relation to Muslims the issue of conversion or apostasy raises significant religious and political considerations. Many Muslims feel considerable disquiet about Article 18 of the International Covenant on Civil and Political Rights 1966 which was adopted at the behest of a Christian delegate from Lebanon despite strong opposition from the Muslim delegates who were in attendance. Christianity's link with the merchants, missionaries and military of the colonial era is still fresh in many minds. The disproportionately strong support that Christian missionary activities receive from abroad also arouses fear and resentment. The adoption of Islam as the religion of the federation and the compulsory subjection of Muslims to the *shari'a* in a number of matters are other reasons why the conversion of a

Muslim out of Islam arouses deep revulsion and anger among the Malay/ Muslim citizens. The situation is exceedingly complex due to the intermingling of politics, law and religion.

Many Muslim scholars argue that repeated references in the Holy Qur'an to the need for tolerance and non-compulsion[5] refer to the freedom of conscience of non-Muslims. Muslims themselves have an absolute duty to uphold their faith. As Islam is the religion of the federation and Malays are, by constitutional definition, required to be of the Muslim faith, all Muslims are liable to prosecution if their conduct is violative of Islamic precepts. No Muslim can lay a claim to opt out of *shari'a* laws — the constitutional guarantee of freedom of religion notwithstanding. The notion that freedom to believe includes the freedom not to believe is unlikely to be accepted in Malay society and has been rejected in national courts.[6] Despite international norms to the contrary in Article 18 of the Universal Declaration of Human Rights and Article 18 of the International Convenant on Civil and Political Rights (that freedom of religion includes freedom to change one's religious belief), the impact of local culture and beliefs cannot be discounted. Others argue that Islam is a religion of persuasion, not force. The proposal to detain apostates may run counter to the spirit of Islam which is one of tolerance for the disbeliever.

It is noteworthy that the Holy Qur'an nowhere prescribes a wordly punishment for apostates even though it is stated repeatedly that their conduct shall incur the wrath of Allah (SWT) in the hereafter.[7] In fact Surah Ali 'Imran 3:86–89 recognizes the possibility of repentance and reminds us that Allah is all-forgiving. Only if the apostate turns against the Muslim community is he to be seized and killed (Surah Nisa 4:89). The Grand Imam of Al-Azhar, Sheikh Muhammad Sayyed Tantawi is of the view that as long as the apostates do not insult or attack Islam or the Muslims, they should be left alone. "Action should not be taken against them on the basis that they renounced Islam. Only when they insult Islam or try to destroy the religion, one should act (against them)."[8] Tantawi bases his opinion on Surah An-Nisa (4:137): "Those who believe, then disbelieve, again believe and again disbelieve, then increase in disbelief, Allah will not forgive them nor guide them in the right path". The difficulty is that there is a known *hadith* ordering that apostates should be advised, imprisoned, and if they still persist, then beheaded. Some Muslim scholars like Professor Hashim Kamali are of the view that the *hadith* must be read in the context in which it was made — in times of war, emergency and grave threat to the Islamic community. They also point out that the Prophet never ordered the execution of an apostate.

In response to the Muslim *volksgeist,* a number of states have, in the last few years, enacted rehabilitation laws that permit detention and re-education of converts out of Islam. Variously referred to as Restoration of Aqidah or apostasy or *murtad* laws, these enactments shake constitutional theory to its roots. They pit state law on apostasy against the Federal Constitution's guarantee of religious liberty. They pit national law against international law. They put Article 11 of the Constitution on a collision course with the conservative interpretation of religious freedom in Islam. From a constitutional law point of view, apostasy laws raise difficult constitutional issues under Articles 11, 5, 3, 10 and 12.

Article 11: The freedom in Article 11(1) is broad enough to permit change of faith. Though Article 11(4) restricts propagation of any religion to Muslims, the law nowhere forbids voluntary conversion of a Muslim to another faith. In the case of *Minister v Jamaluddin Othman* [1989] 1 MLJ 369 the Supreme Court implicitly acknowledged the right of a Muslim to convert to another religion. A similar sentiment was expressed in *Kamariah bte Ali* [2002] 3 MLJ 657.

Article 5: Forced rehabilitation will be an interference with personal liberty guaranteed by Article 5(1). *Habeas corpus* may be applied for.

Article 3: The *aqidah* (basic faith) laws cannot be saved by Article 3's declaration that Islam is the religion of the federation because Article 3(4) clearly states that "nothing in this article derogates from any other provision of this Constitution". This means that Article 3 cannot override Article 11.

Article 10(1)(a): Article 10(1)(a) guarantees speech and expression. A *murtad* (convert out of Islam) may claim that the rehabilitation law violates his rights under Article 10 unless aspects of public order can be used to defend the *murtad* law.

Article 10(1)(c): Article 10(1)(c) guarantees the right to associate. Inherent in this right is the right to disassociate. See *Dewan Undangan Negeri Kelantan v Nordin b. Salleh* [1992] 1 MLJ 343 about the right to leave a political party and join another.

Article 12: Article 12(3) says that no person shall be forced to receive instruction or take part in any ceremony or act of worship of a religion other than his own. The forced rehabilitation laws will fall foul of this guarantee.

The *aqidah* laws are triggering a massive constitutional debate that pits religion against the Constitution and disturbs the delicate social fabric that has held all Malaysians together for forty-seven years. At the moment the following judicial attitudes and conflicts have emerged. According to the High Court the act of exiting from a religion is not part of freedom of religion — at least not in the case of Muslims: *Daud Mamat v Majlis Agama* [2002]

2 MLJ 390. A contrary view was recently expressed by the Court of Appeal in an appeal from a Kelantan High Court decision. It was held that a Muslim is not forbidden from renouncing Islam: *Kamariah bte Ali lwn Kerajaan Negeri Kelantan* [2002] 3 MLJ 657. But this renunciation cannot be done unilaterally. A Muslim who wishes to declare apostasy must first get the *shari'a* court to confirm that he/she has left the religion. A statutory declaration of apostasy is not enough. The matter has to be determined by the *shari'a* courts using Islamic law: *Daud Mamat* [2002] 2 MLJ 390 and *Mad Yaacob Ismail* [2002] 6 MLJ 179. Until the act of renunciation is validated by the *shari'a* court, a Muslim is deemed to be a person of the Muslim faith: *Kamariah bte Ali* [2002] 3 MLJ 657.

A Muslim cannot escape the jurisdiction of the *shari'a* court by a unilateral act of renunciation. The *shari'a* court continues to have jurisdiction till the issue of status is determined at law. In the absence of an inquiry by the *shari'a* court, the civil court must accept a Muslim to be still a Muslim till the *shari'a* court has made a pronouncement. Civil courts should not interfere with decisions of the *shari'a* courts because of Article 121(1A). The issue of whether an individual is an apostate or not was one of Islamic law and not civil law.

(g) Schools of Islamic Thought

Many state enactments declare that the *shari'a* law applicable to Muslims shall be the law of the Shafie school of Islam. This poses problems for Muslims of other schools of Islamic thought.

HUDUD LAWS

In the last few years a number of state assemblies, as part of their quest for an Islamic state, are enacting "*hudud* laws" — that is, laws relating to crimes and punishments that are laid down in the *shari'a*. The states are claiming to exercise this jurisdiction on the ground that under the federal constitution, Islamic penal law is in state hands. This is an overstatement for a number of legal reasons.

First, under Schedule 9, List II, Item 1, states have authority relating to "creation and punishment of offences by persons professing the religion of Islam against precepts of that religion, *except in regard to matters included in the Federal List*" (emphasis added). This means that any matter assigned to the federal parliament is outside the legislative competence of the states. In Schedule 9, List I, Item 4, criminal law and procedure, administration of justice, jurisdiction and powers of all courts, creation of offences in respect of any of the matters included in the Federal List *or dealt with by federal law* are in federal hands. It is well known that theft, robbery, rape, murder, incest, unnatural sex are all dealt with by the federal Penal Code. Therefore, the states are not permitted to enact *hudud* laws on these criminal matters even though these crimes are also crimes against Islam.

Second, Schedule 9, List II, Item 1 clearly provides that *shari'a* courts "shall have jurisdiction only over persons professing the religion of Islam". This means that *shari'a* courts have no power to apply the *hudud* laws to non-Muslims.

Third, the jurisdiction of the *shari'a* courts is not inherent but must be derived from federal law. The Constitution, in Schedule 9, List II, Item 1 says that *shari'a* courts "shall not have jurisdiction in respect of offences except in so far as conferred by federal law". The relevant federal law is the *Syariah* Courts (Criminal Jurisdiction) Act 1965. It imposes limits on jail terms and fines that the *shari'a* courts can impose. The limit is three years jail, five thousand ringgit fine and six lashes. Any penalty other than these permitted penalties is unconstitutional.

The implication of the above is that the states and the state *shari'a* courts have jurisdiction only over such Islamic criminal offences as are *not* dealt with by federal law *viz*, offences like consuming alcohol, not fasting during *bulan puasa* (fasting month), *zina* (adultery), *khalwat* (illicit privacy) and missing Friday prayers.

In addition to the question as to who has the jurisdiction to enact *hudud* laws, there is the further constitutional problem of enforcement of *hudud* laws and the arrest and detention of *shari'a* offenders. The state authorities are entitled to set-up their own enforcement units. But if they wish to seek the help of the federal police, there are legal dilemmas. The police force is a federal force: Ninth Schedule, List I, Item 3(a). Its powers and functions are derived from the Federal Constitution and from federal laws like the Police Act 1967 (Act 344). Under Section 3(3) of Act 344, the Force shall be employed for "the prevention and detection of crime and the apprehension and prosecution of offenders". The control of the Force in any area or state is in the hands of the commissioner, chief police officer or such police officer as the IGP may specify: Section 6. Section 19 states that every police officer shall perform the duties and exercise the powers granted to him under Act 344 *or any other law at any place in Malaysia where he may be doing duty* (emphasis added). It is arguable that the words in italics could cover state *shari'a* laws. This could mean that police officers are obliged under Section 19 to enforce state laws. It must be remembered, however, that Sections 20(1) and (2) clarify that in the performance of his duties, a police officer is subject to the orders and directions of his superiors in the force and not the order of the state executive. In any case, Sections 3(3), 19 and 20 of the Police Act must be read subject to the constitution which identifies the police as a federal force and confers on it powers and functions which are entirely in relation to the Federal List. Any general powers or duties in Sections (3), 19 and 20 should be read *ejus dem generis* with the specific duties enumerated in Section 20(3) sub-paragraphs (a) to (m). The doctrine of *ejus dem generis* teaches us that if in a statute general words are followed by specific words, then the general words should be interpreted narrowly to make them fall into the *genera* to which the specific words belong. All the duties in sub-paragraphs (a) to (m) are federal duties. The general duties in Sections 3, 19 and 20 must be confined to matters within federal jurisdiction.

As with the police, prisons, reformatories, remand homes and places of detention are in the Federal List: Ninth Schedule List I, Item 3(b). It is, therefore, submitted that state-run rehabilitation centres for "*aqidah* offenders" or *murtads* will be outside the powers of the state authorities.

ISLAMIC STATE

During the last eighteen months an engaging debate has been raging about whether Malaysia is an Islamic or secular state. The non-Muslims of the country are adamant in their assertion that Malaysia's Constitution is, and always was, meant to provide a secular foundation. The opposition Muslim party, PAS, agrees with them that the constitution is secular. But it says this in an accusatory tone and has made it clear that once in power it will amend the basic law to convert Malaysia into an Islamic state. The ruling Muslim party, UMNO, dismisses this proposal on the ground that Malaysia is already an Islamic state and, therefore, no constitutional amendments are needed. It rests its case on the fact that Muslims constitute the majority of the population. The constitutional monarchs at the federal and state levels are Muslims. The political executive, the civil service, the police, the army, the judiciary and the legislatures, while multi-racial, are under the control of Muslims. The federal and state constitutions are replete with Islamic features. Islamic practices are gaining ground. Islamic economic and religious institutions thrive with state support.

It is submitted that the differences of opinion over whether Malaysia is an Islamic or secular state are attributable to semantics — the assignment of different meanings to the same word by participants in a discourse. Opinions are clashing because there is no litmus test or universally agreed list of criteria to typify a social or legal system as theocratic or temporal. The problem is compounded by the fact that there is no ideal or prototype secular or Islamic state that one could hold up as a shining model or paradigm of one or the other. Diversity is as much a part of Islam as of other religions.

DIVERSITY IN ISLAM

As in other religious, political and economic systems, diversity and differences are part of Islamic ideology and of the practice of forty-eight or so Muslim majority countries. The Shi'as and the Sunnis (and within the Sunnis) the Hanafi, Shafei, Maliki and Hanbali schools, are not always in agreement over details. As in every other system that depends on human endeavour for realisation, there is a massive gap between theory and reality and promise and performance. Sympathetic scholars of Islamic history point to the glorious days of the Prophet; to the state under the Constitution of Medina; to the Ottoman Empire; to the eclectic rule of Akbar the Great in India; and to the tolerance and accommodation of Muslim society in Malaysia as mirrors of an Islamic polity. The critics view the arch-conservative interpretations of Islam in Sudan, Saudi Arabia, Nigeria and Pakistan as reflective of the theocratic, puritanical Islamic state. The fanaticism of the Taliban regime in Afghanistan and the terrorist attacks on the World Trade Centre in New York on 11 September 2001 may mislead the detractors to believe that Islam is in a perpetual state of war with non-believers.

In fact the objective reality is that Islam co-existed in harmony with Christianity and Judaism throughout its history. No doubt there are a few incidents of repression as under Moghul Emperor Aurangzeb in India and the Taliban in Afghanistan but these do not match the brutality of the Inquisition, the holocaust against the Jews in Europe, the oppressive practices of European and American colonizers in Mexico, Latin America, Africa and Asia, the annihilation of indigenous peoples in three continents and the enslavement and dehumanization of Africans. Islam is no more to be blamed for September 11 than Christianity for the holocaust in Germany, genocide in Bosnia and the brutalization of Muslims in Palestine, Iraq and Afghanistan.

SECULAR STATE

A secular constitution separates the state from the church and law from religion. The functions of the state are confined to mundane matters and religion is left entirely to religious establishments. There is no legally prescribed official or state religion and no state aid is given to any religion or for any religious purposes. Freedom of religion is, however, generally guaranteed and private religious activities by individuals, groups and associations are not interfered with except on grounds of public order, national security, public health or public morality. Well-known examples of secular states are India, the United States, Singapore and Turkey.

India: In India, the Preamble to the Constitution declares India to be a secular state. There is no official, state religion in India. The constitution has neither established a religion of its own nor conferred any special patronage upon any particular religion. Under Article 27 of the Indian Constitution, the state cannot compel any citizen to pay any taxes for the promotion or maintenance of any particular religion or religious institution. No religious instruction can be provided in any educational institution wholly provided by state funds. Denominational institutions receiving aid from the state can impart religious instruction but cannot compel anyone to receive such instruction without his or his parent's consent.

The attitude of the law towards religion is one of neutrality and impartiality though actual practices diverge from theory. Personal laws are allowed but no one can be compelled to observe them. Also, the state exercises an overriding power to regulate or suppress religious practices that offend morality and public order.

United States: Like India, the United States does not have a state religion. However, many laws of the United States are grounded in Protestant Christianity. Most state constitutions pay deference to God in their preambles. However, in the area of public education, the separation between the church and the state is very pronounced. In 1963 the U.S. Supreme Court in *Abington v Schempp* 374 U.S. 203 (1963) held that Bible reading exercises in public schools were unconstitutional. Public funds cannot be used to support any sectarian activity. In *Engel v Vitale* 8 L.Ed. 2d 601 (1962) state sponsored prayer in public schools was held to violate the constitutional clause that forbade the state from establishing any religion. A high school principal who allowed a group of students to conduct a prayer meeting in his office was prohibited by the state court from using a public premise for a sectarian purpose. In *McCollum v Board of Education* 333 U.S. 203 (1948) releasing students for a short time to enable them to pray constituted unconstitutional use of tax supported property for religious instruction. In the United States distributing religious literature in public schools is not allowed. Wearing a distinctive religious garb by a public school teacher while engaged in the performance of duties can be prohibited. In the interest of maintaining the changing values of a pluralist society, American courts have taken secularism to extremes by trying to remove God from the classroom. Recently the

University of North Carolina prescribed a book *Approaching the Quran: The Early Revelations* by Michael Sells. A Christian organization immediately challenged this as a violation of the First Amendment to religious freedom. *Turkey*: As in the United States, Turkey maintains a strict divide between religion and politics. In 1998 the Turkish Supreme Constitutional Court banned the electorally popular Islamic Welfare Party. A woman MP who chose to wear a scarf to parliament was dismissed from parliament. Schoolgirls who defy the ban on head-covering are expelled from schools. Likewise in Singapore. It is clear, therefore, that in the guise of neutrality, many secular states adopt an attitude of hostility towards organized religions.

THEOCRACY

In contrast with secular states, in theocracies religion is interwoven into the fabric of government. "Theocracy" literally means rule by God. In political science the term has come to mean either one of two things. First, the temporal ruler is subject to the final direction of the theological head because the spiritual power is deemed to be higher than the temporal and the temporal is to be judged by the spiritual. Iran has such a constitutional rule. Second, the law of God is the supreme law of the land. The divine law is expounded and administered by pious men as God's agents on earth. Saudi Arabia and the Vatican are theocracies of this kind.

HYBRID SYSTEMS

The Islamic state discussion is riddled with the error that a state must be either theocratic or secular. In fact, many hybrid versions exist and ideological purity — even if desirable — is not easily possible. Whether the Malaysian polity is "Islamic" or not depends also on whether one views things in a purely *de jure* (legal) way or whether one brushes into the legal canvas the *de facto* realities.

SECULAR FEATURES IN THE FEDERAL CONSTITUTION
(a) Historical Evidence

Malaysia's document of destiny does not contain a preamble. The word "secular" does not appear anywhere in the constitution. However, there is historical evidence that the country was meant to be secular and the intention in making Islam the official religion of the federation was primarily for ceremonial purposes. In the White Paper dealing with the 1957 constitutional proposals it is stated: "There has been included in the proposed Federal Constitution a declaration that Islam is the religion of the Federation. This will in no way affect the present position of the Federation as a secular state...."[9]

(b) Case Law

It was held in *Che Omar Che Soh v PP* [1988] 2 MLJ 55 that though Islam is the religion of the federation, it is not the basic law of the land and Article 3 (on Islam) imposes no limits on the power of parliament to legislate. Islamic law is not and never was the general law of the land either at the federal or state level. It applies only to Muslims and only in areas outlined in Item 1 of List II of the Ninth Schedule. In the law of evidence, for example, the Evidence Act applies to the exclusion of Islamic law: *Ainan v Syed Abubakar* [1939] MLJ 209. The *shari'a* courts have limited jurisdiction only over persons professing the religion of Islam.[10] It must be noted, however, that the High Court in *Meor Atiqulrahman Ishak v Fatimah bte Sihi* [2000] 5 MLJ 375 did not follow the *Che Omar Che Soh* decision. It held that Islam is *ad-deen* — a way of life. Regulations violating Article 3 can be invalidated.

(c) Adat (Custom)

One must also note the very significant influence of Malay *adat* on Malay-Muslim personal laws. In some states like Negeri Sembilan, *adat* overrides *agama* (religion) in some areas of family law.

(d) Constitutional Supremacy

Under Article 4(1) the constitution and not the *shari'a* is the supreme law of the federation. Any law passed after Merdeka Day which is inconsistent with the constitution shall, to the extent of the inconsistency, be void. Under Article 162(6) and (7) any pre-Merdeka law which is inconsistent with the constitution, may be amended, adapted or repealed by the courts to make it fall in line with the constitution. Article 160(2) of the constitution, which defines "law", does not mention the *shari'a* as part of the definition of law. Though Islam is adopted as the religion of the federation, it is clearly stated in Article 3(4) that nothing in this article derogates from any other provision of the constitution. This means that no right or prohibition is extinguished as a result of Article 3.

(e) Higher Status of Secular Authorities

If by a theocratic state is meant a state in which the temporal ruler is subjected to the final direction of the theological head and in which the law of God is the supreme law of the land, then clearly Malaysia is nowhere near a theocratic, Islamic state. *Shari'a* authorities are appointed by state governments and can be dismissed by them. Temporal authorities are higher than religious authorities. Except for those areas in which the *shari'a* is allowed to operate, the law of the land is enacted, expounded and administered by secular officials.

(f) Senior Federal Posts

The Yang Di-Pertuan Agong must, of course, be a Muslim. But Islam is not a prerequisite for citizenship or for occupying the post of the prime minister. Members of the cabinet, legislature, judiciary, public services (including the police and the armed forces) and the commissions under the constitution are not required to be of the Muslim faith. In the Sixth Schedule, the oath of office for cabinet ministers, parliamentary secretaries, speaker of the Dewan Rakyat, MPs and senators, judges and members of constitutional commissions is quite non-religious in its wording and does not require allegiance to a divine being or to Islam.

(g) No Constitutional Amendment

Despite the process of Islamization since the early eighties, no constitutional changes have been made to declare Malaysia an Islamic state or to put the *shari'a* on a higher pedestal than the law of the constitution. Article 121(1A), added by Act A704 in 1988 insulates the *shari'a* courts from interference by the civil courts in matters *within the jurisdiction of the shari'a courts*. If the *shari'a* courts exceed their jurisdiction a high court declaration is a distinct possibility. Proponents of the Islamic state must remember that amending the constitution to declare Malaysia as an Islamic state will require a two-thirds majority in parliament plus the consent of the Conference of Rulers and the Governors of Sabah and Sarawak.[11]

ISLAMIC FEATURES IN THE FEDERAL CONSTITUTION

(a) Constitutional Recognition of Islam

In a secular constitution there is no prescribed official religion and no state aid is given to any religion or for any religious purposes. The reality of life and the law in Malaysia is quite different. The word "Islam" occurs at least twenty-four times in the constitution.[12] The word "*shari'a*" occurs three times[13] and the words *"Mufti"*, *"Kadi Besar"* and *"Kadi"* at least once each.[14] The Constitution of Malaysia in Article 3(1) provides that Islam is the religion of the federation but all other religions may be practised in peace and harmony.

(b) Religious Pluralism

Acceptance of religious pluralism is entirely in line with Islam. In the Qur'an in Surah al-Baqarah (2:256) it is stated: "Let there be no compulsion in religion". In Surah al-Kafirun (109:1-6) it is stated: "O you that reject Faith: ... To you be your way and to me mine." In Surah Yunus (10:99) the Holy Qur'an reminds us that Allah (the most high) could have made the entire mankind alike and so no compulsion should be employed to change people from one belief to another. "If it had been thy Lord's will, they would all have believed, all who are on earth. Will you then compel mankind against their will to believe?"

Islam shows the hightest respect for Judaism and Christianity. In Surah al-Baqarah (2:136) it is stated:

> "...we believe in Allah, and in that which has been revealed to us and in that which was revealed to Ibrahim and Ismail and Ishaq and Yaqub and the tribes and in that which was given to Musa and Isa and in that which was given to all the prophets from the Lord. We do not make any distinction between any of them and to Him do we submit."[15]

Respect for all previous prophets is part of a Muslim's articles of faith. In the sixth year of Hijrah, Prophet Muhammad granted to the monks of St. Catherine, near Mount Sinar, a charter of rights:[16] They were not to be unfairly taxed (2) no bishop was to be driven out of his bishopric (3) no Christian was to be forced to reject his religion (4) no monk was to be expelled from his monastery (5) no pilgrim was to be detained from his pilgrimage (6) nor were the Christian churches to be pulled down for the sake of building mosques or houses for Muslims (7) Christian women married to Muslims were to enjoy their own religion (8) if the Christians should stand in need of assistance for the repair of their churches or any other matter pertaining to their religion, the Muslims were to assist them.

Similar treaties with the Jews of Medina and the Christians of Najran in Yemen were signed.[17] Ameer Ali says of the treaty at Najran: "Has any conquering race of faith given to its subject nationalities a better guarantee than is to be found in the words of the Prophet?"[18] Even "idol-worshippers" are not to be abused. Surah An'am (6:108) states: "Do not abuse those whom they worship besides Allah". Surah al-Tauba (9:6) commands that "if any pagan asks you for asylum, grant it to him so that he may listen to the word of Allah and then escort him to where he can be secure". If enemies from other countries attacked the non-Muslims in an Islamic state, Muslims are asked to fight in order to protect the freedom of religious worship of the non-Muslims. Non-Muslims have the right to keep their languages and customs, to establish their own schools and colleges and to be visited by missionaries. In the Turkish empire, Christians were represented in the State Council. In the Mughal Empire in India state aid was given to build and restore Hindu temples. In Egypt the oldest churches were built during the pre-colonial (Islamic) period.[19] If a non-Muslim minor is taken a prisoner of war and if his parents die, the child has the right to continue with the religion of his father.[20]

In sum, the general history of Islam is one of tolerance towards other religions. The Constitution of Malaysia honours this spirit. It provides a foundation for religious liberty by guaranteeing this right in many articles of the constitution, namely, Articles 3(1), 8, 11, 12 and 150(6A). In addition, the guarantees of freedom of speech, assembly and association in Article 10 also impact on freedom of religion. Islam is the religion of the federation. But all other religions may be practised in peace and harmony: Article 3(1).

In respect of religion, every person has the right to three things: to profess, to practise and, subject to Article 11(4), to propagate his religion: Article 11(1): The first refers to beliefs and doctrines. The second refers to exhibition of these beliefs through acts, practices and rituals. The third is about attempts at propagation. The right to beliefs and doctrines is generally regarded as absolute. The last two aspects are, everywhere, subject to regulation on grounds of public order, health, morality and so forth.

Does freedom of religion extend only to those practices and rituals that are essential and mandatory or does it also cover practices that are non-essential and optional? *Halimatussaadiah v PSC* [1992] 1 MLJ 513 implies that a non-mandatory practice (like wearing the *purdah*) is not protected by Article 11. The case also distinguished between beliefs and practices. The latter may be regulated if they lead to public disorder, affect public health or public morality. However *Meor Atiqulrahman Ishak v Fatimah bte Sihi* [2000] 5 MLJ 375 correctly holds that the constitutional freedom extends to practices (like wearing a *serban*) which, though not mandatory, are part of the religious tradition. The right to religion is available not only to individuals but also to groups and associations: Article 11(3) and 12(2). Every religious group has the right to manage its own affairs, establish and maintain institutions for religious purposes, acquire and own property and administer it: Article 11(3). All religious groups may establish and maintain institutions for religious education: Article 12(2). Note, however, that the above rights are subject to local authority laws on planning permissions. The rights above are available to citizens as well as to non-citizens: Article 11(1).

There is no compulsion on anyone to support a religion other than his own. No person shall be compelled to pay any tax the proceeds of which are specially allocated to a religion other than his own: Article 11(2). The implication is that imposition of tax to support one's own religion is constitutional. For example a Muslim cannot refuse to pay *zakat* (obligatory religious tax) and *fitrah* (charity given at the end of the fasting month). There is to be no discrimination on the ground of religion in relation to the rights of students to education or in public support for educational institutions: Article 12(1) and 8(2). No person shall be required to receive instruction in or to take part in any ceremony or act of worship of a religion other than his/her own: Article 12(3). However a person can voluntarily participate in other people's religious activities. There can be no discrimination on the ground of religion against employees in the public sector; in the acquisition, holding or disposition of property; and in any trade, business or profession: Article 8(2). A preventive detention order cannot be issued on the ground that a convert out of Islam is involved in a programme for propagation of Christianity amongst Malays: *Minister v Jamaluddin bin Othman* [1989] 1 MLJ 368. Article 150(6A) provides that freedom of religion cannot be restricted even in times of emergency by an emergency law under Article 150.

(c) Rukun Negara

In the *Rukun Negara* (the principles of state policy) faith in God is declared to be a cardinal principle of state policy.

(d) Implications of Article 3(1)

The implication of adopting Islam as the religion of the federation is that Islamic education and way of life can be promoted by the state for the uplifting of Muslims. Article 12(2) provides that it shall be lawful for the federation or a state to establish or maintain Islamic institutions, provide instruction in the religion of Islam to Muslims and incur expenditure for the above purposes. Thus, taxpayers' money can be utilized to promote Islamic institutions and to build mosques and other Islamic places of worship and to keep them under the control of state authorities.

(e) Islamic Courts

Islamic courts can be established and *shari'a* officials can be hired. The jurisdiction of the *shari'a* courts is protected by Article 121(1A) against interference by ordinary courts.

(f) Muslims Subject to Shari'a Laws

All Muslims are subjected to Islamic law in matters of succession, testate and intestate, betrothal, marriage, divorce, dower, maintenance, adoption, legitimacy, guardianship, gifts, *waqf* (charitable endowments), *zakat, fitrah, baitulmal* (public treasury) or similar Islamic religious revenue. A Muslim cannot opt out of Islamic law.[21] He/she can be compelled to pay *zakat* and *fitrah*.

State enactments can seek vigorously to enforce Islamic morality amongst Muslims. For example beauty and body building contests are forbidden to Muslims in many states. In areas permitted by the Ninth Schedule, Islamic civil and criminal laws are applied to all Muslims.

Item 1 of List II of the Ninth Schedule permits state legislation to create and punish offences by persons professing the religion of Islam against the precepts of that religion. However, the power of the state to enforce Islamic criminal law is limited by the words "except in regard to matters included in the Federal List" or "dealt with by federal law".

(g) Preaching to Muslims Regulated

Propagation of one's religion to others is part of the constitutional right under Article 11. However this right is subject to one important limitation. Missionary activity amongst Muslims may be regulated. Under Article 11(4) state law and (for federal territories) federal law may control or restrict the propagation of any religious doctrine amongst Muslims. This Article is directed not only at non-Muslim attempts to convert Muslims but also at propagation to Muslims by unauthorized Muslims. Application of such laws, however, poses a serious constitutional objection. *Shari'a* courts cannot have jurisdiction over non-Muslims and it appears that a federal criminal court will have to try a non-Muslim whose proselytising zeal violates a state law.

(h) State Constitutions

All state constitutions in Malay states prescribe that the Ruler of the state must be a person of the Islamic faith. Some state constitutions require that the Menteri Besar and state officials like the State Secretary shall profess Islam. Except for Sarawak, Islam is the official religion in all states.

(i) Concept of a "Malay"

The concept of a "Malay" is inextricably tied up with observance of the religion of Islam.[22]

(j) Islamic Economy

In the financial field Islamic monetary institutions are being vigorously promoted. Among them are Bank Islam, *Takaful* (Islamic insurance), Tabung Haji, Pilgrims Management and Fund Board, Amanah Ikhtiar Malaysia, Qarad Hasan (interest free loans), *jual janji* (similar to mortgage), *waqf, Bait-ul-mal, zakat* and *fitrah*.

(k) Islamization

The Islamization policy of the government has won Malaysia many admirers abroad. At the world stage Malaysia is recognized as a model Muslim country.

Government-supported Islamic institutions abound. There is a National Council for Islamic Affairs, State Councils of Muslim Religion, Fatwa Committees, the Islamic Research Centre, the Department of Religious Affairs, UIAM and IKIM. Islamic practices: Quran competitions are held; the azan and Islamic programmes are aired over radio and TV. TV1 and TV2 devote at least fifteen hours a week to Islamic programmes. Islamic salutations and prayers are offered at most government functions; Islamic form of dressing is becoming increasingly mainstream. In many government departments, Qur'anic verses are recited over the public address system at the beginning of the day.

CONCLUSION

Malaysia has a commendable record of religious harmony and religious freedom. This is not to deny that in the last two decades a number of thorny issues have emerged. On the issue of an Islamic versus a secular state, it can be stated categorically that the Malaysian legal system is neither fully secular nor fully theocratic. It is hybrid. It permits legal pluralism. It avoids the extremes of American style secularism or Saudi, Iranian and Taliban type of religious control over all aspects of life. It mirrors the rich diversity and pluralism of its population. It prefers pragmatism over ideological purity; moderation over extremism. It walks the middle path. It promotes piety but does not insist on ideological purity. Muslims are governed by divinely ordained laws in a number of chosen fields. In other fields their life is regulated by Malay *adat* and by non-ecclesiastical provisions enacted by democratically elected legislatures. Non-Muslims, in turn, are entirely regulated by secular laws. Though they have legitimate concerns about some administrative decisions, there is no evidence whatsoever that the country's legal pluralism is being disturbed. No non-Muslim is being subjected to Muslim laws though Muslims are being increasingly exposed to the *shari'a*.

Those who view Islam with antipathy view the increasing Islamization of society with consternation. Many of them do whatever they can to demonize the religion. The bin Ladens, Mullah Omars and Shaikh Yassins of Muslim societies and the arch-conservative and literal interpretation of holy texts by regimes in Saudi, Sudan, Pakistan and the Malaysian states of Kelantan and (till early 2004) Terengganu give them much to condemn. But many Muslim scholars see the resurgence of Islam as the correction of an imbalance; as a counter to the hegemonic influence of the dominant Western civilization with its massively successful appeal to hedonism, consumerism and capitalism. It is not wrong to suggest that the rise of Islamic influences has added to and not subtracted from the pluralism of Malaysian society. For whatever it is worth, Islam offers an alternative worldview of economics, politics and culture. This worldview has to be tested in the fires of scrutiny. It has to compete with a whole range of powerful and deeply entrenched forces from the past and the present. At the world stage Islam has just emerged from the shadows of the last few centuries to claim a right to compete for a place in our hearts and minds. In Malaysia the future is likely to see action and reaction, pull and push and a symbiosis among the many factors and forces that have shaped and are shaping the political, social and moral landscape in Malaysia.

Given the multi-racial, multi-cultural and multi-religious composition of Malaysian society, the imperatives of coalition politics, the demands of a federal polity, the power of the non-Malay electorate, the forty-seven-year old political tradition of compromise and consensus, the increasing democratization of life, the greater sensitivity to human rights, the emergence of many powerful NGOs including those espousing women's issues, the juggernaut of globalization, the pulls of secularism and modernism, the glitter of a capitalistic, hedonistic and consumer-based economy, the power of the international media to shape our values, and the overwhelming control that Western institutions wield over our economic, cultural and educational life, it is unlikely that Islam will have a "walk-over" in Malaysia and will sweep away everything in its path. Malaysian society is, and is likely to remain, a cultural mosaic. Islam in Malaysia will continue to co-exist with modernity, with Malay *adat* and with the dominant American and European culture that shapes our worldview, our thinking processes and our framework assumptions.

Notes

1   *Bowman v Secular Society* (1917) Appeal Cases 406. See also (1991) 1 AllER 306–23 for the controversy about Salman Rushdie's *Satanic Verses*.
2   Ministry of Education Circular KP PP0129/210 dated 5 February 1969.
3   *Meor Atiqulrahman bin Ishak v Fatimah bte Sihi* [2000] 5 MLJ 375. See Dr. Abdul Aziz Bari, "Islam in the Federal Constitution: A Commentary On The Decision Of Meor Atiqulrahman", [2000] 2 MLJ cxxix.
4   "Where Religious Worship Centres Can Be Located", *New Straits Times*, 22 December 2000, p. 10.
5   Holy Qur'an Surahs 2:256; 109:1–6; 10:99.
6   *Daud Mamat v Majlis Agama Islam* [2002] 2 MLJ 390.
7   Surahs Muhammad 47:25, 27–28; Ali 'Imran 3:86–89; Bawarah 2:217; Nahl 16:106
8   *The Star*, 29 August 1998, p. 22.
9   M.Sufian Hashim, 'The Relationship between Islam and the State in Malaya', *Intisari* 1, no. 1 (1962): 8.
10 Refer to Schedule 9, List II, Item 1.
11 Article 159(5) & 161E. The "basic structure" argument may also be invoked to resist any revolutionary constitutional change.
12 Articles 3(1), 3(2), 3(3), 3(5), 11(4), 12(2), 34(1), 150(6A), 160(2), Fourth Schedule, and Ninth schedule, List II, Item 1.
13 Articles 121(1A), 145(3), Ninth Schedule, List II, Item 1.
14 Article 132(4)(A).
15 The equivalent Christian name for Ibrahim R.A. is Abraham; for Ismail R.A. is Ishmael; for Yaqub R.A. is Jacob; for Musa R.A. is Moses; and for Nabi Isa is Jesus Christ.
16 Ibn Hisham *Sirah*, p. 718.
17 Hamidullah, *Introduction to Islam*, Kuwait, IIFSO Publication, Kuwait, p. 171.
18 Ameer Ali, *The Spirit of Islam*, London, 1922, p. 273.
19 See Abdur Rahman Doi, *Non-Muslims Under Shariah*, 1979, p. 77–82.
20 Ibid., p. 81.
21 However in many areas Muslims are allowed to have a choice between *shari'a* provisions and ordinary civil laws. Among these areas are banking, trusts, adoption and a whole range of commercial transactions.
22 See definition of a "Malay" in Article 160(2).

14

THE ISLAMIC STATE: ORIGINS, DEFINITION AND SALIENT ATTRIBUTES

Mohammad Hashim Kamali

INTRODUCTION

This chapter begins with an introductory section which sets out some of the uncertainties concerning the concept and definition of an Islamic state, a brief history of developments, and a literature review. The remaining part of the discussion focuses on the salient attributes of an Islamic state: whether the Islamic state proposes a limited as opposed to a totalitarian government, whether it can be characterized as a civilian state as opposed to a theocracy, and whether it would be justified to characterize the Islamic state as a qualified democracy. The last section of this paper briefly addresses the Islamist demand for the establishment of Islamic state, and some comments on recent developments in Malaysia. What is attempted here is a selective account of some of the characteristic features of an Islamic state and does not claim to be exhaustive.

PREVAILING UNCERTAINTIES

Much of the ambiguity concerning the basic concept of an Islamic state is due to the under-developed state of Islamic constitutional law when it is compared to the private and personal law branches of the *shari'a*. This was in turn a result of the prevalence of dictatorship and dynastic rule in much of the Islamic history which stifled the natural development of ideas on politics and government. Scholarly attention was consequently focused on matters of worship, matrimonial law, property and inheritance, etc., which are far more developed when compared to constitutional law and government. What is more is that most of what happened in the centuries following the fall of the Righteous Caliphate represented a departure from the normative principles of Islam.

A former Mufti of Egypt, Shaykh Ahmad Huraydi wrote that the political order that prevailed in the Muslim lands from the Umayyad rule down to the end of the Ottomans did not, on the whole, comply with the principles and teachings of Islam. Those who wrote on Islamic government and administration often focused their attention on dynastic practices which did not reflect the Islamic principles of government but mainly expounded the history of government in those times and "there is a huge difference between the two".[1]

This was due partly to a continuing rift between the *ulama* and government which had started with the replacement of the Righteous Caliphate with monarchy by the founder of the Umayyad dynasty, Mu'awiya (d. 680 CE). Mu'awiya's coercive methods to obtain the pledge of allegiance (*bay'a*) for his son Yazid by threat of force marked the onset of political distortion and disenchantment of the *ulama* with the Umayyad rulers. The situation deteriorated when the Prophet's grandson, Husayn, challenged Yazid's leadership and was brutally killed together with his followers in the tragic incident of Karbala. The *ulama* questioned the legitimacy of these rulers and insisted on the enforcement of *shari'a*, which was increasingly being replaced by administrative decrees, resembling those of the Roman and Persian empires.

Abu Hamid al-Ghazali's (d. 1111 CE) *magnum opus, Ihya' Ulum al-Din* (*Revivification of the Religious Sciences*) was an attempt to revive the *shari'a* and make a fresh start in that direction. A similar attempt was made two centuries later by Taqi al-Din Ibn Taymiyya (d. 1328 CE), the author of *al-siyasa al-shar'iyya*, to revive the increasingly isolated *shari'a* into the practice of government. The question over legitimacy remained unresolved and so was the rift between the *ulama* and government. The *ulama* were for the most part isolated from government hierarchy and remained uninvolved in the day-to-day management of affairs. They wrote little on politics and government and much of what they wrote was viewed with reservations by the rulers.

Two different models of Islamic government featured in this narrative of disequilibrium and discord, and both remained somewhat inconclusive. The early caliphate captured the imagination of Muslims as the valid precedent and has retained its appeal to this day. The second of these was hereditary monarchy that prevailed over the centuries after the collapse of the Righteous Caliphate, until it was abolished by the Ottoman Turks in 1924. The early caliphate offered a vision in respect mainly of its ideals and principles, but it was too under-developed in its institutional set up to provide a model and prototype. Dynastic monarchy did not provide a model either due to problems over legitimacy and a questionable record of adherence to the *shari'a*.

The Shi'ite scholar, Shaykh Ja'far al-Subhani, acknowledged that one does not find a comprehensive work on the form and structure of an Islamic state as many of the works written by Sunni scholars were actually premised on the *status quo* and were basically descriptive of the governments of their times. This is the case even with al-Mawardi's *al-Ahkam al-Sultaniyya*, (Ordinances of Government) which pays more attention to the realities of the Abbasid state of his time rather than the foundational guidelines of the Qur'an and Sunnah. What needs to be done is to take a fresh recourse to the normative guidelines and avoid tainting those guidelines with the precedent of dynastic rule.[2]

At around the same time when Subhani spoke of the deviations of the past governments, Vatikiotis drew attention to the Islamic resurgence of recent times to say that Muslims in the Middle East were critical of the prevailing "alien order which many Muslims consider unsuitable and inadequate for their societies…". Vatikiotis added: "One observes that neither in Iran so far nor among any of the militant Islamic movements elsewhere is there a clear idea of the nature of the Islamic state or government they wish to establish."[3]

Selim al-'Awwa noted that the Islamic revolution of Iran stimulated Islamic scholarship and many researchers have since written on issues of constitutional law in Islam. Yet despite this welcome development, "many issues of interest to Islamic political thought and constitutional law remain shrouded in ambiguity which tend to cause hesitation and impede research".[4] It is perhaps the present generation of researchers who will contribute to the development of constitutional law in a way "that would suit the requirements of our age and address issues of concern to us at present".[5]

Juristic works on the caliphate are on the whole concerned with the methods of designation of the caliph, his rights and duties and a certain institutional blueprint on the judiciary, vizierate, and departmental structures for the army, taxation, police duties and so forth. This literature on the whole does not address modern developments, including the nation state itself, and constitutional themes on democracy, separation of powers and so forth. Muslim jurists of the pre-modern era wrote about the caliphate, *dar al-Islam*, *dar al-harb* (abode of Islam, abode of war) and envisaged a monolithic *umma* (muslim community) ruled by a single caliphate. The term îIslamic stateî occurs, for the first time it seems, in the writings of Rashid Rida (d. 1935). The term has been used since by individual writers as well as states, such as Pakistan, Iran, Afghanistan, etc. Pakistan's vision of an Islamic state is manifested in its Constitutions of 1956 and 1973 which declare sovereignty as a prerogative of God, and the Qur'an and Sunnah as basic sources of legislation. A republican system that is accountable to the people and conducts its affairs through consultation is also envisaged. Numerous model constitutions of Islamic state have sprung up in the recent writings of Muslim jurists, but consensus has yet to emerge over the definition and basic features of an Islamic state.

The Islamic state in the writing of scholars such as Rashid Rida, Syed Qutb, Maududi, Qaradawi and others is basically a *shari'a* state which is committed to the enforcement of *shari'a*. This idea seems to have a parallel in the Hanafi definition of *dar al-Islam* (the abode of Islam) which refers to a territory that is ruled by the *shari'a* even if the majority of its inhabitants happen to be non-Muslim. The other three schools, namely the Shafi'i, Maliki and Hanbali consider a place *dar al-Islam* if the majority of its inhabitants are Muslim who are also free to practice their faith without interference and oppression. It is a place where the rituals of the faith such as the Friday prayer, the *adhan* and other religious duties are publicly observed. The question that arises here is: would it be accurate to equate *dar al-Islam* with the Islamic state given the fact that *dar al-Islam* preceded the nation-state and was predicated in an entirely different set of socio-political realities?

SALIENT FEATURES

The salient features of an Islamic state that are addressed in some detail in the following pages are (a) that the Islamic state proposes a limited government; (b) it is a civilian state and (c) it is a qualified democracy.

(a) Limited Government

Islam advocates a limited government in which the individual enjoys considerable autonomy. There are, for example, restrictions on the legislative capabilities of the state, which may not introduce laws contrary to Islamic principles. Legislation must also meet the requirements of consultation and consensus. The state power is constrained by reference to the clear injunctions of the text which are neither made by the state nor does it have authority to overrule and abrogate them. The Islamic state may not issue commands contrary to the *shari'a*, but if it does so, the individual is not bound by obeying it. The head of state represents the community which has elected him in the first place and has authority to depose him in the event of a flagrant violation of the law.[6]

Islam does not advocate a totalitarian government as many aspects of civilian life remain outside the domain of law and government. Muslim jurists have thus distinguished the religious (*dini*) from juridical (*qada'i*) obligations and maintained that only the latter are enforceable before the courts. Most of the religious aspects of the individual's life in society are private and non-justiceable. Even some of the religious duties such as prayer, fasting, the *haj*, and almost all of what is classified as recommendable, reprehensible and permissible (*mandub, makruh, mubah*) are not legally enforceable. The private and civil rights of the individual are also immune, by the express injunctions of *shari'a*, against encroachment by others, including the state. No government agency, nor even the *shari'a* courts, have powers to grant discretionary changes in the private rights and properties of individuals, without the consent of the person concerned.[7]

The head of state and judge enjoys but limited powers to grant a pardon to a convicted offender, or to order discretionary punishment for unstipulated violations. The deterrent (*ta'zir*) punishments are open to court discretionary powers in respect of determining the quantitative aspect of the punishment only for conduct which is prescribed by the *shari'a*. The judges have no powers to create an offence, without valid evidence in the sources, on discretionary grounds. There is, moreover, no recognition in the *shari'a* of any privileged individual or group and no one, including the head of state, enjoys any special immunity or status before the courts of justice.[8] To quote Joseph Schact on this, "the solutions provided by Islamic law go decisively and consistently in favour of the rights of the individual, of the sanctity of contracts, and of private property and they put severe limits to the action of the state in these matters".[9]

The state's accountability to the community is in the present day Muslim countries articulated in their written constitutions which have become a common and generally accepted feature of government. These constitutions serve to a large extent as instruments of democracy — a more organized manifestation, in other words, of *bay'a* (fealty) and *shura* (consultation), and they are on the whole consistent with Islamic principles.[10]

In response to a question whether constitution-making was at all acceptable to Islam, Rashid Rida has issued the following *fatwa*: since a constitution is basically designed to delineate the limits of the state power and clarify the state's commitment to the basic rights of the people, it is acceptable to Islam.

If enacting a formal constitution operates as a check on despotism, there is no question over its compatibility with the *shari'a*. In the event where the constitution contains rules that may be repugnant to the teachings of Islam, only the part that is so repugnant may be set aside but not the whole of it. Rid, added that in the writings of Muslim jurists one also finds instances where they made errors in their *ijtihad* (independent reasoning) and in the books they have authored. One ought to isolate and reject the views that are erroneous but not the whole of their endeavour. The error must be corrected at an early opportunity so that the community is protected against deviation. Mahmud Hilmy has concurred with this and confirmed that there is nothing in the *shari'a* against enacting a written constitution.[11]

The powers of the Islamic state are also limited in respect of taxation. The *shari'a* thus lays down the following criteria which the government must observe in the imposition of tax: (1) Tax must be just and proportionate to the ability of the taxpayer; (2) it must apply equally to all without discrimination; (3) taxation must aim at the minimum of what is deemed necessary; (4) the well-being of the taxpayer must be observed in the determination of quantity and methods of collection; and (5) Taxation must observe the time limit of one calendar year for the yield or profit to materialize.[12] Both Abu Yusuf and Mawardi have emphasized moderation in tax by stating that it must in no case deprive the taxpayer of the necessities of life.[13]

(b) Theocratic or Civilian?

If theocracy refers to a government by religious leaders who exercise spiritual authority, such as that of the Pope in the Middle Ages, then the Islamic state does not qualify. In a theocracy the leaders claim to represent God and exercise powers such as the pardoning of sins. The Islamic state is simply not vested with such authority.[14] "The Islamic State", wrote Qaradawi, "is not a theocracy: it is a civilian state (*dawla madaniyya*)". It is civilian because it comes into being by election, homage and consultation and the head of state is accountable to the people. Citizens are also entitled to give him counsel and advice that may alert him to his error.[15]

Turabi wrote on in a similar vein: "It should be clearly understood that an Islamic state is not a theocracy", adding that it is not the government of the *ulama* nor is it a government by men only, to the exclusion of women. Women played a considerable role in public life during the time of the Prophet and they took part in the election of the third Caliph 'Uthman.[16] Another commentator noted that the Islamic state is committed to administer justice and protect the people's right and liberties and enable them to lead an honourable life.[17] Sayyid Qutb maintained that the Islamic state is not confined to any particular form or model, but it is committed to the enforcement of *shari'a*. That does not, however, make the Islamic state a theocracy as the *shari'a* itself does not approve of theocratic government.[18]

Zaydan refuted the view that the *shari'a* is all concerned with religious and worship matters. This is admittedly one aspect of it, but the *shari'a* also addresses government matters, issues of justice, rights and liberties from a wider perspective. On these matters the *juris corpus* of *shari'a* aspires to objectivity. The rules of justice in *shari'a*, for example, do not distinguish between Muslims and non-Muslim; they are basically objective and humanitarian.[19]

Theocratic government demands unquestioning obedience of its citizens and that naturally discourages individual freedom. Islam has, on the other hand, recognized the individual's right to disobey an unlawful command, just as it also restrains the government from issuing such a command and imposing on people's freedom.[20] Fathi Osman observed that the Islamic government is a people's government (*hukuma sha'biyya*) wherein the ruler is elected by the people and mandated to administer justice and uphold their basic rights in accordance with a set of objective rules.[21]

Qaradawi concurs that the Islamic state is neither a theocracy, nor is it totally secular (*'ilmaniyya*) as it does not seek to isolate religion. On the contrary, it has a duty to protect religion and enable the people to observe it. The lawful and unlawful (*halal, haram*) that are expounded in *shari'a* are observed by the Islamic state. The state maintains the religious values, yet it is not a theocratic state. Every member of the community, man and woman alike, is entitled to give sincere advice to the ruler and also to engage in the promotion of good and prevention of evil.[22]

The civilian character of the Islamic state has, however, been exposed to doubt in recent years as a result partly of the Islamic revolution of Iran 1979 which brought an *ulama*-led government into power, and Iran looked, to all intents and purposes, a theocratic state. Two other historical events have also been widely cited in support of the claim that the Islamic state was theocratic. These are the two statements made respectively by (i) the third Caliph ʿUthman, and (ii) the Abbasid Caliph Jaʿfar b. al-Mansur. I shall elaborate on these quotations first before discussing Iran.

(i)   Just before assassinating the Caliph 'Uthman, his assailants asked him to relinquish his position as caliph, a demand which the caliph declined and said, "no, by God I shall not remove the garment with which God has adorned me with". Some commentators saw this as an affirmation, by the deceased caliph, of the religious character of the caliphal office, and the view somehow continued to reverberate that the caliph was the chosen of God.[23] The Mu'tazila rationalists maintained that the caliph was an elected representative of the community and had no claim to holiness whatsoever. This view eventually gained ground and is now generally accepted to be in keeping with valid precedent: The slain caliph had said nothing during his thirteen years in office to change the basic position that the caliph was accountable to the people. It is further added that he had probably referred to the *bay'a* which brought him into office and he consequently saw it as a trust that could not be nullified by the aggressive act of the assailants.[24]

(ii) The Abbasid Caliph Ja'far b. al-Mansur (d. 158/775) is quoted to have said in a mosque sermon:

> O people! I am God's appointed authority in His earth (*sultan Allah fi ardih*), and I rule with His divine help and endorsement. I am guardian of His property and I act in accordance with His will and what I give, I do so by His permission …

Mutawalli who quoted this commented that most people had taken this statement from the literary work of an Andalusian author who was not a jurist and the quotation was also less than accurate.[25] Qaradawi concurred with Mutawalli and added: even if the Caliph al-Mansur's statement were accurate, it is best to treat it as an isolated incident which does not command authority. "We are not bound by al-Mansur's precedent on this." Qaradawi added that it was possible al-Mansur had meant that he was at the service of God's *shari'a* and its executor, not that he was a repository of divine authority as such. Qaradawi also quoted in this connection an incident where the Caliph al-Mansur had issued an explicit order to the then judge of Basra, Sawwar b. 'Abd Allah, in a land dispute between a merchant and an army commander — that the land should be given to the latter. The judge apparently wrote back to say "the evidence brought before me shows that the land belongs to the merchant, and I cannot take it away from him without evidence". The caliph wrote again: "By God … you shall give it to the army commander." And when the judge wrote again in equally emphatic terms repeating his earlier message, the Caliph al-Mansur conceded and even praised God for the firm stand that the judge had taken on the cause of justice. Qaradawi has also recounted two other similar cases which show that al-Mansur did not see himself as someone above the law and he was, in fact, a learned man and knew very well the limits of his authority *vis-a-vis* the *shari'a*. Could it be true then to hear the same caliph arrogating divine authority to himself? The truth is that claims of theocratic rule are unacceptable to the *shari'a* and Islamic thought hardly leaves the matter open to doubt.[26]

IRAN'S REVOLUTIONARY EXPERIENCE

Commentators who had earlier characterized the post-revolutionary Islamic Republic of Iran as a theocratic state would have noted that Iran itself had wanted to cast off that image and has gradually moved in that direction. Ayatollah Khomeini's theory of the guardianship of the jurist (*vilayat-e faqih*) and his own religious personality evidently lent support to the theocratic image of the Islamic Republic, especially in the early years of the revolution. But Iran under President Khatami has become a keen supporter of civil society and is now a leading influence in the advocacy of civilian rule and commitment to people's rights and liberties.

Qaradawi who addressed this issue in his 1997 publication also maintained, even before Khatami, that the impression of a theocratic state was less than accurate. The leading offices of state in Iran, including those of the President, the Supreme Leader, and the *majlis* (council) were all elective. Ministers and government officials did not cease to be taken to task by the *majlis* and the Islamic republic has itself made no claim to be a theocratic state. On one occasion in 1984 the *majlis*, for example, removed no less than seven ministers by a vote of non-confidence in accordance with the constitution.[27]

The Shi'ite doctrines on leadership and imamate are also different from those of its Sunni counterparts. The Sunnis who are in the majority, maintain that caliphate and government are elective and do not partake in the dogma and belief structure of Islam. The Shi'ites, on the other hand, consider imamate as a part of the Shi'ite theology and the *imam*, being the chosen of God, receives his title through hereditary succession from within the household of the Prophet. The Shi'ite *imam* is decidedly a theocratic figure and also believed to be infallible. The Shi'ite *imam* is the successor of the Prophet and has in theory direct authorization from God to manage the temporal and spiritual affairs of the Muslim community.[28] But then the last living *imam* of the Shi'a Imamiyya went into occultation over 1000 years ago, during which time the mantle of the occult *imam* was carried by his deputy (*na'ib-e imam*) who leads the Shi'ite community but who is not infallible. In the absence of Prophet and *imam*, the affairs of state are determined in accordance with the will and consent of the community through consultation. This is to all intents and purposes the same position as the Sunni doctrine of *khilafa* has taken. This position is reflected in the views of a leading Shi'ite leader of

Lebanon, and President of the Shi'ite Supreme Council, Muhammad Mahdi Shamsuddin, as discussed below.[29]

Ayatollah Khomeini's doctrine of *vilayat-e faqih* took a step further the Shi'ite doctrine of imamate and its underlying theme of the awaited *imam*. In the absence of a living *imam*, Khomeini (himself a deputy *imam*) entrusted the leading jurist to assume the leadership of the community and act as *na'ib-e imam*. But the question of the occult Imam remained problematic. Ayatollah Mahdi Shamsuddin's concept of *vilayat al-umma* restored to the *umma* itself the authority which Imam Khomeini had entrusted in the leading *faqih* (authority of the Muslim community).

Mahdi Shamsuddin explained that following the Prophet's demise, the *umma* became the locus of political authority, according to the Ash'arites and the Sunnis, but only the *imam* had title to authority and leadership, according to the Shi'ite doctrine. 'Ali b. Abu Talib was the first *imam* to inherit that authority and the succeeding *imams* carried the title after him. The twelfth *imam* has remained absent for a long time and only God knows when he will return, in which case the *umma* assumes his authority during the time of his absence. The community exercises in turn its authority through elective and consultative methods.[30]

This is a path-breaking development, which is how Selim al-'Awwa and Tawfiq al-Shawi have both appraised it for the potential it offers toward establishing a common basis of identity between the Sunni and Shi'ite approaches to leadership. Tawfiq al-Shawi sees Mahdi Shamsuddin's *vilayat al-umma* as a logical extension, indeed the matrix, of *imam* Khomeini's doctrine of *vilayat-e faqih*, which was basically an elective office; the Sunnis only differed with it in that they did not stipulate that the candidate must be a *faqih* (cleric). Mahdi Shamsuddin has effectively restored that choice back to the community.[31]

Selim al-'Awwa observed that the basic nation of *vilayat al-umma* was a point of agreement between the arbitrators who tried to settle the leadership dispute between 'Ali and Mu'awiya in the year 41/662. Had there been a confirmation of this then, no one would have disputed the *ummatic* locus of political authority. Khomeini's notion of *vilayat-e faqih* changed the Shi'ite doctrine which had postponed the establishment of an Islamic state until the return of the last *imam*. *Vilayat-e faqih* enabled the *faqih* to establish an Islamic government during the *imam*'s absence, and Mahdi Shamsuddin's concept of *vilayat al-umma* is an extension of the same logic; it marks a welcome beginning for a common doctrinal position to Islamic government among all Muslims.[32]

All of these tend to suggest that Islam favours not a theocracy but a people's government. The reader will also note that at no time had the Iranian state arrogated divinity to itself due to the absence of a living *imam*. This being the case, neither the Shi'ite doctrine during the time of occultation, nor the post revolutionary experience of Iran provide an argument by which to characterize the Islamic state as a theocracy, even among the Shi'ite community, let alone the wider majority of the Sunnis.

A QUALIFIED DEMOCRACY

Democracy is basically predicated in a set of principles most important among which are a recognition of the inherent worth of every human being, a representative and participatory government, acceptance of the rule of law, equality of all citizens before the law, and a high level of tolerance of unconventional views and beliefs. Islam contains a set of basic principles which "make it highly responsive towards many of the moral and legal prerequisites of democracy".[33] If democracy means a system of government that is the opposite of dictatorship, Islam is compatible with democracy "because there is no place in it for arbitrary rule by one man or a group of men".[34] A whole generation of Muslim scholars have tried to redefine concepts such as *bay'a* (pledge of allegiance) and *ijma'* (general consensus) in ways that may deviate from their traditional usage, but they are "no more removed from their original meanings than modern European models of democracy are from the ancient Greek *demes* (the people)".[35]

Among the differences commentators have noted in comparing democracy to an Islamic state, one is the attribution of sovereignty to God in Islam, but to the people in a democratic state. In a democracy the people may bring any legal order or system they wish for themselves whereas an Islamic state is bound by implementing the *shari'a*. Furthermore, democratic aims are generally material aims whereas Islam seeks both material and spiritual values. Democracy may not regulate personal morality whereas this too is of concern to an Islamic order.[36]

Taha Husayn observed that the political system in early Islam was neither democratic nor did it rest on absolutism as understood by the Greeks and Romans; it was a purely Arab system of government to which Islam added its own requirements. Muhammad Husayn Haykal similarly observed that the system of *shura* (consultation) in early Islam did not constitute a check on the powers of the caliph. Even though the caliph had to consult the community, he was not answerable to it.[37] Al-Ris has responded and expressed some reservations. Firstly, if by "purely Arab" it is suggested that the Islamic state is ethnocentric, then it must be said that Islam does not advocate ethnicity. Secondly, to say that the Islamic state was not democratic also does not reflect the fact that the people's consent, homage and welfare (*maslaha*) lay at the foundation of the sate of Medina. The commitment of that state to justice, equality and people's rights also went a long way toward democracy as a government of the people, by the people, for the people. Al-Ris adds, however, that while the Islamic state subscribed to these values, it was not identical with democracy. The people's will is sovereign in a democracy but in Islam the *shari'a*, although generally supportive of it, also introduces limitations to it. In a Western democracy, the people's sovereignty recognizes virtually no limitations whereas in an Islamic state the Qur'anic injunctions on equality and justice may not be violated in the name of people's sovereignty. Al-Ris concludes that the Islamic state and democracy have aspects in common just as they also differ in certain other respects. It is in this way *sui generis* as it has characteristics of its own.[38]

In Hassan Turabi's assessment, an Islamic state is not exactly a direct government of the people by the people: it is rather a government of the *shari'a*. But in ìa substantial sense, it is a popular government since the *shari'a* approves the convictions of the people and, therefore, their direct will".[39]

Selim al-'Awwa is critical of the view some jurists have taken that consultation was only recommended and not an obligatory requirement. This position is indefensible in view of the Qur'anic command (3:159) addressed to the Prophet asking him to consult the community, and also the Prophet's own practice of frequent recourse to *shura*, followed by the precedent of the Pious Caliphs and the Companions after him. Thus "I find it strange to see that some have considered *shura* only advisable but not obligatory".[40] Al-'Awwa then cites al-Qurtubi in support of the position that *shura* is a cardinal principle of Islamic government and an obligation of the Islamic state to implement.[41]

A conflict may exist between the idea of commitment to a divine law and the democratic notion of sovereignty. Yet the Islamic state may be described as a qualified democracy. This is because the community is the locus of authority that can hold the government to account and may ultimately depose it. The *shari'a* also vests the people's representatives with the authority to pass consensus-based legislation through *ijma'*.[42] This is the basic premise of a minority view among Muslim scholars that sovereignty in the Islamic state belongs to the *umma*. Others have qualified this to say that the *umma* is vested with a limited or "executive sovereignty (*al-sultan al-tanfidhi*)".[43]

Still others have held that the Islamic state exercises a composite sovereignty (*al-siyada al-muzdawija*) of the *umma* and the *shari'a*, which are inseparably intertwined and cannot be meaningfully separated.[44]

Furthermore, the Islamic government must strive to secure the people's welfare. According to a legal maxim of *shari'a* "the affair of the *imam* is judged by reference to the people's welfare-*amr al-imam manut bi'l-maslaha.*" It is the people's welfare on which the success and failure of an Islamic government is to be judged. A government that makes decisions, independently of the people's *maslaha*, thus deviates from its basic terms of reference.[45] "The *shari'a* makes people's *maslaha* as the basic criterion of relations between the ruler and ruled."[46] Qaradawi has consequently characterized the Islamic state as "a state of rights and liberties (*dawlat al-huquq wa'l-hurriyyat*) which is committed to the protection of the rights of life, ownership, right to the basic means of living, right to personal security and honour. These are the essential values (*al-daruriyyat*) which the *shari'a* seeks to protect".[47] Muhammad Asad observed that a state may be described "Islamic" if it incorporates in its constitution the clear and unambiguous ordinances of Islam which have a direct bearing on the community's socio-political and economic life.[48]

Qaradawi has also spoken forcefully against the detractors of democracy in the name of Islam, for Islam advocates the people's government. There is essential harmony between Islam and democracy." Islam has resolutely denounced oppressive and arrogant rulers, the Pharaoh and the Kora, who sought to enslave and humiliate their people. The Prophet Muhammad expressed this vividly in a *hadith*: "when you see my community afraid of calling a tyrant "tyrant" then take leave of it".[49] The ruler in Islam is "agent and employee of the community" who is accountable to the people. This was amply shown in the speeches and sermons of both the first and second caliphs, Abu Bakr and 'Umar. Qaradawi then added that democracy was the fruit of a long-standing struggle in which the people successfully subjugated despotism to the people's will. It is humanity's shared achievement and "we are entitled … to take from others ideas and methods that would benefit us, provided they do not clash with a clear and unequivocal text".[50] Election according to Qaradawi is a form of testimony (*shahada*) by which the electorate testifies to the suitability of the candidate. The electorate is under an obligation to give testimony and consider it "as discharge of electoral duty"[51] to ensure only the strong and trustworthy candidates are elected.

Qaradawi has also discussed political parties as an important feature of modern democracy. Here too, he dismisses the argument many have advanced that Islam rejects political parties. The *shari'a* principles of *hisba* (promotion of good and prevention of evil), and *nasiha* (sincere advice) as well as the right it grants to the public to criticize their government leaders can be given a meaningful role within a multi-party system. Political parties are therefore acceptable in an Islamic state. To curb despotism and oppressive rule, Qaradawi adds, is not within the capacity of individuals acting in isolation. But when the people join together in large numbers, they can influence government policy, in which case there should be no need for acts of rebellion and uprising against oppressive rule as often happened in the past.[52]

The *shari'a* in its broad outline is more democratic than totalitarian. It was due probably to its strong advocacy of the people's rights that totalitarian regimes of the past had difficulty in the implementation of *shari'a*. The ulama communities have also acted, more often than not, as protectors of the people's rights and resisted oppressive governments on their behalf.

Ameer Ali (d. 1929) rightly observed that the *shari'a* gave the people a code which consecrated the principle of self-government, made men equal in the eyes of the law, and made the government subordinate to the law. An examination of the political conditions of the Muslims under the early caliphs tends to depict a popular government administered by an elective chief with limited powers to exercise. At a time of history when everywhere "the masses were in hopeless subjugation, Islam elaborated a political system fundamentally republican in character, stressing the duties of the sovereigns towards their subjects, and the freedom and equality of people."[53]

Muhammad Iqbal (d. 1938) spoke affirmatively of the democratic impulse of Islam but said that the Muslims never effectively developed the elective principle. This was due partly to the Persians and the Mongols, the two great races which embraced Islam and formed governments; they were not only strangers to the elective principle, but actively opposed to it. The Persians worshipped their monarchs as manifestors of divine power, and the Mongols were given to tribalist methods.[54] Iqbal also wrote: "The republican form of government is not only thoroughly consistent with the spirit of Islam, but has also become a necessity in view of the new forces that are set free in the world of Islam."[55] The position of the ruler in the eyes of the *shari'a* is the same as that of an ordinary Muslim. In Islam, the basis of legislation, after the clear injunctions of the *shari'a*, is the agreement of the Muslim community. Iqbal's commentator, Khalifa 'Abdul Hakim characterized "Iqbal's conception of Islamic democracy" as closely aligned with what Islam experienced during its early period. In this "there was no ruling class, freedom reigned everywhere. The state was a welfare state".[56] The rulers were elected on the merit of intellectual and moral excellence.

Asad described the Islamic government democratic and added that democracy as conceived by the West was infinitely nearer to the Islamic conception thereof than to its Greek parallel. For Islam maintains that all human beings are equal and must be given the same opportunities for development and self-expression. Islam essentially envisaged an elective form of government. A government that comes to power by "non-elective means becomes automatically illegal".[57]

The evidence I have examined suggests obviously that there are some differences between the Islamic system of rule and a modern democratic state. Yet there is enough in common between them to justify the characterization of the Islamic state as a qualified democracy.

THE ISLAMISTS AND THE ISLAMIC STATE

The Islamist demand in the Middle East and elsewhere in the Muslim world to replace the political order in their respective countries with an Islamic state which is committed to a strict implementation of the *shari'a* has become one of the principal themes of their campaign. They have obviously come to the conclusion that the nation state of the post-colonial era has failed to deliver the claims and promises it typically made to bring prosperity, modernization and good government. The Islamist claim is admittedly not without substance as democracy and the people's basic rights have not taken root and the majority of Muslim countries have experienced totalitarian regimes that also fell short of the people's expectations. Yet the claim that bringing an Islamic state would remedy the situation and provide effective solutions to problems of good government, poverty and corruption is also less than realistic. For engagement in a constructive course of change for the better can hardly claim credibility if it is marked with confrontation and violence. Selim al-'Awwa has rightly observed that the Islamists have exaggerated their case when they say that the only way for a better future is through establishing an Islamic state. This is erroneous as it is reductionist of Islam and tends to narrow down the wider scope of Islamic teachings. For Islam's primary focus is not so much on politics and government as it is on reforming the individual and providing moral and religious guidance for an orderly life in society. Islam provides a *shari'a* which lays down a certain number of specific rules whereas for the rest Islam provides general principles on religion, morality and law, and also some guidelines on government. To say that establishing an Islamic state is of central importance to Islam and identify this as the only way to reformation (*islah*) of the individual and society is therefore overstated. It is even a greater mistake for the Islamists to validate recourse to violence in order to secure political power. For Islam advocates consultation and consensus and when these are abandoned in favour of coercive methods, the Islamic identity and basis of that approach becomes decidedly questionable.[58] These modern Islamists resemble the Kharijites of the early days of Islam who also validated the use of force as means to political power and they consequently lost ground and earned themselves the epithetic designation "the outsiders" who had abandoned the mainstream and consensus-based Islam.[59]

If the Islamists have a programme and agenda, they must surely offer it for consultation and win public support for it through participation and consensus. If they have a viewpoint to project on issues of public concern, they can promote it through a variety of methods and formulas that Islam has provided for such purposes. This would include sincere advice (*nasiha*) to fellow citizens and leaders, and constructive criticism of the authorities (*hurriyat al mu'arada*). On matters of expert and technical nature, the *shari'a* entitles the qualified person to carry out *fatwa* (considered opinion or verdict) and *ijtih,d* (independent reasoning). All peaceful means of expression, including media and broadcasting, may be utilised for information and dissemination of ideas. The main limits to freedom of expression that the *shari'a* has specified are avoidance of harm to others, slander and libel, blasphemy and sedition.[60] The Islamists are certainly expected to utilize the peaceful and participatory methods that Islam recommends. Recourse to the use of force is validated for self-defence and fighting injustice mainly on the personal level. There is certainly no support in Islam for recourse to coercive methods in order to gain political power and establish a government. In the event where the government itself becomes oppressive and engages in criminality and aggression, the individual is entitled not to obey it. But only the community as a whole is entitled to take collective action to depose an unlawful government, if this is possible, without engaging in civil strife and violence. This is nowadays only feasible, in my view, through a vote of no confidence and impeachment, but I do not propose to engage in further detail on this.

Recent developments in Malaysia, especially Prime Minister Dr. Mahathir's announcement, in late 2001, that Malaysia was an Islamic state, might have sounded less than convincing to begin with. This was undoubtedly an important development and in many ways unexpected, yet the government has not changed that position despite some hesitations that are bound to exist on account of the multi-religious composition of Malaysian society. The prime minister has actually repeated that announcement in some of his subsequent statements in Malaysia and abroad. This is by no means accidental. As it is, Islam is an integral part of Malay identity, side by side with the Malay language and Malay custom. These are, in fact, the three ingredients often cited in the definition of Malayness, and the religious rituals as well as the moral and cultural teachings of Islam are generally observed among the

Muslims of Malaysia. Islam also plays a visible role in the ruling party UMNO (United Malay National Organization). Some of the developments on the Islamic front such as the introduction in 1993 of the *Hudud* (prescribed punishment) Bill in Kelantan and more recently in Terengganu in 2002 have been received with reservation and criticism by the federal government. The federal government has made it known that the *hudud* bill provisions, in both cases, violate the Federal Constitution and the state jurisdictional limits in regard to the imposition of the *hudud* punishments.

The present writer has also been critical of the somewhat dogmatic manner that these punishments have been formulated in the proposed enactments of Kelantan and Terengganu. Yet this writer does not propose to engage the reader with details over this but merely to say that despite the critique advanced by this writer and many others on the juridical aspects of the *hudud* bill,[61] there has been no fresh attempt or proposal to take an *ijtihad*-oriented approach (that is, creative interpretation in a given socio-political context) to the *hudud* so that the prevailing conditions of Malaysian society are adequately reflected in the proposed laws.

CONCLUSION

There is general agreement on the necessity of leadership and a system of rule that manages the community affairs in accordance with the basic principles of Islam. But evidence is inconclusive on the question as to what form and structure it should have. This leads one to the conclusion that the Islamic state is more of an idea and concept than an institutional form. An Islamic state is thus any system of rule that upholds the injunctions of Islam on equality and justice, on consultation, and the basic rights and liberties of the people. It is a civilian, constitutional and representative system which is accountable to the people, strives for the people's welfare and upholds the morality and dogma of Islam. Non-Muslims are entitled in an Islamic state to follow and practice their own religion free of interference. They are also allowed to practice their own laws and traditions pertaining to personal status matters. Any state that is committed to these principles may be regarded as an Islamic state regardless of the organizational form and model it may represent.

Notes

[1]   Shaykh Ahmad Huraydi as quoted in Fu'ad A. Ahmad, *Usul Nizam al-Hukm fi'l-Islam* [Principles of Government] Alexandria: Mu'assasa Shabab al-Jami'a, 1411/1991, p. 15.

2   Ja'far al-Subhani, *Ma'alim al-Hukuma al-Islamiyya* [Signposts of an Islamic
    Government], lecture series compiled by Ja'far al-Hadi, Beirut: Dar al-Adwa',
    1405/1984, pp. 76–77.
3   P.J. Vatikiotis, "Islamic Resurgence: A Critical Review" in *Islam and Power*,
    edited by Alexander S. Cudsi and Ali E. Hillal Dessouki. Baltimore and London:
    the John Hopkins University Press, 1981, pp. 193, 196.
4   Mohamed Selim el-Awa, *al-Fiqh al-Islami fi Tariq al-Tajdid* [Islamic Law in Its
    New Form], 2nd edn., Beirut: al-Maktab al-Islami, 1419/1998, p. 44.
5   Ibid.
6   Cf. M.H. Kamali, "Characteristics of the Islamic State," *Islamic Studies* 32
    (1993), p. 32; Tawfiq al-Shawi, *al-Mawsu'a al-'Asriyya fi'l-Fiqh al-Jina'i al-Islami*
    [Contemporary Encyclopedia of Islamic Criminal Law], Cairo: Dar al-Shuruq,
    1421/2001, vol. 2, p. 286; Mustafa Kamal Wasfi, *al-Nizam al-Dusturi fi'l-Islam
    Muqarinan bi'l-Nuzum al-'Asriyya* [Constitutional Government in Islam
    Compared to Contemporary Constitutional Orders], 2nd edn., Cairo: Maktaba
    Wahba, 1414/1994, pp. 14–15; Yusuf Qaradawi, *Min Fiqh al-Dawla fi'l-Islam*
    [The Jurisprudence of State in Islam], Cairo: Dar al-Shuruq, 1417/1997, p. 58;
    Manzuruddin Ahmed, "The Classical Muslim State", *Islamic Studies* 1 (1962):
    90.
7   Cf. Kamali, "Characteristics of the Islamic State", n. p. 32.
8   Ibid., p. 33; el-Awa, *al-Fiqh al-Islami fi Tariq al-Tajdid* [Islamic Law in Its New
    Form], note 5, pp. 170–71.
9   Joseph Schact, "Islamic Law in Contemporary States", *The American Journal of
    Comparative Law* 8 (1959): 19.
10 Cf. Tawfiq al-Shawi, *al-Mawsu'a al-'Asriyya* [Contemporary Encyclopedia of
    Islamic Criminal Law] 1, no. 6: 114–15.
11 Muhammad RashÓd Rid,, *Fatawa Imam Muhammad Rashid Rida* [The Verdicts
    of Imam Muhammad Rashid Rida], compiled by Salah al-Din Munjid and
    Yusuf Khuri, Beirut: Dar al-Kitab al-Jadid, 1390/1970, pp. 805–08; Mahmud
    Hilmy, *Nizam al-Hukm al-Islami* [Systems of Governance in Islam], 6th edn.
    Cairo: no publisher, 1401/1981, p. 122.
12 Cf. 'Abd al-Wahhab Khallaf, *al-Siyasa al-Shar'iyya* [Shari'a Oriented Policy],
    Cairo: al-Matba'a al-Salafiyya, 1350/1970, p. 59; Umar Chapra, *The Economic
    System of Islam*, Karachi: University of Karachi Press, 1971, p. 63; Kamali,
    "Characteristics of the Islamic State", p. 33.
13 Abu Yusuf Ya'qub b. Ibrahim, *Kitab al-Kharaj* [Book on Taxation], 2nd edn.,
    Cairo: al-Salafiyya, 1352 A.H., p. 152; Abu'l-Hasan al-Mawardi, *Kitab
    al-Ahkam al-Sultaniyya* [Book on Ordinances of Government], 2nd edn., Cairo:
    al-Babi al-Halabi, 1386 A.H., p. 194.
14 Cf. Kamali, "Characteristics of the Islamic State", p. 37; Diya al-Din al-Ris,
    al-Nazariyyat al-Siyasiyya al-Islamiyya [Islamic Political Theories], 7th edn.,
    Cairo: Dar al-Turath, n.d., p. 377.
15 Qaradawi, *Min Fiqh al-Dawla* [Islamic Law and State], n. 6, pp. 57–58; See also

Anwar A. Qadri, *Islamic Jurisprudence in the Modern World*, 2nd edn., Lahore: Ashraf Press, 1981, p. 270.

16   Hasan Turabi, "The Islamic State", in *Voices of Resurgent Islam*, edited by J. Esposito. New York: OUP, 1983, p. 243.

17   Salem Azzam, ed., *Islam in Contemporary Society*, London: Longman, 1982, p. 258.

18   Sayyid Qutb, *al-'Adala al-Ijtima'iyya fi'l-Islam* [Social Justice in Islam], 2nd edn., Cairo: 'Isa al-Babi al-Halabi, 1373/1954, p. 98.

19   Cf. Abd al-Karim Zaydan, *al-Fard wa'l-Dawla fil-Shari'a al-Islamiyya* [The Individual, the State, and the *shari'a*], 2nd edn., Gray: Indiana: International Islamic Federation of Student Organizations, 1390/1970, p. 7.

20   Cf. 'Abd al-Hamid Mutawalli, *Mabadi Nizam al-Hukm fil-Islam* [Foundations of the Systems of Government], Alexandria: Manshat al-Ma'arif, 1974, p. 92f.

21   Fathi Osman, *al-Fikr al-Qanuni al-Islami* [Islamic Juridical Thought], Cairo: Matba'a Mukhajmar, n.d., p. 119.

22   Qaradawi, *Min Fiqh al-Dawla* [Islamic Law and State], n. 6, pp. 31, 34.

23   Cf. Ibn al-Athir, *al-Bidaya wa'l-Nihaya* [The Beginning and the End], Beirut: Maktabat al-Ma'arif, vol. 17, p. 180.

24   Qaradawi, *Min Fiqh al-Dawla* [Islamic Law and State], n. 6, pp. 60, 66; Fahmi Huwaydi, "Akdhubat al-Hukm al-Ilahi," *al-Ahram*, 14/10/1986 as quoted by Qaradawi.

25   'Abd al-Hamid Mutawalli, *Mabadi Nizam al-Hukm fi'l-Islam* [Foundations of Islamic Government], Alexandria: Mansa'at al-Ma'arif, 1974, p. 190.

26   Qaradawi, *Min Fiqh al-Dawla* [Islamic Law and State], n. 5, pp. 68–70 (also referring to Jalal al-Din al-Suyuti, *Tarikh al-Khulafa'* [The History of the Caliphs], Beirut: Dar al-Fikr, p. 241).

27   Qaradawi, *Min Fiqh al-Dawla*, n. 5, p. 72.

28   Cf. Zafir al-Qasimi, *Nizam al-Hukm fi'l- Shari'a wa'l-Tarikh* [System of Rule in *Shari'a* in Jurist History], 2nd edn., Beirut: Dar al-Nafa'is, 1977, p. 297; A.K.S. Lambton, *State and Government in Medieval Islam*, OUP, 1981, p. 298.

29   Al-Shawi, *al-Mawsu'a al-'Asriyya* [Contemporary Encyclopedia of Islamic Criminal Law] 2, no. 6: 105.

30   Mahdi Shamsuddin's views are conveyed in his two works *Nizam al-Hukm wa'l-Idara fi'l-Islam* [Governance and Administration in Islam], Beirut: 1997 and *al-Ijtimac al-Siyasi al-Islami* [Social Justice in Islam] — cited by both Selim el-'Awwa and Tawfiq al-Shawi as in the following notes.

31   Tawfiq al-Shawi, *al-Mawsu'a al-'Asriyya* [Contemporary Encyclopedia] 1, no. 6: 106.

32   Muhammad Selim al-'Awwa, *al-Fiqh al-Islami fi Tariq al-Tajdid* [Islamic Law in its New Form], 2nd edn., Beirut: al-Maktab al-Islami, 1419/1998, pp. 71–72.

33   Hamid Enayat, *Modern Islamic Political Thought*, London: Macmillan Press Ltd., 1982, p. 126.

34   Ibid., p. 128.

35 Ibid., p. 135.
36 Cf. Baqir Sharif al-Qurshi, *Nizam al-Hukm wa'l-Idara fi'l-Islam* [Governance and Administration in Islam], Najaf (Iran); Matba'a al-Adab, 1966, p. 104f.
37 Both views quoted in Mazheruddin Siddiqi, *Modern Reformist Thought in the Muslim World*, Islamabad, Islamic Research Institute, 1982, pp. 132–33.
38 Al-Ris, *al-Nazariyyat al-Siyasiyya al-Islamiyya* [Islamic Political Theories], n. 14, pp. 372–85.
39 Hassan Turabi, "The Islamic State", in *Voices of Resurgent Islam*, p. 244.
40 Al-'Awwa, *al-Fiqh al-Islami* [Islamic Law in Its New Form], n. 5, p. 60.
41 Ibid., p. 61; *al-Qurtubi, Tafsir al-Qurtubi* [Qurtubi's Commentary], 4, Beirut edn., p. 249.
42 For details on *ijma'* see Kamali, *Principles of Islamic Jurisprudence*, Cambridge: The Islamic Texts Society, 1991, p. 168f.
43 Zaydan, *al-Fard wa'l-Dawla* [The Individual, the State and *Shari'a*], p. 25. For further detail on sovereignty see M.H. Kamali, "The Limits of Power in an Islamic State", *Islamic Studies* 28 (1989): 324; Wasfi, *al-Nizam al-Dusturi* [Constitutional Order], p. 17.
44 Al-Ris, *al-Nazariyyat al-Siyasiyya*, n. 14, p. 385.
45 Cf. Wasfi, *al-Nizam al-Dusturi*, n. 6, pp. 97–98; al-Shawi, *al-Mawsu' al-'Asriyya*, n. 6, vol. I, p. 106, and vol. II, p. 452.
46 Tawfiq al-Shawi, *al-Mawsu' al-'Asriyya*, n. 6, vol. 1, p. 104.
47 Al-Qaradawi, *Min Fiqh al-Dawla fi'l-Islam*, n. 6, pp. 48–49.
48 Muhammad Asad, *The Principles of State and Government in Islam*, Berkeley: University of California Press, 1961, p. 17.
49 Qaradawi, *Min Fiqh al-Dawla*, n. 6, pp. 130–47.
50 Ibid.
51 Ibid., p. 138.
52 Ibid., pp. 147–61.
53 Syed Ameer Ali, quoted in Siddiqi, *Modern Reformist Thought*, n. 38, p. 119.
54 Quoted by Siddiqi, Ibid., p. 127.
55 Muhammad Iqbal, *The Reconstruction of Religious Thought in Islam*, Lahore: Ashraf Press, reprint 1982, p. 157; see also Siddiqi, *Reformist Thought*, p. 127.
56 Siddiqi, *Reformist Thought*, n. 38, p. 128 (quoting Khalifa 'Abdul Hakim, *Fikr-e Iqbal* [Iqbal's Thought], p. 266).
57 Asad, *Principles of State*, n. 49, p. 36.
58 Cf. al-'Awwa, *al-Fiqh al-Islami*, n. 5, pp. 48–49.
59 Ibid., p. 46.
60 For details on this and other violations of the freedom of expression see M.H. Kamali, *Freedom of Expression in Islam*, Cambridge: The Islamic Text Society, 1997.
61 See for details M.H. Kamali, *Punishment in Islamic Law: An Enquiry into the Hudud Bill of Kelantan*, Kuala Lumpur, Institut Kajian Dasar, 1995. A subsequent edition of the book was published by Ilmiah Publishers of Kuala Lumpur, 2000.

PART FOUR

Impact of September 11 on Islamic Thought and Practice

15

SEPTEMBER 11 AND ISLAMIC MILITANCY IN POST-NEW ORDER INDONESIA

Noorhaidi Hasan

INTRODUCTION

On 11 September 2001, a tragedy occurred in the United States. Three jetliners hijacked by terrorists struck the World Trade Centre and the Pentagon, the principal symbols of American hegemony. Another hijacked jetliner tried to crash into the White House but failed, and plummeted into an open field in Pennsylvania. Within the space of twenty minutes, the twin towers of the World Trade Centre and part of the Pentagon collapsed, with the loss of more than three thousand lives. Mass hysteria and sorrow immediately afflicted not only American society, but also all civilized nations throughout the world. They strongly condemned the attacks and sent their sympathies to the victims. As an immediate response to the attacks, President George W. Bush proclaimed a "global crusade" against "terrorism". He asked the entire world to join an anti-terrorist coalition, in order to defeat Osama bin Laden and his internationally operating terrorist network, Al Qaeda, which was accused of being responsible for the attacks. He even took a vow to retaliate by bombing Afghanistan, a country ruled by the Taliban regime and considered to have provided a haven for Osama bin Laden and his organization. From this tragedy, the world has apparently entered a new phase of global war, following the collapse of the Soviet Union and the end of the cold war.

Various effects have been produced by the September 11 tragedy and its aftermath. Direct reactions to the tragedy appeared in different parts of the world. In the West there emerged sporadic attacks against Muslim immigrants and their symbols of existence, indicating the increase of anti-Islam sentiment. Such a sentiment was intertwined with the fear of the threat of terrorism associated with Islam, exacerbated by the anti-terrorist campaigns by the United States. Similarly, in the Muslim world, reactions to September 11 arose in many places, but with different concerns, where protests against George W. Bush's proclamation of a global war were voiced. These reactions significantly correlated with the increase of anti-American sentiment in particular and the rise of Islamic radicalism in general. Witnessing these events, it is difficult to deny that the clash between the Western world and the Muslim world is somehow really legitimizing Huntington's thesis about the clash of civilizations.[1]

Indonesia is one of the Muslim countries in the world witnessing the move of Islamic radicalism to the centre of the discursive space. A variety of radical Islamist groups have come to the fore, demanding the implementation of the Islamic *shari'a,* conducting *razzias* on cafes, discotheques, and casinos, and most importantly, in the name of *jihad,* sending thousands of their militia troops to some trouble spots. By doing so, they have been extremely active in bringing the radical Islamic discourses into the public sphere and providing models for their application. It is of interest that, in the wake of September 11, they have become more vocal and active in producing their discourses and somehow succeeding in dominating the Indonesian public sphere.

The purpose of this chapter is to look at how the September 11 tragedy and its aftermath contributed to the increasing popularity of the radical Islamist discourse in the recent political landscape of Indonesia, and how this phenomenon would naturally influence thoughts, discourses, and practices of Muslims in the country. It will focus on the radical Islamist groups and their discourses in relation to September 11 and its aftermath, and shall examine the reactions against September 11, after which event an anti-American coalition was established. Secondly, this essay will analyze the rise of radical Islamism in post-New Order Indonesia. Thirdly, it will look at how events post-September 11 will have various effects on Islam in the country — in relation to the legitimacy of the radical Islamist groups, the expansion of *jihad,* and the quest for an Islamic state.

ANTI-AMERICAN COALITION

Immediately after George W. Bush had proclaimed a global crusade against terrorism, various Islamist groups in Indonesia took to the streets to voice their protests against the United States. The masses from the Front Pembela

Islam (Defenders of Islam Front), the Front Pemuda Islam Surakarta (Surakarta Muslim Youth Front), the Kesatuan Aksi Mahasiswa Muslim Indonesia (the United Action of Indonesian Muslim Students), the Himpunan Aksi Mahasiswa Muslim Indonesia (the Collaborative Action of Indonesian Muslim Students, Hammas), the Gerakan Pemuda Islam (the Islamic Youth Movement), the Front Hizbullah (the Front of the God's Party), the Majelis Mujahidin Indonesia (the Council of Indonesian Holy Warriors), the Partai Bulan Bintang (Crescent and Star Party), and the Partai Keadilan (Justice Party) flooded the streets around the American Embassy in Jakarta.[2] They rejected George W. Bush's determination to retaliate the September 11 attacks by bombing Afghanistan, and questioned the accusations he had made that Osama bin Laden was behind the attacks. For them, such accusations constituted part of an ongoing conspiracy to destroy Islam.

When the threat of the U.S. military retaliation became reality, anti-America demonstrations staged by the various Islamist groups became larger and more widespread. They condemned the attacks and demanded the government sever its diplomatic ties with the United States. Such demonstrations occurred not only in Jakarta but also in half a dozen other cities, such as Surabaya, Makasar, Medan, and Solo. The demonstrations were followed by the burning of the Stars and Stripes flag and billboards of McDonald's and KFC (Kentucky Fried Chicken) franchise restaurants. In line with the upsurge of the demonstrations, the Front Pemuda Islam Surakarta and the Laskar Pembela Islam issued a threat to expel American citizens in particular and Western people in general. Although this threat has never been acted upon, it undoubtedly brought about some anxiety among most Western expatriates who lived in Indonesia.

Some elements of the radical Islamist groups gravitated towards two major Islamic militia groups, the Laskar Pembela Islam and the Laskar Mujahidin Indonesia, which went a step further, by calling for *jihad* against the United States and its related interests. They opened venues for the registration of holy warriors prepared to go to Afghanistan. Another Islamic militia group, the Laskar Jihad, preferred not to involve themselves in the demonstrations, based on the belief that demonstration is an expression of democracy which is in opposition to the principle of absolute authority of God. Nevertheless, this particular militia group stated that 10,000 holy fighters were prepared to undertake *jihad* in Afghanistan. Ja'far Umar Thalib, the leader of this group, sought to mobilize and fuel the emotions of his followers to prepare a resistance against the United States and what he called all manifestations of its arrogance.[3] Even though these threats primarily remained rhetorical, some leaders of the radical Islamist groups made it known that a dozen of their holy fighters had landed in Afghanistan.[4]

A number of established Muslim organizations were forced to align themselves with the anti-American sentiments spread by the radical Islamist groups. The Indonesian Council of Ulama (MUI, Majelis Ulama Indonesia), a semi-governmental body of *ulama*, for instance, issued a call for *jihad* against the United States, which, by attacking Afghanistan, was perceived to have opposed justice and the principle of presumption of innocence.[5] Yet, this call was clarified by the secretary general of the institution, stating that what they meant by *jihad* in the call was not an armed war but rather a serious (peaceful) attempt to assist Afghan Muslims who would face the attacks of the United States and its allies.[6] Similarly, the Nahdhlatul Ulama and the Muhammadiyah, the two largest moderate Muslim organizations, condemned the attacks and labelled them an aggression against Afghan innocents. For them, the United States had no reason to attack Afghanistan before they had secured evidence of the involvement of Osama bin Laden in the September 11 attacks.[7]

The September 11 tragedy, followed by the attacks of the United States and its allies on Afghanistan, has apparently unified the various Islamist groups into one same concern, rhetoric, and action. With different flags, they staged demonstrations together to voice their sympathies to Afghan Muslims and yell their anti-American slogans. From their perspective, Afghan Muslims have become the victims of the arrogance of the United States, which, by bombing Afghanistan, had proclaimed a war against Islam and positioned themselves as the greatest enemy of Muslims. Using such rhetoric, they succeeded in building what they called an "action alliance" to resist the arrogance of the United States.

The action alliance, born out of the concern demonstrated by the radical Islamist groups with September 11 and its aftermath, has undoubtedly changed the landscape of Islamism in present-day Indonesia. These events have redefined the points of reference for legitimacy in the context of competition for authority: the various Islamist groups obtained a rare opportunity to enhance their legitimacy as the defenders of the Muslim *umma*. The image of a Muslim world facing a holy war against "a coalition of unbelievers", following George W. Bush's decision to retaliate against the September 11 attacks, has been presented by the radical Islamist groups in the country as proof of an ongoing evil conspiracy to destroy Islam. When many Muslim groups remained silent in responding to such a "critical situation", the radical Islamist groups came to the fore to demonstrate themselves as the most committed defenders of Islam. This step succeeded in pushing millions of Indonesian Muslims to stand at their side.

RADICAL ISLAMISM IN POST-NEW ORDER INDONESIA

Since the collapse of the New Order regime, Islamic radicalism has engulfed the political arena of Indonesia. We note, for instance, the emergence of the Laskar Pembela Islam, the Laskar Jihad, the Laskar Mujahidin, as well as other minor radical Islamist organizations. But, before September 11, their actions were still very much defined by their different, often competing political interests. The Laskar Pembela Islam, for instance, had been primarily concerned with issues of morality brought about by the efflorescence of cafes, discotheques, and casinos in different parts of Jakarta. For this concern, they frequently swept venues they accused of being dens of iniquity and they covered these actions with the slogan *al-amr bi al-ma'ruf wa nahy 'an munkar,* a Qur'anic phrase meaning enjoining good and forbidding evil, claiming that they were seeking to diminish evils and implement the *shari'a.* The Laskar Pembela Islam is the paramilitary division of the Front Pembela Islam led by Habib Rizieq Husein Shihab (b. 1965). Recruiting its membership from jobless youth, gangsters (*preman*), as well as students from a number of traditional Islamic schools (*pesantren*) and members of mosque youth organizations affiliated with some key figures in the organization, this particular militia group is believed to have often received orders from some civilian and military elites to stage demonstrations and put political pressure on their rivals.

Another Islamic militia group, the Laskar Jihad, preferred to focus on *jihad* actions on the Moluccan islands and other trouble spots in Indonesia. It became the most active group in sending its *jihad* fighters to the spice-islands. It consists of around 10,000 young members, militants who prefer to wear *jalabiyyah* (long flowing robes) and long beards, demonstrating their willingness to martyr themselves for God. The Laskar Jihad is a paramilitary division of the Forum Komunikasi Ahlu Sunnah wal-Jama'ah (the Communication Forum of the Followers of the Sunnah and the Community of the Prophet),[8] FKAWJ for short, which was established by Ja'far Umar Thalib, and officially inaugurated at a *tabligh akbar* (mass religious meeting), in Solo, Central Java, on 14 February 1998.[9] The foundation of this organization was intended as an umbrella for the followers of the contemporary Salafi movement, adopting the most puritanical style of Islam, known as Wahhabism.[10] This movement was brought to Indonesia in the mid-1980s by some Saudi Arabian returnees, who have studied with a number of prominent Salafi *ulama* at that centre of the Muslim world and been involved in the Afghan war. Their attempts to disseminate this particular (non-political) movement received enthusiastic responses from university students.[11] Through a process of mobilization in a climate of major changes following the collapse of the New Order regime, the network of the contemporary Salafi communities resorted to direct political activism and served as the main composition and backbone of the Laskar Jihad.

Unlike the Laskar Pembela Islam and the Laskar Jihad, which never explicitly questioned the format of the modern nation-state, their concern with the establishment of an Islamic state, which has been covered in their struggle for the application of the *shari'a,* has driven the actions of the Laskar Mujahidin Indonesia. It is a loose alliance of a dozen minor Islamic militia groups scattered in various regions, whose existence cannot be disassociated with the clandestine Negara Islam Indonesia (NII, the Islamic State of Indonesia) movement. The umbrella organization of the Laskar Mujahidin is the Majelis Mujahidin Indonesia (Indonesian Holy Warrior Assembly), established during the so-called "first national congress of *mujahidin"*[12] which took place in Yogyakarta in August 2001. This organization is led by Abu Bakar Baasyir, acting as *amir al-mujahidin,* the leader of holy warriors, and the leader of *ahl al-hall wa al-aqd,* the advisory council of the assembly.[13] He is known as an old figure among the radical Islamist groups who had for a long time actively resisted Suharto. Together with Abdullah Sungkar, Abu Bakar Baasyir established the Ngruki Pesantren, a conservative Islamic boarding school in Solo, Central Java. Both were arrested in the 1970s for allegedly leading the Jama'ah Islamiyyah (JI, the Islamic group), which tried to start the so-called *komando jihad (jihad* command) rebellious movement against Suharto. They fled to Malaysia to escape another prison term and did not return until after the fall of Suharto in 1998. Giving a speech in the first national congress of *mujahidin,* Abu Bakar Baasyir proclaimed that the application of the *shari'a* was absolutely essential, and argued that its rejection must be countered by *jihad.*[14] The executive committee *(lajna tanfidhiya)* of this assembly responsible for its day-to-day administration is under the leadership of Irfan S. Awwas, who served nine years of a thirteen-year prison sentence for his activities associated with the Negara Islam Indonesia movement.

Other Islamist groups to actively promulgate anti-America slogans were youth organizations and university-student organizations either linked to certain political parties from the Islamist end of the spectrum or to prominent Islamist figures. The Gerakan Pemuda Islam, for instance, is a youth organization mobilized by the Partai Persatuan Pembangunan, an Islamist party led by Vice-President Hamzah Haz, putting the enforcement of the *shari'a* as one of its main agenda.[15] A number of local leaders of this party in

Surakarta, who still have close ties with Abu Bakar Baasyir and other former Jama'ah Islamiyyah leaders, sponsored the establishment of the Front Pemuda Islam Surakarta. Furthermore, the Kesatuan Aksi Mahasiswa Muslim Indonesia is linked with the Partai Keadilan which was a permutation of the Muslim Brotherhood movement. This party was established by young intellectuals influenced by such Islamist ideologues as Hasan al-Banna and Sayyid Qutb. The Kesatuan Aksi Mahasiswa Muslim Indonesia somewhat resembles the Himpunan Aksi Mahasiswa Muslim Indonesia, which is a loose alliance of Islamist-inclined university-student organizations in several universities in Jakarta. Both were established to challenge the left-inclined university-student organizations, which emerged in the days leading to the fall of Suharto.[16]

The rise of the radical Islamist groups in post-New Order Indonesia can be seen against the backdrop of the relation between Islam and the state during the New Order. In order to maintain the political stability required by the process of modernization and development, the New Order marginalized and repressed expressions of political Islam. The marginalization of political Islam, whose apogee occurred when the state successfully forced all socio-political organizations to accept the Pancasila as their sole foundation, inevitably created a feeling of deprivation and frustration among its constituency. However, the inability of the state to fulfil its promises in providing employment and economic prosperity, except for a few segments of the society, brought about a kind of legitimacy crisis which developed particularly from the end of the 1980s. In its attempt to restrain the spread of this crisis, the state sought to introduce a strategy of conservative Islamization, particularly focused on the accentuation of the Islamic symbols in the public discourse, or accommodating the religious socio-political powers.

The constituency of Islamism naturally welcomed the shift of the New Order's policy on Islam with enthusiasm. They soon affiliated themselves with it, or at least felt that they were going in the same direction. They saw this as a promising opportunity and they believed that in this way they would be able to change the fate of their society, their nation, and their state — not to mention bringing about changes at their own private level. This strategy appears to have succeeded in "subduing" a variety of Islamist oppositions.[17] Alongside the Islamization strategy run by the state, Islamic activisms had the opportunity to proliferate in university campuses, which in turn became a fertile soil of the transnational Islamic movements. All these developments have broadened the Islamist constituency, who became frustrated, with their hopes, by dramatic turn of events after the collapse of the New Order regime.

In the transitional situation following the collapse of the New Order regime, all groups sought to place themselves as authoritative interpreters of

Islam in order to have a place in the public sphere. They became involved in what Dale F. Eickelman and James Piscatori call "competition and contest over both the interpretation of symbols and control of the institutions, formal and informal, that produce and sustain them".[18] Because of the major changes taking place in the transitional situation, some of them used the opportunity to transform themselves into political parties, and by so doing, became engaged in the on-going process of the political system. Some others have consistently viewed the existing system of government as illegitimate and rejected the idea of compromise and participation. They used popular politics to attract the sympathy of the masses and direct public opinion.

OSAMA BIN LADEN: STRATEGIC ALLIANCE OR SYMBOLIC CAPITAL?

In the wake of September 11, the name of Osama bin Laden came into the political arena of Indonesia. In the demonstrations and actions staged by the radical Islamist groups, demonstrators held up the photographs of Osama and called out his name. While showing bin Laden's photographs, they displayed the slogan: "Death to the great Satan, America!"[19] In their orations, the heroism of bin Laden in leading what they called a holy resistance against an evil plan to destroy the Muslim *umma* was proclaimed. He was perceived as not only a victim of the arrogance of the United States and its evil plans to destroy Islam, but also a symbol of resistance against its hegemonic power. In a relatively short time, this charismatic leader became the idol and hero of thousands of people who felt deprived in the fast current of social change and globalization.

The eruption of Osama bin Laden into Indonesia's public sphere raised many suspicions about the existence of the linkage between his Al Qaeda network and some radical Islamist leaders, particularly from the three major Islamic militia groups.[20] It is quite problematic, however, to verify such suspicions, before we are able to secure evidence about the existence of such a linkage. Indeed, a number of leaders of the Islamic militia groups have taken part in the Afghan war and some of them have even met with bin Laden. Ja'far Umar Thalib, the leader of the Laskar Jihad, for instance, made it known that during his engagement in the Afghan war he had in fact met Osama. An emissary of Osama has even visited him in Ambon in order to offer financial and arms supports.[21] Nevertheless, Ja'far Umar Thalib denied such a connection, stating that bin Laden is a sectarian Muslim (*khariji*). He published various articles in the media organs of the Laskar Jihad to support his claim. Website of his organization even posted a *fatwa* issued by the late Saudi grand *mufti* 'Abd al-'Aziz 'Abd Allah Bin Baz, confirming that Osama is an erring sectarian for his rebellion against the Saudi regime. Long before September 11 Ja'far Umar Thalib had already condemned bin Laden as a sectarian Muslim in one of his articles published in 1996.[22]

It is worth mentioning that the relation between Ja'far Umar Thalib and some Saudi official *ulama*, who legitimized the presence of American troops in their country, has been quite visible. Ja'far Umar Thalib stayed in the Middle East, particularly Yemen and Saudi Arabia, from 1991 to 1993, when a heated conflict between bin Laden and Saudi official *ulama* collaborated by the royal family, took place. There he succeeded in establishing close links with the official *ulama*, including 'Abd al-'Aziz 'Abd Allah Bin Baz (d. 1999), Muhammad Nasr al-Din al-Albani (d. 1999), and Rabi' Ibn Hadi 'Umar al-Madkhali. Upon his return to Indonesia, Ja'far Umar Thalib frequently requested *fatwa* from them before doing certain actions. Such a relationship is quite difficult to imagine if Ja'far Umar Thalib is part of Al Qaeda, considering the fact that one of the primary targets of the Al Qaeda is to expel the presence of American troops in the Middle East, particularly Saudi Arabia.

On the other hand, the existence of a kind of operational co-operation between Abu Bakar Baasyir and Osama bin Laden is easier to imagine. While denying direct contact with Osama, Abu Bakar Baasyir and some of his colleagues in the Majelis Mujahidin Indonesia brazenly spoke of their admiration for him. A number of translated books published by al-Wihdah press owned by Irfan S. Awwas include introductory remarks by bin Laden.[23] Abu Bakar Baasyir was even suspected of having links with some radical Muslims, including Abu Muhammad Jibril Abdurrahman,[24] Taufik Abdul Halim,[25] Fathur Rahman Ghozi,[26] and Agus Dwikarna,[27] arrested in Singapore, Indonesia and the Philippines, all of whom were allegedly involved in terrorist activities in those countries. Rohan Gunaratna, the author of *Inside Al Qaeda, Global Network of Terror,* recently alleged that Abu Bakar Baasyir has been responsible for the operations of the Jama'ah Islamiyyah, which he claims as an Al Qaeda cell in Southeast Asia. In this network, it is believed that there is Riduan Isamuddin, better known as Hambali, who is suspected to be the principal Jama'ah Islamiyyah operative in the region, planning several terrorist attacks in Singapore. He was also suspected to be responsible for the Christmas 2000 bombing campaign in several cities in Indonesia.[28] Nevertheless, due to its secrecy, concluding that there is operational co-operation between Abu Bakar Baasyir and Osama bin Laden, without considering the internal dynamics of Islam in Indonesia itself, as has been done by Gunaratna, who excessively bases his analysis on intelligence sources as well as magazine and newspaper reports, remains problematic.[29]

Apart from the possibility of the existence of Al Qaeda network in Indonesia, the significance of bin Laden apparently lies more at a symbolic level. He became a symbol of courage, and resistance altogether, representing the feeling of thousands of young people who have suffered very much from the enduring crisis afflicting Indonesia. He was believed to have been able to teach the arrogant Americans a lesson. Like a football star, his fame was used by some businessmen who reaped the benefits by selling "Osama bin Laden" T-shirts. They knew that Osama bin Laden was marketable; teenagers from various cities in Indonesia were proud of wearing such a T-shirt.[30] The heroic image conjured up by Osama bin Laden was used by the radical Islamist groups for their domestic political ends. Within the context of competing for authority, they sought to rely on this figure in order to enhance the legitimacy of defending the Muslim *umma* at the local-national level. As if they were telling the *umma* that, together with bin Laden, they were seeking to defend the interests of the *umma,* one that had been perceived as being neglected by the mainstream Muslim groups.

ZIONIST-CUM-WESTERN CONSPIRACY

In line with the rise of Osama in the public sphere of Indonesia, the discourse of Zionist-cum-West conspiracy to destroy Islam has become more frequently heard. Many people believed that the events of September 11 were intentionally designed by Jews to trigger the anger of the world against Islam, and by doing so, to attain the legitimacy to kill Palestinians. There still continue to be many people pointing to the absence of many Jewish workers in the World Trade Centre when the terrorist attacks occurred. According to one of the articles in *Suara Hidayatullah,* the increasing brutality of the Israeli army against Palestinians is not only an expression of the current anti-Islamic attitude of the Jewish state, but also proof of Israel's participation in the attacks.[31] Such a suspicion was also put forward by the president of the Partai Keadilan Hidayat Nurwahid, who argued that right when the United States proclaimed a war against "Islamic terrorism", Israel openly attacked Palestinians, and the attacks were supported by the United States.[32]

Actually, the discourse of the Zionist-cum-West conspiracy is not novel in Indonesia. This discourse has had a long history. It came to the country in the 1970s from a number of Arabic texts produced in the Middle East following the failure of Arab countries in defeating Israel in the 1967 war.[33]

One of the Islamist media that actively campaigned this discourse was *Media Dakwah*, the official publication of the Dewan Dakwah Islamiyah Indonesia (DDII, the Indonesian Council of Islamic *Da'wa*) in an effort to counter the proliferation of liberal thoughts advocated liberal Muslim thinkers.[34] The discourse of the Zionist-cum-West conspiracy has continually been produced by the proponents of the various Islamist groups in Indonesia to drive their certain political interests.[35] When Suharto's position was threatened, for instance, this discourse resurfaced in the form of a theory that it was the Jews, represented by George Soros, who were responsible for the deepest economic crisis ever faced during the New Order. Similarly, when the conflict on the Moluccan islands became heated, this discourse was again recalled by the radical Islamist groups. The dispatch of the Laskar Jihad voluntary fighters to the islands was among other things based on the reason that Moluccan Muslims were being attacked by their Christian enemies supported by a "Zionist-cum-Crusader conspiracy".[36]

However, in the wake of September 11 and its aftermath, Indonesian Muslims became more frequently exposed to the speculation about the Zionist-cum-West conspiracy. A variety of Islamist media organs, including *Media Dakwah, Suara Hidayatullah, Sabili, and Jurnal Islam*, were highly rigorous in making reports on the existence of this conspiracy. This kind of discourse has even entered food stalls in the streets and become the hot topic discussed by different segments of Indonesian Muslim society. Even when the pressures increased on the Indonesian Government already viewed thus far as too passive in facing the challenge posed by the radical Islamist groups, many people interpreted this as part of such a conspiracy. For instance, various Islamist groups reacted angrily to Singapore's Senior Minister Lee Kuan Yew's accusation that Indonesia had become a nest for terrorists. They immediately mobilized their own masses to condemn Lee Kuan Yew whose country is deemed to be the centre of Jews in Asia attempting to destroy Islam in the region.[37]

Within the context of the increase of the Zionist-cum-West conspiracy discourse, American products became the target of the radical Islamist groups. McDonald's franchise restaurants in Indonesia, for instance, were forced to publish an announcement that the owner was an indigenous Indonesian *hajj* in order to avoid such attacks. The importation of chicken thighs from America was rejected by the radical Islamist groups and supported by the MUI. Recently, the anti-Zionist-cum-West conspiracy manifested themselves in the call for a boycott against American products, ranging from cigarettes, to shirts, perfume, accessories, and even Coca-Cola.[38] The radical Islamist groups tried to prove the involvement of McDonald's, for instance, with the

Zionist-cum-West conspiracy, pointing to the fact that McDonald's has given donations to the Jewish United Fund, which is considered to be responsible for the flows of money from the United States to Israel, used by the latter to kill Palestinians.[39]

THE REVIVAL OF *JIHAD*

Islamism has long been associated with *jihad*. This concept has been considered to provide legitimacy for the radical Islamist groups in using violence to challenge regimes in power and reconstruct the existing social-political systems. Beginning in the 1970s, the revolutionary character wrapped by *jihad* has defined the strategy taken by various Islamist movements across the Muslim world. However, Gilles Kepel (2000) observes that in the last decade, the popularity of *jihad* has declined, in line with the failure of the radical Islamist groups to significantly challenge regimes in power and the existing political systems. This failure gave a lesson for Islamists to change their revolutionary strategy and take a more compromising way, and this became the main character of Islamism in the last decade. As a result, moderate Muslims took over the control over the public sphere in many Muslim countries, while radical Islamists who have been marginalized withdrew themselves from the political arena and waged sporadic violence.[40]

In the wake of September 11, the popularity of *jihad* has returned to the public sphere of the Muslim world. This holds true for the case of Indonesia, where *jihad* has become one of the most important vocabularies in the recent popular political discourse. The New Order regime was almost paranoid about the use of this term and repressed any groups trying to use it. After the collapse of the New Order, *jihad* came back into the political arena of Indonesia and reached its peak of popularity after September 11. *Jihad* is referred to by many people in their daily discussions responding different issues. When a group of people sought to topple a provincial governor, for instance, they called such an action *jihad* and demanded people to join.

The September 11 events and its aftermaths have apparently paved the way for the revival of *jihad* to the public spheres of Indonesia. The rhetoric developed by the radical Islamist groups that a coalition of "belligerent unbelievers" led by the United States is threatening Muslims, legitimized this revival of *jihad*. Based on the example taken from the attacks of the United States and its allies on Afghanistan, the radical Islamist groups describe the present-day situation as a hostile situation that obligates Muslims to wage a holy war. For the proponents of the radical Islamist groups, in such a situation *jihad* is the only answer. They interpreted *jihad* as a mechanism to protect Muslims from the attacks perpetrated by their enemies. A number of radical Islamist leaders emphasize that in this kind of situation an engagement in a "holy war" against "belligerent unbelievers" is a duty that should be fulfilled by all Muslims as proof of their commitment to Islam. For them, this is the true *jihad*, the greater *jihad*. The obligation to conduct *jihad* in this kind of situation is emphasized by, for instance, Fauzan al-Anshari, an activist in the Laskar Mujahidin, while condemning a young writer who argues that *jihad* is a religious symbol frequently used for temporary political interests: "The commitment to *jihad* is parallel with the belief in God. Whoever believes in God must prove his belief by conducting *jihad*. Those who reject *jihad* simply prove that they do not believe in God".[41]

The term *jihad* can be loosely translated as "to struggle" or "to expend effort" towards a particular cause. The term was originally used to refer to one's personal struggle against one's own mortal failings and weaknesses, which would include battling against one's pride, fears, anxieties, and prejudices. In one of the Prophet Muhammad's *hadith*, this personal existential struggle is described as the *jihad akbar* (greater *jihad*). Alongside the *jihad akbar* there is the concept of *jihad asghar* (lesser *jihad*), associated with armed war for self-preservation and self-defence. In the classical and modern literature of *jihad*, the defensive nature of this *jihad asghar* has always been emphasized.[42]

In line with the increase of anti-America sentiments, the defensive character of *jihad* has changed to be aggressive: it is no longer considered as self-defence. *Jihad* is no longer merely interpreted as a holy struggle to defend Muslims from hostile assailants, but also as an active effort to retaliate against the attacks by Muslim enemies. Abu Bakar Baasyir, for instance, points out, "Violence in the framework of *jihad* is allowed to resist against belligerent unbelievers attacking Muslims."[43] Within this context, *jihad* has even been linked to the concept of martyrdom. For radical Muslims, *jihad* must be pursued by Muslims in order to reach the rank of martyrs. With such a reading, suicide bombers might be appraised as martyrs. Terrorist actions aimed at causing losses on the side of the Muslim's enemy are even included in the meaning of *jihad*. A number of examples about the heroism of the Prophet's Companions in resisting their enemy were put forward in order to legitimize such a position. The actions of young people in Palestine were appraised as similar to what the Prophet's Companions did. *Sabili* writes:

> From an Islamic perspective, all actions done by a Muslim in order to materialize the interests of the *umma* and honour Islam can be categorized as *jihad*, including pursuing martyrdom, inflicting losses on the side of Muslim's enemies, motivating Muslims to go to *jihad*, keeping the secret of the *umma*, and enervating the spirit of Muslim's enemies.[44]

In extended scope of its meaning, *jihad* is also presented as a way to liberate Muslim *umma* from any influence of the infidel West. Within this context, they called upon Muslims to boycott products of the United States and this was perceived as part of *jihad*. In one of its editorial notes, *Jurnal Islam* writes:

> We must be aware that what they (the enemies of Muslims) are doing needs to be challenged with *jihad*, in the form of empowering the economy of the *umma* in all aspects of life, so that we are not constantly exploited by the interests of Jews and Christians. It is the time to conduct *jihad* by boycotting all products of the United States.[45]

THE FAILURE OF NATION-STATE

The existence of nation-state has long been criticised by the proponents of Islamism. The introduction of this system by the West to the Muslim world has brought about discontent among many people. Traditional authorities that have so far enjoyed privileges from their society, particularly, were forced to leave their position and give it to new elites produced by the system of modern nation-state. For Islamists in general, the modern nation-state adopted by their governments does not serve the ideological, political or economic interests of Muslims. Instead, it serves the interests of the dominant world powers. Islamism, which emerged partly as a form of protest to the system, sought to offer an alternative: the Islamic state. They believe that an Islamic state can withstand and even correct Western domination and the corruption of their authoritarian regimes.[46]

The September 11 tragedy has given a new legitimacy for Islamists and especially radicals to continue their struggle to challenge the modern nation-state. The system of nation-state is perceived to be no longer capable of protecting Muslims from the Zionist-cum-West powers perpetrating their effort to destroy Islam. In this situation, the only system considered able to protect Islam and the Muslim *umma* is the Islamic state — even though the Islamists themselves are unclear about its form, substance, role, relevance and practicality in the contemporary era. For several groups, the perfect form of the Islamic state is the Islamic caliphate established at an earlier period denoting the zenith of Muslim power. The Sabab Hizb al-Tahrir Indonesia, for instance, chose the Islamic caliphate as an alternative and they sought to campaign for the triumph of this system. For this group, this is the time to revive the Islamic caliphate that has been buried under the hegemony of the nation-state.[47]

This kind of discourse has become more frequently heard in the Indonesian public sphere and this served as a catalyst facilitating the further proliferation of the discourse of the application of the *shari'a*. The issue of the application of the *shari'a*, which had earlier come to the fore, has become more articulated. In various provinces and regencies, including West Sumatra, Riau, Banten, South Sulawesi, Gorontalo, Tasikmalaya, Cianjur, and Madura, there emerged demands for the implementation for the *shari'a*, along with the autonomy packages offered by the central government. The proponents of the radical Islamist groups in each region demonstrated their jealousy of the province of Aceh which succeeded in implementing the *shari'a*.[48] Representatives of the Islamic groups in parliament, particularly from the Partai Bulan Bintang and the Partai Keadilan, tried to include the *shari'a* into the Constitution of Indonesia in various sessions when the amendment of the constitution was discussed.

For the proponents of the Islamist groups, the application of the *shari'a* is necessary as a way to protect Muslims from the attacks of the Zionist-cum-West conspiracy working to destroy the Muslim *umma* in different ways. A clear example of how the West is perceived as perpetrating the threat against Islam is demonstrated by Adian Husaini in *Buletin Laskar Jihad*. In his essay, Husaini accuses the West of already having been planning an agenda to destroy Islam for several decades through opinion, the spread of iniquities, and armed war as in Afghanistan. According to him, this problem must be answered by the application of the *shari'a*.[49]

The application of the *shari'a* is also viewed by the Islamist groups as the answer to the crisis afflicting Indonesian society, which is perceived as an impact of the application of a secular system. For them, the secular system was imposed by the West and this system has generated a society that is brutal, sadistic, and licentious. The Islamist groups took a line of equivalence between the crisis, the spread of immorality and the secular system. For the proponents of the Islamist groups, the way to escape this disaster is the *shari'a* alone, whose implementation will bring stability, morality, and prosperity to the country. The *shari'a* is thus seen as an alternative and a solution to the crisis and it is believed to be able to create a fair and prosperous society.[50]

By demanding the application of the *shari'a* and emphasizing the Zionist-cum-West conspiracy, the radical Islamist groups questioned the legitimacy of Megawati's government and the system adopted. They believed that the government has neglected its responsibility to facilitate the application of the *shari'a* as its rejection to revive the Jakarta Charter is evidence as is indifference to the fate of Afghan Muslims attacked by the United States. One of the clear

examples of how the radical Islamist groups view Megawati is demonstrated
by the opinions of Habib Rizieq Shihab, who argues:

> When the United States brutally attacked Afghanistan, Megawati did
> not say anything, did not react... This shows that she does not care of
> the fate of Muslims. Instead, she tried to repress anti-America movements,
> and this also means that Megawati is a collaborator of America and
> Zionist.[51]

In a similar tone, Abu Bakar Baasyir says that, "Megawati's government
has been co-opted in the U.S.-cum-Zionist network, because of her
dependence on the United States".[52] The arrests of some radical Islamist
leaders provoked an angry reaction from the radical Islamist groups. The
Islamist organs, like *Sabili, Suara Hidayatullah,* and *Buletin Laskar Jihad,*
described the arrest of Ja'far Umar Thalib, for instance, as part of Megawati
administration's attempt to "woo the United States". They condemned
Megawati for being incapable of facing the political pressures of the United
States. For them, Megawati has been co-opted in the political interests of
the United States, and is controlled by Jews.[53]

CLASH BETWEEN LIBERAL ISLAM AND CONSERVATIVE ISLAM

In their efforts to dominate the field of discourse, the radical Islamist groups
faced challenges from the elements of Muslims advocating liberal Islam. Such
a challenge has particularly emerged from a group calling themselves Jaringan
Islam Liberal (JIL, Liberal Islam Network). Established in March 2001 by
several young Muslim thinkers from different religious backgrounds, this
group was enthusiastically welcomed by moderate Muslims, both from the
Nahdhlatul Ulama and the Muhammadiyah, who still constitute the vast
majority of Indonesian Muslims. The programmes organized by the Liberal
Islam Network received enthusiastic responses from many Muslims of both
organizations. In organizing their programmes, the proponents of the Liberal
Islam Network have received financial support from foreign funding agencies,
such as the Ford Foundation and the Asia Foundation.

The proliferation of liberal Islamic discourse in favour of democracy,
human rights, gender equality, freedom of thought, and progressiveness
became the main goal of the Liberal Islam Network. They consistently reject
the concept of totality in Islam, the implementation of the *shari'a* imposed by
the state, the identification of *jihad* with armed holy war, as well as gender
inequality.[54] In order to reach a broad audience, the Liberal Islam Network

have used various media channels, including the internet, newspapers, magazines, radio, and television. They regularly opened discussion forums, published articles in various newspapers, and broadcasted talk shows with liberal Muslim thinkers.

In the wake of September 11, the tension between the proponents of radical Islam and liberal Islam has turned into an open clash. A number of proponents of the Liberal Islam Network have been intimidated and even attacked physically by the followers of the radical Islamist groups. The rise of the Liberal Islam Network has indeed triggered the anger of a number of the radical Islamist leaders, including Ja'far Umar Thalib and Habib Rizieq Shihab. They accused the Liberal Islam Network to be part of the conspiracy to destroy Islam. According to Ja'far Umar Thalib, the difference between the Laskar Jihad and the Liberal Islam Network is like the difference between Islam and *kafir*, implicitly excommunicating his liberal opponents. Some members of the radical Islamist groups persecuted one of the proponents of the Liberal Islam Network when he published an article that was considered as humiliating Islam. *Suara Hidayatullah* condemned the liberal Muslims as masked secularists rejecting the notion of totality in Islam.[55] It has published a feature forecasting the destruction of the Indonesian nation-state due to the proliferation of the liberal Islam's notions.[56]

Since most activists of the Liberal Islam come from the State Institute for Islamic Studies, usually abbreviated as IAIN, the IAIN also received harsh critiques from the radical Islamist groups. They staged demonstrations to protest the IAIN. They even changed the meaning of the abbreviation from Institut Agama Islam Negeri to become *Inkar Allah Ingkar Nabi,* meaning denying God and denying the Prophet.[57] The IAIN is even condemned as the voice of Orientalist and West liberal ideas, which have an agenda to destroy Islam. A number of liberal thinkers from the IAIN, such as Nurcholis Madjid and Harun Nasution, are constantly damned by the Islamist groups as responsible for the proliferation of liberal Islamic ideas.[58]

CONCLUSION

The wave of Islamic militancy, demonstrated by the rise of the various radical Islamist groups, has become the hallmark of the political landscape of Indonesia since the collapse of the New Order regime. The social-political instability following the collapse of the New Order regime, when competing groups and interests attempted to win the contest for power, played such a crucial role in the rise of the radical Islamist groups, which have been extremely active in bringing the radical Islamic discourse into the public sphere. Being legitimized by the events following the September 11 disaster, the radical Islamic discourse has become increasingly dominant in the public sphere. The rise of Osama bin Laden as a cult hero in the radical Islamic discourse after 11 September has strong appeal among young people who feel deprived in the situation of deep economic crisis afflicting present-day Indonesia.

The September 11 disaster and its aftermath have enhanced the basis of legitimacy of the radical Islamist groups. In the midst of the contestation over religious symbols, the retaliation made by George W. Bush against the September 11 terrorist attacks was taken by the radical Islamist groups as an example of a tangible threat against Islam. The terrorists demonstrated themselves as heroes of the resistance against the hegemonic power. Within the context of facing the threatening enemies, the key concepts in the radical Islamic discourses, including the *shari'a, jihad*, and anti-Westernism, have increasingly enjoyed attention in the popular political discourse in the country. The events that have followed in the wake of September 11 also accelerated the deterioration in the relations between the Indonesian Government and the Islamic opposition in the country. The government is condemned as indifferent to the fate of Muslims who form the majority of the Indonesian people. The legitimacy of the government and its political system has constantly been questioned.

With September 11 the tension between radical Islam and liberal Islam has increased to the extent that it has turned into an open clash. The battle between the proponents of the two groups will continue for many years to come. Nevertheless, with the rise of the Liberal Islam Network and support given by the established Muslim organizations to the liberal discourse, there is some hope in believing that the wave of Islamic militancy that has engulfed Indonesian since the collapse of the New Order regime will end soon. However, this will be very much defined by the political stability of the country, in which the military has always played a crucial role. In reading the story of the Islamic militancy wave in Indonesia, we must understand the nexus between the interests of some political (military and civilian) elites and the needs of some old and new (religious) social actors to reinforce or search for a particular identity.

Notes

1   Samuel P. Huntington, *The Clash of Civilizations and the Remaking of World Order*, New York: Simon&Schuster, 1996.

2   See the report made by Harold Crouch, "Indonesia: Violence and Radical Muslims" *Indonesia Briefing*, Jakarta/Brussels: International Crisis Group, 2001.

3   Ja'far Umar Thalib, "Mampuslah Amerika", *Buletin Laskar Jihad*, 10 (October 2001): 9; see also Ja'far Umar Thalib, "Menyikapi Gertakan Si Pengecut dan Penakut," *Buletin Laskar Jihad*, 11 (November 2001): 6.
4   See "Relawan Jihad Indonesia Masuk Peshawar," *Republika*, 9 October 2001. According to this report, at that time there had already been 300 Indonesians in Peshawar, who were prepared to enter the Pakistan-Afghanistan border and assist Taliban against the United States.
5   "MUI Desak Pemerintah Bekukan Hubungan Diplomatik Dengan AS", *Kompas*, 8 October 2001.
6   See, for instance, "MUI Putuskan Hubungan Dagang dengan Amerika", *Buletin Laskar Jihad*, 11 (November 2001): 10-11; see also Ja'far Umar Thalib, "Antara Solidaritas Lokal dengan Solidaritas Interlokal," *Buletin Laskar Jihad*, 12 (December 2001): 6.
7   "PB NU Kecam Agresi AS Terhadap Afganistan", *Kompas*, 8 October 2001; "PP Muhammadiyah Ajak Dunia Islam Galang Solidaritas", *Kompas*, 9 October 2001.
8   This term is not to be confused with the doctrine of *ahl al-sunna wa al-jama'a* developed by the Nahdhatul Ulama (NU).
9   As for the Laskar Jihad, see Noorhaidi Hasan, "Faith and Politics: the Rise of the Laskar Jihad in the Era of Transition in Indonesia, *Indonesia* 73 (April 2002): 145–69.
10 The contemporary Salafi movement is an attempt to reinforce traditional Wahhabism minus-politics, sponsored by Saudi Arabia, in which the thoughts of Muhammad ibn 'Abd al-Wahhab (1703–87), who drew inspirations from the teachings of Ahmad ibn Taymiyyah (1263 to 1328), a medieval thinker of Hanbalism, the strictest of the four legal schools of Sunni Islam, are given a particular emphasis.
11 The transformation of the Ihya al-Sunnah network into political activism resulted in a fragmentation in the Salafi network in Indonesia. There are two major groups which still maintain their "non-political" stance: Jama'ah As-Sunnah and Jama'ah As-Sofwa.
12 This congress discussed one central theme: the enforcement of the Islamic *shari'a* was deemed highly necessary to curb the various problems and disasters afflicting Indonesia today. Within the context of the implementation of the Islamic *shari'a*, the notions of *khilafa Islamiyya* (Islamic caliphate), *imama* (imamate) and *jihad* (holy war) were also brought up. On detailed information of the results of the congress, see *Risalah Kongres Mujahidin I dan Penegakan Shari'a Islam*, edited by Irfan S. Awwas, Yogyakarta: Wihdah Press, 2001.
13 About the organizational structure of the Majelis Mujahidin Indonesia, see Majelis Mujahidin Indonesia, *Mengenal Majelis Mujahidin Indonesia: Untuk Penegakan Shari'a Islam*, Yogyakarta: Markaz Pusat Majelis Mujahidin, 2001.
14 Awwas, *Risalah Kongres Mujahidin*, (2001): 139.
15 However, it must be noted that this party is quite pragmatic in its approach.

16   As for the Himpunan Aksi Mahasiswa Muslim Indonesia, see Chaedir Bamualim
      et al. *Radikalisme Agama dan Perubahan Sosial di DKI Jakarta*, research report,
      Jakarta: PBB IAIN Syarif Hidayatullah and Bappeda Pemda DKI, 1999/2000,
      p. 70.

17   See Robert W. Hefner, *Civil Islam: Muslims and Democratization in Indonesia*,
      Princeton: Princeton University Press, 2000, pp. 128–43.

18   See Dale F. Eickelman and James Piscatori, *Muslim Politics*, Princeton: Princeton
      University Press, 1996, p. 5.

19   "Kecam AS, Bantah Singapura", *Detik.com*, 24 April 2002.

20   In mid-December 2001, the head of the State Intelligence Agency (BIN), A.M.
      Hendropriyono, announced that the government had found evidence of an
      Al-Qaeda training camp in the Poso region of Central Sulawesi. According to
      him, the camp had been used by foreigners, most of whom were based in Spain,
      but they were assisted by Indonesian groups. But several days later, Hendropriyono
      withdrew his claim, see "BIN Temukan Bekas Kamp Latihan Al-Qaeda di Poso",
      Kompas, 14 December 2001.

21   Interview with Abu Zaki Ery Ziyad, the public relation of the Laskar Jihad,
      30 October 2001.

22   Ja'far Umar Thalib, "Memahami Hukum Jama'ah, Imamah dan Bai'at", *Salafy*
      12 (1996): 8–13.

23   See, for instance, Lembaga Studi dan Penelitian Islam Pakistan, *Membangun
      Kekuatan Islam di Tengah Perselisihan Ummat*, translated from *Al 'Amal al-Islami
      Bain Dawa'i al-Ijtima'i wa Du'aat al-Niza'i*, Yogyakarta: Wihdah Press, 2001.

24   Co-founder of the Majelis Mujahidin Indonesia, Abu Muhammad Jibril
      Abdurrahman was arrested by Suharto in 1979 and in jail until 1981. In order
      to avoid a second arrest by Suharto, he fled to Singapore in 1985, and he was
      engaged in the Afghan war from then on. During his engagement in the Afghan
      war he became acquainted with some militant Islamics such as Abdullah Azzam,
      the founder of Al-Qaeda. As for the biography of this figure, see Abu Mohammad
      Jibril Abdurrahman, *Karakteristik Lelaki Shalih*, Yogyakarta: Wihdah Press, 2001,
      pp. 9–11.

25   Taufik Abdul Halim is a young Malaysian, arrested by the Indonesian police
      who accused him of being responsible for a bombing in Atrium Senen, Jakarta.
      As for the connections between Abu Bakar Baasyir and Taufik Abdul Halim, see
      "Poros Jakarta-Kuala Lumpur, Buih Pepsi Cola", *Gatra*, 28 August 2001.

26   An alumnus of the Ngruki Pesantren established by Abu Bakar Baasyir, Fathur
      Rahman Ghozi has studied in Lahore, Pakistan, and long lived in the Philippines,
      see "Teroris Internasional dari Madiun", *Adil*, <www.detik.com>, 31 January
      2002.

27   Agus Dwikarna, the leader of the Laskar Jundullah, one of the faction in the
      Laskar Mujahidin Indonesia, was arrested along with Tamsil Linrung and Abdul
      Jamal Balfas. See "Detained Indonesian is associate of pro-bin Laden cleric:

Philippines", AFP, 17 March 2002. While the last two were later released, Dwikarna was sentenced by the Philippine for 10 years; see "Agus Dwikarna Divonis 10-17 Tahun", *Republika*, 13 July 2002; see also "Indonesian Linked to Al Qaeda Cell", *CNN*, 19 July 2002.

28   See his latest book, *Inside Al Qaeda, Global Network of Terror*, London: Hurst & Company, 2002, pp. 198–203.

29   Cf. Sidney Jones, "Al Qaeda in Southeast Asia: The Case of The "Ngruki Network" in Indonesia", *Indonesia Briefing*, Jakarta/Brussels: International Crisis Group, 8 August 2002.

30   Compare with the case of Malaysia, see Farish A. Noor, "Mr. Osama Comes to Town: The Manifold Uses of the Image of Osama ben Laden in the Contestation over Islamic Symbols in Malaysia", unpublished paper, presented to ISIM Staf Seminar, February 2002.

31   "Bisa Jadi Yahudi Otaknya", *Suara Hidayatullah*, <www.hidayatullah.com>, October 2001.

32   "RI Kutuk Keras Agresi Militer Israel", *Kompas*, 2 April 2002.

33   Martin van Bruinessen, "Yahudi sebagai Simbol dan Wacana Pemikiran Islam Indonesia Masa Kini," in *Spiritualitas Baru: Agama dan Aspirasi Rakyat*, edited by Ahmad Suaedy et al., Yogyakarta: DIAN/Interfidei, 1994.

34   See R. William Liddle, "Media Dakwah Scripturalism: One Form of Islamic Political Thought and Action in New Order Indonesia", in *Towards a New Paradigm: Recent Developments in Indonesian Islamic Thought*, edited by Mark R. Woodward, Arizona: Arizona State University, 1996, pp. 328–29.

35   See James T. Siegel, "*Kiblat* and the Mediatic Jew", *Indonesia* 69 (April 2000): 9–40.

36   Ja'far Umar Thalib, "Menyangkal Makar Yahudi dan Nashara", *Salafy*, 31 (1999): 30–33.

37   "Demo Anti Lee", *Gatra*, 27 February 2002.

38   "Boikot Produk Amerika-Zionis", *Suara Hidayatullah*, April 2002.

39   "McDonalds, Amerika dan Zionis, Setali Tiga Uang Perangi Islam", *Jurnal Islam* 93, no. 2 (6 June 2002).

40   Gilles Kepel, *Jihad: The Trait of Political Islam*, London: I.B. Tauris, 2000, pp. 366–67.

41   Fauzan Al-Anshari, "Jihad dalam Perspektif Syariah (Pelajaran Untuk Sukidi)," *Republika*, 18 January 2002.

42   For a detailed discussion on the concept of *jihad* in classical and modern Islamic literature, see Rudolph Peters, *Islam and Colonialism: The Doctrine of Jihad in Modern History*, The Hague: Mouton Publishers, 1979; concerning the rules of *jihad* in Islamic law see Majid Khadd[u]ri, *War and Peace in the Law of Islam*, Baltimore: the Johns Hopkins Press, 1955, pp. 55–73.

43   Abu Bakar Baasyir, "Islam Agama Damai", interview, *Republika*, 11 October 2002: 5.

[44] See "Bom Syahid Satu Jalan Menuju Surga", *Sabili*, accessed on 27 April 2002.
[45] "Mari Berjihad, Boikot Produk Zionis Amerika", *Jurnal Islam* 93, no. 2 (6 June 2002).
[46] See Ahmad S. Mousalli, *Moderate and Radical Islamic Fundamentalism: The Quest for Modernity, Legitimacy, and the Islamic State*, Gainesville: University Press of Florida, 1999, p. 69.
[47] Sabab Hizb al-Tahrir Indonesia, "Permusuhan Kaum Kafir", *Al Islam*, <www.al-islam.or.id>, accessed on 27 June 2002.
[48] As for the demands for the implementation of the Islamic *shari'a* in various provinces and regencies, see, for instance, a special report of *Tempo*, national biweekly magazine, "Siapa mau Syariat Islam" 36, no. 30 (5–11 November 2001).
[49] Adian Husaini, "Umat Islam Wajib Melawan Arus Opini Barat", *Buletin Laskar Jihad*, 17 May 2002; see also Adian Husaini, *Rajam Dalam Arus Budaya Syahwat: Penerapan Hukum Rajam di Indonesia dalam Tinjauan Syariat Islam, Hukum Positif & Politik Global*, Jakarta: Pustaka Al-Kautsar, 2001.
[50] "Deklarasi penerapan Syariat Islam", *Republika*, 15 March 2002.
[51] Habib Muhammad Rizieq Shihab, "Kita Tidak Takut pada PDIP", *Jurnal Islam* 91, no. 2 (17–23 May 2002): 4.
[52] Abu Bakar Baasyir, "Pemahaman Mega Soal Islam Dangkal", *Jurnal Islam* 91, no. 2 (17–23 May 2002): 5.
[53] See "Dukungan Mengalir", *Republika*, 8 May 2002; and "Pimpinan Ormas & Parpol Akan Temui Ja'far", *Republika*, 9 May 2002.
[54] See the website of the liberal Islam, <www.islamlib.com>.
[55] "Islam Liberal, Sekularis Berkedok Muslim", *Suara Hidayatullah*, February 2002.
[56] Abdillah Razak, Idris Rustamaji, "Tragedi Presiden Uzil Bashar Afdhalla", and "Jakarta, Maret 2038", *Suara Hidayatullah*, February 2002.
[57] "IAIN: Ingkar Allah Ingkar Nabi", *Suara Hidayatullah*, August 2001.
[58] "Pluralisme: Rahmat atau Laknat", *Suara Hidayatullah*, August 2001; see also Adian Husaini, "32 Tahun Gerakan Nurcholis Madjid: Kecanggihan atau Kepalsuan?" *Suara Hidayatullah*, March 2002.

References

Abdurrahman, Abu Mohammad Jibril. *Karakteristik Lelaki Shalih.* Yogyakarta: Wihdah Press, 2001.

Al-Anshari, Fauzan. "Jihad dalam Perspektif Syariah (Pelajaran Untuk Sukidi)". *Republika*, 8 January 2002.

Awwas, Irfan S., ed. *Risalah Kongres Mujahidin I dan Penegakan Shari'a Islam.* Yogyakarta: Wihdah Press, 2001.

Baasyir, Abu Bakar. "Pemahaman Mega Soal Islam Dangkal". *Jurnal Islam* 91, 17–23 May 2002.

Bamualim, Chaedir et al. *Radikalisme Agama dan Perubahan Sosial di DKI Jakarta,* research report. Jakarta: PBB IAIN Syarif Hidayatullah and Bappeda Pemda DKI, 2000.

Crouch, Harold. "Indonesia: Violence and Radical Muslims". *Indonesia Briefing*. Jakarta/Brussels: International Crisis Group, 2001.

Eickelman, Dale F. and Piscatori, James. *Muslim Politics*. Princeton: Princeton University Press, 1996.

Gunaratna, Rohan. *Inside Al Qaeda, Global Network of Terror*. London: Hurst & Company, 2002.

Hasan, Noorhaidi. "Faith and Politics: the Rise of the Laskar Jihad in the Era of Transition in Indonesia, *Indonesia* 73 (2002): 145–69.

Hefner, Robert W. *Civil Islam: Muslims and Democratization in Indonesia*. Princeton: Princeton University Press, 2000.

_____. "Globalization, Governance, and the Crisis of Indonesian Islam". A paper presented to Conference on Globalization, State Capacity, and Muslim Self Determination, University of California-Santa Cruz, 7–9 March 2002.

Huntington, Samuel P. *The Clash of Civilizations and the Remaking of World Order*. New York: Simon & Schuster, 1996.

Husaini, Adian. *Rajam Dalam Arus Budaya Syahwat: Penerapan Hukum Rajam di Indonesia dalam Tinjauan Syariat Islam, Hukum Positif & Politik Global*. Jakarta: Pustaka Al-Kautsar, 2001.

_____. "Umat Islam Wajib Melawan Arus Opini Barat". *Buletin Laskar Jihad*, 17 May 2002.

Jones, Sidney. "Al Qaeda in Southeast Asia: The Case of The 'Ngruki Network' in Indonesia". *Indonesia Briefing*. Jakarta/Brussels: International Crisis Group, 8 August 2002.

Kepel, Gilles. *Jihad: the Trait of Political Islam*. London: I.B. Tauris, 2000.

Khadduri, Majid. *War and Peace in the Law of Islam*. Baltimore: the Johns Hopkins Press, 1955.

Lembaga Studi dan Penelitian Islam Pakistan. *Membangun Kekuatan Islam di Tengah Perselisihan Ummat*, translated from *Al 'Amal al-Islami Bain Dawa'i al-Ijtima'i wa Du'aat al-Niza'i*. Yogyakarta: Wihdah Press, 2001.

Liddle, R. William. "Media Dakwah Scripturalism: One Form of Islamic Political Thought and Action in New Order Indonesia". In *Towards a New Paradigm: Recent Developments in Indonesian Islamic Thought*, edited by Mark R. Woodward. Arizona: Arizona State University, 1996.

Majelis Mujahidin Indonesia. *Mengenal Majelis Mujahidin Indonesia: Untuk Penegakan Syari'ah Islam*. Yogyakarta: Markaz Pusat Majelis Mujahidin, 2001.

Mousalli, Ahmad S. *Moderate and Radical Islamic Fundamentalism: The Quest for Modernity, Legitimacy, and the Islamic State*. Gainesville: University Press of Florida, 1999.

Noor, Farish A. "Mr. Osama Comes to Town: The Manifold Uses of the Image of Osama ben Laden in the Contestation over Islamic Symbols in Malaysia". Unpublished paper, presented to ISIM Staff Seminar. February 2002.

Peters, Rudolph. *Islam and Colonialism: The Doctrine of Jihad in Modern History.* The Hague: Mouton Publishers, 1979.

Sabab Hizb al-Tahrir Indonesia. "Permusuhan Kaum Kafir". *Al Islam*, <www.al-islam.or.id>, 27 June 2002.

Shihab, Habib Muhammad Rizieq. "Kita Tidak Takut pada PDIP". *Jurnal Islam* 91 (17 May 2002).

Siegel, James T. *"Kiblat* and the Mediatic Jew". *Indonesia* 69 (2000): 9–40.

Thalib, Ja'far Umar. "Memahami Hukum Jama'ah, Imamah dan Bai'at". *Salafy* 12 (1996).

_____. "Menyangkal Makar Yahudi dan Nashara". *Salafy* 31 (1999).

_____. "Mampuslah Amerika". *Buletin Laskar Jihad* 10 (2001).

_____. "Menyikapi Gertakan Si Pengecut dan Penakut". *Buletin Laskar Jihad* 11 (2001).

_____. "Antara Solidaritas Lokal dengan Solidaritas Interlokal". *Buletin Laskar Jihad* 12 (2001).

Van Bruinessen, Martin. "Yahudi sebagai Simbol dan Wacana Pemikiran Islam Indonesia Masa Kini". In *Spiritualitas Baru: Agama dan Aspirasi Rakyat*, edited by Ahmad Suaedy, et al. Yogyakarta: DIAN/Interfidei, 1994.

_____. "Contending Varieties of Muslim Politics in post-Suharto Indonesia". A paper presented at the international colloquium "L'islam politique a l'aube du XXIeme siecle", Tehran, 28–29 October 2001.

16

THE IMPACT OF SEPTEMBER 11 ON ISLAM IN SOUTHEAST ASIA

Bernard Adeney-Risakotta

INTRODUCTION

Mahatma Gandhi was reputedly asked what he thought about the impact of the French Revolution. With characteristic modesty he replied, "It's too soon to tell." Certainly it is far too soon to tell what will be the impact on Southeast Asian Islam of the September 11 attack on New York and Washington. Indeed it may be many years, or even decades before a deep analysis is possible. I thus share these reflections with the awareness that they are tentative and incomplete.

Islam in Southeast Asia is extremely diverse. Therefore the impact of September 11 is quite different for different segments of Islam. Islam, as it is practised in the real world,[1] is not a single, monolithic entity. The Muslim community is neither the "greatest threat to democracy and freedom", nor the "greatest hope for human civilization against the decadence of the West". There is both danger and hope in this community, but it should neither be demonized nor idealized.

In spite of the diversity of Islam, it is useful to compare "Southeast Asian Islamic" perceptions with "Western perceptions" of the events associated with September 11. Of course these are ideal types that should not be reified. In reality, many Muslims are closer to the "Western" perception, just as many Non-Muslim Westerners are closer to a "Muslim" interpretation of September 11. There is no unified "Muslim" or "Western" perception, but many perceptions grounded in different interests, values and assumptions. Nevertheless, ideal type analysis is useful for exposing basic assumptions that lead to very different perceptions of the same events.

THE SYMBOLIC CONTEXT OF SEPTEMBER 11 AND THE WAR ON TERRORISM

The horrific events of September 11 are linked to a whole complex of other events, both prior and subsequent to that fateful day. Neither Muslims nor non-Muslims can evaluate the attacks on U.S. targets on September 11 in isolation from the "war on terrorism" that has dominated the Western controlled media ever since. The war on terrorism first targetted the Taliban in Afghanistan. Even though a majority of Asian Muslims did not approve of Taliban interpretations of Islam, the attack on Afghanistan was seen by many as an attack on an Islamic nation, and by extension as an attack on Islam. Repeated assurances by Western leaders that Islam was not the target did not seem convincing to most Muslims in Southeast Asia.

The George W. Bush administration's attack on Iraq retrospectively projected this war into the past and the future. The war took on a symbolic, transcendent meaning by tying together George Bush's rhetoric with his father's Gulf War against Saddam Hussein and Iraq. The war on terrorism is thus identified with earlier conflicts with Muslim states like Iraq, Iran and Palestine. The emotions and responses of people to the September 11 attack are made infinitely more complex by tying them into the Middle East conflict. From the point of view of most Muslims, the Israeli oppression of the Palestinians is at the heart of the Middle East conflict. The failure of the United States to restrain Israeli attacks on Palestinian territories is thus emotionally linked to the attacks on symbolic targets in the United States itself. With a remarkable economy of symbolic representation, some Muslims even associate the attack on September 11 with the defence of innocent Palestinian children.

Sympathy for the victims of September 11 was soon drowned out by anger and fear, prompted by the U.S. response. While most Muslims condemned the September 11 "tragedy", the attacks on Afghanistan and Iraq provoked a far more emotional response. On the one hand, even radical Muslim figures quickly distanced themselves from Al Qaeda and spoke disparagingly of the Taliban. On the other hand, many Muslims feared that the war on terrorism was a thinly disguised attack on Islam. The attack on Afghanistan was widely perceived as unjust, brutal and an act of revenge carried out on innocent people. In Indonesia, respected leaders of Nahdlatul

Ulama (NU), Muhammadiyah and Majelis Ulama Indonesia (MUI), joined with more radical Muslim groups in condemning the U.S. attack on 7 October 2001. This was the first time since the fall of Suharto that all the Muslim organizations were united on an issue. In fact, both NU and Muhammadiyah had to restrain their more hot-headed members from going to fight on the side of the Taliban. Anger against American unilateral militarism seemed to far outweigh the anger against the terrorists.

While the Western media focused on the brutality of the Taliban and the liberation experienced by Muslims who were freed from a repressive regime, the Indonesian press tended to zero in on the civilian victims of the U.S. attack. Just as it was easy for Americans to identify with the victims of the September 11 attacks, but not with the victims of the Afghanistan war, so it was easier for Indonesians to identify with Muslim victims of U.S. bombings than it was to identify with middle class or wealthy workers in the World Trade Centre towers. September 11 seemed like a Hollywood action movie, and in any case, was faraway. This sense of remoteness changed, at least for Indonesians, with the dramatic bombing of two nightspots in Bali on 12 October 2002. As the television screens filled with images of burned and mangled Western bodies, many Indonesian Muslims felt an anguish over terrorism that they had not experienced before.[2]

NATIONALISM AND MUSLIM SOLIDARITY AFTER SEPTEMBER 11

The tragedy of September 11 had a profound impact on experiences of nationalism. In the United States, patriotism surged and the whole nation was caught up in an emotional experience of solidarity that had not been seen since World War II. Most Americans felt that the attacks on the twin towers in New York were attacks on them as a people and as a nation-state. For different reasons, nationalism has also been on the rise in Europe, fuelled by resentment towards immigrants.

In contrast, the war on terrorism did not stimulate much nationalism among Southeast Asian Muslims. September 11 was an attack on "others", far away. In contrast, the attack against Afghanistan on October 7 was perceived as an attack on "us", but the "us" was not a single nation. Muslims do not feel threatened as nations by the war on terrorism, but rather as the *umat Allah* (the people of God). The war on terrorism sparked strong feelings of solidarity among Muslims of different nations who feel unjustly targetted by the powerful West. Among Muslims, religious solidarity grew at the expense of nationalism.

While it is too soon to anticipate the long-term effect of September 11 on nationalism, many writers have argued that diverse forces of globalization are weakening the power of nationalism. Vaclav Havel observed that:

> There is every indication that the glory of the nation-state as the culmination of every national community's history, and its highest value — the only one, in fact, in the name of which it is permissible to kill, or for which people have been expected to die — has already passed its peak.[3]

While American nationalism rises and the right of the state to monopolize violence is assumed as self-evident in the West, in the Muslim world the moral authority of the state is met with cynicism and the use of violence to defend religion is gaining credibility. It appears that Southeast Asian Muslims are more likely to kill or die for their religion than to kill or die for their country.[4]

Muslims in Southern Thailand and the Philippines may still put their hope in nationalism, in the form of a struggle for their own state over against the dominant majority. However even in these cases, the struggle for independence is often linked to pan-Islamic rhetoric that elevates religious ties above all national loyalties.

In contrast, nationalism among Muslims in Singapore appears to be defined by pride in economic prosperity and the enforced harmony between races and religions. Singaporean Muslims show little desire to share in a pan-Islamic identity that might involve them in the problems of their neighbours. On the contrary, Indonesian and Malaysian Islam are perceived as a threat to Singaporean nationalism.

The perceived threat that most Muslims feel in Southeast Asia tends to undermine nationalism. According to conventional wisdom, external threats tend to increase nationalism. That is indeed what has happened in the United States, where the threat is perceived to be against the whole nation. The state appears to be the only actor that can protect the people from terrorism. Solidarity with the nation-state has been strengthened in ways scarcely imaginable just a year ago. Before September 11, terrorism was a vague and distant threat to most Americans. After watching the twin towers collapse in slow motion hundreds of times on television, and listening for weeks to harrowing tales of heroism and grief, the nation became united by a mixture of fear and pride that was further strengthened by the quick military victory in Afghanistan. The mysterious anthrax attacks also reinforced the fear and the solidarity of American society.

In contrast, the external threat perceived by Southeast Asian Muslims is not primarily a threat against the nation-state. Rather, it is a threat against Islam and the Muslim way of life. For Muslims, this is not a new threat, but part of a long historical memory. It is not only tied in with recent conflicts such as the Gulf War and the Middle East conflict between "Palestinian Muslim Arabs" and "American Jewish Israelis", but it is also linked to the ancient conflicts between Muslims and Christians going back to the Crusades. For Southeast Asian Muslims it is most vividly linked to their recent struggles against colonialism. The West is not primarily perceived as the home of democracy, decency and freedom (as Bush believed), but rather as the source of colonialism, injustice and oppression. The poverty, weakness and fragmentation of the Islamic world are a shameful result of Western domination.

After World War II, the struggle against colonialism focused loyalties on the newly emerging nation-states in Southeast Asia. Nationalism united diverse peoples in a common cause that transcended religious difference. But the overheated expectations of nationalism have brought great disappointment to many Muslims throughout Southeast Asia, especially since the economic crisis of 1997. In Indonesia, the collapse of the economy and the ongoing political, economic, social and cultural crisis also brings foreign domination in the form of dependency on the International Monetary Fund (IMF) and the sale of national assets. The chasm between the wealth and power of the West and the poverty and instability of Indonesia is punctuated every day by the Western-dominated mass media. The lifestyle of people in the West, as portrayed by the media, is not only a source of envy, but also of revulsion. Just as people are drawn to the sex and violence of Hollywood TV shows, even so their distaste for the perceived decadence has fuelled the return to religion as a source of value and meaning. Islam is seen as a source of identity and pride over against the West, as well as a programme for the salvation of the world.

In Indonesia, the nation state has proved a bitter disappointment. The state seems powerless to overcome ethnic conflict, rampant corruption, or the weakness of the economy in a rapidly globalizing marketplace. Even the grief experienced after the Bali bombings did not unite the nation behind the government, but rather stimulated fresh criticism of the inability of the government to prevent such a tragedy. Of course, nationalism of a separatist variety is still strong in Indonesian provinces like Aceh, but that only weakens loyalties to the broader nation-state. Ironically, leaders of the Aceh Freedom Movement (GAM), not only distance themselves from Al Qaeda and, the tensions springing out of radical Islam, but claim that they are true nationalists, fighting against Javanese Islamic fanatics.[5]

It would be a mistake to underestimate the power of nationalism in Indonesia, especially when the economy is in such shambles. Indonesian nationalism may be deeper than it appears during a time of economic and political turmoil. Even though there is widespread disillusionment with an ineffective government, there are many small signs of a deep nationalism in Indonesia. Nationalism and support for the central government are not necessarily synonymous. Currently, feelings of national solidarity are at an all-time low and separatist movements are vigorous in many areas. Nevertheless, the diverse communities of this sprawling archipelago have built a sense of common destiny and national unity during the past century that will not easily disappear.[6]

The Bali bombings of 12 October 2002 provoked widespread horror in Indonesia, and immediate condemnation from all segments of society. The emotional impact of these bombs in Indonesia appears greater than the emotional impact of September 11. Of course this response is partly motivated by dread of dire economic consequences, such as the collapse of the vital tourist industry and withdrawal of foreign investments. However the anguish displayed was somewhat surprising. Many Muslims expressed a sense of deep shame that such a senseless massacre could occur in Indonesia. Some articles suggested that Indonesia was under attack from foreign enemies. Others called it "a wake-up call" for the nation.

Many articles made oblique or directly disparaging reference to statements by certain Muslim politicians who had claimed that there were no terrorists in Indonesia. As the Defence Minister put it, "Terrorism is right there before our eyes."[7] In contrast with September 11, no one expressed any sympathy for the bombers. Whoever did the bombing is seen as an enemy. There is some speculation that the U.S. Central Intelligence Agency (CIA) may have planted the bombs to discredit Islam and stimulate support for the war on terrorism. However speculations of this sort provoke little support among most Indonesian Muslims.[8] The Bali bombings may have a more profound effect on Indonesia than the September 11 attack. But no one, including the bombers, can know what that effect will be in the long run. The United States' unilateral war against Iraq certainly increases Muslim sympathy for radical Islam.

On the whole, the aftermath of September 11 has alienated Southeast Asian Muslims from the West. Many Muslims feel that pan-Islamic identity is a more effective vehicle than nationalism for resisting Western domination. Most Southeast Asian Muslims do not reject nationalism, but many see it as subordinate to their religious identity. Benjamin Barber contrasts the impact of Western-dominated globalization with the appeal of primordial identities, both of which undermine the nation-state. He writes:

> *Jihad* and *McWorld* operate with equal strength in opposite directions, the one driven by parochial hatreds, the other by universalising markets, the one re-creating ancient sub national and ethnic borders from within; the other making national borders porous from without. Yet Jihad and McWorld have this in common: they both make war on the sovereign nation-state.[9]

In one sense, this analysis is simply wrong. Islamic *jihad* is no less universalizing than capitalist globalization. As Anthony Reid observed, "Barber could have no idea how globalized the *jihad* side of this equation would become in the hands of Al Qaeda."[10] Indeed, universal religions such as Islam are no less globalizing than "McWorld", and not just in the hands of Al Qaeda. The worldwide impact of religion is far greater than the spectacular havoc caused by a few terrorists. Religious solidarity in Islam always exceeds national borders. Muslims would certainly deny the idea that *jihad* is "driven by parochial hatreds". Rather, true *jihad* is understood by Muslims to mean struggle for truth, justice and survival. Only rarely should it take the form of armed struggle, but even then it is defined as defensive, in response to aggression. Very few Muslims in Southeast Asia would agree that the attacks on September 11, or the bombs in Bali, could be considered defensive *jihad*. Even radical Muslim leaders, who have long expressed hostility to the West, condemned the WTC and Bali attacks. Why then do some Muslims openly express their admiration for Osama bin Laden?

AMBIVALENT AND CONTRADICTORY EMOTIONS

Responses of Muslims to September 11, in the post-colonial context of Southeast Asia, are complex and ambivalent. At a rational and emotional level, most Muslims were horrified at the terrible loss of civilian life on September 11. Nevertheless, the symbolic nature of the targets could not help but invoke a kind of delight at the audacity and bravery of fellow Muslims who were able to attack the WTC in New York and the Pentagon in Washington, two of the central symbols of the capitalist and military world order. Muslims have long felt humiliated and powerless in face of hegemonic Western powers that determine the economic and cultural structure of the modern world. The Muslim terrorists who were willing to sacrifice their lives in attacking American symbols of power are felt to be heroic, even if their deeds are considered terrible.

While a few Muslims might openly rejoice at the success of the attacks on September 11, the great majority could never condone such massive destruction. However, they could still feel a secret pride and suppressed pleasure in the success of the attacks. Evidence for this ambivalence can be seen in the simultaneous denial that Osama bin Laden was behind the attacks, coupled with his elevation into a Muslim hero. At a rational level, mass murder at a scale seen on September 11 is opposed to all the main teachings of Islam. Even those who call for a *jihad* against the West, repeatedly claim that Islam is a religion of tolerance, under which all religions can live in peace. All Muslims condemn terrorism, but definitions of terrorism differ.

Another dynamic in ambivalent Muslim reactions to September 11 is the vigorous Muslim belief in the sovereignty of God and the doctrine of fate, or destiny (*nasib, takdir*). The use of language in the Indonesian press underscores this point. Almost always the September 11 attacks are described as a "tragedy" (*tragedi 11 September*). A tragedy is something terrible that was fated — there is little that one can do about it. According to one form of this belief, the September 11 attacks were the will of God. That does not necessarily mean that the massacre was right or justifiable. Even if it was a great sin, it was a sin that God permitted. Like all tragedies, it must be accepted as the will of God.

According to Muslims, the proper response to tragedy is to submit oneself (*pasrah*), to the will of God and examine oneself to search for the meaning of the tragedy. Some Muslim leaders simultaneously deplored the attacks and called on the United States to practise introspection. If God allowed this tragedy, then perhaps it meant that Americans should repent of their sins. No less a figure than Hamzah Haz, the Vice-President of Indonesia, commented that the September 11 tragedy might in some sense pay for the sins of America. There was sympathy for the suffering of the victims, yet at the same time a conviction that the attacks on symbols of worldwide capitalism and American militarism were part of the sovereign will of God.

Haz, along with Amien Rais, reacted angrily to charges from the West (and Singapore), that Indonesia was becoming a haven for terrorists. Both Haz and Rais were widely quoted as saying that "There are no terrorists in Indonesia, *insy'allah*." Since both men have ties to violent and radical Muslim groups such as Laskar Jihad, they should be in a position to know. However the word *insy'allah* is a tricky qualification. It could be interpreted as meaning, "There are no terrorists in Indonesia, unless it is the will of God."[11] In any case, both men quickly withdrew their rash statements after the Bali bombings.

Obviously it would be a grievous error to equate these views with the perceptions of all Muslims in Southeast Asia. In many articles Muslim leaders from all the Southeast Asian nations repeatedly make the point that Islam is not the source of terrorism and that Islam is not an enemy of the West. However, the unilateralism shown by the United States and the tendency of President Bush to demand unconditional support for the "war on terrorism" also provoke widespread negative comment. Bush's use of words such as "crusade" and "axis of evil" to describe Iraq, Iran and North Korea, together with his attack on Iraq and threats against any country that "harbours terrorists" stirred up deep resentment among Southeast Asian Muslims. Even a progressive Muslim leader such as Aburrahman Wahid lashed out at the hegemonic intentions of Western leaders towards Muslim states.[12]

DEFINITIONS OF TERRORISM

The emotional and political complexity of responding to September 11 is highlighted by the apparent lack of agreement on the definition of terrorism. In press accounts, it appears that all groups agree in condemning terrorism. However the meaning of terrorism is far from clear. For example, a report in the respected Indonesian newspaper, *Kompas*, quotes the head of Nahdlatul Ulama for East Java (PWNU Jawa Timur) as questioning whether, from the point of view of Islam, the tragic attack on the WTC and the Pentagon should be considered acts of terrorism.[13] In contrast, the U.S. aggression on Afghanistan in which many civilians were killed, is often cited as an example of terrorism. Ironically, no one seems to question whether or not the Bali bombings were terrorist bombings.

Explicit attempts to define terrorism are often contradictory or unclear. For example, a definition from a radical Islamic source (that claims to be "as clear as the noon sun"), suggests that terrorism is,

> ...the practice of violence, or intimidation with violence, that contains the political motive of undermining the authority of a country, or commanding a country to address certain problems, or influencing the leaders of a country by throwing out various rumours, or disturbing the economy of a country to cause a crisis and political instability, with the ultimate goal of changing the *status quo* that is supported by law and accepted by the people.[14]

In this definition, terrorism is not defined by the means used (which include violence, intimidation, commands, rumours and economic aggression), but rather by the motives and injustice of the agent.

The same writer distinguishes terrorism from *jihad* and defines international terrorism as "carried out by great nations in the name of a new world system, although behind them stands an economic *mafia*, a weapons *mafia* and the channel of ancient and modern colonialism".[15] In contrast, the writer argues that terrorism should not be considered "merely actions of provocation, or activities intended to create fear and riots".[16] In other words, the main agents of terrorism are the Western nation-states and the violent acts of individuals are merely provocation, not terrorism.

In Western discourse, terrorism is defined by its means and its targets, not by its motives or the justice of its cause. Terrorism is usually considered a political weapon in which innocent civilians are deliberately killed or injured with the express purpose of causing terror among the general population. From this perspective, terrorism is a violent attack against innocent people carried out by private individuals or groups for a larger political purpose. In contrast, many Muslim sources routinely characterize U.S. bombing of cities in Iraq and Afghanistan, or Israeli attacks on Palestinian cities, as terrorist in nature because of the high number of civilian casualties. From a Western perspective, suicide bombings in crowded Jewish cities are terrorist acts. But many Muslims would not agree. Rather, it is the Israeli army, financially supported by the United States that carries out terrorist attacks on Palestinian civilians.

From a Western perspective, if a bomb explodes in a public place and injures one person, that is terrorism; whereas when a government conducts a military attack against a predefined enemy, even if a thousand civilians die (as "collateral damage"), that is an act of war, not terrorism. The crucial difference between terrorism and the lawful acts of governments, from a Western perspective, is not the justice of the cause nor the number of civilian casualties, but rather that terrorism is conducted by private parties who deliberately target civilians to induce public terror. In contrast, acts of war are carried out by legally constituted governments against specifically defined enemies, and civilians are not deliberately targetted.

The Western definition of terrorism is premised on a particular view of the state, based on the idea of a social contract in which the government (Hobbes' *Leviathan*), monopolizes the means of violence. In exchange the individual is granted freedom from fear or arbitrary harm. This view posits the individual as the fundamental unit of value whose freedom and protection is the goal of the social contract. In contrast, many Muslims in Southeast Asia distrust the legitimacy of governments, and especially the dominant powers of the current world order. The fundamental paradigm of society is not a social contract, but rather the family. Likewise the most fundamental value is not the freedom and safety of the individual, but rather the glory of God and the well being of the *umat*. People are tied together by blood and fate, not by the free choice of individuals.

From this perspective, the defining characteristics of terrorism include the number of casualties and the injustice of the terrorists in carrying out acts of violence based on motives of greed and national interest. For example, several articles in the Indonesian press that condemned the U.S. attack on Afghanistan, suggest that the attacks were really motivated by material interests in gaining access to uranium or in establishing an oil pipeline. Similarly, it is often suggested that Israeli attacks on Palestine are motivated by the Jewish desire to control all of the territory on the West Bank of the River Jordan.

Many Muslims perceive the U.S.-led war on terrorism as hypocritical because the lives of the victims of September 11 are valued more highly than the lives of Muslim civilians who are killed in the bombing of Afghanistan (or Iraq). The assumption behind this commonly stated perception is that the totality of an action, including its motives and its effects must be considered to determine whether or not an act is terrorist in nature. While Westerners focus on terrorism as a brutal weapon that must be eliminated because it threatens the sanctity of individual life, Southeast Asians feel that their lives have never been very safe, not least of all because of the domination of the global capitalist system. From this perspective, the Western distinction between intended victims and accidental victims does not carry much weight. Some Muslims feel that they have been experiencing terrorism for a long time and now finally the United States is getting a taste of its own medicine.

There is no way to determine which of the definitions of terrorism is "true" or "correct". Anyone is free to make his or her own definition, provided it is clear and consistent. Different definitions point to different interests, values and political agendas that are rooted in different perceptions of events. Definitions of terrorism should exclude attacks on military targets and non-violent political actions. The tendency to equate terrorism with any coercive political act that is considered evil should be avoided. There are many forms of evil, including actions that harm many innocent people. But they should not all be called terrorism. If all forms of injustice are called terrorism, the term loses its analytical usefulness. The Bali bombings may have reduced the gap between polarized perceptions founded on stereotypes of Islam versus those of the West. The bombing of a crowded restaurant[17] filled with foreign tourists seems to fit everyone's definition of terrorism.

WHO ARE THE TERRORISTS?

Differences in the definition of terrorism may lay behind the widely expressed scepticism in the Muslim world about who in fact carried out the attacks on the twin towers of the WTC and the Pentagon. While the Western press treats the guilt of Osama and Al Qaeda as an established fact, many doubts are expressed by Muslim spokespersons. Conspiracy theories abound, including the common charge that the Israeli Secret Service (Mossad) masterminded the attack in order to discredit the Muslim world. Even some non-Muslims in Indonesia seemed to believe the unfounded rumour that the Jews had all been warned ahead of time not to enter the WTC on the day of the attack.[18] Reports in the Indonesian press discounted the video released by the United States in which bin Laden expressed his fore-knowledge and pleasure at the success of the attacks. An article in *Kompas* approvingly quotes Muslim spokespersons from all over the world who made statements that the video was a fake that had been engineered by the United States to make bin Laden look guilty.

Paradoxically, Osama also became a hero to many Muslims in Southeast Asia. In Yogyakarta for instance, many young people sported T-shirts showing pictures of Osama bin Laden. Surprisingly, even progressive liberal Muslims took up the fad. The ambivalence of this position is effectively expressed in a Malaysian article from a radical Muslim magazine that asks whether or not Osama bin Laden is really a vicious terrorist (*pengganas*). After commenting on his "clean" and "sweet" face, the article gives an elaborate argument to show that the American case against Osama is a fabrication and that probably the Jews were behind the attack. However the article ends ironically by saying that, even if Osama planned the attacks, he had good reasons, because he was defending the nations and religion of Islam against American aggression.[19] The article displays a thinly disguised delight in the vulnerability of the United States, which has finally been paid back a little, for all of its arrogance and evil towards the Muslim world.

At a rational level Osama bin Laden cannot be considered both a mass murderer and a heroic martyr. Paradoxically, he must simultaneously be absolved of guilt and yet praised for his audacity. At one and the same time, he plays the role of scapegoat, sacrificial victim and a figuratively risen saviour. The French philosopher, Rene Girard, argues that all religions are grounded in societal attempts to manage violence by selecting a scapegoat who becomes a sacrificial victim and who is finally elevated to the divine status of saviour.[20] Girard's theory is developed especially from his analysis of the Greek tragedies. One need not accept the totality of his theory in order to see that the dynamic he portrays offers a partial explanation for many religious beliefs and practices. Like Oedipus, Osama commits a great crime and becomes the target and scapegoat for the sins of all Muslims. Like Oedipus too, he is exiled and hunted by the almost supernatural military powers of the West. Finally like Oedipus, bin Laden is raised to almost god-like status through his sufferings. Symbolically it does not matter whether he is killed or not. He will live forever in the lives of his followers.

If there are doubts about Osama bin Laden's guilt, there are even greater doubts about who can be defined as a terrorist in Southeast Asia. When Lee Kuan Yew suggested that Singapore could not be secure because Indonesia was a haven for terrorists, the response in Indonesia was swift and full of outrage. The vehemence of these denials was puzzling, especially since the head of the Indonesian intelligence had admitted to an Al Qaeda training camp in Sulawesi, and the experience of terror in Indonesia has been common for a long time. Even the word is common in Indonesian discourse (*teror/diteror*). However, the vehement denials make more sense if considered in light of the conflicting definitions of terrorism and the qualifying word, *insy'allah*. Of course the denials can also be read as simple political expediency to avoid becoming the target of U.S. scrutiny.

THE POLITICAL IMPACT OF SEPTEMBER 11 ON SOUTHEAST ASIAN STATES

Even if the emotional impact of September 11 on Southeast Asian Muslims was remarkably uniform, the political impact varied enormously from country to country. The pattern of formal political responses in Muslim majority states was similar in different countries, that is, to condemn the September 11 attack and also condemn the attack against Afghanistan. However the political impact was different. The established governments of the three majority Muslim nations in the region seemed to have benefitted from September 11. The governments in Malaysia, Indonesia and Brunei each claim to be moderate Muslim states who are threatened by political opposition from Muslim radicals.

The United States has suddenly become very interested in the Muslim world and is in search of "Muslim" nations who will co-operate in the war against terrorism and demonstrate that it is not a war on Islam. For the first time since the Cold War, the United States again appears to have a global agenda. In order to further the cause, the United States must avoid the dangerous "clash of civilizations" thesis and find allies in the Muslim world. In short, the United States is looking for exemplary Muslim countries that can demonstrate that Islam is not antithetical to modernity, economic development or democratic political stability. Islamic states in Southeast Asia appear to be the best candidates. Unlike Middle Eastern, African and South Asian Islam, the Muslim states of Southeast Asia have a reputation for inter-religious tolerance, openness to modernity and adaptability. Southeast Asian Muslim states in a post-colonial, post September 11 climate, walk a fine line between maintaining their legitimacy as Islamic nations opposed to Western hegemony, and moderate, modern states that co-operate in the war against terrorism.

1. Malaysia

In Malaysia, Prime Minister Mahathir Mohamad benefitted the most from the new world climate following September 11. He was transformed in Western perceptions, from an ageing, discredited tyrant (following his vicious political "assassination" of Anwar Ibrahim), into a model of Islamic moderation. Mahathir defended his reputation as an independent Muslim leader by sharply criticizing the Western attack on Afghanistan. However he also strongly condemned the September 11 attacks and acted swiftly to arrest suspected Islamic radicals (including the son of Nik Abdul Aziz, the leader of the opposition Islamic party, Parti Islam SeMalaysia or PAS). He portrayed the opposition party as Islamic extremists and declared that Malaysia was already an "Islamic state", in fact, a politically stable, prosperous, modern and "democratic" Islamic state.[21]

Since Malaysia is heavily dependent on U.S. investments,[22] Mahathir was anxious to head off identification of Islam with *jihad* while at the same time co-opting his political opposition's demands for a Muslim state. Mahathir's suppression of political rivals, who are branded as Islamic militants, has brought Western approval and support. As a leader he is portrayed as a "shining light" of the Muslim world. At least in the short run, Mahathir seems to have played his cards very well. However, the question is still open concerning what kind of Muslim state Malaysia is becoming.[23] In particular the possibility of democratic inclusion of dissident Muslim and non-Muslim voices in Malaysian politics appears to be very vulnerable.

2. Indonesia

Similar to Malaysia, Indonesia has also positioned itself as a moderate Muslim nation that verbally supports the war against terrorism even though it did not endorse the war against the Taliban. However unlike Malaysia, Indonesia has not taken any dramatic steps in arresting suspected terrorists. On the contrary, suspected Indonesian terrorists who were arrested in the Philippines, were released as a result of high-level Indonesian state intervention. According to the U.S. Ambassador to Indonesia, the United States is nevertheless "very happy" with the co-operation of Indonesia "behind the scenes". Since no substantial co-operation has been evident in public, we are left to wonder what has gone on, if anything, behind the scenes. At the start of the attack on Afghanistan, the public outrage in Indonesia was so strong that there were many calls for breaking off diplomatic relations with the United States. However, even conservative leaders recognized that such an action could be very costly, in light of Indonesia's current economic dependency.

It is clear that the United States is very concerned that Indonesia should not continue its gradual drift towards "Islamic fundamentalism", and the former will to do all it can to support a relatively moderate regime such as that of President Megawati. For the first time since the early 1970s Indonesia is in a relatively strong bargaining position with the United States. During the Cold War, the United States also had a strongly felt global agenda: containing the spread of communism. With this in mind they were willing to support the Indonesian economy and overlook Suharto's excesses, as long as he was a bulwark against communism. Suddenly there is now a new global mission: the war on terrorism. Indonesia has signed on in theory and is beginning to receive the first payoffs. In addition to a far more accommodating U.S. ambassador, the main evidence of this is a renewal of U.S. support for the Indonesian military. Both the ascension of Megawati to the presidency and the tragedy of September 11 strengthened the role of the military in Indonesia. Whether this will, in the long run, strengthen or undermine moderation and stability in Indonesia is still an open question. Even more questionable is the impact of U.S.-supported, military dominance on human rights and democracy in Indonesia.

Since the Bali bombings of 12 October 2002, there have been strident calls in the Indonesian press for proactive and vigorous action to combat terrorism. The Indonesian Government has called in experts from several Western countries, including the American Federal Bureau of Investigation (FBI), to help find the people responsible for the bombings. Such action would have been unthinkable before 12 October. There are also renewed calls for closer co-operation between Indonesia and international agencies, including the military and intelligence services of the United States.

3. Thailand

In Southern Thailand, Malay Muslims have waged a low-level "terrorist" campaign for independence ever since the 1960s.[24] The Thai Government alternated its policies over the years, between assimilation, repression and accommodation of the Malay Muslim minority. However none of these policies have "worked" and Malay Muslim resentment against the Thai Government remains strong. In the late 1990s, thawing relations between Thailand and Malaysia resulted in the denial of safe havens in Malaysia for Thai Muslim separatist fighters. As a result of the arrests of major figures and surrender of others, it appeared that the insurgency was drawing to a close. However, between October 1998 and August 1999, fifty "terrorist" attacks took place. In April 2001, the remnants of different revolutionary groups (PULO, New Pulo and BRN), merged under the name *Bersatu* (United), and carried out a dramatic attack that killed one boy and injured forty.[25]

It is very hard to calculate the effect of September 11 on the Muslim separatist movement in Southern Thailand. From a material point of view, September 11 strengthened the warrant of the Thai Government in dealing harshly with dissidents and increased the teamwork between Thailand, Malaysia, Singapore and Indonesia in searching out terrorists. Insofar as there may have been a link between militants in Thailand and Al Qaeda or other international militant organizations, worldwide attention and the destruction of terrorist networks will render the militants more vulnerable. On the other hand, the psychological impact of September 11 on worldwide Muslim radicalism should not be underestimated. Similar to the situation in Malaysia, September 11 has strengthened the military hand of the government in Thailand to repress radical dissidents. However it is questionable whether military repression can quell a struggle for independence that has been going on in Southern Thailand for hundreds of years.

4. The Philippines

The most dangerous trouble spot in Muslim Southeast Asia continues to be Mindanao, the Philippines. Unlike Thailand, where Muslim rebels are relatively few in number and under-supplied, the Muslim insurgency in Mindanao is large, complex and well armed. Three groups of separatists compete for influence and use different methods. The Moro National Liberation Front (MNLF) emphasizes a nationalist Moro ideology and reached a compromise agreement with the Philippine Government in 1976, which granted autonomy to the Moro people in return for an end to armed struggle.

Radical elements refused to honour this agreement and formed the Moro Islamic Liberation Front (MILF), in 1980. The MILF continues the armed struggle under the banner of a more radical Islamic ideology. This group currently has more than 11,000 soldiers, an impressive armoury of modern weapons and international sources of funding.[26] The MILF is a military operation fighting a guerrilla war against the Philippine Government to establish a strict Muslim, Moro state. As such it does not fit within the conventional Western definition of terrorism. The Abu Sayyaf Group (ASG) is more violent and radical than the MILF. Formally established in 1992, ASG uses terrorist tactics to expel all non-Muslims from Moro territory. They currently number about a thousand fighters and have become infamous for kidnappings, robberies and brutal massacres of non-Muslims.

MNLF is primarily nationalist and secondarily Islamic. MILF is primarily Islamic and secondarily nationalist. However, ASG is Islamic and internationalist, and hopes to unite all the Muslims of Southeast Asian into one fundamentalist Islamic state. ASG has attracted intense scrutiny from the United States, not only because they still hold two American tourists as hostages, but also because they are reliably linked to Al Qaeda and other international terrorist networks. As the closest ally to the United States in Southeast Asia, the Philippines offered the most comprehensive backing for the war on terrorism. After September 11, President Gloria Macapagal Arroyo not only supported the U.S. attack on Afghanistan, but even offered the use of Philippine naval bases. This was an astonishing change of policy in light of the painful decision ten years ago to evict the U.S. military from these bases.[27]

Somewhat to the consternation of her ASEAN (Association of Southeast Asian Nations) neighbours, Arroyo also invited U.S. military support for strikes against ASG. For the first time since the Vietnam War, American soldiers were involved as "military advisers" in Southeast Asia. As a loyal ally, the Philippines can expect to receive substantial financial and military support from the United States in their war against ASG. While the battle against ASG may be amenable to a military solution, Moro independence is a more intractable problem for which financial and military aid provide no easy solution. A perceptive article by Thomas M. Mckenna questions the standard account that explains Moro nationalism as the result of centuries of oppression of Muslims by Spanish and American colonial powers.[28] Even if Moro Islamic nationalism is a more recent result of local dynamics, it remains to be seen if September 11 will strengthen international Islamic identity in the region, thereby strengthening the separatist movement, or conversely, create more international pressure for a negotiated solution. In either case, the Philippine Government will need to avoid falling back into a dependent military relationship with the United States which will be unpopular both domestically and harmful to regional ties with Muslim states that are wary of Western hegemony in the region.

CONCLUSION

In this chapter, an "ideal type" analysis was used, supported by empirical observations of the responses of Muslims, to clarify some differences between the perceptions of Westerners and Southeast Asian Muslims. In doing so, the real differences between different streams of Islam have been deliberately obscured. This chapter does not delve deeply into the impact of September 11 on Muslims in particular local communities — it attempts only to provide a broad overview. Local communities of Muslims are constantly creating new meanings to mediate the conflicting values and demands of their life in the real world. From this perspective, there is no single "impact" of September 11 on Muslims in Southeast Asia. Not only are there different streams within Islam, but real communities of Muslims are part of an ongoing process of interpretation and adjustment to reality. The impact of September 11 is not like the impact of a jetliner crashing into a skyscraper, but is more like a process of negotiation and dialogue. Islam in Southeast Asia is not static. The impact of September 11 is a changing reality whose long-term results are not yet clear. Just as the Bali bombings may have changed the impact of September 11 on Islam in Indonesia, so too, the American war against Iraq changed many perceptions and political realities.

This study favours the political and "public" face of Islam over the local, everyday responses of the great majority of Muslims. Islam is not defined by her most vocal spokespersons, nor by her most powerful political leaders, but by the living response of millions of Muslims who are trying to live their lives in submission to God and at peace with their neighbours. It pays attention to symbolic, conceptual, doctrinal and psychological factors in Muslim responses to September 11 as tools for understanding the dramatic differences between Muslim and Western perceptions of the same events.

In reality the differences between Southeast Asian Muslims and Westerners are not as dramatic as they might appear in this chapter. Many Westerners are very critical of the Bush administration and many Muslims admire the power of the United States in responding to her perceived enemies. In the long run, the differences among Muslims in their attitude to the "West" are as great as the differences between Muslims and Westerners. Similarly, the differences among Westerners are no less sharp than the differences between Westerners and Southeast Asian Muslims.

Nevertheless, an attempt has been made to flag some major, paradigmatic differences between Southeast Asian Muslims and the West. These include differing symbolic and historical contexts of interpretation, different views of the individual and the nation-state, different emotions rooted in different perceptions of ultimate reality, and different definitions of terrorism and terrorists. While these differences should not be minimized, the different paradigms do not necessarily contradict each other. Rather, they are like different languages and different symbol systems used to describe the same events. Southeast Asians are already adept at speaking several languages and moving in and out of different symbol systems. The language of Western modernity is not foreign to most Muslims. Unfortunately the language of Islam is still foreign to most Westerners. The world will be a safer place to live if more and more of us learn to be "bilingual".

Notes

1   In this chapter "Islam" does not refer to the ideal religion, revealed by Allah to the Prophet Mohammed. Rather it refers to the real people who practice this religion in many part of the world. Islam as a religion in the world, and Muslims as an empirical community are not ideal, nor are they monolithic and static. Rather they are diverse and changing all the time.

2   I wrote this article before the Bali bombings which occurred just days before the deadline for final revisions of this publication. Four bombs exploded in three locations: Kuta, Denpasar and Manado (North Sulawesi). The two bombs in Kuta killed around 200 people, most of them foreign tourists, and left hundreds more seriously injured or crippled. The Denpasar bomb was near the United States Consulate and the Manado bomb was near the Philippine Consulate. Neither of these smaller bombs caused any fatalities.

3   Vaclav Havel, "Kosovo and the End of the Nation-State", address to Canadian Parliament in *The New York Review of Books*, 10 June 1999, pp. 4–6. Cited in Anthony Reid, "Indonesians, Acehnese and the Modern Nation-State", unpublished paper, *Jurnal Anthropologi* Conference, Bali, 2002.

4   Even in S. Philippines, the more nationalistic MNLF has been losing influence to the more religiously oriented MILF and ASG.

5   See, Timo Kivimaki, "Two Acehnese Views of the post-September 11 World", *NIAS nytt: Nordic Newsletter of Asian Studies*, no. 4 (December 2001): 18.

6   In my opinion, even many Indonesians are unaware of how strong are the commonalties of culture, economic interest, language, history and religion, that have tied them together as a nation over the past century. Unfortunately this theme cannot be developed in this chapter.

7   Bambang Susilo Yudhoyono, quoted in *Kompas* 14 October 2002, p. 1.

8   An American observer made the ironic comment that even though the CIA is involved in many bloody activities, they do not normally kill large numbers of white people.

9   Benjamin Barber, *Jihad vs. McWorld: How Globalism and Tribalism are reshaping the World*, New York: Ballantyne, 1995, p. 6. Cited in Anthony Reid, "Indonesians,

Acehnese and the Modern Nation-State", unpublished paper, *Jurnal Anthropologi* Conference, Bali, 2002.

¹⁰ Reid, Ibid.

¹¹ In Indonesian the meaning is ambiguous. It could also be translated, "God willing, there are no terrorists in Indonesia." In this construction "*insy'allah*" serves as a pious affirmation of hope that there are in fact no terrorists, whereas the former interpretation might even justify the presence of terrorists as the will of God.

¹² "Gus Dur Kecam Hegemoni Negara Barat terhadap Negara Islam", *Kompas*, 14 December 2001. Gus Dur did, however, caution Muslims not to equate American political leaders with American society as a whole.

¹³ "NU Jatim Bahas Masalah Terorisme dan Anthrax", *Kompas*, 2 November 2001.

¹⁴ Jam'ah Amin, *Jihad Bukan Terorisme: Detik-detik Kemenangan Islam*, Jakarta: Darul Falah, undated, about 2000, pp. 139–40.

¹⁵ Ibid, pp. 140–41.

¹⁶ Ibid., p. 143.

¹⁷ While I have never been there, I was informed that one of the "nightclubs" bombed in Kuta was an excellent seafood restaurant that features a second rate band in the evening. The bombing took place on a busy Saturday night.

¹⁸ For example, a non-Muslim Indonesian student, reflecting accounts in the press, expressed to me his conviction that Jews had been warned before-hand and that probably the Jewish Government orchestrated the hijackings of the planes. The irony of accusing the Jews while protesting that there is insufficient evidence to prove that Osama bin Laden was behind the assault seems strikingly irrational. Even if there were insufficient evidence to prove bin Laden did it (and this is doubtful), there was at least enough evidence to demonstrate that he was a very likely suspect, whereas there is no evidence whatsoever that the Jews attacked the WTC.

¹⁹ See, Dato' Dr. Hassan Ahmad, "Osama bin Laden — 'Pengganas' atau Apa?", *Dewan Masyarakat*, December 2001, pp. 8–10. The argument is a little like saying, "We didn't do it, you did it to yourself, and even if we did do it, you deserved it!"

²⁰ Rene Girard, *La Violence et le Sacre*, Paris: Grasset, 1972.

²¹ See, David Camroux, "Malaysia: Winners and Losers", *NIAS nytt: Nordic Newsletter of Asian Studies*, no. 4 (December 2001): 8. For a complementary analysis see, Shamsul A.B., "Beyond 11 September: A Malaysian Response", *NIAS nytt*, no. 4 (December 2001): 6.

²² "…the U.S.-based large corporations form the biggest collective investor in the Malaysian economy dependent on manufacturing". Shamsul A.B., ibid., p. 6.

²³ See, Patricia A. Martinez, "The Islamic State or the State of Islam in Malaysia", *Contemporary Southeast Asia* 23, no. 3 (December 2001): 474–503.

²⁴ Actually conflicts between the Malay Muslims of S. Thailand (the Kingdom of Patani) and Siam may date back to the fifteenth century and certainly to the

eighteenth century, when the Siamese state finally established control over Patani. Whether the current insurgents should be termed terrorists or freedom fighters depends on your point of view. See Peter Chalk, "Militant Islamic Separatism in Southern Thailand", in *Islam in Asia: Changing Political Realities*, edited by Jason F. Isaacson and Colin Rubenstein, New Brunswick, NJ: Transaction, 2002. This informative book was compiled prior to 11 September 2001 and is marred by the tendency to equate Islam with militant fundamentalism.

25 Chalk, "Thailand" in Isaacson and Rubenstein, 2002, p. 179.

26 Peter Chalk, "Militant Islamic Extremism in the Southern Philippines" in Isaacson and Rubenstein, 2002, p. 196.

27 Sophie Boisseau du Rocher, "The Philippines: the Triple Aftermath of 11th September", *NIASnytt*, no. 4 (December 2001): 26–27.

28 Thomas M. McKenna, "Appreciating Islam in the Muslim Philippines: Authority, Experience, and Identity in Cotabato", in *Islam in an Era of Nation-States: Politics and Religious Renewal in Muslim Southeast Asia*, edited by Robert W. Hefner and Patricia Horvatich, Honolulu: University of Hawaii Press, 1997, pp. 43–73.

CONCLUSION
Addressing the Challenge of
Political Islam in Southeast Asia

K. S. Nathan and Mohammad Hashim Kamali

Political Islam as an issue affecting our present and future, will remain a matter of great concern to Muslims as well as non-Muslims in this region, and the world as well. Parts I and II have highlighted the complexity involved, and the problematique associated with translating theory and doctrine to reality. Indeed, this is the biggest challenge facing all Muslims: to adapt, modernize, reform, and reinvent their social systems in as much as the non-Muslims too are doing the same — to develop relevant models of economic, political, social, cultural and religious life — that can empower us without undermining our freedom to choose, while at the same time enabling us to positively address the multi-faceted challenges confronting humanity in the twenty-first century. In this conclusion, the focus is not on "doctrinal Islam" but on "applied Islam", that is, the political and strategic dimensions of Islamic activity as it affects Muslims and non-Muslims alike.

A question naturally arises whether Islam is inherently political or whether politicization of Islam is a historical phase and a circumstantial development brought into sharp relief in the latter part of the twentieth century. Political Islam emerged partly as a reaction to European colonialism and partly as an aspect of the nationalist movement that struggled for independence in the former colonies. For Islam is basically a faith and a state of mind founded on its renowned five pillars, namely, prayer, fasting, the hajj, the *zakat* obligation to help the poor, belief in God and the hereafter. These are not inherently political and Muslims can practise their religion without any political engagement in a party or government, or even in the absence of a government. Islam admittedly does not preclude government from the scope of its teachings, yet it remains to be said that state and government are not essential to the religion.

The question whether Islam is a religion (*din*) only, or both religion and state (*din wa dawla*) was addressed in the early decades of the twentieth century by Shaykh 'Ali 'Abd al-Raziq, a former judge and professor of the famous Al-Azhar Universityin Cairo, and at one time also Minister of Awqaf (religious endowments) of Egypt, who published a book bearing the title *al-Islam wa Usul al-Hukm* (Islam and the Principles of Government) in 1926. Raziq's principal argument and conclusion was that Islam was essentially a religion and that state and government were not an integral part of its basic message and teaching. The book aroused much controversy especially in the conservative circles of the ulama, and a debate that has continued more or less ever since. The book has been translated into several languages and numerous books were subsequently published in response to Raziq's arguments. Many have advanced rigorous reactions and debates, but 'Ali 'Abd al-Raziq's book has never been dismissed either as a heresy or one devoid of substance.

What is of interest to us here is the time frame and the circumstantial setting which prompted 'Ali 'Abd al-Raziq to write that book. The Shaykh published his book soon after the spectacular downfall of the caliphate in Turkey which caused controversy and unrest among Muslims almost everywhere — Muslims who had seen and perceived the caliphate as an aspect of Islam and its symbol of political unity for almost the entire thirteen centuries of Islam's history. 'Ali 'Abd al-Raziq was also not the first to introduce that subject, for he basically followed and substantiated the conclusion that the ulama and government of Turkey had already proclaimed and publicized during the months leading to the final abolition of caliphate in 1924. The basic thesis was that the caliphate was not an integral part of Islam.

The early 1920s marked a time when the course of events pointed to what may be seen as the depoliticization of Islam, if one may use the expression. It seems in hindsight that the world has witnessed a dramatic turnaround, within the same century, and the diametrically opposing assertions that shows Islam, in the eyes of its advocates, now known as Islamists, in a totally different light. The tide of circumstance has brought us full circle and political Islam is in the forefront of the public image of the religion, especially in the eyes of the present generation of non-Muslims. The truth is perhaps somewhere in between, but it is not our purpose to delve into this argument any further. The basic point is that political Islam is no more than a controversial interpretation that may well prove to be a temporary and a passing phase.

Muslims, like everyone else, are obliged by the challenges and exigencies of modernization to abandon the idea and comfort of living in the past, and acquire religious and political confidence to live with plurality and diversity as the precious and permanent assets of our common cultural heritage in Southeast Asia. Non-Muslims too are equally obliged to understand the essence, direction, and future course of global Islam as it manifests itself in both the public and private spheres. In human history, religious issues have always remained contentious, exacerbated as they are by the difficulty in separating the secular from the sacred, and by the complexities involved in translating religious doctrine to concrete practical applications in the context of modernization, multi-culturalism, and globalization.

To take a parochial view of Islam does not do justice to the wider aspects of its teachings. Among the world religions, it may be said that Islam stands out for its acceptance of religious pluralism as an integral part of its teachings. Non-Muslims are granted the freedom to practise their own faith and they have a recognized and a protected status according to the clear text of the Qur'an (2: 256; 10: 99 and 109:6). Islam can never be quoted in support of unjust killing, be it of a Muslim or of anyone else. In this regard, it may be surmised: had the Muslims enjoyed a protected status under Christianity, the massacres and ethnic cleansing of Serbrinica may not have occurred! Islam advocates peaceful relations in society with its own followers and those of other faiths. Those who resort to violence and terror, Al-Qaeda, Jema'ah Islamiyyah and their likes, misquote and deface the principles of Islam. Jihad is quoted in support of merciless killing of innocent by-standers. However, it must be emphasized that both violent *jihad* and suicide bombing are far removed from the correct understanding of *jihad*. What we have witnessed and are still grappling with is also indicative of a widening gap, indeed a disconnect, in communication and understanding between Islam and the West, and more particularly between the United States and the world of Islam.

While Islam *per se* does not pose a problem to modern governance and management of religious diversity, it is its political dimension seized upon by its most conservative and radical elements that have aroused concern and suspicion both amongst the moderate Muslims and non-Muslim strata of the populace. Rightly or wrongly, the September 11 tragedy produced a significant, even if incorrect, impact upon the perceptions of non-Muslim states, societies, and individuals about the dangers arising from the ability of a small group of ultra-conservative radicals who are prepared to use force and violence to implement their controversial agenda and vision of an Islamic world order. The Taliban regime's imposition of a very austere and puritanical socio-legal order on the Afghan people during its five-year rule (1996–2001), with severe restrictions on human rights, and especially women's rights, has not augured well for the establishment of an "Islamic state" in the context of twenty-first century. Not only the international community, but also the moderate strata of the Afghan populace, indeed the vast majority of Muslims, opposed the Taliban vision and practice of Islam. This is borne out by the fact that even after five years in office, only three Muslim countries had established diplomatic relations with the Taliban. It seems that modernity and the accompanying challenges of development, industrialization, and globalization of Islam arguably has not brought about a more liberal, enlightened, egalitarian, and just world order, that is, a system of internal growth and development as well as external interaction that is evidently more progressive, open, democratic, and enlightened *vis-à-vis* the present secular-oriented world order.

In Southeast Asia, especially in Muslim majority countries like Indonesia and Malaysia, the debate is ongoing about the merits and demerits of establishing an Islamic state — a debate that has not been well received by the West, especially after the 9/11 tragedy despite the more moderate posture of these countries on Islamic issues. The immediate result, even for the incumbent regimes, was to further tighten internal security laws, ostensibly to arrest and detain suspected Al Qaeda and Jema'ah Islamiyyah (JI) operatives whose goal it is to advance their self-styled Islamic agenda by targetting institutions, infrastructures, and regimes friendly to the West, all in the name of Islam. These operatives have clearly succeeded in tarnishing the image even of the moderate strata of Muslims who abhor terrorism and violence. And the only superpower today, the United States, is pursuing a vigorous and activist foreign policy based on fear — the fear of another September 11 tragedy occurring within its borders. To overcome this fear of Islamic terrorism, President George W. Bush is even willing to travel further to effect regime change(as has already happened in Afghanistan in November 2001 and Iraq in April 2003), besides organizing and leading a global war against international terrorism, including direct military involvement in Southeast Asia. Violence breeds violence and it is unrealistic to expect that terrorism can be fought and terminated through recourse to violent methods. The U.S. foreign policy is widely criticized for its undivided emphasis of military means to combat terror, and also for the indiscriminate use of such means. What does one normally do when a crime is committed? Seize the perpetrator or start air raids and bombing of a whole country, such as in the case of Afghanistan? The terrorists who had planned their escape are still at large but an unknown and certainly large number of defenceless villagers including women and children were killed by the U.S. bombing raids on eastern Afghanistan in the last quarter of 2001.

The feeling is widespread among the world Muslims that the U.S.-led campaign against terrorism has addressed the symptoms, but not the causes, of this ugly phenomenon. The lead-up to the 9/11 tragedy reflected the widespread frustrations of Muslims about inequalities and unjust situations brought about by the West. But instead of addressing those frustrations and its allied conflicts, a unilateralist approach is being taken to deal with terrorism. Those who continue to see 9/11 as the cause, and what happened after as the effect, have surely missed the point to see what brought on that human tragedy in the first place. Violence appears as the first, not the last, resort to political manoeuvres. The ever increasing scale of senseless violence, such as in the case of suicide bombing, point to the collapse of basic human reason. Those who resort to this absolute nihilism must have lost faith in humanity and are driven by the grim reality of no hope and no purpose to make life worth living. The world after 9/11 has become a bewildering place as if all liberal notions of universal reason, freedom, tolerance and the rule of law since the enlightenment have lost their validity and relevance, deserving only to be flushed away in the face of resurgent ancient savageries. This also brings to mind of course the apparently uncivilized treatment of prisoners in Iraq's Abu Ghraib prison in the hands of the Americans and their European allies.

The Bush doctrine of pre-emption not only contains strategic implications for regional and world order, but also would invariably produce consequences for both the Muslim and non-Muslim worlds. In particular, Muslim states, organizations, and individuals are obliged to decide on what would be the best strategy or strategies to advance the interests of the Islamic world without necessarily triggering a major confrontation with the world's current superpower. Given the lack or absence of effective leadership from the Muslim World unlike the existence of a coherent power(United States) centre in the Western world, the successful pursuit of global Islam would necessarily have to stem from stronger internal social, political, economic, intellectual, and cultural foundations.

Admittedly, one of the major strategic implications of global Islam is the tendency among vocal sections of the Muslim population to create an Islamic state on the grounds that the present secular state and international system has failed to deliver both in the moral and material realms of life. However, it is equally pertinent to note that international terrorism has by and large failed to achieve its stated objectives of revolutionizing the domestic and international order in favour of the terrorists' agendas for socio-political change. If anything, 11 September 2001 has set the clock back for the expansion of global Islam as the nation-state system is now marshalling all its resources at its command to combat, if not defeat, this menace to regional and world order. The Islamic state, for all its virtues, still remains undefined in terms of its operational principles and practice in a pluralistic context. Muslim theologians and politicians offer contending versions of the Islamic state in terms of what is desirable and what is possible. Indeed, the "Islamic state" is a highly contested site for Muslim clerics, political authorities and revolutionaries determined to implement their own version of an Islamic order for their own societies and for the world. Unfortunately for these religious enthusiasts, its antithesis, the nation-state is proving all the more resilient in using nationalism to contain if not defeat transnational ideologies — in the same way that International Communism was defeated just over a decade ago.

On the positive side, September 11 has inspired if not urged Muslims and non-Muslims to engage in further dialogue with a view to emphasizing commonalities and minimizing differences in the true spirit of mutual tolerance and coexistence. Moderate Muslims too have become more aware that theocracies in the context of modern, twenty-first century developments and requirements have become anachronistic, thus creating a grater need to use human wisdom in mixing the religious and secular spheres. It is true that Islam does not make a water-tight division between religion and politics — indeed religion should guide all spheres of life including politics. Yet given human ambitions, proclivities and frailties, power and politics are ultimately used to determine the religious sphere in the interest of the power-holders. Christianity in Europe prior to the Lutheran Reformation of the early sixteenth century suffered from the corruption resulting from the collusion of religion and politics — a problem that was finally settled, not in months, but after 150 years when in 1648 the Peace of Westphalia established the foundations of the modern nation-state with religion essentially confined to the private sphere. Whether Islam is capable of a similar Reformation is an issue that can only be settled by the Muslims. Nevertheless, the past record of human history suggests that change can be brought about as much from internal dynamics as from external stimulation.

September 11 could well serve as a benchmark for all civilizations. The Western-oriented nation-state system could well be suffering from certain inherent weaknesses arising from a monopoly of power by a singular state or a group of states, resulting in a very uneven distribution of wealth, resources and influence. Muslim reactions against perceived injustices of the present world order should be addressed if the aim is to identify and resolve the root causes of international terrorism — the 11 September 2001 attacks in the United States, the 12 October 2002 Bali bombing, the 5 August 2003 J.W.

Marriott hotel bombing in Jakarta, and the 11 March 2004 attacks on a commuter train in Madrid being among its manifestations. Greater introspection on the part of the Muslim world in terms of reforming outmoded religious practices and infusing the religion with creativity and practicality would lend credence to the moderate voices within Islam that are urging change. Finally, the space for inter-faith dialogue has certainly expanded post-9/11, and perhaps this is one of the more positive strategic consequences for promoting a healthy dialogue of civilizations towards the common pursuit of peace, progress and prosperity for all.

The rapid development of the course of mainly negative forces and events since 9/11 requires continuous engagement in self-assessment and consultation of what needs to be done and how the existing approaches to issues can be improved and refined. This publication has touched on an analysis of such issues and stimulated a cross-section of mainly Muslim, but also some non-Muslim, opinion on the diagnostics of the problem-ridden state of Muslim-non-Muslim relations. The post-9/11 era opened new vistas for reflection, analysis, and research as the course of events has accelerated so much as to outpace the reflective engagement of a coterie of scholars within even a short period. This edited volume mainly looks at the basic issues of concern to the Muslims and non-Muslims of Southeast Asia. But the wider aspects of globalization, terrorism, and Muslim-West relations have only partially, if at all, been the focus of discussion and analysis. There remains scope for further consultative engagement, and widening of the avenues of communication and research to deepen the climate of understanding among the Muslims and non-Muslims of Southeast Asia to reflect on and recommend feasible solutions to issues of concern to this region and beyond.

NOTE ON CONTRIBUTORS

Azyumardi Azra is Professor of History at Universitas Islam Negeri Syarif Hidayatullah (UIN, or State Islamic University) in Jakarta, Indonesia. He received his advanced degrees from Columbia University, including an M.A. (1988) from the Department of Middle Eastern Languages and Cultures, and an M.A. (1989), M. Phil. (1990), and Ph.D. (1992) from the Department of History, Columbia University. He has held teaching and research fellowships in Southeast Asian Studies at several institutions including the Oxford Centre for Islamic Studies and St. Anthony's College, Oxford University (1994–1995), University of Philippines, Diliman (1997), Harvard University (Asia Centre), and New York University where he was Distinguished International Visiting Professor at the Department of Middle Eastern Studies (2001). His publications include *Pergolakan Politik Islam* [Tension of Islamic Politics], 1996; *Islam Reformis* [Reformist Islam], 1999; *Renaisans Islam di Asia Tenggara* [Renaissance of Islam in Southeast Asia] (National Book Award, 1999); and *Islam Substantif* [Substantive Islam], 2000, as well as chapter contributions in numerous books and journals.

Johan H. Meuleman holds a *Doctorandus* of Arts from Vrije Universiteit, Amsterdam (1978) majoring in economic and social history, and a Doctor of Arts from the same university in 1984. Since 2001 to the present, he is a Research Fellow on "Islam in Indonesia" at the International Institute of Asian Studies, Leiden. He is also a volunteer lecturer at the Islamic University of Europe in the Netherlands. He has over 30 scholarly publications (books, articles in international and Indonesian journals, contributions to collective publications) in English, French and Indonesian including topics such as the history of Islam in Southeast Asia (particularly Indonesia), and social and intellectual developments in Southeast Asian Islam. His several publications include "Indonesian Islam between Particularity and Universality", *Studia Islamika* (Jakarta), July–September 1997.

Carmen A. Abubakar is a Professor, and Dean of the Institute of Islamic Studies (IIS) of the University of the Philippines (UP) in Diliman, Quezon City. She holds a B.S.E. (Bachelor of Science in Education) from Norte Dame College, Jolo, Sulu (1966), M.A.T. (Master of Arts in Teaching, 1973), and Ph.D. in Philippines Studies (1990) from the University of the Philippines, Diliman. Her research areas concern Muslim society in general and women in particular, and she has published several articles and given lectures on these topics. She is the president of the Research Association of Islamic Social Sciences (RAIS), a non-stock, non-profit research and extension organization focused on the concerns, needs and conditions of Muslims in the Philippines and the contemporary Muslim world. She has published widely on the society and culture of the Muslims in the Philippines.

Bahtiar Effendy is currently Deputy Director of the Institute for the Study and Advancement of Business Ethics, (LSPEU Indonesia), and Lecturer at the Faculty of Graduate Studies, State Islamic University, Jakarta. He also holds concurrent teaching positions at the University of Indonesia, University of Jayabaya and University of Muhammadiyah, all in Jakarta. He holds a B.A. in 1983 and Doctorandus in 1986 from State Institute for Islamic Studies, (IAIN) Jakarta, before pursuing his graduate studies in the USA, in Southeast Asian Studies at Ohio University (M.A., 1988) and Political Science at Ohio State University (M.A., 1991 and Ph.D., 1994). His research interests have focused on Indonesian politics, Indonesian Islamic politics, Islam and democracy, and politics of the developing areas. His many publications include *Islam and the State in Indonesia*, 2003; *Teologi Baru Politik Islam*, 2001; and *Masyarakat Agama dan Pluralitas Keagamaan*, Yogyakarta: Galang, 2001.

Mohamed Aslam Haneef is currently Associate Professor of Economics at the International Islamic University Malaysia (IIUM), Kuala Lumpur, where his teaching and research interests include Islamic Economics and Economic Development. He earned a B. Econs. (Hons.) from IIUM in 1987, and M. Econs from the University of Malaya in 1991 before pursuing doctoral studies at the School of Development Studies, University of East Anglia,

(Ph.D., 1994) in Norwich, United Kingdom. From 1996–99, he was Head of the Department of Economics at IIUM, and has held visiting appointments as Commonwealth Fellow at Oxford Centre for Islamic Studies and as Fulbright Fellow at the Centre for Muslim-Christian Understanding, Georgetown University, Washington D.C. His publications include *Contemporary Islamic Economic Thought: A Selected Comparative Analysis*, 1995; *Economics and Society*, 1998; and "Islam and Economic Development in Malaysia — A Reappraisal", *Journal of Islamic Studies* 12, no. 3 (2001).

Shamsul A.B. is concurrently Director of the Institute of the Malay World & Civilization (ATMA) and the Institute for Occidental Studies (IKON) at Universiti Kebangsaan Malaysia, Bangi. He holds a B.A. (1973) and M.A. (1976) in Anthropology & Sociology from the University of Malaya, Kuala Lumpur, and Ph.D. in Social Anthropology from Monash University, Melbourne(1983). He researches, lectures and writes extensively on the theme "politics, religion, culture and economic development" with an empirical focus on Malaysia and Southeast Asia. He has held various fellowships and visiting professorships in Europe, India, Japan, Australia and Southeast Asia. His publications include the award-winning book, *From British to Bumiputera Rule*, Singapore: ISEAS, 1986. His most recent major publications are *Japanese Anthropologists and Malaysian Society*, Osaka: Minpaku, 1998, co-editor with T. Uesugi and *The Challenges of Critical Academia*, Special Issue of the Journal *Inter-Asia Cultural Studies* 2, no. 2 (August 2001), co-editor with Allen Chun.

Zainah Anwar is presently the Executive Director of Sisters in Islam (SIS) — a non-governmental organization founded in 1988, and which advocates the rights of Muslim women within the framework of Islam. She earned a Diploma in Mass Communication (Journalism) from the MARA Institute of Technology in Shah Alam, Selangor, Malaysia in 1975, then went to the United States to obtain her M.Sc. degree in Journalism from Boston University (1977), and a M.A. in Law and Diplomacy from Fletcher, Tufts University in Boston (1986). Her book, *Islamic Revivalism in Malaysia: Dakwah Among the Students* (1987) has become a standard reference in the study of Islam in Malaysia.

Patricia A. Martinez is currently an Associate Professor at the Asia-Europe Institute, University of Malaya, Kuala Lumpur, Malaysia, where she also heads the Intercultural Studies Programme. She holds a B.A. (Second Class

Upper Honours in English), University of Malaya (1982), M.A. in Christian Theology from the Maryknoll School of Theology, USA (1994), M.A. (Comparative Study of Religion) from Temple University, Philadelphia, USA (1997), and Ph.D. in Religion (specialization: Islam) from Temple University, USA (2000). She has also obtained a Diploma in Arabic from Al-al bayt University, Jordan (1998). She has presented numerous papers locally and internationally on gender issues, political Islam, civil society, Islam and globalization, and the development of Islam in the context of plural societies in Malaysia and Southeast Asia. She has also published widely on these subjects in local and international journals, and books including *Complex Configurations: The Women's Agenda for Change and The Women's Candidacy Initiative*, in *From Moral Communities to NGOs in Malaysia*, edited by Meredith Weiss and Saliha Hassan, London: Curzon Press, 2002.

Peter G. Riddell is currently Professor of Islamic Studies and Director, Centre for Islamic Studies, London School of Theology in Northwood, Middlesex, UK. He holds a B.A. (French & Indonesian) from Sydney University, Australia in 1974, M.A. Qual. (1979) and Ph.D. (1985) in Islam & Linguistics from the Australian National University, Canberra. He taught Arabic and Islamic Studies and Christian-Muslim Relations at ANU and also at St. Mark's National Theological Centre in Canberra between 1990–95. He also taught Modern Southeast Asian History at the London School of Oriental and African Studies from 1999-2001. Prof. Riddell has published widely on the study of Islam and Muslim-Christian Relations. His numerous publications include a book on *Islam and the Malay-Indonesian World: Transmission and Responses*, 2001; "The Diverse Voices of Political Islam in Post-Suharto Indonesia", in *Islam and Christian-Muslim Relations* 13, no. 1 (January 2002); and "What is Islam?" in *Terrorism: Asking Questions, Seeking Answers*, edited by Riddell, Peter and Peter Cotterell. London: LBC Centre for Islamic Studies & Muslim Christian Relations, Occasional Paper No. 3, January 2002.

Lily Zakiyah Munir is Founder and Director of the Centre for Pesantren and Democracy, a newly established NGO with a mission to promote democracy and human rights education in pesantrens and grassroots Muslim communities. She holds a B.A. in the Teaching of English as a Foreign Language (TEFL) from the Institute of Teaching and Education (IKIP), Surabaya (1973), Doctoranda in TEFL from IPKI, Jakarta (1976), and M.A. in Medical Anthropology from the University of Amsterdam, Netherlands (2000). She is also a Research Fellow in the Islam and Human Rights

Programme of Emory University's School of Law in Atlanta, Georgia, USA. From 1985 to the present, she has served as a member of the central board of Muslimat Nahdlatul Ulama (MNU), a women's organization under the auspices of the NU, one of the biggest Islamic organizations in Indonesia. She has presented numerous papers on gender and women's rights in Islam.

Syed Farid Alatas is currently an Associate Professor at the Department of Sociology, National University of Singapore. He holds a B.Sc. in Economics from the University of Oregon (1983), M.A. (1988) and Ph.D. (1991) in Sociology from The Johns Hopkins University, Washington, D.C., USA. A Malaysian national, he had his schooling in Singapore and lectured at the Department of Southeast Asian Studies, University of Malaya prior to his appointment at NUS. His book *Democracy and Authoritarianism: The Rise of the Post-Colonial State in Indonesia and Malaysia* was published by Macmillan (1997). His recent articles include "The Study of the Social Sciences in Developing Societies: Towards an Adequate Conceptualization of Relevance", *Current Sociology* 49, no. 2 (2001); "Eurocentrism and the Role of the Human Sciences in the Dialogue Among Civilizations", *The European Legacy* 7, no. 6 (2002); and "Academic Dependency and the Global Division of Labour in the Social Sciences", *Current Sociology* 51, no. 6 (2003).

Abdul Rashid Moten is currently Professor at the Department of Political Science, International Islamic University Malaysia, where his teaching and research interests include methods of political inquiry, issues in the Islamization of political science, comparative politics, the politics of South Asia and the Middle East and the Islamic political experience. He received his education at Dhaka University, Bangladesh (Political Science, B.A. Hons. 1969, M.A. First Class 1970), Villanova University, Pa., USA, (Political Theory, M.A. 1974) and at the University of Alberta, Canada (Comparative Politics & International Relations, Ph.D. 1982). His numerous publications include *Revolution to Revolution: Jama'at-e-Islami in the Politics of Pakistan*, 2001; *Political Science: An Islamic Perspective*, 1996; *Islam and Revolution: Contribution of Sayyid Mawdudi*, 1988; and "Civil Society and Participatory Politics in Malaysia", in *Politics, Administration and Change*, no. 36 (July–December 2001), Australia. He has taught in universities in USA, Canada, Nigeria and Malaysia. He is the editor of *Intellectual Discourse*, a journal of IIUM.

Shad Saleem Faruqi is currently the Legal Adviser to Universiti Teknologi MARA (UiTM), Shah Alam, Selangor, Malaysia and Professor of Law at the Faculty of Law of UiTM. He holds a B.A. in Government from

Wesleyan University in Connecticut, USA (1966), LL.B. (1968), LL.M. (1970) from Aligarh Muslim University in India, and a Ph.D. in Law from the International Islamic University Malaysia (IIUM), Kuala Lumpur (1991). From 1999–2002 he served as Assistant Vice-Chancellor (Legal Affairs) at UiTM. He has authored numerous articles and books including *Human Rights, Globalisation and the Asian Economic Crisis*, 1999; and *Media Law in Malaysia*, 2000. He is, or has been, a consultant on constitutional and media law issues to international organizations in the United States, Maldives, Philippines, Singapore, Kampuchea, Fiji, Indonesia and Malaysia.

Mohammad Hashim Kamali was born in Afghanistan, and is currently a Professor of Islamic Law and Jurisprudence at the International Islamic University Malaysia (IIUM) in Gombak, Kuala Lumpur. He holds a B.A. (Law and Political Science) from Kabul University (1965), LL.M. in Comparative Law (1972), and a Ph.D. in Islamic and Middle Eastern Law (1976) from the University of London. Dr. Kamali has taught at the Institute of Islamic Studies of McGill University in Montreal, Canada, and has held several Visiting Fellowships including one at the Institute for Advanced Study in Berlin in 2000–01. He has participated in over a hundred national and international conferences, published 13 books and over 80 academic articles. His publications include *Principles of Islamic Jurisprudence*, Cambridge, 1991; and *Islamic Commercial Law: An Analysis of Futures and Options*, Cambridge, 2000. His book *Law in Afghanistan*, Leiden: 1985, is also a work of reference in the field.

Noorhaidi Hasan is currently conducting research towards his Ph.D., focusing on radical Islam in the era of transition in Indonesia at the International Institute for Asian Studies (IIAS), Leiden, the Netherlands, since April 2001. He received his B.A. in Islamic Law in 1994 from the Shari'a Faculty of the State Institute for Islamic Studies, Yogyakarta, where he was appointed a Lecturer and researcher until 1997. He earned his M.A. in Islamic Studies from Leiden University, Netherlands in 1999, and M.Phil. (2000), at the International Institute for the Study of Islam in the Modern World (ISIM), also at Leiden. His publications include "In Search of Identity: the Contemporary Islamic Communities in Southeast Asia", *Studia Islamika* 7, no. 3 (2000); *Radikalisme Agama dan Perubahan Sosial Politik di Indonesia*, co-author, Jakarta: Pusat Bahasa dan Budaya, IAIN Syarif Hidayatullah, 2001; "Islamic Radicalism and the Crisis of the Nation-State", ISIM Newsletter, no. 7 (2001), and "Faith and Politics: the Rise of the Laskar Jihad in the Era of Transition in Indonesia," *Indonesia*, Cornell: SEAP, April 2002.

Bernard T. Adeney-Risakotta is currently Professor of Social Ethics in the Graduate Programme at Duta Wacana Christian University in Yogyakarta, Indonesia. He is also a regular guest professor at the Islamic State University, Sunan Kalijaga and Gadja Mada University. He holds a B.A. (Hons.) from the University of Wisconsin, Madison (1970), B.D. (Hons.) in Theology, Ethics, and Asian Religions from the University of London (1974), and a Ph.D. in Religion and Society from the Graduate Theological Union (with the University of California), Berkeley (1982). Dr. Adeney-Risakotta has written extensively on religion and society, including: *Just War, Political Realism and Faith*, 1988; *Strange Virtues: Ethics in a Multicultural World*, 1995; *Etika Sosial Lintas Budaya*, 2000; and *Kekuasaan, Agama dan Kekerasan di Indonesia* (forthcoming).

ABOUT THE EDITORS

K.S. Nathan is currently a Senior Fellow at the Institute of Southeast Asian Studies, Singapore. He holds a B.A. Hons. (Second Class Upper) in History, from the University of Malaya in Kuala Lumpur (1971); Ph.D. in International Relations from Claremont Graduate University in California, USA (1975); LL.B. Hons. (Second Class Upper) from the University of London (1992), Certificate in Legal Practice (C.L.P.) from the legal Profession Qualifying Board, Malaysia (April 1996), and LL.M. from the University of London (November 1996). He served as Deputy Dean of the Faculty of Arts & Social Sciences, University of Malaya from 1982–84. Prior to joining ISEAS in April 2001, he was Professor of International Relations at the University of Malaya until 2001. His numerous publications are in the field of international relations, ASEAN regional security, and Malaysian politics and foreign policy. More recently, his research interests include political Islam and international terrorism with special reference to Southeast Asia.

Mohammad Hashim Kamali is currently Professor of Islamic law and jurisprudence at the International Islamic University Malaysia in Kuala Lumpur. He holds a B.A. (Law and Political Science) from Kabul University (1965), LL.M. in Comparative Law (1972), and a Ph.D. in Islamic and Middle Eastern Law (1976) from the University of London. He is a Fellow of the International Institute of Islamic Thought, Herndon, Virginia. He is a member of the International Advisory Board of *Islamic Studies* (Islamabad), *al-Taidid* (IIUM, Kuala Lumpur), *the American Journal of Islamic Social Sciences* (USA), and *Religion and Law Review* (New Delhi). He is the author of numerous books, including *Principles Islamic Jurisprudence* (Cambridge 1991), *Freedom of Expression in Islam* (Cambridge 1997), and *Islamic Commercial Law: An Analysis of Futures and Options* (Cambridge 2000). He received the Isma'il al-Faruqi Award for Academic Excellence twice, the first time in 1995 and subsequently in 1997.

www.ingramcontent.com/pod-product-compliance
Lightning Source LLC
Chambersburg PA
CBHW020810100426
42814CB00001B/15